# CREATING

## A

# WORLD ECONOMY

Merchant Capital, Colonialism,
and World Trade, 1400–1825

Alan K. Smith

SYRACUSE UNIVERSITY

Westview Press

BOULDER • SAN FRANCISCO • OXFORD

Copyright © 1991 by Westview Press, Inc.

Published in 1991 in the United States of America by Westview Press, Inc., 5500 Central Avenue, Boulder, Colorado 80301, and in the United Kingdom by Westview Press, 36 Lonsdale Road, Summertown, Oxford OX2 7EW

Library of Congress Cataloging-in-Publication Data
Smith, Alan K.
    Creating a world economy : merchant capital, colonialism, and world trade, 1400–1825 / Alan K. Smith.
        p.  cm.
    Includes bibliographical references and index.
    ISBN 0-8133-1110-1. ISBN 0-8133-1109-8 (pbk.).
    1. Commerce—History.  2. International trade—History.
3. Economic history.  4. Capitalism—History.  5. Colonies—History.
I. Title.
HF479.S65  1991
382′.09—dc20                                                                      91-10221
                                                                                 CIP

Printed and bound in the United States of America

The paper used in this publication meets the requirements
of the American National Standard for Permanence of Paper
for Printed Library Materials Z39.48-1984.

10    9    8    7    6    5    4    3    2    1

# CONTENTS

# PREFACE

This is the first part of a two-volume study on the development of the world economy. It deals with what is termed the first world economy, which is seen as an entity that was shaped by the emergence of merchant capital in early-modern Europe. The study ends in the early nineteenth century, when the world created by merchant capital was supplanted by a new world economy that was the response to the growing influence of industrial capital. In essence, the earlier period is viewed as one of gestation, during which the influence of the capitalist mode of production was first extended to diverse parts of the world. The latter period, which will be dealt with in the second volume, covers the maturation of the capitalist mode of production under the influence of industrialization and the consequent quasi-permanent impact it had on the world.

Whereas only a few years ago such a study might have been considered daring and novel, so many have recently appeared that books on the world economy are now quite commonplace. I can remember a roundtable conference at Columbia University in the late 1970s at which many of the participants, my own graduate students included, sat in awe of Immanuel Wallerstein and his audacity for even contemplating so brash an undertaking as a study of the modern world. Scarcely a decade later, a publisher could indicate its lack of interest in my project with the terse observation that the "last thing that the world needs" is another book on why it was only Europe that became wealthy.

Nevertheless, it seems to me that the topic is sufficiently broad to allow for multiple interpretation, especially because many of those whom the siren has enticed to accept the challenge come from such diverse academic backgrounds that the same basic scenario is viewed in a multitude of different lights. Moreover, the subject matter is sufficiently important that if each study contributes only a few additional insights into the problem, ultimately the general fund of information will greatly aid in the overall understanding of the dynamics that dominate the modern world.

In a sense, however, it is ironic that I should have undertaken the present study, as southern Africa, the area in which I specialize, is scarcely mentioned. That I should find myself so far from my academic base can be traced to the disillusionment that overtook a generation of idealistic

Africanists. Naively believing that postindependence Africa could live up to its promises of a new type of humanistic socialism, we were rudely awakened by the realities of the 1970s. It became obvious that the failures prevalent almost everywhere could no longer be rationalized by blaming them on aberrant personalities such as Idi Amin or the influence of a small number of manipulative compradors. Once nudged out of my insularity, I soon became aware that Africa's problems were not unique. Rather, they were shared by most other areas of the so-called Third World. The problem became to identify why this seemingly irreversible trend had been established.

The investigation began as a matter of personal curiosity. At every stage, however, the answer to each particular problem always seemed to be a little further removed in time and place. Understanding the processes that unfolded at any given point in history seemed to depend on understanding what had preceded. Before I realized it, I was seeking the answers to the problems of twentieth-century Mozambique in sixteenth-century Europe. More and more, these answers appeared to have been enmeshed in the phenomenon of the development of capitalism and the processes it set in motion. It was equally important to understand why capitalism developed where it did and nowhere else. Thus, I unwittingly undertook an investigation that took me far away from my roots but whose promise seemed worth the effort. Such an investigation, though, because of the vastness of the subject, will always be incomplete and imperfect. Yet, however imperfect the results may prove to be, the very centrality of the questions raised is justification enough to warrant their investigation.

So many people have provided help that to list them all would require another volume. Mention, nevertheless, should be made of many of my former graduate students who challenged me to think in somewhat untraditional ways. Members of the Department of History at Syracuse University have helped me at all stages of planning, especially in terms of bibliographical suggestions. Malcolm Valentine, Don Warren, Jim Newman, and Ed Steinhart read earlier drafts and contributed valuable criticism. Finally, my special thanks and gratitude to Rob Gregory; I could never have completed the project without his help.

*Alan K. Smith*

# CREATING
A
# WORLD
# ECONOMY

# 1

# INTRODUCTION

This volume represents an attempt to write history on a global scale. More specifically, it seeks to investigate the dynamics of the creation of what is referred to as the first world economy and to identify the component parts of that structure. The term itself refers to a vast economic system in which various regions played different roles. It is not, however, defined purely by economics. Rather, social systems both affected and were affected by the specific forms of participation assumed by each of the contributors to the overall system. Thus, the world is seen not as being composed of separate entities, each independently charting its own destiny, but every system is part of a larger whole, which presents certain opportunities and also imposes certain constraints on the direction that each may take.

A generation ago in Western literature, world history was interpreted as something quite different. The world was assumed to be virtually synonymous with Europe, although a sort of perverse cultural imperialism extended its frontiers to include Egypt and the Fertile Crescent. As is aptly pointed out by the title of Eric Wolf's recent study, the rest of the world was composed of people without history.[1] Even in university courses that carried the title "world history," India and China were given scant mention; the Muslim world emerged from obscurity only when Europe chose to crusade against it; and Africa, the Americas, and southeast Asia simply did not exist. Thus, for all intents and purposes, the history of the world began with classical antiquity, marched through the Middle Ages, and eventually erupted into the glory of the modern European nation-state.

More recently, however, some scholars have included the rest of the world in their world histories. This is especially true of the works of the prolific historians L. S. Stavrianos and William McNeill. Each devotes considerably more attention to other parts of the globe than Europe and successfully defuses any notion that such phenomena as invention, progress, and "civilization" were European monopolies. However, although this body of scholarship makes an invaluable contribution by highlighting many of the achievements of diverse cultures around the world, it does not seek to focus on the reasons for the relative success of Europe vis-à-vis the rest of the world.[2]

Some modern scholars, however, have addressed the question of why only Europe was able to achieve sustained growth. Although this suggests tacit recognition of the existence of the rest of the world, it in no way acknowledges parity. In fact, in many instances, this new approach is as ethnocentric as that of the earlier generation, which had completely ignored the wider world. For although they were more aware of societies and cultures beyond the borders of Europe, they paid scant attention to the study of that world. Rather, they assumed that failure for most parts of the globe was preordained and natural. Thus, instead of sensing the need for in-depth comparative analyses, these authors continued to place themselves entirely within a European framework. As a result, their investigations are limited to locating the prime mover that enabled Europe completely to outdistance Africa, Asia, and the Americas.

A key example of this phenomenon appeared with the publication of *The Rise of the Western World.* Its authors, Douglass North and Robert Thomas, categorically state that "this book explains that unique historical achievement, the rise of the Western world." They continue that "we submit . . . that the development and expansion of a market economy during the Middle Ages was a direct response to opportunity gained from the specialization and trade made feasible by population growth." Moreover, they take European superiority as a given. Seemingly with little investigation of the problem, they conclude that much of Latin America, Asia, and Africa, even in recent times, failed because of inefficient economic organization.[3]

In *How It All Began*, Walt Rostow addresses the same problem. He, too, is impressed by the genius of the West, although he sees a different source as being the prime mover in its success. Rostow argues that "the central thesis of this book is that the scientific revolution is the element in the equation of history that distinguishes early modern Europe." Moreover, even if his source material appears inadequate for the task, he does devote some attention to the wider world. Nevertheless, the conclusion is that "the decisive weakness in traditional societies was on the demand side: in the lack of innovators, of men moved by economic incentives or perceptions actively to seek changes in technology."[4]

Yet another scholar who was fascinated by the question of European hegemony was E. L. Jones. As might be expected, *The European Economic Miracle* discovers a different main catalyst behind the miracle. For Jones, European expansion overseas was decisive. "Europe," he observes, "discovered an unprecedented ecological windfall. Europe was sufficiently decentralized and flexible to develop in response. . . . This conjunction of windfall and entrepreneurship happened only once in history." Insofar as he believes that the process that led Europe to industrialization was achieved "by pure accident," his book lacks some of the disguised ethnocentricism of the other studies. Moreover, a significant percentage of the volume is devoted to the wider world. Unfortunately, these sections concentrate on the failures of these societies, virtually ignoring their impressive accomplishments.[5]

The most recent contribution to the literature was coauthored by Nathan Rosenberg and L. E. Birdzell. Like several other studies, *How the West Grew Rich* devotes scant attention to societies beyond Europe. In a fashion similar to Rostow, the authors place great emphasis on Western innovation and experimentation as being crucial in the development of capitalism. "The immediate sources of western growth," they contend, "were innovations in trade, technology, and organization." This was aided by decentralization, which served to prevent any single source from inhibiting this growth. Under these circumstances, European technology was able to improve rapidly. There thus emerged in Europe and, they imply, nowhere else a dynamic system propelled by the transition to capitalism.[6]

Capitalism is also the key variable in the work of Immanuel Wallerstein, whose two volumes on *The Modern World System* constitute the most controversial and most important of the contributions that seek to answer the question why Europe was relatively so successful. Although his background was originally that of an Africanist and one feels that he is more sympathetic to the societies of the wider world, the focus of his studies is also almost exclusively on Europe. He sees trade within Europe itself as having been particularly important because it allowed certain regions to specialize in commodities of higher value. Whereas others emphasize the importance of the decentralized nature of early-modern Europe, Wallerstein believes that the creation of strong state machineries, which were capable of underwriting economic advance, was crucial. Where these elements were prominent, the degree of skill in the labor force was advanced and economic growth was fomented.[7]

If *The Modern World System* is Eurocentric in its focus, it is very different in its deductions. More so than any of the other authors, Wallerstein sees the emergence of Europe as having contributed not only to its own advance but also to the development of a highly structured world economy. Consisting of a capitalist core centered in northwestern Europe, a rather nebulously defined semiperiphery, a periphery, and areas that were "external," this world economy formed a multiregional economic system, with each of the component parts contributing in different ways. One key variable was the form of labor control and specialization. As one descends the ladder from core through semiperiphery to periphery, one finds the transition from skilled to semiskilled to unskilled labor. Moreover, the amount of naked coercion required in the more advanced regions is much less than in the peripheries. Thus, even though Wallerstein concentrates on Europe, his major concern is with an entity, however ill-defined, that is much larger and constitutes an integrated whole.[8]

Although he also stresses the decisive nature of capitalism and also employs an avowedly Marxist analysis, Eric Wolf's approach and conclusions are very different. To begin with, his is the only volume in which more attention is devoted to the wider world than to Europe. In looking at non-European societies that were dominated by the tributary mode of production, he finds a crucial weakness in that they were dominated by the "competition between classes of non-producers for power at the top." Europe, on the other hand, was saved by capitalism, which (unlike Weber, Wallerstein, or Frank) Wolf sees not as a lineal development from the tributary mode but "as a qualitatively new phenomenon." This emergence of a new mode of production, in turn, was facilitated by overseas expansion. He observes that "the crisis of feudalism was solved by locating, seizing, and distributing resources beyond the European frontiers." In the process, producers in different parts of the world were drawn into a common web of exchange. By the era of the industrial revolution, capitalism, which he emphasizes must be capital in production, had taken root.[9]

Although an extensive critique of the various authors cited could be undertaken, it seems less appropriate than a general commentary on what remains to be done and the ways in which the approach I adopt here will be different from those that others have presented. Because the attempts of those who try to broaden perspectives by expanding their outlook far beyond their specialized bases are subject to attack from so many different directions, no particular benefit would be derived from emphasizing points of disagreement. Yet questions remain about the very questions that have been asked and whether an alternative approach can be suggested. One wonders if it is possible to write a history that is global, interpretative, and offers insight into the basic dynamics of the processes that prepared the world for its current shape.

One major deficiency of the literature, although to varying degrees there are exceptions, is the treatment of the wider world. In some instances it is totally ignored; in others, its history is either truncated or abused. This fault should be corrected not only in order to gain a better balance in the world-view of those who even consider the question of human development, but also to provide precious clues to the evolution of societies in general. For growth, which is interpreted to mean the increasing ability to master the material environment and to make it produce more, at one time or another proceeded at a faster rate on every other continent than it did in Europe. This fundamental observation should open some eyes with respect to the kind of questions that should be asked. So, too, should Peter Farb's harsh judgment that for most of the past ten thousand years "northern Europeans . . . live[d] in squalor and ignorance, producing few cultural innovations."[10] One task of this study, therefore, will be to take a look at the achievements of societies in the wider world, thus providing a better comparative background for an understanding of the forces that shaped Europe and subsequently a new world economy.

Equally important as the growth of the wider world was its inability to maintain its momentum. There are those who believe in natural cycles and therefore deduce that after a period of flowering of material culture in a given society, a form of decadence sets in. In one sense this is a comfortable theory because most of the great achievements of the past were overtaken by periods of decline. Yet this is a particularly unsatisfying answer in that it leaves to cyclical oscillation the intriguing question of why peoples who erect great monuments or produce fine textiles or harvest abundant crops should some centuries later live in poverty and squalor. A look at the wider world provides clues to the puzzle of the failure of continued growth and focuses on the challenges that were to face Europe as well. It will be seen that although some of the patterns that determined this decline were particularistic, others were more universal. Moreover, I will argue that almost everywhere the main problems were social in origin. Thus, rather than some mysterious traditional conservatism, it was the frailty of manmade institutions in the wider world that deflected growth. In essence the wider world fell victim to its inability to resolve the social question of the distribution of its resources.

Medieval Europe passed through cycles not very different from those experienced elsewhere. From humble beginnings in about the eleventh century, it started a lackluster growth that by the thirteenth century brought it to the technological limit it was capable of achieving under the constraints of its social structure. Ironically and crucially, Europe's date with destiny was postponed by a most unlikely source. This was the Black Death, which by suffocating so many people enabled the rest to breathe. Subsequently, technological improvements in Europe, buttressed by social change, would begin radically to alter its position vis-à-vis its material resources. This, however, was not the end of the story. How successfully a particular region within Europe was able to benefit from the new opportunities would be related to a class struggle unique to that region. Ignoring this fundamental dichotomy, scholars often speak of Europe as an entity, all parts of which made similar strides forward. This is a crucial misunderstanding, as a full grasp of the reasons for European failures is important for understanding the reasons for European successes.

The Europe that emerged in the sixteenth century armed with a technology that made continuing growth possible also sought to intensify its contacts with the wider world. In a sense this represented a dramatic departure from the past. For it involved the unprecedented establishment of intimate contact between various parts of the world that paved the way for permanent interaction. The Portuguese, the Spanish, and the Venetians, pioneers in these endeavors, received strong support from their respective governments. While the Portuguese and Venetians competed for the spice trade of Asia, the Spanish began an intensive colonization in the Americas. Initially unchallenged by their northern counterparts, the aggressive Mediterranean fortune seekers began to tap the wealth of hitherto inaccessible or unknown sources. Although these European states glittered for a time during the sixteenth century, they ultimately failed to prosper from their windfall discoveries. The literature abounds with particularistic reasons why each failed to take advantage of its opportunities. In this study emphasis will be placed on how the experiences of these countries fit into a more generalized pattern, specifically showing that they suffered from the contradictions inherent in their respective social structures, which it seems no amount of wealth could have corrected.

The literature is equally aware that while the western and central Mediterranean were experiencing downward cycles similar to those previously undergone in the wider world, something new and distinctive was taking place in the northwestern corner of Europe. It has been named capitalism. When, why, and how it appeared has produced a voluminous and oftentimes contentious series of debates.[11] Many authors who have attempted to determine the reasons for European success have adopted one of the prominent positions in that debate. That is, they place misguided emphasis on the commercial revolution in late medieval Europe instead of focusing on the crucial social changes that took place in a few select regions.

For it is important to note that, quite by chance, well before the Netherlands and England emerged in their mature forms, unique modifications had taken place in their respective social structures. Minor though many of these changes may have seemed at the time, ultimately they would prove decisive in the transition to capitalism. Whereas elsewhere the social structure continued to be heavily weighted in favor of traditionalism, in the Netherlands and England new forces emerged that were capable of offering competition. That the Netherlands was ultimately unable to take full advantage of the opportunity whereas England was able to make continuous progress, demonstrates that the outcome was not inevitable. England, however, avoided the pitfalls that not only ensnared the Dutch but had also hindered social formations in other parts of the world. The crucial watershed must be seen as having been the English Civil War. Traditionalism was defeated, capitalism became entrenched as the dominant mode of production, and neither England nor the world economy would ever be the same again.[12] Thus for almost three centuries the northwestern corner of Europe would form the core of the first world economy.

The emergence of capitalism in northwest Europe facilitated the creation of peripheries. Unlike other global histories, this study will attempt to give a specificity to a term that is usually used in the most random ways. Although spatial location played a part in the creation of peripheries, the term as used here, has little to do with geography. Rather, it refers to certain regions whose social relations of production were transformed by their integration with the core of the world economy. Specifically, as a response to market opportunities that a growing Europe was creating and the structures that the mercantile capitalist mode of production was establishing, social change was being imposed in such diverse regions as eastern Europe, western Africa, northeastern Brazil, and many of the Caribbean Islands. Whether these changes took the form of a reemergence of serfdom or the implantation of chattel slavery, the periphery should be defined as those regions where the social system became dominated by coerced labor, which, in turn, reflected a response to the emergence of a world economy. The periphery, then, is not a vague notion but a category naming regions where a specific and concrete social order arose from and responded to the needs of capitalism.[13]

At the same time capitalism created the periphery, it also established dependencies. Whereas peripheries might exist either as independent entities or as colonies, a dependency derived its status from its colonial position. Although the two categories may have shared some superficial similarities, there were also fundamental differences between them. These stemmed from what was produced, the nature of the organization of production, and the resultant social relations. Thus, whereas production in the periphery required coerced labor, the dominant tendency of labor organization in the dependencies was in the opposite direction. Labor organization, in turn, reflected both what was produced and the priorities of the organizers of production. For example, because the commodities exported by the peripheries served as complements to the economies of the core, the organizers of production in each sphere had every reason to be satisfied with the basic structure of the system and hence tacitly to desire its perpetuation. Output in the dependencies, on the other hand, may have competed with metropolitan production, and therefore, at least at various times, the colonial power may have deemed it necessary to regulate or even to suppress colonial economic development. As a result, quite unlike the situation that prevailed in the peripheries, in the dependencies the organizers of production had less reason to be satisfied with the system and its continuation.[14]

As suggested by the existence of colonial dependencies, the colonial powers of Europe formed another important component of the first world economy. During the seventeenth century, the Spanish and Portuguese pioneers of overseas settlement were joined by the English, French, and, to a lesser extent, the Dutch. These additions contributed to the proliferation of the area of settlement. Frontier regions of Spanish America, the interior of Brazil, the eastern seaboard of North America, and the myriad of islands in the Caribbean all were colonized during this century. In many instances the colonies formed important adjuncts to the metropolitan economies. In fact, depression in the colonies or even a significant slump in trade could have an enormous negative impact in the metropolis. Thus fortunes on both sides of the Atlantic became increasingly intertwined.

Although the first world economy continued to grow and become more complex, many areas of the world still remained external to the new system. Eastern Africa, India, Ceylon, Indonesia, southeast Asia, China, Japan, and the Middle East all are included in this category. The criterion for determining membership was not whether a particular region engaged in long-distance trade with the core or other parts of the world economy. For in fact there was great variation in the degree to which the respective territories pursued overseas commerce, ranging from the limited participation of isolationist Ming China and Tokugawa Japan to the intensive export economies of Java and Mughal India. Rather, what distinguished the external areas from the other categories was that participation in commercial relations was discretionary and that, even where trade was fairly substantial and important, it seems to have had little lasting impact on the structures of the respective social formations.

By the eighteenth century the component parts of the first world economy were in place. Largely because of the maturation of capitalist relations of production in England, that small island nation was able to dominate world trade. Not surprisingly, the colonial powers of western Europe were envious of that supremacy. They were jealous not only of England's rule over a flourishing and diverse colonial empire but also of its ability to infiltrate rival colonies. The Continentals were not content with their situation. Convinced that England's overall supremacy stemmed from its economic base, they sought to emulate, duplicate, and even outdo their island rival. By adopting policies that have commonly been referred to as "mercantilistic," each independently set out to transform its economy and make it more productive. Nevertheless, despite sometimes significant state sponsorship of the efforts to promote growth, the results were disappointing. Although their respective economies grew at rates faster than in the seventeenth century, the gap between them and England continued to grow. The principal reason was that the traditional state of Europe could not compete successfully as long as its basic contradictions remained unresolved. To have done so would have required a similar conversion to capitalist relations of production. This, however, was not a viable option, as none of the Continentals had produced a class capable of challenging the existing order, and the forces of tradition and privilege were unlikely to preside voluntarily over their own demise.

Undeterred by their economic failures, the Continentals adopted a more direct challenge to England's hegemony. In essence, they chose warfare as a means to accomplish what they were unable to achieve by peaceful competition. Thus, throughout the eighteenth century, various combinations of powers sought to defeat England on the battlefield. They hoped that victory would enable them to win generous economic concessions. Because the constant warfare was fought in many parts of the world, the concerned parties felt the need to strengthen their colonies so that they could defend themselves against foreign interlopers. It was also perceived that it would be necessary to make them more dependent on the metropolis if it was to reap the benefits that it should derive from having colonies. What ministers in European capitals did not foresee was the extent to which the colonials would both resent and resist these new departures. When the various metropolises refused to back down, the colonials resorted to revolution. Although it would take fifty years before the process was completed, eventually every revolution succeeded. Yet the world economy into which they emerged was to be radically different from the one from which they had tried to escape.

Because the independence movements coincided with the gestation of the industrial revolution, the way was being cleared for the creation of a new world economy. Industrialization would generate new demands in the core, while it in turn sought to impose new conditions on the former dependencies, on the peripheries, and even on the external areas. Not only would there be a reshuffling of the roles played by the various component parts and an enlarging of the scope of the world economy, there would also be a redefinition of the terms of incorporation into the larger whole. Much of the nineteenth century would be devoted to this reorganization.

Before one considers the stages of evolution of the first world economy, however, one might make a few observations concerning the degree of interaction and integration among various parts of the world prior to the fifteenth century. Only by taking this into account can one appreciate how much this system departed from the conditions that had previously prevailed. Eric Wolf provides one approach to the problem. Perhaps because of his anthropological background, in the introductory sections of his volume Wolf seeks certain unifying factors. To this end he identifies ecological zones that horizontally crisscross the globe. Whatever the continent, he notes, peoples who lived in environments of the same basic makeup made remarkably similar adjustments. The forest dwellers of Africa, Asia, and the Americas, for example, found solutions to their problems that shared a great deal of resemblance. Likewise, desert peoples coped with their harsh environments in similar ways. Thus Wolf concludes by emphasizing the case for the unifying factors in the human historical experience.[15]

The social and political institutions developed by peoples in different parts of the world also bore striking similarities. Because it raises such crucial questions concerning the development of capitalism in Europe, one such system that merits elaboration is feudalism. Historians of the European experience have applied the term to the setting of the later Middle Ages. Its component parts are said to consist of a subject peasantry, service instead of salary, the supremacy of a specialized class of warriors, ties of obedience and protection, fragmentation of authority, and a natural economy. When these scholars compared European institutions with those of other societies, they generally concluded that those of Europe were unique and that the term *feudalism* could be applied with accuracy only to the European experience.

A minority of scholars, however, denied that feudalism was a uniquely European institution. Edwin Reischauer, for example, wrote that "feudalism is not merely a chance array of facts in early European history, but is a fundamental . . . form of human organization."[16] For when one looks at the core institutions of feudalism rather than superstructural trappings such as chivalry, one sees that they fall into the wider category that has been broadly defined as the tributary mode of production.[17] What all feudal systems had in common was the supplanting of a previous state or kinship structure by a class of seigneurs as the dominant force in society. The new ruling seigneurs established the right to extract by extra-economic coercion the surplus of the producers. In addition, they proceeded to arrogate the right to administer arbitrary justice. The producers, however, retained rights, the most important of which was continued access to the means of production as long as they met their obligations to their overlords. As will be seen, these conditions prevailed in many parts of the world as well as in medieval Europe.

In addition to broad similarities in their cultural evolution, migration connected various regions of the world. Often movement was so gradual as to be almost imperceptible. Thus, in the Americas, after crossing the land bridge that was formed in the Bering Strait during the last ice age, humans slowly meandered southward until they reached the southern tip of South America about 9000 B.C. It is reckoned that this represented an advance of only eighteen miles per generation. On the other hand, the dispersal of populations could be fairly rapid. This occurred in Africa, where between roughly the third century B.C. and the third century A.D., peoples speaking Bantu languages occupied the southern half of the continent.[18]

Migration was equally important in Asia. For millennia the Indian subcontinent served as a magnet to groups of migrants and invaders from the northwest. It is estimated that approximately two thousand years ago Indians became an important influence in southeast Asia, where many elements of Hindu culture were bequeathed. In this region they encountered populations that millennia before had migrated from the northern interior of China and Tibet. In fact, southward migration appears to have been the dominant tendency in much of east and southeast Asia. Thus, Chinese-speaking peoples gradually permeated southward from the Yellow River to the Yangtze and south China, while Burmans migrated southward along the Irrawaddy, the Thais descended the Chao Phraya, the Khmers moved down the Mekong, and the Vietnamese followed the Red River. Similarly, Indonesia, Polynesia, and Australia were settled by people who originated in Malaya.[19]

Often, seemingly without the aid of large-scale migration, knowledge of various kinds circulated over vast distances. Whereas it was once fashionable to assume that abstract ideas about such institutions as kingship were transferred over long distances, most modern scholars believe that the independent evolution of these notions is the more likely probability. The transfer of techniques concerning material culture, however, is a much stronger possibility. Although scholars agree that there were more sites of the independent invention of agriculture than had previously been believed, in many areas both the knowledge of cultivation and the introduction of new crops came from outside influence. An even stronger case can be made for metallurgy, as the techniques are often so esoteric that they are unlikely to have had multiple origins. This is especially true of the production of iron, which was so similar in so many parts of the world that it probably originated in only a few areas.

Most of the world was also linked by commercial exchanges. This often involved remarkably long distances and extremely arduous journeys. Both the passage over the Great Silk Road at tremendously high elevations from China to the Middle East and the crossing of the Sahara Desert from the Western Sudan to North Africa were just such grueling undertakings. The readiness of traders to embark on lengthy journeys shows that few areas were untouched by the phenomenon of long-distance commerce. For example, it has recently been postulated that by the tenth century direct links, probably by sea, had been forged between North and South America.[20] Despite the ubiquity of trade, however, the Indian Ocean remained the most important conveyor of goods, attracting commodities from such distant places as Japan, at one extreme, and Rome and East Africa, at the other.

Although there were many points of contact among the various regions of the world, it is critical to emphasize how relatively unimportant these were in terms of their ability to create conditions of integration. For example, although some transhumant pastoral people such as Turkish-speaking herders of Central Asia might maintain contacts with an ancestral homeland, migrations were usually unidirectional. Ties between the migrants and their points of origin generally appear to have been completely severed. It should also be noted that the knowledge that a given society received from diffusion probably represented only a small percentage of the general fund of information. Even when exposed to new ideas, conservative human nature is likely to resist the implementation of new techniques unless they are of such clear-cut superiority over the extant technology that not to adopt them would be foolhardy.

One should also not overestimate the role of international trade in forging linkages of substance between distant lands. For with the exception of a few commodities, it consisted mostly of the discretionary exchange of luxuries such as gold, jewels, spices, and ceramics. Moreover, because the volume was relatively small and it was designed to satisfy the whims of aristocracies, it rarely formed an integral part of the regional economies. Thus one can follow the conclusion of L. S. Stavrianos, who notes that prior to the sixteenth century, "there were parallel histories of separate peoples rather than one unified history of mankind."[21]

Even before the sixteenth century, however, social processes that would eventually lead to a radical reconstruction of the world and impose integration upon it were already in gestation. Similar beginnings were made in various parts of the world, but only in Europe were they carried to fruition. This is rather surprising, as the pad from which Europe would launch its great leap was significantly more modest than those of many contemporary societies. It therefore becomes necessary to attempt two inquiries. The first is to investigate both the achievements of the different areas of the wider world and the reasons why they were unable to maintain their momentum. The second will involve focusing on Europe to see how it was able to avoid the pitfalls that hampered its contemporaries.

# 2

# THE WIDER WORLD

Because Europe has established an overwhelming and continually accelerating technological lead with respect to the wider world, Westerners often assume that this is a situation that has always prevailed. Nothing, however, could be further from the truth. In most instances, the technological advances that accompanied Europe's emergence into the early-modern era had been anticipated elsewhere. In fact, with the exception of the contributions of ancient Greece, none of the major technological innovations that were responsible for material progress in human civilization was first developed in Europe.

Rather, it was the wider world that spawned sophisticated agricultural systems, pioneered the development of metallurgy, witnessed the perfection of a wide variety of mechanical inventions, and uncovered many keys to abstract knowledge. Moreover, prior to the fifteenth century, in many parts of the world these techniques were applied in such a fashion as to create physically and socially impressive societies that far surpassed anything achieved in medieval Europe. The main question to be dealt with is why the wider world was unable to consolidate the early lead it enjoyed. Before addressing that issue, however, it will be necessary to describe the achievements that were attained by peoples in widely separated parts of the globe.

## THE AGRICULTURAL BASE

Perhaps the single most important achievement of the wider world was the agricultural revolution—the process by which man the hunter, the gatherer, or the fisherman was converted into a producer of food. The domestication of plants was to have radical repercussions in a variety of ways. First of all, it enabled human beings to abandon a nomadic or transhumant life-style for a reasonably settled existence. To a greater extent than had prevailed previously, humans were able to become dominant over the environment. This, in turn, provided the backdrop that allowed population to increase by geometric proportions, forever changing mankind's relationship both with the surroundings and with other humans.

Since scholars once believed that the agricultural revolution involved a significant technological breakthrough that was unlikely to have occurred in several different places, they often assumed that agriculture began in one place and that its knowledge subsequently diffused elsewhere. The most likely candidate was considered to be the so-called Fertile Crescent located in Mesopotamia between the valleys of the Tigris and Euphrates rivers, although some authorities did admit of the possibility of a separate origin in southeast Asia. More recently, recognized wisdom has begun to lean toward a viewpoint that stresses the possibility of multiple independent sites of origin. It has even been suggested that plant domestication in Ethiopia and Persia may have predated that of Mesopotamia.[1] It would also appear that agriculture was practiced from a very early date in Thailand. Moreover, others have argued the case for the independent origin of both savanna and forest agriculture in West Africa. Similarly, it is believed that Mesoamerica, Andean Peru, and the Caribbean coast of South America all developed agriculture without reference to other areas for tutelage. Thus, although the knowledge of agriculture seems to have diffused into Europe, India, and China as well as percolating from the centers of its inception, it no longer seems necessary to consider the beginning of plant domestication as an esoteric phenomenon.[2]

Since in secular terms the time separating the appearance of agriculture in various parts of the world was minuscule, diffusion of agricultural knowledge seemed a likely explanation of the rapid permeation of this revolutionary technology. It now would seem that the transition had much more to do with population growth pressures that were being imposed on various groups around the world. More specifically, it would appear that as gatherers human beings had had a knowledge of seeds and their propagation for some time. As long as population densities remained low, however, the "effort-price" of agriculture—that is, the amount of input in terms of time invested vis-à-vis the yield to be harvested—remained unattractive. As population densities increased and natural food became more difficult to procure, the "effort-price" pendulum began to favor cultivation. Thus, it must be emphasized that this transition was not merely fortuitous. Rather, it represented a deliberate decision by groups whose growing populations were being threatened by the inability of the natural environment to guarantee all of their needs.[3]

The best demonstration of this hypothesis can be seen by looking at the example of the Americas. Here, as elsewhere, human beings lived mainly as hunters, benefiting from the large herds of game that had crossed the land bridge from Asia to take advantage of the virgin vegetation of the Americas. Suddenly, beginning about ten thousand years ago, the climatic phenomenon known as the Altithermal, during which the temperature became warmer and the atmosphere became drier, drastically changed the environment. Glaciers melted, the land bridge closed, water sources dried up, and vegetation disappeared and along with it the animals that had formed the staple of the human diet. It cannot be coincidental that it was shortly after the disappearance of the big game that the first traces of horticulture in the Americas are to be seen. In lieu of animals to prey upon, agricultural products became a much more attractive proposition, and people began to use knowledge that previously had remained latent in their minds.[4]

Because of its implications for subsequent human development, it is difficult to think of a better phrase than the "agricultural revolution" to describe the transition of human beings from parasites on the environment to producers of their own sustenance. But the term demands an immediate qualification. In most regions many thousands of years elapsed between the time when it was first practiced and the time when it became an almost universal undertaking. Surprisingly, for example, in light of what was subsequently to transpire in terms of its meteoric growth and innovative capacity, China was to be a relative latecomer to cultivation. Nor should one think of agriculture as having immediately and irrevocably subsumed other modes of existence. Quite the contrary, it was a slow and tedious process by which it became the major source of sustenance among most peoples. In parts of Mesoamerica, for example, it was to be many thousands of years after the first domestication of plants that agricultural produce came to make up the staple of the human diet.[5]

Nor did mastering the science of horticulture come easily or quickly. Initially, virtually the only tool available to the cultivator was the wooden digging stick, a fairly inefficient implement. As a result, in most areas of the world, farmers initially resorted to a method that is popularly known as slash and burn. Swidden, its more academic name, involved clearing fields with the use of fire and sometimes sowing the seeds in the ashes that were left. Although slash and burn is often viewed as being a primitive technique, it is ineffective only insofar as the long fallow periods required to regenerate the soil necessitate that there be extensive tracts of land relative to the population. Over time, in many areas ways were found to make more efficient use of the land. One such device was crop rotation, a process by which a given plot would be planted with a series of different crops. Because each of the succession of plant forms made different demands on the soil, the same piece of land could be maintained in permanent usage. This tendency toward constant usage of the soil was also abetted by the use of a wide variety of fertilizers, which artificially restored the nutrients that the plant life had taken away.

After millennia of trial and error, different staples began to emerge in the various regions of the world. Although maize formed part of one of the richest and most diverse plant complexes on earth, it clearly emerged as the dominant crop in Mesoamerica. It evolved from a wild grass whose fruit was no bigger than a thimble to the huge cobs with which we are familiar today. Part of the reason for its prominence in Mesoamerica was that it was ideally suited to the temperate climate of the highlands of·the *mesa central*. Moreover, several harvests could be produced annually, and maize possesses an extremely high nutritional value: When it replaced manioc as the staple among groups of Indians on the Caribbean coast, there was an immediate and significant growth in population.[6]

In other parts of the world, wheat came to be the dominant crop. Whether or not it was first domesticated in Persia or in the Tigris-Euphrates Valley, it had diffused over a wide area well before the Christian era. Its cultivation spread first to the Nile Valley and North Africa, then as far east as India and China. It did well in areas that featured winter rains and even better in fertile river valleys, where regular flooding made possible the harvesting of several crops each year. Therefore, where its cultivation was feasible, wheat came to supplant other grain crops, even though the latter may have been cultivated for a considerable amount of time.[7]

Wet rice was the third major staple that was developed in the wider world. Like wheat, it came to be cultivated over a vast expanse of territory that included Madagascar, parts of East Africa and India, most of southeast Asia, China, and Japan. The example of Japan demonstrates how important it could be. Composed of four main, but extremely mountainous islands, Japan had little arable land with which to work. Under such conditions it was essential to find a staple that could make maximum use of the limited land resources. That the islands were able to support dense populations throughout Japan's history is testimony to the high yields of wet rice, arguably the highest per acre of any domesticated plant. In fact, in parts of southeast Asia, yield ratios of 100:1 were attained, and a combination of wet and dry and early and late varieties enabled rice to be grown throughout the year.[8]

Whereas some regions placed heavy emphasis on one staple, others exhibited a truly remarkable diversity. None was more interesting than the complex that was developed in Greater Peru. The unusual terrain at once necessitated a unique adaptation and provided the backdrop for a unique synthesis. The Andean world has often been characterized as vertical, as the terrain rises precipitously from the narrow coastal belt to the high Andes of more than fifteen thousand feet within a few hundred miles of the coast. Although each elevation called for a different solution in terms of what was grown and under what conditions, the result was a diversity in production rivaling that of any region of the world. The tropical products of the coast yielded to maize as the intermediate altitudes were reached. Finally, all had to surrender to the remarkable potato, able to prosper at what for other plants were forbidding altitudes. Andean cultivation became so specialized that twenty-four different varieties of potato were adapted to different mini-environments. Because the varying climates provided a myriad of growing seasons, farmers sought to acquire plots at different elevations, thus allowing them to maximize annual production.[9]

Equally interesting, if only because it is less well known, was the flowering of agriculture in the Arab world between roughly A.D. 700 and 1100. North Africa and the Middle East had always been firmly entrenched in the complex that produced wheat with the aid of winter rainfall. Partly because of the stability and unity brought by the Arab conquest of the seventh century and partly because of the increased contacts with the wider world that followed in its wake, a miraculous transformation took place. "The Arab agricultural revolution," as Andrew Watson calls it, stemmed largely from the Arab world's Indian connection. Rice, sugar, cotton, and citrus fruits, among other tropical plant forms, all diffused from India during this epoch. All summer crops, these represented a windfall that made it possible to use land that previously had remained idle during many months of the year. Everywhere throughout the Arab world, but especially in Mesopotamia and Egypt, large surpluses came to be produced, as three harvests were yielded annually.[10]

There are those who argue that the pinnacle of agricultural production in the wider world was achieved in the Indian subcontinent. These claims are based partly on the expertise that was developed and partly on the range of plant life that was produced. In this regard the environment of the subcontinent was particularly favorable, as it included river valleys, the broad plains of the north, diverse highlands, subtropical regions, and a variety of specialized minizones. There is evidence of double-cropping of grains from an early date, with wheat and barley being sown in the winter and dry rice and millet during the summer. By at least the advent of the Christian era a variety of other crops, including sugar, citrus fruits, and wet rice, had been added to the complex. Such a level of sophistication was reached that industrial crops like cotton, jute, hemp, and silk came to play a large role in the overall agro-industrial complex. The proponents of the primacy of Indian agriculture would point not only to its diversity but also to its yields, as they were reputed to be exceedingly high.[11]

Most serious disagreement about the primacy of Indian agriculture would probably come from those who argue the case for China. Chinese civilization was based in the north along the Yellow River valley, but its agricultural development was rather unimpressive. Although wheat replaced millet as the staple somewhat before the beginning of the Christian era, its propagation was slow in evolving. Its maturation as a staple crop many centuries later, however, coincided roughly with an era when Chinese civilization was gravitating southward toward the Yangtze Valley. There they not only learned wet-rice cultivation from northern southeast Asia but proceeded to perfect it in a way never previously accomplished. Through careful seed selection the Chinese were able to produce drought-resistant strains and others whose harvest times were progressively reduced from six months, to one hundred days, to sixty days, and finally down to forty days. The multiple-cropping of both wheat and rice enabled an agricultural special-ization that was perhaps unequaled. Chinese farmers concentrated on timber, vegetables, fruits, sugar, hemp, oils, paper, silk, and even fish farming among other specialties. The very success of the Chinese prompted Mark Elvin to conclude that "by the thirteenth century . . . China had what was probably the most sophisticated agriculture in the world."[12]

That agriculture in the wider world became as productive as it did was not accidental. Rather, it resulted from experimentation, building upon what had been learned, and, frequently, heavy inputs of labor and capital. It is not coincidental that what may have been the first agrarian manual in the world appeared in eighth-century China, followed soon thereafter by one of Arab authorship. Similar thoughtfulness prompted Mexicans to invent and perfect *chinampa*. In order to ensure proper early gestation, seedlings were first planted in fertile mud that had been dredged from the bottom of shallow lakes. A similar principle and technique underwrote the cultivation of wet rice. Seedlings were planted individually in the paddies until they had reached the proper stage of growth and could be safely transplanted. The work has been described as tedious, backbreaking, and awfully muddy. These and a whole range of other innovations and sacrifices were the catalysts that contributed to high levels of productivity.[13]

In many parts of the wider world the knowledge of how to harness water and to use it to maximum advantage was an important agricultural improvement. This was especially true in regions where the climate was extremely dry. For example, because there is virtually no rainfall in coastal Peru, the regions beyond the river valleys were chronically in need of water. Although irrigation had a long antiquity in the area, one of the main achievements of the Incas in the fifteenth century was to revive coastal agriculture by rebuilding and enlarging the systems of irrigation. The Sudanic zones of western Africa were equally hostile to agriculture, with the very short rainy season followed by a prolonged dry one. Nevertheless, diverting the waters of the Niger River and its tributaries, the Sudanic peoples used wells, flooding, and the *shaduf* (a device for raising well water and distributing it over the fields) to irrigate a vast expanse of territory that otherwise could not have been cultivated. Although nature created these as harsh lands, humans transformed them to the extent that they amply supplied the needs of the farmers, the cities, and the numerous livestock. Directly to the north of the Sudan, the Arab world also faced problems of water management. It met the challenge in a similar fashion. According to Andrew Watson, "it would only be a slight exaggeration to say that there was hardly a river, stream, oases, spring . . . or predictable flood that was not fully exploited."[14]

In many ways the Chinese system of water management was even more remarkable. For, whereas the peoples of the arid zones were obliged to come to grips with their problem of drought, the Chinese were blessed with abundant resources of water. Oftentimes in human history, however, abundance has led to wasteful treatment of the resource. The Chinese, on the contrary, perceived that careful control of water could significantly improve their already productive agriculture. Making full use of the many river systems of southern China, the government created agencies whose sole purpose was the coordination and management of water. Canals connecting rivers and streams, aqueducts and dams for storing water, irrigation ditches to deliver it to the desired locations, terracing to prevent its escape, sluice gates to maintain the desired water levels, and devices for both raising and lowering water all formed part of a water management system unrivaled anywhere in the world. The prominence of water control led one early Western scholar to refer to China as an "hydraulic society."[15]

Iron was another key component of the agricultural cycle, although there were great variations in its relative importance. The archeological record suggests that knowledge of smelting was perfected in southwest Asia around 3500 B.C. Although there is debate concerning other areas of independent invention, more so than is the case with agriculture, it can be said that the proliferation of smelting was probably due to diffusion. Some representative dates of its arrival in various parts of the world are: Nok in northern Nigeria, about 900 B.C.; northern India, around 800 B.C.; China, about 600 B.C.; Meroe in the Sudan, around 500 B.C.; Japan, about A.D. 100; and the southern third of the African continent, around A.D. 300.[16]

Notably absent from the list is the American continent, which because of its isolation was to be deprived of the contact that would have taught it the processes necessary for the manufacture of the tools required to deal with its difficult environments. Without iron, much of the potentially fertile American continent could not be profitably exploited, thus, in part, severely limiting the possible growth of American civilization. Just how crucial iron was to conquest of an environment can be gleaned from the contemporaneous, even synonymous, spread of agriculture and iron throughout most of the African continent. Whereas most of Africa, however, continued to depend on the hoe as the principal agricultural tool, elsewhere plows came into general usage. Nowhere was this more evident than in India, where heavy plows made their appearance fully two millennia before they would become common in Europe.[17]

The role of domestic animals as factors of production varied considerably. In Mesoamerica, where they were virtually unknown, in most of Africa south of the Sahara, where the disease-ridden environment prevented their survival, and Japan, where arable land was too valuable to allow for pasturage, animal power did not add much to the process of production. In South America, as well, their contribution was limited to the wool provided by the alpaca and the limited carrying capacity of the llama. Even in China they played a minor role, as the Chinese preferred to keep land in arable production rather than devoting some of it to pasture. The situation in southeast Asia, however, was very different, insofar as oxen and water buffalo were essential components in the process of wet-rice cultivation. The most sophisticated use of animal power, however, was in India, where oxen, buffalo, and even elephants were made to work for man. As early as the beginning of the Christian era, there are reports of up to twenty-four oxen being harnessed to the heaviest plows.[18]

Before considering other aspects of developments in the wider world, some qualification and generalization might be appropriate. Not all peoples participated equally in the general surge forward. Quite the contrary, on every continent there remained groups who were either strangers to agriculture or who practiced it inefficiently. Nevertheless, it should be emphasized that on every continent during the critical period between roughly A.D. 1000 and A.D. 1500 there were societies whose agricultural potential far surpassed that of Europe. Sophisticated crop rotation, high-yielding staples, and the extensive use of fertilizers, iron, animal power, and irrigation were just some factors that distinguished agriculture in the wider world from that of Europe. "In many ways," writes Peter Farb, New World agriculture "was superior [to that of the Old World]. Indians cultivated a wider variety of plants than did Europeans at the time of the discovery of North America and they used horticultural techniques that were in many cases more advanced."[19] It should be noted that an even stronger case could be made for other areas of the world.

## MATERIAL PROGRESS IN THE WIDER WORLD

The large agricultural surpluses produced throughout the wider world freed many segments of the populace to engage in nonagrarian specialization. Delving into a broad range of activities, over time these societies were able to improve on a variety of skills. Material, social, and intellectual considerations were all part of an equation that contributed to increasingly complex social formations. Any objective assessment comparing the achievements of the wider world with those of Europe prior to the fifteenth century would have to conclude that the former were far more impressive.

Among the most notable achievements of the wider world were its intellectual ones. Although they remained isolated from other cultures, Mesoamericans were able to invent for themselves many sophisticated techniques, including a complex calendrical system, a hieroglyphic script, and painting. Africans mastered sculpture, carving, and music. Across the ocean in India, Hindu culture was noted for art, music, literature, and the drama. Hindu influence was also prevalent throughout southeast Asia, where Sanskrit functioned as a lingua franca and provided the medium for literature and philosophical debate. The Arabs, on the other hand, can perhaps be considered to have been more pragmatic. They excelled at algebra, trigonometry, optics, medicine, law, and geography.[20]

For sheer scope in intellectual and practical prowess, however, none could approach the Chinese. By the time of the Sung (A.D. 960–1275), heavy emphasis had come to be placed on the scientific and the technological. In addition to pioneering such studies as algebra, physics, and mechanical engineering, the list of their inventions is truly astonishing. Among those that eventually diffused to the West are magnetic science, quantitative cartography, cast iron, and the double-acting principle of rotary and longitudinal motion. One should bear in mind the conclusion reached by Joseph Needham, the historian par excellence of Chinese science. "West European technology," he writes, "may be said to have been less advanced than that of any Old World region" prior to the fifteenth century.[21]

Urbanization was also a pervasive phenomenon that emerged throughout the wider world. In many regions, in fact, congregating in towns was of considerable antiquity. Even before the founding of the Old Kingdom more than five thousand years ago, for example, the Nile Valley from Upper Egypt to the Mediterranean supported numerous cities. In northern India, archeologists date the remains of an urban culture known as the Harappa to about 2600 B.C. Even in America urbanization began at an early date; its origins can be traced to the Olmec site of Monte Alban, which was begun about 1100 B.C. Thus, at a time when many Europeans were still in a seminomadic state, urbanization had taken root in many parts of the world.[22]

Although most urban sites might aptly be characterized as towns, others grew into substantial cities. Arab geographers of the eleventh century described Kumbi Saleh, the capital of the Sudanic state of Ghana, as a very large city, which was divided between a "pagan" half and a Muslim half. Further to the south, in the forest belt, the two main streets of Benin City are said to have crossed at right angles and to have extended four miles in a straight line in each direction. Benin City, however, would not appear to have been as large as Teotihuacan, the dominant city in Mesoamerica during the classic period (c. A.D. 300–900). Founded in the sixth century, Teotihuacan had an estimated population of between two and six hundred thousand inhabitants. Despite its nomadic heritage, the Arab world produced cities that were at least as large as those in the Americas. For example, while it reigned as capital of the Arab empire during the ascendancy of the Abbasid caliphate (founded A.D. 762), Baghdad had a population that probably exceeded five hundred thousand. Urbanization, however, reached its apogee in China. During the southern Sung period (1135–1275), Kai'feng, Peking, and Nanking each had a population of more than a million, and some estimates credit Soochow with as many as two million residents.[23]

Although a whole range of activities usually took place within a given city, many were primarily specialized. Some, such as the Mayan cities of the Yucatan peninsula and the Hindu temple cities of India, functioned mainly as religious centers to which people made regular pilgrimages. The raison d'être of others was commerce. Such diverse places as the cities bordering on the southern Sahara Desert or the port of Canton in China, as well as innumerable sites in between, were concerned with long-distance trade.[24] Generally speaking, however, the largest cities were administrative centers. The court, its retinue, the bureaucracy, and the many retainers necessary to support the establishment were gathered together in these locations. Tenochtitlan, the Aztec capital; Delhi, seat of the sultanate in India that bore its name; and Kai'feng, elevated to the status of capital during the Sung dynasty in China, are but three examples of the general pattern.[25]

Many groups in the wider world also demonstrated the capacity to apply their craftsmanship on a grand scale. For the combination of technological skill and organizational ability involved in their building, the pyramids of Old Kingdom Egypt are probably unequaled in history. They were, however, surpassed in size, if not in technological know-how, by the step pyramids of Mesoamerica. Mesoamericans, especially the Maya, also produced massive and brilliant stone stela, some of which weighed more than fifty thousand tons. For sheer beauty and elegance, however, the ornate palaces constructed by Hindu princes were unsurpassed. Similarly, the Khmers of Cambodia and the Burmans during the Pagan empire were noted for their extremely fine architecture, especially their Buddhist temples.[26]

Two remarkable achievements by the Chinese serve as a final example. The Great Wall, which was constructed in antiquity to keep "barbarians" out of the country, extended more than two thousand miles along China's northern border. Perhaps even more impressive, however, was the Grand Canal. Constructed over many centuries and at the cost of many thousands of lives, it eventually linked central China with the capital, which by the time of its completion had been transferred to the northern city of Peking.[27]

Specialized skills were also used in commodity production. In almost every area, the manufacture of cloth was an important undertaking. Peru, because of the unique combination of access to alpacas and the unusually cold climate, was one of the few regions where wool was the staple. In the western Sudan, the Arab world, and the Indian subcontinent, the production of cotton textiles was emphasized. Although the Arabs were reputed to be particularly adept at cotton manufacture, primacy in this field belonged to the Indians, whose fine cloths were unrivaled anywhere in the world and were to remain so until the industrial revolution. Similarly, Indian silk was of high quality, although it was probably not of the same standard as that produced by the Chinese. The Chinese, in turn, were particularly impressed by the luxury textiles of the Persians, especially their gold- and silver-threaded cloth and their unique velvets.[28]

Iron was the other industry of overwhelming importance. Whether manufactured by the village blacksmith in Africa or produced in the factory-type enterprises of the Arab world, it was a commodity that was needed in both war and peace. Indian iron stood out for its strength and durability and was used for a whole range of agricultural tools, including plows, sickles, axes, and spades. The Japanese were also adept at high-quality production. Their swords, often said to be composed of steel, were in high demand throughout a vast area.[29] In this endeavor, as in so many others, however, the Chinese surpassed the rest. In addition to being of first-rate quality, the quantity of iron output was truly staggering. Robert Hartwell notes that during the eleventh century, the annual production was in the neighborhood of 150 thousand tons—a figure, he hastens to point out, that was five times greater than that of England and Wales in 1640.[30]

In the most advanced economies some aspects of production took on a distinctly modern tone. In India the *khakarna* system gathered under one roof numerous artisans who created to the specifications of the owner. Similarly, in the Arab world shipyards, mills, and foundries operated on a scale that presupposed large sums of capital invested in production. The range and magnitude of such enterprises was even larger in China. Coal, alum, ships, salt, and paper were among the more important mass-produced commodities. Hartwell concludes that these activities were "undertaken on a scale of operation and absolute level of output that [was] not common in any other national economy before the end of the eighteenth century."[31]

Such large undertakings could only take place where financing could be arranged. In the south of India, merchant guilds, which have been described as multinational in their focus, provided this function. Family partnerships seem to have played the same role in China, although the scale of some enterprises suggests that more complex arrangements must have been available. The evidence, however, would seem to indicate that the Muslim world had the most advanced financial institutions. As Elihu Ashtor notes, in addition to the lending activities of merchant guilds, banking developed at an early date. He adds that by the eighth century, "huge sums" were deposited in these banks and that credit arrangements with the productive sector were the norm.[32]

Operations of this nature suggest that the labor force as well was at least partially modern in its composition. In the absence of better data it is impossible to quantify what percentage of total output was produced in which sector, although it is likely that simple artisan manufacture predominated. Nevertheless, there clearly emerged a class of worker who depended exclusively on wages for a livelihood. Although the proletarianization of the labor force appears to have been mainly an urban phenomenon, rural labor was also used in commodity production. "Putting out," especially in the production of textiles, became a common practice in many parts of the world. There is also evidence of the growth of an agricultural proletariat, which was obliged to labor for its more fortunate neighbors.[33]

Commodity production and the market went hand in hand. Indeed, there existed an intensive regional trade on every continent. Mexicans not only descended from their highlands toward the coastal plains to procure the tropical commodities of the forest, but after the eleventh century they seem to have made direct contact with South America. In western Africa, groups known variously as the Dyula and the Wangara carried goods throughout the savanna and into the southern forests. Similarly, following the Arab conquest, the worlds of Iberia, North Africa, and the Middle East achieved a remarkable degree of commercial integration.[34]

Markets and commerce were equally important in South and East Asia. Even in India, which was noted for internal isolation during its medieval period, there were signs of road building and a general revivification of trade by the tenth century. As was the case in so many other spheres, however, it was China that stood head and shoulders above the rest. Aided by its vast network of paved roads and canals, the country was converted into one giant internal market. It certainly inspired awe in the fourteenth-century Italian traveler Marco Polo who, speaking solely of the valley of the Yangtze, wrote that "in the amount of shipping it carries and the volume and the value of its traffic . . . it exceeds all the rivers of the Christians put together and their seas into the bargain."[35]

In addition to the regional trades, there existed a long-distance trade that drew most of the globe into its nexus. The notable exceptions were the Americas, which until 1492 remained a separate world, and Europe, which was too impoverished and underdeveloped during its Middle Ages to play a significant role. Some of this commerce was carried overland via such famous trade routes as the trans-Sahara or the Great Silk Road from China to the Middle East. Of the two, the crossing of the Sahara appears to have been used more consistently, partly because there was no waterborne alternative and also because it seems not to have been as vulnerable to the depredations of marauders as was a seven-month-long journey through the mountain passages that dominated the linkage between the Orient and the West.[36]

Both the greater security and the lower costs contributed to the growth of seaborne commerce in the Indian Ocean, which became much more important than that transported by land. At various times, Hindus, Ethiopians, Persians, Arab and Indian Muslims, and the Chinese were the leading participants. Their business brought them to such entrepôts and termini as Ormuz, Aden, various sites along both the Malabar and Coromandel coasts of India, Ceylon, Srivijayya, and Canton. The commerce involved the circulation of a staggering array of commodities from such distant places as the forests of West Africa, at one extreme, to the islands of Japan, at the other. Needless to say, it included the products of virtually every place in between.[37] By the fifteenth century, the port of Malacca on the Malay peninsula had become what was probably the most important entrepôt in the world. "At one single entrepôt," writes John Cady, "virtually all types of marketable seaborne products of the vast Asian continent and the East Indies islands were available for exchange."[38]

International commerce was almost exclusively the province of the specialist merchant. It was not uncommon for traders to take up semipermanent or even permanent residence in a foreign land. For example, Dyula merchant communities were to be found dispersed throughout most of West Africa. In a similar fashion, Hindu groups from South India crossed into Ceylon, where they served the foreign princes. Some cities, Alexandria and Canton, for example, housed merchants from many different places. In certain cases the contact became so intimate that the alien traders were assimilated into the communities. Quite ironically, in view of the later Chinese ostracism of foreign traders, many of those who resided in Canton became sinicized. The most successful merchants, whether resident at home, itinerant, or permanently stationed abroad, often made huge profits. This was equally true of the guilds of South India, the Karamis of North Africa, and the Co-hung of China.[39]

Nevertheless, in many regions merchants were viewed with a great deal of ambivalence. The traditional Japanese and Chinese social orders looked upon traders with contempt; in India the merchant castes ranked very low in the social hierarchy. Moreover, increasing Hindu social prejudices against travel abroad seemingly contributed to the Hindus' loss of their once prominent position in international commerce. Despite these prejudices, however, at the peaks of economic growth of the various regions, merchants came to be viewed in a more favorable light, at least by local rulers. In both North Africa and South India they were granted special favors in return for providing subsidies to the state. Even in Sung China, special decrees removed the official stigma that accompanied merchant status. Sons of merchants were even allowed to compete in the civil service examinations, as long as they themselves did not actively engage in commerce. Thus the possibility developed that a new element might emerge into the social hierarchy.[40]

At the other end of the spectrum of social acceptability were the large landowners. Often the genesis of their wealth in landed property was their relationship to individuals who were well placed in the traditional social structure, which had once been dominated by ties of kinship. As most societies expanded, however, there came to be alternative means of attaining the same position. As the Aztec conquests proceeded, for example, land was distributed in private fief to those who had distinguished themselves in battle. In China, merchants often invested in land, demonstrating a distinct preference for social standing at the expense of potential commercial profits. Whereas the Chinese merchant-turned-gentleman tended to become a conservative rentier, his Arab counterpart was more dynamic. In fact, the term *improving landlord* would not be out of place. During the heyday of the agricultural revolution, land became increasingly concentrated in the hands of the practitioners of the new agriculture, that is, those who were willing to invest more capital and labor into their estates.[41]

As is indicated by the transfer of landed property in the Arab world, in many regions, especially during periods of economic vibrance, there emerged the notion of land as a fully alienable commodity. In the fifteenth century, for example, private title to ownership of estates was opened to members of the Aztec aristocracy. Whereas private ownership of land was reserved for the Aztec nobility, in South Asia and the Arab empire peasants were considered to be freeholders of their land. In ninth-century China, under an arrangement known as the "equitable field system," by which peasants were made into freeholders, the state tried to ensure peasant ownership. Even where notions of communal tenures persisted, as was the case in the Muslim world, their existence was being threatened by the trend toward private ownership of land. "In practice, if not in legal theory," writes Andrew Watson, "the early Islamic world recognized that virtually all land was owned by an individual who had the right to sell, mortgage, or will it" as he so chose.[42]

In addition to the possibility of aggregating land through private acquisition or gaining wealth through commercial pursuits, there were other means of achieving social mobility. Excelling in military service often brought with it rewards bestowed by a grateful ruler. Passage into and upward through the government bureaucracy was another way of securing advancement. In theory this was especially true in imperial China. Through an elaborate system of examination and grading, all positions in the hierarchy were supposed to be within the reach of the man of talent, although success in passing the exams presupposed a thorough and often expensive education in the doctrines of Confucius.[43]

Bureaucratic control of the state epitomized by imperial China was only one of a variety of forms of exercising political control. At one extreme was the thoroughly centralized state, perhaps best typified by the Inca despotism that ruled over virtually every detail of the lives of its subjects. Another solution to the problem of regulating large territorial units was to maintain only a modicum of central control, leaving the day-to-day workings of the empire in provincial hands. This approach, for example, was chosen by both the Guptas of northern India and the Malians of the western Sudan. Finally, the Aztecs did not administer their empire at all. Rather, it was conceived of as a number of tribute zones, each of which was left to run its own affairs, as long as the periodic requisitions were surrendered to the central treasury.[44]

The state in the wider world often grew to considerable proportions. Sometimes this was facilitated by topography. For example, in India the plains to the north of the Vindhya Mountains were consolidated into vast empires on at least three different occasions. In part this resulted from the relatively easy communication in this region. Similarly, given coherence by the Niger River, the savanna of the western Sudan spawned the vast empires of Mali and Songhai.[45]

On other occasions, however, empires were created no matter what difficulties the environment posed. For most of their history the Chinese were able to maintain unified control over a huge territory, despite imposing physical obstacles. "Only an appreciation of the geographical difficulties which China had to overcome," writes Joseph Needham, "can give an idea of the immensity of the task of unification which the Chinese accomplished."[46] Perhaps the greatest task of all, however, was achieved by the Incas. Without the aid of a network of rivers to facilitate communication or animals that were capable of being mounted, they nevertheless constructed a vast empire in the rugged terrain of the Andes Mountains. Linked together by a centrally planned network of roads and bridges that had no equal in the contemporary world, at its peak the empire extended twenty-five hundred miles from north to south.[47]

Periods of maximum economic growth often coincided with the apex of state authority. Occasionally this was the result of the stability that a state imposed on domestic matters and the security it provided for travel and trade. The approach to economic matters could vary considerably. Sometimes governments chose to play an active role, as in Mauryan India, where the administration participated directly in a wide variety of important economic undertakings. Similarly, the economy of the Incas was fully managed from above, with specified quotas of different products assigned to the various segments of the population.[48] On the other hand, the state might foment development by pursuing a policy of nonintervention in economic matters. Whereas previous Chinese dynasties had meddled with the economy, during the Sung there was a conscious policy of laissez-faire.

According to Laurence Ma, this contributed to the fantastic growth of that era, a growth he considers to have been leading in the direction of "incipient capitalism."[49] At the height of prosperity of the Arab world, its rulers followed a similarly enlightened policy. It was based on the principles of laissez-faire, low taxation on commerce, and rebates to those who irrigated their land.[50]

The unfolding of developments in the wider world raises interesting questions. From the perspective of A.D. 1000, it would have been inconceivable that the wider world would lag and Europe would surge ahead. On each and every count that would have been considered in reaching a prognostication—including agricultural productivity, scientific knowledge, industrial output, and organizational capacity—the wider world clearly had a sizable lead. Moreover, a social scientist who had been denied knowledge of subsequent events might reach the same conclusion. For not only was the material achievement of the wider world much greater than that of Europe, but harbingers of the factors that would ultimately determine modernity were already in evidence. These included land viewed as a commodity, capital accumulation, capital in the process of production, monetized economies, lending institutions, and a working class divorced from the means of production. The wider world indeed seemed braced for the takeoff into modernity.

## ABORTED GROWTH

The breakthrough into modernity, however, did not take place in any region of the wider world. Quite the contrary, each fell victim to regression, stagnation, or a leveling off of progress. Whether the changes were temporary or relatively permanent, some of the reasons were unique to particular areas; others answered to rules of a more general nature. This section is devoted to a description and analysis of these phenomena in order to establish a basis for comparison with Europe. Specifically, it will demonstrate how similar historical process was in both regions. Moreover, it will perhaps provide the foundation for identifying the slight differences between them, differences that ultimately would prove crucial.

It is fairly easy to date the point at which a given region passed its pinnacle and began to decline or level off. For example, the fortunes of India began a downturn with the demise of the Gupta empire in A.D. 495. Rather remarkably, throughout both North and South America, the ninth century was the watershed. Although political fragmentation had been a constant factor within the Arab world almost from the inception of the empire, material and cultural decline can be dated from about the twelfth century. The case of China is somewhat more problematical, as the process was more gradual than elsewhere; nevertheless, it is fairly accurate to state that after the overthrow of the Sung dynasty by the invading Mongols in 1276, China never regained the dynamism of its past.[51]

Once the formidable Gupta empire began to disintegrate into its component parts, India entered what could be called its middle ages. Indian merchants came to play an increasingly minor role in both international and domestic commerce. In fact, the level of commerce itself seems to have reduced significantly. Fewer coins were minted and the amount of money in circulation apparently dwindled. With the decline of the once imposing royal courts, craftsmen drifted back to their villages, presumably to take up tillage of the soil. The guilds disintegrated, and craft regulation increasingly became the province of a powerful caste system that began to control more and more of Indian life.[52]

In Mesoamerica the period of downturn is referred to as the postclassic. Dating from roughly A.D. 900, it was a period of little material or cultural innovation. Not only was there no new construction, but that which had been built previously was allowed to fall into ruin. Cities that were once vibrant centers were abandoned. It was a time marked by internecine warfare, as is indicated by the fact that Mayan gods, which previously glorified fertility, came to emphasize prowess in battle. Various attempts, such as that of the Toltecs, to impose unity all ended in failure. As a consequence of the power vacuum, numerous groups from the north began to infiltrate the Valley of Mexico. One was a nomadic band known as the Aztec. By the fifteenth century, after having long served as mercenaries, they emerged as a power in their own right, and for almost a century they pillaged and plundered a wide region of Mesoamerica.[53]

By the twelfth century, the synthesis that had been combined to create the "economic miracle" in the Arab world had fallen apart. Even at the peak of productivity, the economy rested on a delicate balance of forces. When increased military activity upset that balance, an immediate downturn took place. The systems of irrigation, so painstakingly constructed, were allowed to fall into disuse. Soil eroded to the extent that formerly productive land reverted to desert. There was also a marked decrease in the quality of industrial production and in output. Even the formerly vigorous commercial sector experienced a recession, which ultimately would provide an opportunity for enterprising Italian merchants to infiltrate the region.[54]

The case of China is somewhat different insofar as the economic decline was not as drastic as it was elsewhere. Yet for almost a century the country was subjected to an often devastating foreign rule during which there was a significant downturn in population. Although indigenous rule was returned with the accession of the Ming dynasty in the late fourteenth century, China would never regain the glories of the southern Sung. For example, the output of steel reached only 50 percent of what had been produced previously. The country increasingly turned inward, and the level of overseas commerce was tremendously reduced. As population levels rose during the fifteenth and sixteenth centuries, labor became more abundant and hence cheaper. Under these circumstances it became economically more viable to depend on inexpensive labor rather than invest capital in improvements. Quite incredibly, the society that had invented much more than any other ceased in any way to be innovative.[55]

Among the reasons responsible for the general downturn in many regions of the wider world were the contradictions inherent in the institution of the state. Although it might foster economic growth through the implementation of wise policies, the state often overextended itself in pursuing political goals that brought few concrete returns. Military expenditures were one major drain. For instance, when the Mauryan army faced Alexander and the Greeks, it is said to have numbered 650 thousand infantry, 30 thousand cavalry, 9 thousand elephants, and 8 thousand chariots. Similarly, by the era of the Ming dynasty, the armed forces of China were significantly larger than those that had been commonplace in India. The standing army consisted of some three million men, each outfitted with standardized equipment, and the navy was composed of sixty-five hundred of the finest ships in the world. Impressive as these statistics are, they disguise the great strains that the support of such large military establishments placed on the revenues of the respective states.[56]

Plunder was a rather simplistic solution some chose in order to replenish depleted resources. The Cholas of South India, for example, not only began the institutionalized raiding of their neighbors but extended their operations into Ceylon. The Aztecs of Mesoamerica likewise regularized the art of raiding and extortion. Initially this course of action might prove successful because of the element of surprise. As the potential victims became alerted to the dangers and began to take measures to resist, however, the cost of raiding greatly increased. The Aztecs were in the painful process of learning the ramifications of raiding as a mode of existence when the first Europeans arrived. For as the total wealth of the social formation diminished drastically, competition within Aztec society for the decreasing spoils began to open fissures that would ultimately accrue to the benefit of the Spanish.[57]

Rather than engaging in predation as a matter of policy, most states viewed taxation of an industrious peasantry as the ideal manner of raising revenue. This was especially necessary because the strength of the upper classes enabled them successfully to resist taxation. Thus the state often sought to stabilize the position of the peasant. Such a policy was adopted in India, where the state fought a concerted campaign against slavery in order to ensure itself of a peasantry capable of paying taxes. Similarly, throughout the Arab world efforts were made to protect settled cultivators from the depredations of nomadic marauders. The "equitable field system" inaugurated in China during the T'ang dynasty had the same purpose. It envisaged guaranteeing the peasantry access to sufficient land so that they could provide the government with ample revenue. The policy of these states, had it been enacted with moderation, might have succeeded. But because the peasants seemed so vulnerable, states found it difficult to resist the temptation to place increasing burdens on them. Eventually, even these normally inarticulate members of society sought to ameliorate their condition.[58]

Most of the disaster that overtook the Arab world was also due to the policies enacted by states desperate for revenue. After taxing the peasantry to the brink of ruin, Arab governments began to look elsewhere for funds. The obvious choice was the buoyant economy. Even though prosperity had abounded while laissez-faire had been the prevailing philosophy, expedience obliged administrations to intervene in economic matters. Disastrous results followed. The granting of monopolies came to supersede free trade. Such heavy taxation was imposed on workshops that those which survived produced a distinctly inferior product. The state bit the hand that fed it, and by the time it realized what it had done, many areas had already reverted to a natural economy.[59]

Although the Chinese state was not as parasitic as those of the Arabs, the policies adopted by the bureaucrats in the service of the Ming emperors may also have had deleterious effects. Making use of their superior naval techniques, in the early fifteenth century the Chinese embarked on a series of voyages of trade and exploration throughout the Indian Ocean. Under the leadership of Admiral Cheng-Ho, the first of these expeditions consisted of many ships and carried a crew of 27,870. Subsequent voyages were also on a large scale. One scholar has even suggested that it appeared that China was on the verge of establishing a "thalassocracy."[60]

Nevertheless, the Ming dynasty did a sudden volte-face. The government decreed that foreigners were no longer welcome in China and that Chinese could no longer travel abroad. One theory as to why this course was chosen is that after hundreds of years of intermittent construction, the completion of the Grand Canal so improved internal communications that self-sufficiency became an option. Another is that the scholar-bureaucrats who administered the empire were frightened that the changes that might result from such new departures would threaten their ascendancy, and they lobbied successfully against foreign contacts.[61] One consequence of isolation was that a strong navy was no longer necessary and thus was not maintained. Isolation may have bequeathed an even more important legacy: Because it occurred at a time when Chinese science had become less innovative, China might have benefited from being able to learn from other areas of the world. By choosing self-sufficiency, however, the Chinese denied themselves this possibility.

In its desperation to find short-term solutions to serious problems, the state often paved the way for its own destruction by instituting policies that encouraged the emergence of a rival feudal mode of production. This was especially the case in the Arab world. Having taxed the peasants to the point of exhaustion and having disrupted the productive sectors to the extent that they were no longer vibrant, the state unwittingly began to mortgage its long-term future. In order to prolong its existence, the state granted land to mercenaries and surrendered privileges of future tax collection to those with ready cash. Although these were initially deemed to be short-term arrangements, as the state became weaker, the grantees began to assert hereditary privilege. Simultaneously, peasants, either rack-rented by the state or left at the mercy of rapacious tax collectors, began to recommend themselves to any seigneur who could protect them against the multiple demands of the hostile world in which they lived. Others, who borrowed in the hope of escaping from their plight, also found themselves bound to the soil when they could not repay their debts. Thus the tendency was for the formerly free peasantry to be converted into serfs.[62]

It has been argued that the middle ages of Indian history also witnessed the feudalization of the Indian social formation. As the organizational capacity of central authority diminished, rulers resorted to entrusting subordinates with the administration of the countryside. Although these positions were initially conceived of as forming part of the state bureaucracy, the tendency was for them to become hereditary in the family of the original grantee. According to R. S. Sharma, in some regions peasants became completely subordinated to the authority of their lord. He states that "in some areas the beneficiary was empowered to evict the peasants as well as make them stick to the soil. . . . These factors rendered the economic subjection of peasants . . . as complete as that of their European counterparts."[63] Although Sharma is not alone in depicting a feudal Indian economy, another school of thought denies its existence. These scholars, however, appear to be guided by a too Eurocentric definition that would conform to a model such as the one postulated by Marc Bloch instead of viewing feudalism in its larger context within the tributary mode of production.[64]

Some scholars prefer to use the term *manorial* to describe the phenomenon that overtook China, as the authority of the state never completely eroded, but the distinction would seem to be based largely on semantics. For despite its continuing existence, the state proved impotent in the struggle with the large landowners for control of the peasantry. The equitable field system resolved neither the problems of the peasant nor those of the state. Most peasants did not have sufficient resources to survive a bad season, pay their debts, and meet their tax burdens. Either through debt peonage, sale of their land, or recommending themselves to a local magnate to avoid taxation, over a period of centuries the peasantry became enserfed. Whereas the later Sung rulers fought an unsuccessful rearguard action against the rise of seigneurialism, the Ming dynasty accepted it as a fait accompli. As a result, the terms of tenancy worsened to the extent that some peasants came to be viewed as the personal property of their lord.[65]

The most elaborate and certainly the most long-lived feudal complex came into being in Japan. With the demise of the Yamato state in the ninth century, a rural anarchy prevailed that was presided over by a class of knights known as samurai. As their number proliferated and the power of each greatly decreased, a new class of military official, the daimyo, was able to overthrow the samurai and establish huge fiefs for themselves. In the meantime, the peasantry had been converted into full-scale serfs. Some had recommended themselves to avoid taxation; while others had sought protection from the widespread violence in the countryside. Even those who had not voluntarily surrendered were unable to resist being forcibly incorporated into the feudal regime. Classical feudal property relations were set up: The peasant was confirmed in the ownership of his land in exchange for a generous subsidy extracted by the lord.[66]

The general failure of the wider world as it manifested itself in a resort to feudalism and decreasing levels of productivity was also partially related to the social systems of inheritance. For almost everywhere property was divided among heirs. The demise of the samurai, for example, was directly related to the extensive subdivision of their properties that left the owners without any effective power. In both India and the Muslim world as well, partiable inheritance was the rule. In China not only did division among heirs prevail but neo-Confucian doctrine also prescribed that wealth should be shared. The result was that it became very difficult to maintain capital accumulation on a significant scale. It has been noted, for example, that a Chinese family rarely succeeded in preserving its wealth for more than a few generations.[67]

A discussion of inheritance patterns and capital accumulation also raises the question of the role of kinship and communal patterns of ownership as deterrents to progress. Unfortunately, because this is a question historians have almost completely ignored, most of our notions are derived from the work of social anthropologists who did their research during the twentieth century. Their findings overwhelmingly demonstrated the persistence of kinship in most parts of the wider world, making it easy to assume that this has been a constant throughout history.

Yet it is possible to imagine another scenario. During times of economic growth, kinship ties are likely to have been reduced in importance because security became less of a concern than acquisition. When a downturn occurred, however, its importance as a buttress against uncertainty is likely to have revived. This would appear to have been the case in China. Hilary Beattie dates the revival of the extended family to the sixteenth and seventeenth centuries, when families began acting as corporate units in order to ensure that one of their number would achieve a bureaucratic post and thus guarantee tax exemption for the entire family.[68] If, as appears likely, the resurgence of kinship was repeated elsewhere, by hindering the accumulation of capital it was part and parcel of the general economic decline. Nevertheless, the timing would suggest that it was an effect rather than a cause of that decline.

Religion and belief systems in general also played an important role in shaping the direction of social process. A crucial factor in Islamic history was that Muhammad died while doctrine was still being formulated and before mechanisms of arbitration had been determined. As is common in many systems of belief, Islamic doctrine often appeared contradictory, calling on Muslims to act in different ways when confronted with similar abuses. Holy war, not only against the infidel but specifically against Muslims who were in schism, was viewed as a sacred undertaking. Unfortunately, it was impossible to judge in any objective sense which individuals were infidels and what societies were truly in schism. Nevertheless, there was never a shortage of those who were convinced of the justice of their position and hence willing to impose it on others. The result was an endless succession of reformist movements that constantly threatened the stability of the state, which was in turn obliged to depend on mercenaries for its survival. Thus the cycle of mercenaries, grants of land, and ultimately feudalization in the Arab world was directly related to the nature of Islam itself.[69]

It is much more difficult to assess the role of Hinduism on the Indian social formation. Unlike Islam, which literally exploded onto the world scene, the doctrines of Hinduism were slow in taking shape and only gradually won out over its rivals, Jainism and Buddhism. Nevertheless, as they evolved, these doctrines became more rigid in their prescriptions and came to deemphasize material possessions. Scholars postulate that one of the few concrete ways in which this can be said to have affected the Indian economy was in the sphere of overseas trade. Indians are believed to have been extremely active throughout southeast Asia as merchants and perhaps as colonists at an early date. Subsequently, however, a proscription on Brahminic travel abroad developed and seems to have become the norm for all Hindus. This increasing passiveness on the world scene, it is argued, probably had detrimental effects on the total structure of the Indian economy, for a dynamic incentive to increased production was suppressed.[70]

Yet there are flaws in the hypothesis. South Indians, who were as or more affected by these same doctrines, did not end their overseas ventures. In fact, during the later stages of the Indian middle ages their involvement in trade increased. Thus, even if Hinduism was a factor in dissuading some groups from partaking in overseas commercial endeavors, it must have functioned in concert with other factors peculiar to those regions where it served as a disincentive.[71]

Just as Islam in the Arab world and Hinduism in India were important doctrines, Confucianism played a significant role in China. Rather than constituting a formal religion, the teachings of Confucius and the way they were subsequently reinterpreted provided a moral ethic of the way in which a society should function. Once again, emphasis was placed on stability rather than change. With the passage of the law that required the state to be administered by those who had passed the civil service examination, Confucian principles triumphed. The greatest victory of the Mandarins, the bureaucrats who now ran the day-to-day affairs of the empire, would appear to have been in steering the country away from foreign contacts. They were also largely responsible for discouraging the development and use of firearms. From the Mandarin perspective, these changes might have had revolutionary repercussions for China, repercussions that not only threatened Confucian stability but also the position of the Mandarins as the guardians of that order.[72]

Demography also contributed to the end of progress in the wider world. Because of a remarkable series of demographic studies pioneered by Woodrow Borah and Sherborne Cook, the scholarly community is relatively well informed about the size of the indigenous population of preconquest America. It is estimated that in 1492 a surprising 22 percent of humanity lived on the American continents. Of more significance is that technology had not kept pace with this population explosion. Stating it differently, decline in

the Americas would appear to have come about because, given the technological limitations of its inhabitants, there were too many people for the
environment to support. The Spanish historian Jaime Vicens Vives succinctly
summed up the situation when he noted that "even before the arrival of
the Spaniards, the aboriginal population was headed for disaster."[73] Although
the situation in China was not as chronic, demographic considerations also
seem to have had a negative impact. Once the Mongols had been overthrown,
population increased so rapidly that there was soon a surfeit of labor. The
result was that the surplus so diminished the costs of labor that much of
the incentive to improve technology was lost. It was not until later centuries
that a full Malthusian crisis befell the country, but the effect of having
too many people had already begun by the fifteenth century.[74]

The contradictions that seem to have accompanied growth in the wider
world, although they are extremely difficult to pinpoint, may also have
been important factors in impeding progress. For a variety of reasons,
however, one must tread warily when addressing the issue. First of all, it
must be noted that societies were often extremely complex in their internal
organization and that the wider world exhibited a comparatively enormous
range of social compositions, thus making generalization extremely hazardous.
Second, one must not fall into the trap of viewing them as traditional in
the sense that they were static. Quite the contrary, growth was usually
accompanied by social change that frequently contradicted the vision of
the ideal society. New sectors, which were often engaged in production
and distribution, came to occupy a more important position in society
than their status merited. At the same time, however, traditional elements
in these societies, which did not necessarily participate significantly in
enhancing material growth, still expected their normal or even an enlarged
share of the surplus as their natural right. Thus, diverse segments within
a given social formation were thrust into a position to compete for the
resources that were produced.

Although for long periods the synthesis that made growth possible was
able to survive the contradictions of competing interests, eventually it broke
down. Each region had its own particularistic way of succumbing to the
problems, but a fair generalization is that during times of extreme pressure
on resources, there were breakdowns in the mechanisms for the social
distribution of the surplus product. For example, it is postulated that among
the Maya as populations grew faster than the ability of technology to meet
the new needs, poverty increased among the producers. Eventually, it is
assumed, because the peasants could no longer satisfy their own needs
while still meeting the exactions of both the state and the priesthood, they
staged a massive revolt that forever changed Mayan society.[75]

The ultimate breakdown in the Arab world, on the other hand, although
also the result of diminishing resources, took on a different character. As
the constant warfare sapped the abilities of states to meet their military
requirements, they chose a solution that seems to have led to their own
demise. In order to attract mercenaries to their service, they were obliged

to make grants of land and their revenues. As they were reluctant to relinquish ultimate sovereignty to a new class of feudal lords, however, they opted to limit these grants to relatively short periods of time. The results were counterproductive. Having no permanent stake in the lands over which they presided, before it became apparent that they would be able to make their control hereditary, the seigneurs chose to plunder them for immediate profit rather than to develop them for long-term gains. In India, too, as central authority and its ability to reward its retainers ceased to exist following the demise of the Guptas, the rapacious soldiers and officials formerly under state control took advantage of the power vacuum to loot the peasantry of virtually all it possessed. Thus, looking at the broad spectrum, it appears that in many instances short-term expediences led to the sacrifice of long-term objectives. Ultimately, given the priorities established by certain interest groups, the victim was the productive sector and the victimized the underremunerated producers.[76]

## CONCLUSION

After millennia of growth, by 1500 most of the wider world was unable to sustain the dynamism that had marked its genesis. The degree to which there was a divergence from the progress that had been universally established as the norm differed significantly. With too many people, Indian America faced the gravest crisis. Yet had it come into contact with visitors other than the Spanish and the Portuguese, visitors who had peacefully introduced a new technology at greatly reduced social costs, perhaps America might have overcome the dilemma. Unlike in the Americas, decline in the Arab world was not as absolute. Although the technical and intellectual achievements of the golden age were not to be duplicated, nor was a basic prosperity returned to the productive sector, during the fifteenth and sixteenth centuries much of the Muslim world was to be reunited under the formidable power of the Ottomans, a force that posed a continuous threat to Europe throughout the sixteenth and subsequent centuries. The Chinese experience was similar. After the disastrous Mongolian invasion, China was reunited under the Ming and Ch'ing dynasties. Nevertheless, although in terms of a traditional state one historian has described eighteenth-century China as the "most awe inspiring state in the world," it could not duplicate the achievements of the past.

With respect to Africa, there were no cataclysmic events nor any precipitous decline; states continued to rise and fall as they always had. Similar processes could be observed in southeast Asia as well. Although the Khmers in Cambodia and the Pagan empire in Burma met their demise, any void they left was filled by Vietnamese and the establishment of the Thai hegemony. Japan, in comparison, represents an enigma. Dominated by a feudal mode of production and almost constant warfare, it was still able to make significant progress while most of its contemporaries were languishing. Nevertheless, despite the absence of catastrophe in any of these regions, by the fifteenth century they had already attained the pinnacles of their achievement. Finally, at least by the tenth century, India experienced a revival of its fortunes, which culminated with the creation of the Mughal empire in the sixteenth century. In many respects it was as impressive as any of its predecessors, but it no longer remained in the forefront of world development. This, indeed, is a judgment that could be applied to the wider world as a whole: It had surrendered the vast lead that it had once possessed.

It is easier to describe the nature of and to list the factors that were responsible for the decline of the wider world than to understand why they were decisive. Certainly, with the exception of population pressure, the problems were social in nature insofar as they were man-made. Why various peoples were unable to reverse the trends is an enigma Western historians have facilely explained away by conjuring up the demon of the "traditional mentality," which, conveniently, in their terms, worked in ways different from the Western mind.[77] This solution, however, cannot please anyone who is aware of the accomplishments of the wider world. Societies that created the science, architecture, and commodity production discussed in this chapter cannot simply be dismissed by damning them with the curse of traditionalism.

A more fruitful approach would be to investigate the contradictions that accompany the process of growth. Indeed, growth would seem to exacerbate the latent tensions in any social formation, for the rewards for those who are able to arrogate the surplus become proportionately higher. The competition that took place, however, was of a negative sort. It did not take the form of outproducing and outselling. Rather, the main arena of conflict was the social distribution of what had already been produced. In essence, it was easier, especially for the more powerful elements in society, to be parasitical than productive. Stating the equation somewhat differently, because of the relative ease with which it could be accomplished, the stronger elements in society unwittingly chose the numerous paths that would hinder progress instead of the road that would foment growth. The failure of the wider world ultimately lay in its inability to produce a class capable of reversing the cycle. Even in Europe, however, finding a way to break through the barrier of cyclical growth and stagnation was not to be an easy achievement.

# 3

# MEDIEVAL EUROPE

In its premodern phase, Europe passed through a number of cycles. As was the case of the wider world, it experienced both peaks and troughs. It differed, however, insofar as its peaks were less majestic and its low points more devastating, occasionally bordering on the disastrous. Nevertheless, the factors responsible for both the successes and the failures Europe underwent were frequently quite similar to those that took place elsewhere. Yet despite the similarities in the historical processes that dominated both spheres during much of their history, as Europe edged toward what would become its early-modern period in the years after 1500, its experience began to diverge both from its own past and from the path followed in the wider world. In the absence of a centralization capable of imposing unitary structures, free rein was given to a diversity of competing forces. Although many of the different groups ultimately pursued goals in conflict with one another, obtaining the desired ends frequently required cooperation, concession, and compromise among interests that otherwise had little in common. Because the combinations that emerged differed from one region to another and the weight and power of any given interest might vary significantly across the Continent, Europe came to be composed of various syntheses of social, political, and economic systems. Although as Europe prepared to enter its early-modern phase it was unclear which, if any, of them, would ultimately prove successful in leading the way toward sustained growth, the Middle Ages provided the nurturing ground for those forces and combinations that would overcome seemingly insuperable obstacles.

## THE ANTECEDENTS

The period that preceded the European Middle Ages was one of great political oscillation. Ushered in by the hegemony associated with the Roman Empire, it subsequently covered an era that has come to be known as the Dark Ages, experienced an ill-fated attempt to recapture the glories of Rome, and finally ended in a devastating series of invasions staged from the fringes of the Continent itself. Although the rise and fall of dynasties during this era have captured much attention in the scholarly literature, production and the productive forces that underwrote the social formation were important determinants of the events that took place. For, unlike the situation in the wider world, where the expansion of the material base went hand in hand with the growth of larger social formations, the outstanding feature of early European history was the low level of pro- ductivity that underlay social structures. This, in turn, was related to the relations of production, which were often characterized by their servile nature. Thus, despite ephemeral success in consolidating political authority, prior to the late Middle Ages Europe was unable to sustain the limited momentum that, on occasion, it was able to generate.

The Roman Empire that emerged during the first century prior to the Christian era was an impressive creation. In the northwest and west its dominions included Gaul, Britain, and the Iberian peninsula. Across the Mediterranean, much of North Africa had been conquered and was ad- ministered by Roman officials. In the east, although much of the Hellenic tradition survived, the world of the Greeks was also fully incorporated into the Roman Empire. Syria and Palestine represented the easternmost extensions of Roman power. It was an entity given coherence by a massive system of paved roads that facilitated administration and made possible the rapid transfer of personnel. Because the empire ultimately relied on coercion to maintain its hegemony, the ability to move troops to areas of rebellion was most important. In this regard, by the third century, as problems both within the empire and on its fringes began to mount, the standing army of Roman legions was increased to the level of some 650 thousand men.[1]

The Roman world did not differ significantly in most respects from other empires, although it had its peculiarities. In theory the emperor was omnipotent, despotic, and absolute. Yet in practice his decisions were rarely arbitrary, for he was advised initially by the senate and subsequently by a council known as the consistory. Moreover, the sprawling size of the empire dictated that a good degree of decisionmaking be left in the hands of the military governors of the provinces. Within the empire itself, most free Romans enjoyed a good life. There were tax exemptions and even free distribution of bread. Although most prominent Romans were landowners, many resided in cities and towns for much of the year. Administrative and residential units, as opposed to production centers, urban areas nevertheless formed an integral part of the Roman world.[2]

Nevertheless, Rome was a predominantly agricultural society. To sup- plement the large supplies of grain that were expropriated from the North African provinces, the Roman heartland produced a wide variety of Mediterranean crops, such as grapes, olives, wheat, barley, peas, and beans. Some of the cultivation was undertaken by individuals known as *coloni*, who were usually tenants on the large estates that the Romans called *villa*. But most productivity, agricultural or otherwise, was the province of slaves, large numbers of whom worked in gangs on agricultural estates. Others were responsible for the limited range of industrial activities required for daily existence. Rome, indeed, was heavily dependent on the institution of slavery for the production of its necessities.[3]

Despite its impressive achievements, Roman growth was based on profound weaknesses. In much of the heartland, agrarian techniques were so backward that one-half of the arable had to be retired to fallow each year. Even this expedient, drastic as it was, did not produce adequate yields. Quite the contrary, as incredible as it might seem, yields sometimes were as low as 1:1, that is, for example, for every bean seed planted, one bean was harvested.[4] Part of the problem can be accounted for by the very simple tools that were used. Another part stemmed from the pervasive institution of slavery, which by its nature provided the laborers with no incentive to increase productivity. The slave mode of production, however, had an impact that far transcended the institution itself. Permeated by the ambience of slavery, free Romans came to consider manual labor to be beneath their dignity. This in turn led to the remarkable phenomenon of the virtual absence of any significant technological innovation during the entire period of Roman hegemony.[5]

Rome was adversely affected by slavery in yet another way. Most of the slaves who were incorporated into the social formation were by-products of warfare. As the conquests of the Roman legions became more infrequent and eventually ground to a halt, the supply of slaves also diminished greatly. Legally slaves were chattel whose status was heritable, so the slave population could potentially have reproduced itself. Yet this possibility was mitigated by the preponderance of males in the slave population, nullifying any chance that natural processes could sustain the labor reserve. Some minor relief was provided by the purchase of slaves in various markets. Yet nothing approaching a systematic slave network capable of supplying Rome's needs was ever developed. Thus, as free men continued to eschew certain kinds of labor, productivity in all spheres dropped precipitously during the later stages of the empire.[6]

The falling levels of productivity, unfortunately, coincided with an era in which the demands on the resources of the state were increasing dramatically. By the third century A.D., the borders of the empire were being breached by Germanic-speaking peoples whom the Romans referred to as barbarians. Although most of the infiltrators settled peacefully, others came with the intent to plunder. The most devastating attack occurred in 276, when many cities throughout the empire were laid waste. As a countermeasure, the Romans raised the number of soldiers in their border patrols. This preventative measure, however, greatly increased the burdens on the state.[7]

The state lacked a reservoir of resources that could be tapped in order to cope with its multifaceted problems. Part of the trouble arose because it contained a great number of nonproductive elements. As one historian has noted, "the basic cause of the economic decline of the empire was . . . the increasing number of (economically speaking) idle mouths."[8]

Landowners, for example, did not contribute to the state in proportion to their wealth. In this regard, however, the church was an even greater culprit. Despite its early trials and tribulations in Rome, once Christianity became the established religion, its coffers accumulated vast amounts of wealth. Because the church and the upper echelons remained aloof to the problems the empire faced, the state was obliged to depend increasingly on the taxation of the peasantry. Over time these exactions were raised to intolerable levels.[9]

As the power of the state weakened and the position of the peasantry deteriorated, in the fourth century a new class of people, the magnates, emerged. These appear to have been individuals who were able to engross vast tracts of land. More importantly, they were able to attract peasants to their holdings by protecting them from the exactions of the rapacious tax collector. The *colonus* who sought this protection, however, did so at a price. Although technically the *colonus* remained free, a contract limited his freedom of movement to the extent that he was bound to the soil. Moreover, he was obliged to surrender a generous portion of his surplus to his overlord. As the effectiveness of the state continued to atrophy, the magnates were able to consolidate their position even further by arrogating the right to exercise arbitrary justice without regard to the central administration.[10]

Beset by a multitude of seemingly unending problems, the empire eventually collapsed. It was unable to resist a series of "barbarian" invasions, which in the sixth century brought all semblance of central authority to an end. The undermining of the empire, however, should be seen not as the result of a concerted plan but as a reflection of an advanced state of decay. For initially, at least, the barbarians infiltrated the borders of Rome not to destroy their host but in the hope of enjoying the benefits of inclusion within the Roman social formation. Yet as the centuries wore on, contradictions within that very social formation would render it helpless in the face of external pressure. Because it was unable to make the transition from a parasitic empire based on conquest to one that produced a surplus capable of underwriting the many demands made upon it, the demise of the empire became a foregone conclusion. Thus, by the sixth century, Rome was little more than a vacuum into which the later barbarians were sucked. Under these circumstances the empire succumbed to forces that were much more feeble than the opposition it had easily parried in its heyday.[11]

The Roman tradition, however, survived longer than Rome itself. For administrative convenience, in 324 Byzantium was named capital of the eastern portion of the empire. In many ways, compared with Rome, Byzantium enjoyed several advantages. It was better situated to administer the territories in the Middle East. Moreover, because of the nature of the migratory patterns within Europe, it was not threatened by infiltration from without. Initially, in the absence of an external threat, Byzantium was able to prosper. This resulted partly because the Eastern social system differed greatly from the one that prevailed in the West. Agricultural productivity was dominated by a free peasantry that the state did all in its power to protect. Not only was it state policy to shield the peasantry from arbitrary exactions, but for long periods it was successfully able to oblige the aristocracy to contribute to the general well-being. Under these circumstances it was possible to maintain a strong navy, which in turn enabled the Byzantines to continue to trade throughout the eastern Mediterranean.[12]

Still, Byzantium could not remain immune to challenges from the outside. One of the most formidable was posed by the all-conquering armies of Islam. Syria, Palestine, and Egypt all swiftly succumbed to the onslaughts of the Arab armies. In 717, even Constantinople was besieged, but the Byzantines heroically turned back the assault. Nevertheless, for more than a century Islam would continue to present a serious threat. During the succeeding centuries, provincial revolt, especially in the Slavic regions, would also become endemic. Although the Byzantine state was able to suppress most of these movements, the escalating price the state was obliged to pay took a serious toll on its vibrancy.[13]

The ultimate demise of Byzantium followed a familiar pattern. By the reign of Romanus III in the early eleventh century, the nobility had established the prerogative of exemption from taxation. The timing was particularly unfortunate as the expenses of the state were mounting significantly. Moreover, whereas previously the state had been able to rely on an armed peasantry for most of its defense needs, the necessity to suppress rebellions obliged it to resort to hiring mercenaries who were able to tackle this task more effectively. At the same time, as a cost-cutting measure the collection of taxes was gradually turned over to private tax farmers. In return for their services, they were given access to large tracts of land. Although initially it was stated that these grants were for a limited period, eventually the holders began to view them as hereditary, a process governments began to sanction once the estate owners agreed to use their resources in defense of the state. Soon these great landowners began to compete with and subsequently to undermine the authority of government officials. Once they had accomplished this, it was a relatively simple task to reduce the status of the formerly free peasantry into dependent tenants on their estates.[14]

Long before Byzantium began to decline, decay had already overtaken the West. The many Germanic-speaking peoples who established kingdoms throughout western Europe made no attempts to emulate Rome. The carefully constructed road networks were allowed to fall into disrepair; partly because of the low level of productivity and partly owing to the insecurity that came to prevail over wide areas, overland trade came to a virtual halt. For much of this era, coins ceased to be minted, further depressing trade. Commerce on the high seas also disappeared. One historian has even observed that Westerners became almost completely unaccustomed to seafaring. For these and a variety of other reasons, the period has earned the unflattering title of Dark Ages.[15]

During the eighth and ninth centuries an attempt was made to revive the Roman tradition. Under a series of Frankish kings, the most noteworthy of whom was Charlemagne, the western European center of gravity shifted away from the Mediterranean toward the north. Efforts were made to resuscitate commerce. To this end the state sought to regulate markets and fix prices on many important staples. Mints were established and metal currency was reintroduced. The state even went so far as to promote missions to distant lands in the hopes of stimulating long-distance trade. Nevertheless, central planning was an inadequate solution to resolve the basic difficulties of creating a centralized kingdom in the social and economic milieu of western Europe. For despite what might be regarded as enlightened planning, the major source of wealth of the Carolingian state continued to be derived from plunder and booty. At the other extreme, basic agricultural productivity remained at depths similar to those common during the Roman epoch. It is difficult to imagine that the Carolingian empire could have developed or even endured under these circumstances.[16]

A devastating series of invasions, however, brought the Carolingian experiment to a premature end. The most serious incursions were launched from the north by groups popularly known as the Vikings, who penetrated into the very heartland of Charlemagne's domain and throughout the Continent. Adventurers from Norway plundered Scotland and Ireland, whereas the Swedes concentrated on the Baltic and Russia. For most of Europe, however, the Danes were the primary scourge. As pioneers of the technique of sailing upriver, they were able to gain access to many of the richest territories on the Continent. Their raids became so feared that many regions began paying an annual tribute to avoid the pillage. Eventually, some of the invaders settled down and founded kingdoms, but only after many years of spoliation and much irreparable damage.[17]

Europe also came under siege from the south and the east. By the early eighth century, Muslim armies were threatening Europe's entire southern flank. One thrust passed through the Iberian peninsula and penetrated as far as the south of France. Muslims also invaded and conquered many of the most important Mediterranean islands. Although serious incursions into Europe had been stalled before the end of the eighth century, the Muslim world continued to be perceived as a menace. By the next century a new danger had appeared: the Magyars, Hungarian-speaking horsemen, flowed into Europe from the east. Between 899 and 950 there were no fewer than thirty-three of these raids. Defense against their incursions was particularly difficult, for Europeans were not nearly as adept at equestrianism as were the Magyars.[18]

The invasions of Europe signaled the final phase of a process of deterioration that had continued almost unbroken for a thousand years. During these long centuries, there had been virtually no improvement in agricultural techniques or yields. With the exception of religious centers, cities, once the hallmark of Greco-Roman civilization, for all intents and purposes ceased to be of any significance. Commerce, both within the

Continent and with the East, had become negligible. Finally, even vestiges of central authority disappeared. Thus, as Europe approached what would become its Middle Ages, its prospects were anything but encouraging.

## STABILITY, GROWTH, AND CATASTROPHE

Between the eleventh and the fourteenth centuries, western Europe was to enjoy a respite. It was fortunate insofar as the external forces that had wreaked havoc both on its borders and within its midst largely spent themselves and dissolved without causing additional turmoil. In their wake, however, they left such confusion that it was impossible to recreate even a semblance of central authority. Rather, out of the vacuum there emerged an elaborate variant of the feudal mode of production that came to dominate Europe in the subsequent centuries. Organized in this manner, for a time, a continent desperately in need of tranquillity was able to achieve relative stability. Although part of the price it paid was an extreme localism and near complete autarky, this era enabled Europeans to regroup and to prepare for a revival. Indeed, in the centuries to come the dominant theme would be that of growth. Yet, as impressive as was the expansion, it was almost exclusively quantitative in nature. Eventually, the failure to make qualitative adjustments would expose the structural inadequacies upon which the revival had been based and once again confront Europeans with problems for which they had no solutions.

Decentralization, characterized by the extreme fragmentation of political authority, became the order of the day in the period that succeeded the era of external invasion. Kings, maintaining the exalted title but no longer commanding sufficient resources to oblige compliance or even to staff an administration, began to make grants of authority to subordinates, who, in lieu of salary for their efforts, were empowered to render justice and impose fines within their designated spheres. Because their subordinates were equally lacking in the wherewithal to administer large jurisdictions, they, in turn, conferred similar prerogatives on those who would become their subordinates. By the time the process had reached its natural limitations, most of western Europe was presided over by a complex hierarchy of aristocratic domination. Although many who came to constitute this class had acquired their wealth and status through the violence and depredations of their ancestors, once a semblance of tranquillity and normalcy had been reestablished, the fruits of ancient spoliation were given legitimacy by being anointed with noble status. Thus, the aristocracy came to form part of a system that consisted of several layers of authority, each determined by services that the lower ranks were obliged to perform for the higher in return for a set of privileges that consummated the agreement. The result was a bewildering array of arrangements among barons, earls, counts, dukes, and other titled nobles, the most salient of which was that, although authority theoretically resided in an ascending order of rank that culminated in the king, at each level power was the almost exclusive prerogative of those to whom it had been granted.[19]

Each lord presided over at least one entity that was known as the manor. The manor, in fact, was the classical productive unit of the European feudal mode of production. Ideally, it was divided into three component parts. The demesne corresponded to the lands directly exploited by the lord. This tract of land was cultivated by peasants who owed him labor services. In addition to the demesne, the manor usually consisted of plots reserved for the peasantry. Each peasant household usually had access to several long, narrow strips of land. The rationale was that parcels in these configurations could be plowed more easily. Widely dispersed holdings also tended to equalize the quality of land available to each family, although it did require cooperation among the inhabitants in coordinating planting seasons and regulating fallow periods. Finally, a portion of the manor would be designated as commons and waste. The commons comprised those areas where virtually all residents of the manor, no matter what their status, had the right to graze whatever stock they might possess. Similarly, the waste, land too poor to cultivate, could provide wood for kindling or forage for chickens or goats.[20]

After drawing this classic picture, most scholars caution that manors of this type were probably fairly unrepresentative of the vast majority. For example, demesne production appears to have been more important in France than in England. At the other extreme, the manor sometimes completely lacked a demesne. Nor did manors always consist of one neat, contiguous piece of land. Rather, it was possible for a manor to be composed of farms from several different villages. On the other hand, one village might be divided in such a way that its farms formed part of different manors. Not only in theory but in practice, the variation among types of manors was enormous.[21]

Relations of production on the manor were dominated by the institution known as serfdom. The vast majority of the peasantry were considered to be serfs of one variety or another. The status seems to have represented a dovetailing of the ranks of *coloni* and slaves that had predominated during Roman times. Serfs occupied neither the position of chattel to which slaves were formerly condemned nor did they enjoy the freedom of movement that had been the prerogative of the *coloni*. Rather, most were guaranteed access to the means of production and to a share of what they produced. The price that this security cost, however, was extremely high. Legally they were tied to the soil and obliged to surrender a generous subsidy to their lord, either in the form of unremunerated labor or a significant portion of the harvest. Failure to meet their obligations would result in punishments, fines, or confiscations. Thus, the system was based on extra-economic coercion, which was made possible by the near monopoly of the tools of violence that the seigneurial class possessed.[22]

Just as the classical manor was not necessarily representative of the institution as it existed in practice, the medieval world did not consist exclusively of lords and serfs. Throughout the period there remained free peasant communities that remained legally beyond the nexus of the lord's jurisdiction, although the influence of a powerful magnate could hardly be ignored. Even on the manor itself, however, there existed free men who performed many of the tasks that contributed to its self-sufficiency. Craftsmen such as carpenters and smiths produced most of the limited range of goods required by this materially very simple society. Similarly, administration on the manor was the prerogative of those who were legally categorized as free. Tribute collectors, labor overseers, sheriffs, messengers, and other members of the lord's retinue conspired to ensure that the system functioned smoothly.[23]

Even among the peasantry on the manor there was a wide variety of different statuses that not only distinguished their relations with the lord but also led to significant differences within the class as a whole. The most favored were the allodial tenants, who, in most respects, remained free men. Presumably they had once been modest owners of their holdings. During the periods of uncertainty that accompanied the invasions of the ninth and tenth centuries, they then sought protection of powerful lords. Because they approached him with a degree of collateral, however, many were able to negotiate contracts that guaranteed them fixed rents, full title to property, and the negotiability of their holdings. Others who enjoyed almost as favorable a status were those who recommended themselves during periods when lords were willing to extend generous terms in order to populate their manors.

At the other end of the spectrum were those who were almost completely disenfranchised. Often referred to as villeins, they were bound to the soil, obliged to perform heavy labor, subject to arbitrary increases in their rents, and burdened by any number of fines and dues that the lords could impose virtually at will. In some cases they did not even have access to a plot they could call their own. As the lowest of the low, they were obliged to eke out an existence by a combination of performing labor and taking advantage of the commons and the waste. Thus, even during the high Middle Ages, the peasantry was far from being a homogeneous class.[24]

Whatever his social or legal status, the peasant lived in a world dominated by uncertainty. Compared with counterparts on other continents, the European peasant cultivated the soil in an extremely inefficient manner. First of all, the number and variety of plant forms at the peasant's disposal was extremely limited. This deficiency was compounded by a rudimentary knowledge of seed selection, reliance on the two-field system (which meant that at any given time much of the arable land lay fallow), and the few effective ways of dealing with pests, which often robbed the cultivator of already meager returns. Moreover, the farmer had access to minimal fertilizer. Under these circumstances, yield ratios, even during relatively good years, remained extremely low. During bad years the threat of famine hovered menacingly over the daily life of the rural family. In fact, an attenuated life expectancy, periodic malnutrition, and the very real possibility of starvation haunted most peasants throughout their existences.[25]

The plight of the peasantry was exacerbated by the extremely low level of technology that pervaded the medieval European world. During the high Middle Ages, iron was an extremely scarce commodity, which, even where it existed, was likely to be too expensive for the common tiller of the soil. Moreover, even when iron was used in plows, these remained inefficient instruments. It was more common for plows to be constructed of wood, further hindering their effectiveness in the struggle against an oftentimes hostile environment. And even these rudimentary plows appear to have had only limited usage: Many cultivators were obliged to rely on wooden hoes or, in extreme cases, had no implement other than their bare hands.[26]

Animal power provided little relief. To begin with, it would appear that farm animals were few in number, and partly because it was so difficult to ensure their survival through harsh winters, many were slaughtered in autumn. Although sole ownership of livestock was beyond the means of the majority of the poor peasants, this situation could be partially rectified by communal arrangements in which one team of animals was shared by several heads of households. Nevertheless, even where animals were available, Europeans were unable to make use of their potential. Not only were plows inadequate, but techniques of shoeing and harnessing remained primitive, and farmers were unable to coax maximum efficiency from their draft animals.[27]

Because of the simple agrarian base of European society, many scholars refer to the period as having been dominated by a natural economy. Others disagree, pointing out that trade with the East never completely came to a halt, that local markets continued to function, and that some towns survived throughout the period. Even if these contentions are accepted, however, it still must be concluded that the vast majority of Europeans occupied an autarkical world. They grew the food they ate, manufactured the clothes they wore, and forged the tools they used. With the exception of the upper classes, few ever gazed upon land that did not belong to the manor on which they resided, and they remained completely ignorant of the world beyond. Money played no part in their lives and the acquisition of wealth or even an improvement in their status would have been foreign concepts to most. Presumably, only disaster and natural catastrophe upset what otherwise was a simple and routinized existence.

It is easy to overemphasize the negative aspects of the early Middle Ages. It is true that levels of productivity were extremely inefficient and that vast tracts of the Continent remained unexploited by its still sparse population. Moreover, seafaring and commerce were lost arts as long as coins had ceased to be minted, urban life hardly existed, and poverty and ignorance were the norms rather than the exceptions. Yet there was a positive side to the era as well. Although violence, especially among the upper echelons was far from uncommon, compared with its own past, Europe was relatively tranquil during this period. In essence this was a time of preparation rather than achievement. During the next centuries, this gestation period would prove invaluable for renewed growth.

One of the significant occurrences of the years to come was the sustained growth in population. Historians freely admit that the data they employ are wholly inadequate to make accurate assessments. Nevertheless, they are all agreed on the general tendencies. J. C. Russell, for example, suggests that a European population that probably numbered around thirty-eight million in A.D. 1000 had grown to about seventy-three million in 1340. Most also agree that the major cause of demographic growth was the relative tranquillity that followed the devastating invasions of the ninth and tenth centuries. In the absence of the turmoil that had been a prominent feature of the European scene since the last days of the Roman Empire, population was able to expand at unprecedented rates.[28]

Agricultural output also expanded greatly during these three centuries. The main reasons for this growth were the increase in population and the bringing of new land into cultivation. Until then, Europe had been an underutilized continent with much virgin land. During this period, owing to increasing population pressure, much of the primeval forest was felled and the land brought into agricultural production. At the same time, swamps and coastal marshes were reclaimed. Finally, there was the colonization movement, which involved the migration of mainly Germanic-speaking peoples eastward to the less densely settled territories of Poland and Bohemia. Thus by the thirteenth century, the amount of land in use had been significantly increased.[29]

The high Middle Ages also witnessed the revival of trade. After centuries of inactivity, Europeans once again began to venture into the Mediterranean. This movement was pioneered by a number of Italian cities that competed for commercial dominance. Venice, operating from its Adriatic base, took an early lead. Taking advantage of the problems of the Byzantine empire and the Arab Middle East, the Venetians won a variety of concessions. Spices and textiles from the East made their way to Europe in increasing quantities. Although these developments represented an important departure from the past, it is possible to overestimate their significance. The percentage of Europeans affected by these changes was infinitesimal. Moreover, Europe's productive capacity had not been revolutionized, as suggested by the many ships that sailed to the East in ballast for lack of commodities to trade. Bullion was the only European product that could be exchanged in the East.[30]

Trade also revived in the North Sea. The nature of this commerce, however, differed greatly from that in the Mediterranean. Whereas the commodities traded in the southern regions consisted principally of luxuries imported from the East, the north specialized in more mundane commodities of local origin. Thus the region has been called "a poor man's Mediterranean." Nevertheless, although less valuable than the goods of Asian origin, the fish, timber, wax, and, especially, the woolen cloth that circulated throughout the region probably had a more significant impact on the areas that took part in these exchanges than did the more spectacular luxury trade of the south. Ports from England to Germany and all the way to the Baltic came to be organized in a complex network. Ultimately, various free cities and merchants joined together to form the Hanseatic League, a loose federation that coordinated many trading activities, including who was allowed to trade and under what conditions.[31]

As the high Middle Ages proceeded, linkages between the south and the north came to be forged. Caravans carrying spices and other Oriental goods traversed the Alpine passages from Italy to France, the Low Countries, and Germany. A sea trade with the north was also developed. Lisbon became an entrepôt between the Mediterranean and the northern seas; other goods were shipped from the Cantabrian coast of Spain. By the beginning of the fourteenth century, Italians were making nonstop voyages through the Strait of Gibraltar and dealing directly with the more important ports of the north.[32] This intra-European revival of trade was facilitated by an increase in the amount of coinage in circulation, which, in turn, was made possible by the opening of new mines in the Tyrol and the Harz Mountains. Some gold from the western Sudan also made its way into Europe. Most of this bullion, however, eventually gravitated back toward the Mediterranean, as the terms of trade generally favored the more expensive commodities provided by the Italians.[33]

The resuscitation of trade provided a stimulus to the growth of towns, largely a phenomenon of the twelfth and thirteenth centuries. Whereas most of the urban areas that had survived the Dark Ages had been located in Italy, towns came to be founded in all parts of the Continent. In fact, by 1300 perhaps as many as four thousand dotted the map of Europe. It is believed that most began as temporary encampments at junctures traversed by caravan routes and only gradually assumed a permanent character. Even then, however, most remained extremely small, the majority housing fewer than one thousand permanent residents within their walls. Nevertheless, there were some exceptions to the general pattern. For example, the populations of London, Paris, and some towns in Flanders may have come to exceed twenty thousand inhabitants.[34]

Although commerce appears to have been the main catalyst in the foundation of towns, once they had become established, the range of services they provided was enlarged. Soon skilled craftsmen became part and parcel of everyday urban existence. They provided such necessities as smithing, butchery, and carpentry. The most numerous of the craftsmen, however, were the textile manufacturers, who flourished because of increases in the supply of wool and the improved looms that became available during this era. This led to textile production of varying quality in most areas, but the manufacture of woolen cloth achieved its greatest advances in the Low Countries.[35]

Soon after the inception of craft specialization, organizations known as guilds came into existence. Separate guilds were formed to regulate the functions of each specialty. As they evolved, these institutions came to be dominated by a group of master craftsmen whose status enabled them to control the affairs of the guild, especially the crucial questions of who would be admitted and who would be promoted to the highest rank. Beneath the masters in the hierarchy were a large number of apprentices, who, after having received instruction and practice in manufacturing skills, aspired to join the elite category. At a somewhat later date, the merchant guilds were formed. It would appear that specialist merchants evolved from the earliest and most enterprising craftsmen. Initially having marketed their own products successfully, they came to find it more lucrative to concentrate on commerce at the expense of production. Thus manufacturing and marketing became divorced from each other.[36]

The growth of commerce and towns also affected the countryside in an important way, changing the nature of serfdom itself. Whereas unremunerated labor once formed the core of the institution, by the thirteenth century lords in most areas began to commute these obligations into rents paid in cash. The imposition of money rents was made possible largely by the market that urban areas provided for rural production. Although a majority of the peasants probably welcomed what must have seemed a relaxation in the feudal regime, from the point of view of the lord the move simply made good economic sense. Because population was growing rapidly, the relative value of labor was diminishing. By imposing money rents, lords sought to ensure that their income levels would be maintained and that the burden of marketing the surplus would fall on the shoulders of the peasants. The lord, therefore, theoretically would enjoy the best of two worlds. On the one hand, he was guaranteed the cash with which to purchase the luxuries that increasingly came into vogue. On the other, his income would continue to mount despite the vagaries of harvests and markets.[37]

Many scholars view the change in the nature of serfdom as a precursor to the demise of the feudal mode of production. In his famous "Critique of *Studies in the Development of Capitalism*," Paul Sweezy argued that the combination of the transition from production for use to commodity production, the increasing amount of luxury goods in circulation, the needs of lords for cash, and the attractiveness of towns as regions that offered a better and freer life to peasants, all acted as a dissolvent to the feudal mode of production. As a result, the lords were obliged to make concessions that eventually undermined the "substance" of feudalism.[38]

As attractive as this hypothesis might appear on initial perusal, its theoretical bases can be questioned and its conclusions have little empirical support. As Maurice Dobb points out, there is scant evidence that the widening of the market was a sufficient condition to weaken the extant mode of production. Nor did towns, as suggested by their small populations, act as magnets to serfs trying to evade their feudal obligations. Quite the contrary, there is virtually no evidence that towns sought or even accepted ignorant refugees from the countryside. At any rate, lords during this period seem not to have viewed urban communities as being in any way anathema to their own dominance. Rather, the existence of many of these towns was legitimized by charters they received from the local lord, who viewed them not as insidious cancers within his midst but as potential sectors of growth whose prosperity would handsomely increase his own income.[39]

Indeed, whether or not the change in the nature of serfdom represented a weakening of the feudal mode of production is open to question. First, it should be noted that the changes were brought about neither by peasant militancy nor by negotiation. Rather, they stemmed from unilateral decisions imposed by the lordly class because it considered such changes advantageous to its own interests. Presumably, if the alterations proved unacceptable, the same arbitrariness could be employed in reimposing the labor services that had been commuted. Moreover, labor dues were the only aspect of feudal relations that were changed. Peasants were still denied freedom of movement and were obliged to pay arbitrary fines and dues and to comply with a myriad of other obligations. In the thirteenth century, feudalism, albeit in a slightly altered form, remained as firmly entrenched as ever.[40]

It was not commerce or urbanization that offered the most serious challenge to the feudal mode of production: The crisis was ushered in by the inefficiency of the system. For although the high Middle Ages had witnessed significant growth, there had been little technological improvement, for the social milieu was not conducive to innovation. As B. H. Slicher van Bath has observed, peasants had little incentive to increase productivity because under the terms that prevailed for most of the period they had to surrender the lion's share to the lord.[41] Similarly, although lords might finance quantitative expansion in the forms of colonization and reclamation of land, conditions were not favorable to seeking qualitative improvements. The result, as noted by E. L. Jones, was that there was little technological advance between the epoch of Charlemagne and the thirteenth century.[42] The high Middle Ages, therefore, present a paradox. On the one hand, growth, as exemplified by the increase in population, the founding of towns, the conquest of the forest, and the proliferation of commerce, was everywhere to be seen. Yet, on the other, this growth had not been underwritten by the type of fundamental change that would have been required to sustain it.

By the end of the thirteenth century, clouds had begun to appear on the horizon. Although the mid-1200s have been described as Europe's "halcyon days," by the turn of the fourteenth century, Europe faced insurmountable problems. The major problem was the potential shortage of food. Previously the needs of the burgeoning population could be satisfied by colonizing new lands. By the beginning of the fourteenth century, however, with as many as eighty million mouths to feed and no virgin lands to bring into cultivation, expansion no longer represented a viable option. Equally threatening were the diminishing yields from marginal lands the Europeans had occupied during carefree times of expansion. The crisis was captured by M. M. Postan, who wrote that times of "high yields [from marginal land were] succeeded by long periods of reckoning, when the poorer lands, no longer new, punished the men who tilled them."[43]

By the early fourteenth century, the portents of crisis were already recognizable. With dwindling supplies of food, population levels began to decline. Between 1315 and 1317, a major famine punished much of western

F·irope. As many as 10 percent of the people of Ypres died prior to the harvest of 1316. This disaster, however, was not an aberration; it was only the most fearsome example of what would amount to fifty years of constant hunger. As the fourteenth century staggered toward its midpoint, many inhabitants of Europe found themselves in a weakened condition.[44]

It was, then, a malnourished Europe that in 1348 was brought face to face with the Black Death. The disease itself seems to have been imported into western Europe by black rats, which had traveled from the Middle East aboard Genoese ships. Quickly taking on its more virulent pneumonic form, the plague devastated much of western Europe between 1348 and 1350.[45] Estimates of twenty-four million deaths, or perhaps 40 percent of the European population, are common. Moreover, its toll appears to have been heavier in southern regions and in urban areas. The former because it struck there earliest and the latter because the more intimate contact among peoples helped the disease to spread. Norman Pounds succinctly sums up its significance: "In the whole of European history there has been in all probability no such abrupt reversal of the course of economic development."[46]

Thus, the slow, almost painstaking progress that Europe had managed during the high Middle Ages was threatened by a seeming accident of history. Certainly no sphere of economic or social activity could remain immune to such a disaster. Yet, as unusual as the plague was, it should be seen neither as an aberration nor as the low point of European history. At one level, it can be speculated that had the disease visited during more normal times, it would not have wreaked similar havoc. On another level, despite the pessimism that overtook the Continent, the plague provided Europe with an invaluable reprieve. In essence, the question became, given a second chance, would Europe, unlike the wider world, resolve the contradictions inherent in the process of growth?

## RENEWED GROWTH

European recovery from the ravages of the plague was gradual. For a long time the economy remained in a state of contraction, almost as if still stunned by the cataclysm that had befallen it. Nevertheless, this period was crucial for subsequent development. For during the respite provided by the period of relatively low man-to-land ratios, there was a broadening of the technological base of European society. By the time population levels experienced an upturn and again began to approach the levels of the early thirteenth century, per capita output had also increased significantly. Thus Europe came to be in a better position to face new challenges when they arose. It must be reiterated how important a role the Black Death played in the entire process. As Carlo Cipolla noted, "European development was not halted by a suffocating population pressure. The praise for this restraint, however, does not go to the rationality of Europeans as much as to the blind action of microbes."[47] Therefore, what to contemporaries could only have been considered to be the most catastrophic experience of all recorded time may unexpectedly have turned out to be the salvation of the Continent.

Quite surprisingly, demographic recovery did not follow quickly after the departure of the major outbreak of plague. Although population statistics for the fifteenth century are even less adequate than for preceding centuries, it is believed that a general upturn did not occur until after 1450. There is less agreement on why this should have been. In all probability a number of different factors functioned at the local level, each one of which was more or less important in a given region. It has been pointed out that warfare and its attendant ravages became more common in the fifteenth century. It should also be noted that the plague did not completely disappear overnight. Although there were no continent-wide outbreaks to rival that of 1348–1350, localized epidemics continued throughout the fifteenth century. This, in part, may account for the unusually high infant mortality rates. When periodic famine is added to the list of possible reasons, it becomes obvious that a number of factors contributed to the continued depressed state of population.[48]

Largely because population remained low after the shocks of the fourteenth century, agricultural productivity was one of the few endeavors that soon rebounded from the effects of the plague. In fact, per capita production rose significantly. With many fewer people competing for access to the land, the amount of arable available for each peasant family was greatly enlarged. Nor was it necessary to eke out an existence from marginal lands, which could now be given adequate fallow to enable them to regenerate their productive capacity. Peasants instead concentrated their efforts on the most fertile and rewarding soils and were able to reap greater benefits from their work than had their ancestors.[49]

The increase in agricultural productivity per capita had several important consequences. Because of the abundance of harvests, except during years when natural calamities might upset the normal cycle, peasants were better fed than at any time in their history. This same abundance, however, contributed to the sharp drop in agricultural prices. Fewer consumers meant that demand decreased greatly, and the price of grain remained depressed for more than a century after the catastrophe of the plague. This situation posed a crisis for those who were directly or indirectly dependent on the market. Out of desperation, they sought to convert to crops that would provide higher returns than the staple grains. In England they turned increasingly to grazing sheep for wool that could be sold in the marketplace. In those regions of France climatically compatible, viticulture and the manufacture of wine offered a solution. Similarly, in Germany the production of hops for brewing beer became an adequate substitute for the growing of staple grains. Thus, one of the perverse consequences of the plague was a realization that diversification was possible, and, in these circumstances, extremely desirable.[50]

In comparison with agriculture, craft production recovered slowly, although in the postplague era the individual craftsman may have been better off than his predecessors. Several factors contributed to this situation. Because the mortality rate from the plague was higher in urban than in rural areas, the death rate among craftsmen was proportionately higher than among other segments of society. Production also suffered in that it took a considerable amount of time to train new craftsmen to replace the deceased, whereas almost anyone could take up farming. Moreover, unlike the peasant, who given access to more land could produce larger harvests, the craftsman, in the absence of mechanization, was limited by the constraints of his two hands. Thus, production levels remained low and prices correspondingly high, a situation abetted by the increase in disposable income that low grain prices provided consumers. Paying less for their food yet charging preplague rates for their wares enabled craftsmen to improve their standard of living.[51]

From the latter half of the fourteenth century, the level of commercial activity began to decline. This, in turn, stimulated changes in the patterns of trade. One obvious factor contributing to the depression of the market was that there were fewer consumers. Another was that the late fourteenth and early fifteenth centuries witnessed a bullion shortage in Europe. For centuries bullion had flowed eastward to pay for Oriental imports; this, combined with the shrinking output of the European mines, resulted in a shortage of coinage. Some rulers resorted to the short-term solution of debasing the coins they minted, which only stimulated inflation and created additional barriers to commercial exchange. These general factors, compounded by others that were more specific and localized, led to changes in the structure of trade. Many of the most prominent fairs ceased to be held, as they could no longer be justified by the diminished level of transactions. For a variety of similar reasons, Bruges, once the most important port in the northern seas, lost the primacy that it had enjoyed. During these times of adversity and scarcity, even the common bond that had previously united the merchants of the Hanseatic League began to wear thin, as various cities began to compete in ways that often proved mutually fatal.[52]

By the middle of the fifteenth century, the general downward trend that western Europe had experienced for almost two centuries began to reverse itself. The revival began at different times in different places and was more complete in some areas than in others. Similarly, some aspects of production recovered quickly and thoroughly, whereas others continued to languish. Yet by and large the tendency was in the direction of renewed growth. Perhaps the most important factor in aiding Europe to turn this significant economic corner was the combined technology that came from centuries of slow innovation. Many techniques were of fourteenth- or fifteenth-century invention; others had been available for many centuries. What was novel about the later fifteenth century was that the range of complementary techniques Europeans were able to amass was sufficient to enable them to dominate their environment in ways that had been beyond the capacity of their ancestors.

The revival took place earliest and was most complete in the city-states of northern Italy. At first glance this might have seemed unlikely, Italy having been hit particularly hard by the plague. Nevertheless, building upon the foundations that had been laid during previous centuries, Italians were able to treat the fourteenth-century disaster as only a temporary setback. Banking, mercantile companies, and bills of exchange were much more prevalent than in any other part of the Continent. Capital and credit were readily available, as many Italians gave a liberal interpretation to the church doctrines on usury. Although they had much in common, many of these cities differed in what they emphasized. Milan, described as the most stable of them all, derived its strength from the most sophisticated agricultural base in the region. Florence, on the other hand, had in addition to its commercial and financial network a vibrant manufacturing sector, which produced, among other goods, fine woolen cloth; the city eventually developed a reputation for great wealth and industrial development.

Venice had also developed manufactures, the most noteworthy of which were textiles and glassware.[53] But by the fifteenth century, Venice had not only emerged as the leading maritime power in Italy but had also set in motion a process that might have had important implications for Europe's future relations with the East. Partly because of a commercial treaty that it signed with the decaying Byzantine empire, Venetians obtained advantages in Byzantium that were denied even to the Byzantines. Operating from bases they carved out in the Aegean, the Black Sea, the Middle East, and Egypt, Venetians came to dominate the "country trade" of the eastern Mediterranean by arrogating for themselves the transport of goods within the region. They also captured a virtual monopoly of the spice trade from the East. One notable difference from previous centuries was that Venice's productive capacity, especially that of textile manufacture, was improving whereas that of the Middle East was decreasing: Venetian ships no longer needed to sail in ballast. Rather, Venetian goods came to be marketed in the East, thus reversing the balance of payment trends that had prevailed for over two thousand years and partially stemming the eastward flow of bullion.[54]

As impressive as Italian developments were, ultimately they were probably less important than the continent-wide improvements in agriculture. Whereas the per capita growth in output that followed the plague had basically been quantitative in nature, by the middle of the fifteenth century qualitative change also became apparent. One factor that tended to increase productivity was a greater reliance on horses. Improved techniques in harnessing and shoeing enabled the farmer to utilize their power more effectively. This knowledge occurred at a time when new designs of heavy plows were being diffused throughout Europe. The more sophisticated plow in turn meant that for the first time the European cultivator was able to dominate the heavy soils that make up a significant portion of the Continent. Yield ratios, even on the relatively poor soils, began to increase. This factor, coupled with the almost universal adoption of the three-field system of rotation, meant that the fifteenth-century farmer, unlike his thirteenth- and fourteenth-century predecessor, was able to produce a surplus that would sustain renewed population growth.[55]

Another qualitative breakthrough of the fifteenth century was a significant increase in the productive capacity of Europe. One area in which this could be seen was in the use of inanimate power. Water mills had been introduced as early as the eighth century, but both the scarcity of capital and the mills' lack of flexibility had limited their usefulness. Windmills had also been known since the twelfth century, but it was not until the later stages of the Middle Ages that their proliferation made an impact on production. Lynn White effusively praises the European achievement in this field. "The glory of the later Middle Ages," he writes, "was the building . . . of a complex civilization which rested not on the backs of sweating slaves or coolies but primarily on non-human power."[56]

Mining and metallurgy were also dramatically improved during this period. Much of the credit for this achievement should go to German technicians, who pioneered new methods for digging shafts and extracting ore. It thus became possible to open mines in eastern Europe that could not previously have been exploited with the extant technology. There were also significant improvements in the designs of blast furnaces. These techniques quickly diffused through most parts of the Continent. It is estimated that by the end of the fifteenth century Europe was producing forty thousand tons of iron annually. Although this figure pales in comparison with the statistics for twelfth-century China, it nevertheless meant that iron ceased to be an exotic item that could be utilized only by the fortunate few. Rather, especially among the better-off peasants, its usage became commonplace.[57]

By the second half of the fifteenth century, textile production had both increased and diversified. In certain regions, such as England and Spain, the manufacture of simple woolen cloth increased considerably. Other areas began to specialize in newer and finer cloth. Ironically, these new techniques had been perfected because for some producers the shrinking market during the crisis of the fourteenth and fifteenth centuries made it economically more rational to produce quality cloth for a numerically smaller but wealthier clientele. Thus in many parts of Flanders production goals switched from supplying the diminished mass market to manufacturing luxurious draperies designed to satisfy the upper echelons of society. Textile producers were aided in this endeavor by the importation from Castile of the fine wool provided by the merino sheep. Similarly, Italians developed the art of producing equally high-quality cloth. In this way the Venetians were able to penetrate markets that earlier had been dominated by others. By the later stages of the fifteenth century, then, Europe was producing a much wider range of textiles and was capable of satisfying a variety of tastes and needs.[58]

Improvements in the design of ships that plied the ocean highways were also impressive. That European ships came to be the finest in the world is both ironic and dramatic, especially when it is remembered that only a few centuries earlier seafaring had become an almost completely forgotten skill and that most of the conceptual improvements had been anticipated by both the Arabs and the Chinese. In fact, a good deal of the technology that came to be associated with European ships was copied from others. What was significant, however, was that Europeans not only copied but also realized more fully how these naval designs and nautical skills could be improved upon. The flexible rudder made possible the maneuver of tacking, allowing ships to sail into the wind more easily. New designs in sail construction, the use of the astrolabe, and the increased knowledge of trigonometric charts provided more flexibility on the high seas. Heavy reliance on the compass was as important as any other innovation, for it enabled Italian ships to negotiate the Mediterranean during the winter, a season during which they had traditionally been obliged to remain in port. As the Portuguese would soon demonstrate to the world at large, the combination of these breakthroughs had brought European naval technology to the forefront of contemporary knowledge.[59]

The simultaneous development of firearms was to be equally decisive. Guns had first been used in battle by the Chinese several centuries before. Their invention, however, occurred at a time when Chinese science was ceasing to be innovative, hence their full implications had not been realized. The Ottomans, too, had experimented with cannons, but many of the huge weapons they forged proved to be too unwieldy to be effective.[60] During the fifteenth century, Europeans, for their part, began to exploit the potential not only of cannons but also of smaller arms that could be carried by an individual soldier. Although by modern standards these weapons were crude and primitive, they were soon capable of changing the very nature of warfare. Nothing illustrates this phenomenon better than the use to which firearms were put aboard ships. When the Portuguese reached the Indian Ocean at the beginning of the sixteenth century, they were able to sweep all challengers before them. The implications were succinctly summed up by Carlo Cipolla, who observed that "the gun carrying, ocean going sailing ship . . . was the instrument which made possible the European saga."[61]

As the fifteenth century drew to a close, Europe was armed with a new technology. Even in this sphere, however, there is irony to be found. For much of the basis upon which the improved European technology was built had been invented elsewhere and diffused slowly into Europe over centuries. Disparate sources such as Persia, India, China, and the Arab world provided many of the foundations on which Europe was to build. Speaking of the long-term phenomenon, one historian observed that through Spain and Italy "new goods, processes, [and] technology were introduced into a Europe that was far less developed . . . than the world of Islam."[62] It is even more ironic that the conquests of the dreaded "Mongol hosts" in the thirteenth and fourteenth centuries would play an equally significant role. Yet by imposing peace over a vast area bridging the gap between

China and the West, the pax established during the Mongol century witnessed much travel between Europe and Asia and, with it, the flow of technology, invention, ideas, and innovations from the Celestial Empire to the lands of the "barbarians."[63]

Many tacitly assume that European technical skills had become the finest in the world and that therein lay the key to the process that would enable Europe to establish hegemony over the rest of the world.[64] That progress had been made and that its ships and firearms were superior to the vessels and weapons found elsewhere is beyond doubt. Whether or not, when taking into account the full range of scientific and technical knowledge, we can justify sweeping generalizations about European superiority is more problematical. For many scholars who offer such opinions often appear to be quite ignorant of what had been achieved in the wider world. The relevant point, however, is not to total a quantitative comparison and declare a victor. Rather, it is to understand that Europe was learning to pose new questions and uncover new ways to answer them. Joseph Needham captures the essence of the issue when he observes that "at the Renaissance the method of discovery was itself discovered."[65]

Nevertheless, to debate the issue would largely miss the point. For it would appear that it was not so much the material evolution of this period that would make possible the European saga. Although technology, especially during the early phases of European expansion, was extremely important, the success that certain nations would experience in establishing commercial supremacy was more directly related to social processes evolving simultaneously. As impressive as were the mechanical achievements of the age, it was the changes in the social framework that ultimately would prove to be of greater importance.

## TOWARD MODERNITY

Lynn White speaks of European society of this era as having been molten. Although the comment was intended to refer to technological change, it is perhaps a more accurate evaluation of the social changes that took place during the later Middle Ages. Simply stated, an extremely more complex society emerged. Not only did the roles of the traditional forces change considerably, but new actors appeared to challenge the traditional ordering of society. As the various segments that composed the social and political framework sought to manipulate process to their own advantage, there developed patterns of shifting alliances among the contestants for power. Although the results of this multifaceted struggle would still be indecisive as Europe approached its early-modern period, by 1500 the balance of power had shifted considerably from its medieval origins.

In the postplague period segments of the seigneurial class faced a crisis of enormous proportions. Whereas those who obtained the majority of their income from monopoly rights and tithes remained fairly immune to the economic trends of the day, those who depended on revenues from the rent of their dependent peasants were particularly vulnerable to the altered circumstances. For they had converted the labor services owed by the peasantry into fixed money rents at precisely the wrong time. With the tremendous decline in the number of peasants, the incomes of these lords were greatly reduced. Those peasants who remained paid fixed rents in currencies that were becoming more debased by the day. Few solutions to the lords' problems, however, presented themselves. Cultivation of the demesne with wage labor was not a feasible alternative because the general labor scarcity greatly increased wages. Moreover, the depressed agricultural market made demesne production a very unattractive alternative.[66]

There being no rational economic solution to their problems, lords in many parts of Europe turned to what they considered to be the only solution. This alternative was force: They attempted to reimpose full-scale feudal obligations on the peasants. By arbitrary decree they ordered the peasantry to be bound to the manor. In a similar fashion rents were to be raised, even though what had once been customary tenures had been formalized by the granting of contracts, which offered the security of a fixed rent. In England as early as 1349, legislation known as the Statute of Labourers, whose goal was to rivet the peasantry to the land and to drive down wages, was decreed. On the Continent, similar laws were enacted in France, Castile, Germany, and Portugal.[67]

The lords could not have expected the outcome of their decision: Almost everywhere peasant rebellion broke out on an unprecedented scale. Whether they rose up because their labor services had been commuted more than a hundred years before or because the psychologically depressive years of the postplague era would allow them to tolerate no more cannot be answered. Although the most prominent was the revolt in England in 1380, the process became endemic in many countries. The very boldness of those who first took up arms aroused the envy of others who also raised the cry of revolt.[68] Peasant militancy by itself, however, was not enough to dismantle the extant power structure. In fact, viewed solely as insurrectionary movements of a martial nature, the rebellions should be judged as failures. Nevertheless, their historical significance lay not in their ability directly to overthrow the hegemony of the seigneurial class but in the way that they exposed the contradictions inherent in the feudal system.[69]

For the panicky reaction of the lordly class to the peasant uprisings had as much to do with the freeing of the underlings as did the rebellions themselves. Informally, among themselves, the lords had agreed neither to provide sanctuary nor to accept new recommendations of peasants. Rather, peasants who owed obligations to others were to be returned to their overlords. Yet in the confusion and turmoil that accompanied the rebellions, conditions were ripe for peasants to abscond and seek their fortunes in new environments. At the same time, lords, who began the period with what they considered an insufficient number of rent-payers and who had probably lost control of some of these, faced the specter of permanent ruin. In their quandary, they lost sight of secular historical trends and class solidarity and opportunistically began to compete with one another for a following. The terms of the market under these conditions so favored the sellers of labor that lords were obliged to offer attractive terms. The most important of these were guarantees of freedom of movement and the transfer of property rights. This was the real beginning of the demise of the feudal mode of production.[70]

Freedom, however, did not mean the same thing to peasants in all parts of the Continent. Some won legal rights, but without the hope of becoming owners themselves, they were destined to remain tenants forever. The more fortunate, such as those in many regions of France, not only gained title to their land but also received guarantees against its loss. Others also won the right of freehold tenure, but without the same guarantees as those of their French counterparts. In essence, as Slicher van Bath noted, these individuals received legal freedom in exchange for economic insecurity.[71] In addition to the darker side of the land tenure arrangements, many peasants continued to be subjected to other aspects of the feudal regime that had not been dismantled. In those regions the lords retained the right to impose fines, collect fees, and extract semiservile obligations. This era of transition, in fact, was marked by uncertainty. The lords had not abandoned the struggle for dominance over the peasants. On the contrary, feudal relations continued to prevail in most facets of life in the countryside, and the lords constantly looked for ways of regaining the ground they had lost.[72]

Ironically, during the very period when the aristocracy was losing some aspects of control over the peasantry, in many parts of Europe it was reasserting its power vis-à-vis incipient monarchies. The Iberian peninsula provides a classic study of how the process unfolded. Perhaps owing to their continuing struggle to expel Muslims from their soil, both Portugal and Castile developed relatively powerful monarchies at an early date. Nevertheless, the Portuguese monarchy, which had been particularly strong in the fourteenth century, began to lose control in the fifteenth. Over time, grants of land, which became known as *apanages*, had been made to royal favorites. As civil unrest increased, these nobles, who were usually either close relatives of the royal family or members of the competing Braganza house, took advantage of the turmoil to organize additional revolts, which further weakened the position of the king.[73]

The downfall of the Castilian monarchy began somewhat earlier and was more complete. In the late fourteenth century, a disastrous civil war fought over succession to the throne created a power vacuum that facilitated the reassertion of noble independence. As various factions not only received international support for their candidate but began to develop schisms within their own ranks, conditions of anarchy came to prevail. For much of the fifteenth century, the once proud monarchical office was filled by figureheads whose only distinct function was to provide favors to special interests.[74]

During the fifteenth century, a similar fate overtook the institution of kingship in France and England. Both were profoundly affected by the

Hundred Years' War that they fought against each other during much of the fourteenth and the early years of the fifteenth century. Prior to this prolonged struggle, the French had developed one of the strongest monarchies in Europe. Under its Capetian kings, royal power had expanded from its bases in the Île-de-France to extend over much of the country. Nevertheless, royal pretensions were shaken by the war. Exhausted by the constant demands made on it, the royal bureaucracy eventually proved unable to cope. As corruption became rampant, especially in justice and finance, the administration began to lose its grip on the country. This weakening of monarchical institutions enabled the nobility to reestablish its virtual independence.[75]

Although the Hundred Years' War also placed strains on the English monarchy, it had been fought entirely on French soil and thus did not have a similarly disastrous effect on England. Thereafter a prolonged succession crisis ensued. Known to history as the War of the Roses, in this extended period English barons began to reassert their independence. For the better part of the fifteenth century, private warfare dominated, and the hotly contested throne enjoyed little real power.[76]

The subsequent era, however, witnessed the resurgence of monarchical power in both England and France. In England, this was partially the work of Henry Tudor, who was able to have himself crowned as Henry VII in 1485. This was also partially the work of the recent past, the fratricidal strife that marked the War of the Roses having eliminated so many of the nobility that opposition to Henry bordered on the feeble.[77] Similar occurrences were taking place across the Channel in France, where, during the reign of Louis XI, the monarchy was able to reassert its authority. Ironically, the ability of the crown to reestablish its dominance over the nobility resulted from the depths to which it had previously sunk: When the very survival of the monarchy appeared threatened at several junctures during the Hundred Years' War, the nobles magnanimously agreed to a special tax to be levied on the peasantry. Even after the conclusion of the war, however, this taille continued to be collected. Because the proceeds were used to support the royal army, over time the gap between the strength of the monarchy, on the one hand, and that of the nobles, on the other, widened to the extent that once an effective ruler had ascended the throne, it was a relatively easy matter to suppress seigneurial separatism.[78]

Monarchs were greatly aided in their endeavors by improvements in firearms. Until the fifteenth century monarchical armies had been composed of feudal levies called together for a specific undertaking. For his purposes, the medieval knight had been a superb fighting machine. Decked out in his armor, he was what A. R. Bridbury referred to as the medieval equivalent of a tank.[79] By the fifteenth century, however, monarchs increasingly came to depend on mercenary armies, a process acquiesced to by a nobility not particularly upset at being relieved of burdensome military service. Despite their plebeian origins, the new mercenaries that composed the king's army were more than a match for knights schooled in the warfare of the past.

Firearms and the sheer numbers of the soldiers in his service decisively shifted the balance of power in favor of the monarch. Thus, at one level, firearms popularized warfare.[80]

Cannons were equally decisive in giving kings the advantages. The medieval castle the higher-ranking nobility preferred had evolved into a massive and intricate structure, capable of being breached only with great difficulty. The one way to bring a recalcitrant vassal to heel was via siege, but this was a long, difficult, and expensive undertaking. By the fifteenth century, however, cannons had become much more effective than the original models. They were sufficiently expensive, though, that only monarchs could afford to purchase them on a large scale. Eugene Rice documents the cannon's utility: Whereas in fourteenth-century France it took years to detach one uncooperative lord from his castle, during the reign of Charles VII in the fifteenth century "60 vassals [were] pried out of their castles in one year."[81] Previously monarchs had huffed and puffed, but with the addition of cannons they were also able to blow houses down.

Although monarchies evolved in various parts of western Europe, they differed significantly in their composition. No more striking comparison can be found than between those that occupied the Iberian peninsula. Portugal, on the one hand, was small and relatively homogeneous. Moreover, the feudal tradition had never been strong and the nobility had never enjoyed judicial prerogatives that were as extensive as those of their counterparts elsewhere on the Continent. As a result, strong kings were able to create an effective administration that became the most centralized and rationalized in western Europe.[82]

Spain, on the other hand, consisted of a number of separate kingdoms, which were united only because their respective rulers were husband and wife. Although Ferdinand V and Isabella sought to rule as one sovereign, historically each of the kingdoms had evolved a different constitutional arrangement with its monarch, making it virtually impossible to mobilize their resources toward a common goal. Whereas in Castile they were able to entrench the position of the crown, the Aragonese confederation remained an enigma. There, not only did the seigneurial tradition remain fully in force, but the system of estates, which was able to resist taxation, effectively curbed monarchical ambitions. By the sixteenth century, when young Charles V assumed the throne, the situation had become more complex. Rather than being confined to the peninsula, his authority extended over numerous domains in various parts of the Continent; the complicated arrangements that Charles V was obliged to honor in each greatly exacerbated the difficulties he faced.[83]

Kingship in France and England also represented different variations on the theme of monarchy. Of the two countries, the French crown seemed to have had the greater potential for establishing an absolutist state. From the time of the reassertion of the royal prerogative during the reign of Louis XI, French kings were able to enlarge the sphere of their jurisdiction. In the interests both of weakening seigneurial authority and of meeting the demands of a modern bureaucratic state, French monarchs increasingly replaced the traditional nobility in the administration of its territories with a new class of functionaries. As literate and trained bureaucrats, the nobility of the robe, as these men were called, possessed skills the nobility of the sword completely lacked. Although anachronistic jurisdictions were not eliminated, the tentacles of the state were reaching further into the countryside. This extension of royal power arose from reciprocal factors. Because the monarchy enjoyed an independent tax base that was not subject to control by the *parlement*, the king was free, within limits, to enact new policies implemented by his bureaucracy. These initiatives, in turn, enabled the monarchy to increase its revenue base and thus greatly expand its power.[84]

In comparison with the French crown, the English monarchy functioned under great constraints. There, the institution of parliament remained more vibrant. Although kings in medieval England wielded more power than their counterparts across the Channel, as early as the reign of Edward I, the estates, constituted into a parliament, had obliged the king to agree to enact no financial legislation without their consent. Yet, as was demonstrated by Henry VII, there remained a certain flexibility for an agile king. If a monarch could find adequate revenues without making concessions to Parliament, he was legally quite free to do virtually as he chose. By improving bureaucratic practices of tax collection and instituting other measures, by the latter years of his reign Henry VII was able to increase his revenue threefold. Not only was he able to rule without having to convene Parliament, but because of his unprecedented parsimony he actually left a surplus in the treasury. Thus, more so than elsewhere, a delicate balance of forces dominated the relations between the English king and other segments of society. How these resolved themselves depended upon the mood of the times and the skill and acumen of the reigning monarch.[85]

Throughout Europe, then, a variety of different monarchies were spawned. Yet certain regions chose to reject the idea completely. One of the most notable was the populous area occupied largely by Germanic-speaking peoples. That this should have been the case is somewhat surprising, as the notion of kingship appeared in this region at a relatively early date. In fact, in 962 a large number of different entities agreed to the formation of the Holy Roman Empire, whose principal function was envisaged as the protection of Christianity from external attack. Having both Italian- and Germanic-speaking territories within his purview, the emperor was perceived as a "superduke," who during times of difficulty would lead the defense of this conglomeration of otherwise independent entities. Many emperors, however, wanted to create a more permanent edifice, one that resembled a functioning kingdom. Although such visions remained little more than dreams, in 1239-1240, Emperor Frederick came close to unifying much of Italy and Germany. That he failed was mainly because of opposition from the pope, who was able to thwart his scheme. This was in no way unusual, for, despite the stated goals of each institution, the papacy remained the most adamant opponent of the empire, considering it to be useful when the emperor followed the pope's lead and dangerous when he acted independently. Similarly, the leaders of the menagerie of entities that made up the empire were fearful of centralizing tendencies that might threaten their freedom of action. To this end, they resisted all attempts to have the office made hereditary and insisted upon elections, which they themselves controlled. Thus, faced with an array of opposition and lacking an independent power base from which to operate, Holy Roman Emperors were usually relegated to little more than a ceremonial position.[86]

Although successive Holy Roman Emperors were unable to overcome the influence of Rome, the incipient national monarchies of the later Middle Ages were more successful in asserting their secular rights vis-à-vis those of the papacy. During the high Middle Ages, relations between kings and popes had been delicate, as the claim by the Holy See to universal powers in the secular sphere infringed upon the autonomy of the individual monarchies. The office of kingship remained relatively weak, even within its proclaimed domain, and few kings were willing to confront the papacy directly. As they gained in strength, however, kings became more willing to flex their muscles. A watershed was reached in the early fourteenth century, when ageing Pope Boniface made the tactical error of provoking a confrontation. Outraged because the kings of England and France had levied extraordinary taxes on churches within their realms in order to bolster their shaky finances, Boniface ordered them to rescind their decrees. Moreover, he issued a bull that declared in no uncertain terms papal supremacy in the secular sphere. This, in turn, enraged Philip IV, who dispatched an army to Rome to oblige the pontiff to change his mind. In an almost fairy-tale-like scenario, when captured by French troops, the pope could not stand the strain and promptly died.

The significance of the event, however, far transcended the bizarre scene. "With him," writes Harry Miskimin, "died the medieval phase of the history of the church. The church never recovered the prestige it had lost."[87] The church also suffered from schisms that developed within the papacy itself, which grew to the extent that between 1378 and 1417, rival popes, one residing in Rome and the other at Avignon, vied for control of the church. The position of the church vis-à-vis secular authority never recovered from these setbacks. A subsequent pope might still feel justified in dividing the world into Spanish and Portuguese spheres. Subsequent kings felt equally justified in ignoring his edict.[88]

This period also witnessed an increase in the amount of monarchical influence over urban areas. Yet in many instances this did not necessarily involve confrontations. As towns had grown in numbers and strength during the later Middle Ages, many were able to request and even demand greater freedom from their secular or ecclesiastical overlords. On occasion impoverished lords were obliged to grant greater freedom in return for a subsidy. As urban populations expanded, many of the larger towns found that they were in a position to defend themselves against lords who could not muster equal strength. At the other end of the spectrum, whereas urban strength increased rapidly, it did not grow as fast as that of the monarchies; hence, in many areas even the larger cities found themselves at the mercy of royal control. In both France and England towns were obliged to surrender many of their former independent functions to monarchical supervision. The relationship, however, was often marked more by symbiosis than conflict. The crown might extend generous concessions to towns, which in turn were willing to make equally generous contributions to the royal exchequer. In some instances, the relationship between the two took on the form of a partnership. In Castile, for example, alliances between the two helped to restore central authority, while protecting the towns from the threat of seigneurial power.[89]

There were, however, exceptions to the general phenomenon of the extension of monarchical dominance over towns. In fact, in those areas where urban growth was most pronounced, monarchies either did not develop or were unable to establish complete dominance. This was especially true in northern Italy, where the richest and most powerful cities in Europe were to be found. Any tendency toward the development of monarchy within their respective spheres was thwarted by local oligarchs, who were too jealous of their own prerogatives to allow control to be wrested from their hands. The possibility of centralization over the whole region was also mitigated by the balance of power. Whenever the pretensions of one city-state grew beyond acceptable limits, the others would make a concerted effort to ensure that the upstart did not succeed.[90]

Significant growth in the number of towns also took place in the region referred to as the Low Countries. Although prior to the sixteenth century the towns of Brabant and Flanders did not rival the Italian cities in size or wealth, the area was the most urbanized on the Continent. Perhaps because individually they were smaller, they were less successful in defending themselves against encroachment than their Italian counterparts. During the fifteenth century, by one means or another, most towns in the Low Countries fell under the control of the dukes of Burgundy, who were able to create a loose federation. Nevertheless, although some aspects of their independence were surrendered, they retained a degree of autonomy not shared by those towns located in strong nation-states.[91]

In addition to their evolving relationships with the dominant political authorities, urban areas continued to experience change and conflict in their basic social makeup. One apparently widespread tendency was the rigidification of the structure of the craft guilds. During the early years of their existence, entry into and promotion upward through the grades of the guilds seems to have been a fairly open process. The masters were more concerned with regulating output and ensuring quality than with restricting mobility. As time passed, however, the requirements for attaining the status of master craftsman became more stringent. Most workers, in fact, could not escape from the category of apprentice and therefore were unable to establish their own individual workshops. Over time, as entrance fees were raised and other criteria for promotion were legislated, it became rare for anyone other than the sons of the master to reach this status.[92]

At the same time, the craft guilds were engaged in a vicious competition with the merchants over the right to dispose of their products. The merchants were able to accumulate wealth far more rapidly than could the craftsmen, and they began to use their wealth to dominate urban governments. From this base they passed edicts that determined what was produced and where it could be marketed.[93] In many regions, however, craftsmen refused to accept this encroachment on their freedom without a struggle. Over long periods, there was sporadic violence between the two camps. By the fifteenth century, although merchants remained in the ascendant in most areas, some craft guilds had posed such strong opposition that they were able to gain representation in the urban oligarchy.[94]

Relations between the towns and the countryside were even more complex. From the inception of urban-based guilds, craftsmen were wary of rural competition. To this end, they often went to the extreme of mounting expeditions into their hinterlands to destroy the tools that were required for cottage industry. By the fifteenth century, a new variant had been added to the picture. A small number of merchants came to perceive that their profits would increase significantly if they were able to organize and monopolize rural potential. Often referred to as clothiers, these merchants permeated the rural areas. They distributed yarn to peasant households, occasionally provided them with looms, purchased the woven cloth, and proceeded to market the finished product. The clothier enjoyed several advantages over his urban-based counterpart. The most important was that rural workers were isolated from other workers and from the market. Thus, dealing with a labor force that could neither organize in its own defense nor find an alternative outlet for its products, the clothier was able to pay the rural worker less for the fruits of his labor than those who manufactured the same commodities within the towns received.[95] As was to be expected, the urban areas did not always accept this competition with equanimity. The crafts, because rival production was anathema, and the merchants, because marketing was escaping their control, both sought to undermine the clothiers' endeavors. Nevertheless, although in some instances they succeeded in seriously impeding the development of this cottage industry, the general climate of the time had come to favor the coexistence of rural production and urban manufacture.[96]

In addition to the spectacular rearrangement of institutional power among the various segments that constituted European society during the later Middle Ages, this era also witnessed more subtle but no less important or pervasive changes in the social structure upon which the edifice was built. One notable phenomenon was the deterioration of kinship ties. As early as Roman times, the clan as a corporate entity had become antiquated. The tendency for filial ties to be weakened was accelerated during the age of the great invasions, when even the extended family ceased to command significant loyalty. When the kin group had become an ineffective mechanism of collective security, nuclear family units increasingly began to seek out the best protection they could find. Marion Gibb points out that "the practice of a man seeking lordship provided an alternative social discipline" to that of the kindred group.[97] Although the uncertainties that accompanied the plague led to an ephemeral resurrection of kinship ties, a full reassertion of the primacy of kindred loyalties was aborted. Once the pessimism that the plague had engendered had given way to renewed growth and optimism, familial dependence and obligation seemed less appropriate than it had during the times of economic depression. Thus, whereas in the wider world the trend was toward flirtation with a diminution of kinship ties that was superseded by a return to more primordial forms, in Europe the tendency was in the opposite direction.

In parts of Europe, the end of consanguinity as an important social phenomenon not only resulted from the reaction of the population to external stimuli but was fomented by the policies pursued by various interested parties. In this regard, the church was perhaps the strongest influence. The church equated wealth with power and influence, and one of the most important ways of achieving this end was via bequests; the church therefore sought to eliminate potential competing inheritors. Tailoring its doctrine to suit these ends, prohibitions were placed on close marriage, adoption, polygyny, divorce, and remarriage. Jack Goody notes that because kin beyond the elementary line were completely excluded from inheritance, some 40 percent of the women of Europe were left without heirs.[98]

Similarly, in many areas owners of great estates pursued policies whose logic was to diminish the number of claimants to an inheritance. At one level, where possible, emphasis was placed on primogeniture, thus reducing the importance of collateral lines. At another level, the practice of the payment of dowry was intended to deny descendants of daughters any claim to an inheritance. Even monarchs had a stake in suppressing kinship loyalty, for they sought to have primary allegiance owed to the state. Gibb observed that in the England of King Edward, laws were revised "in such a way that kindred loyalties were reduced to their narrowest scope."[99]

The absence of kin loyalties combined with the emergence of Roman law as the standard legal precedent provided Europe with a unique conjuncture. During the high Middle Ages, when monarchical institutions were impotent, the administration of justice was a prerogative assumed by the lord of the manor. In theory, his adjudication was to be based on customary practices. As feudal tenures fell into abeyance, however, and as the power of monarchies began to revive, there was a transition from the private justice of the manor to a more universal legal system presided over by agents of the crown. Under these circumstances it became necessary to establish a code whose acceptability transcended local practice. In this regard kings were particularly fortunate in that they were able to borrow liberally from the extensive body of precedents that had been codified by the Romans. Of particular significance in this respect were Roman notions concerning land and its ownership. Specifically, in Roman law land was viewed as a fully alienable commodity. The significance is captured by Perry Anderson, who notes that "no other system had known unqualified private property. . . . Rome emancipated private property ownership."[100] The application of this notion of the ownership of land, occurring as it did when kinship was no longer capable of making claims upon private property, meant that in Europe a unique relationship developed between the inhabitants and the land mass they occupied.

Thus by 1500 the social landscape of Europe had changed radically. In fact, it bore scant resemblance to the society that had emerged in the wake of the alien invasions. Church and nobility, the former foundations for authority and stability, no longer were the pillars on which everything rested. In their stead, new forms of organization, which centuries before had been dormant or nonexistent, were struggling to the fore. The changes, however, were not the mere substitution of one anachronistic form for another. Rather, the new social categories, exemplified by the merchant capitalist and the clothier, aspired to goals that were largely unknown in the past. They also functioned in an environment in which the norms of the past were being restructured. These changes, as much as those that were altering the material landscape, would profoundly affect the future.

## CONCLUSION

Prior to entering its premodern phase, Europe underwent a bewildering series of oscillations. It passed through periods of plenty and survived times of scarcity. There were long years of accelerated demographic growth interrupted by intervals of sharp decline. Periods of anarchy and turmoil were interspersed with lengthy epochs of relative tranquillity. With equal facility, Europe was able to maintain itself during times of extreme localism or in the face of resurgent central authority. Thus, in many respects, a pendulum effect in which European fortunes pass from one extreme to another dominated much of its history.

Yet by 1500 a number of trends of a more lineal nature could also be observed. In the social sphere, there was steady progress in the direction of personal liberation. The institution of slavery, which previously had pervaded many areas of the Continent, had become moribund. Moreover, even the personal ties of allegiance that had once bound the majority of its residents to a particular locale had been abolished. Largely because of the breathing space provided by the population downturn that accompanied the plague, a continent that in the eleventh century could only produce enough for basic subsistence had expanded its material base to the extent that generous surpluses became the norm. Under these circumstances, a completely rural and autarkical economy was transformed into one that supported a growing urbanization and an intensified local, regional, and long-distance trade. The technology that supported these changes was constantly being improved, so it appeared that growth and expansion would continue unabated.

By the beginning of the sixteenth century other significant tendencies emerged. By far the most important of these was the rise of monarchical power. After a brief period during the fifteenth century when nobles flexed their muscles for the last time, kings were able to assert their primacy beyond doubt. Thereafter, the aristocracy was obliged to accept a reduced role in both military and administrative affairs. Monarchs were also able to establish dominance over the church. In this regard their greatest achievement was that of obtaining royal patronage of the church, which meant that an individual king gained the right to nominate all of the important clerical positions within his domain and became the final source of adjudication of religious disputes in his kingdom. The relationship between monarchs and towns was more complex insofar as it was more ambiguous. Yet, by and large, thus far the pluses associated with the alliance outweighed the minuses.

The potential for fluidity remained strong. The old guard, as represented by the church and the aristocracy, continued to view their relative decline as a temporary phenomenon. The aristocracy maintained a firm foothold in the countryside and therefore had a solid base from which to launch a counteroffensive. In this regard, one of the principal goals was to reestablish a tight control over the peasantry. Moreover, once the seigneurial class accepted the primacy of the institution of kingship and was no longer considered a threat to royal supremacy, monarchs were likely to find in the nobility a stronger ally than their erstwhile peasant cohorts. For although various kings had found it convenient to make common cause with peasants, towns, and merchants, there were structural defects in these relationships. Various crowns had defended peasants against the reimposition of servile relations, primarily because peasants were viewed as a defenseless source of taxation. Similarly, the relations between monarchs, on the one hand, and towns and merchants, on the other, had largely been self-serving. There were no guarantees that relationships that had once been symbiotic would not become parasitic. At some juncture in the future, then, the alliances that had been forged during years of flux might well be radically restructured.

Thus the potential for a major realignment of the competing forces still remained in early-modern Europe. The new arena, however, was to be the nation-state. In each, the outcome was to be determined by extremely complex struggles. They were influenced by the type of monarchy that prevailed within a given nation-state, the privileges and wealth retained by the seigneurial class, the relative strength of the merchant class, the nature of peasant land tenure, and a myriad of other factors. How these struggles worked themselves out in each nation would be a key factor not only in how each state developed but also in the role that each would play in the world economy.

# 4

# OVERSEAS EXPANSION
# AND DECLINE
# IN THE MEDITERRANEAN

As it emerged from its late medieval into its early-modern phase, Europe had already experienced a great deal of change. The next two centuries, however, not only accelerated the transformation of society on an unprecedented scale but decisively determined who would move ahead and who would lag behind. Greatly influencing these processes was Europe's new global orientation. In addition to expanding commerce from its humble, Mediterranean-based beginnings, Europeans would take up residence in all the continents of the world. This was an an achievement never before accomplished in human history.

Nevertheless, it must be cautioned that expansion did not necessarily bring in its wake everlasting prosperity or even significant benefits to its architects. Rather, whereas the sixteenth century, the era of exploration and initial settlement in the wider world, saw a general prosperity throughout western Europe, the seventeenth century, an age of a more experienced European presence overseas, is often described as an era of crisis. It is probably correct to refer to the later period as having been at best an era of deceleration. Yet Eric Hobsbawm captures the essence of the problem when he emphasizes that what is more important than the degree of overall downturn in Europe is that in this era there was a considerable amount of differentiation in terms of evolving social structures among the leading nations of Europe.[1] Following the lead suggested by Hobsbawm, we must determine the factors that caused certain regions to stagnate while others began to crack the shell that impeded the escape into economic and social modernity.

The sixteenth century witnessed accelerated growth throughout western Europe. This was true of industrial as well as agricultural production. It was also an era of innovation, a time when Europeans began to solve puzzles on their own rather than merely improving on the designs of others. In this regard, the Germans were notably successful. Especially in mining and metallurgy, they pioneered a wide variety of new techniques that transformed the productive capacity of the Continent. Although the population of Europe grew significantly during the sixteenth century, the economic growth differed from that of the thirteenth century. Whereas in the earlier period growth merely reflected an increase in the number of producers, in the later period, in addition to representing the output of a growing population, the rate of economic acceleration was related to real social and technological improvements. That is, in the sixteenth century new forms of social organization developed that were capable of making more effective use not only of technological innovations but also human factors of production. The result was that Europe was more versatile and hence more capable of employing a larger number of components in the process of production.

For the first time Europe also ventured abroad. Unlike previous adventurers into distant parts, the first Europeans to infiltrate the wider world went with sword in hand and the intent of establishing a permanent presence abroad. For the pioneering Portuguese and Spanish, this seemed to be necessary, as peaceful trade did not appear to offer the possibilities of lucrative returns. The attitude they carried with them reflected both their immediate European heritage of plunder and conquest as a mode of existence and the awareness that their respective material bases could not produce a staple that could turn a profit in the wider world.

Even though their methods were crude, the principal legacy of the initial Iberian expansion was to repatriate significant amounts of bullion from the wider world to Europe. From West Africa the Portuguese imported the gold of Guinea, which had previously traversed the Sahara. Although a fraction of this gold had crossed the Mediterranean into Europe, most of it had been dispersed throughout the Arab world and into the vast trading networks of the Indian Ocean. The Spanish discovered unprecedented sources of silver in the Americas. Considering the degree to which the uncertainty of bullion supplies had influenced economic performance in medieval Europe, the sudden appearance of an abundance of metal was to have a lasting impact on the course of subsequent economic development.

How the import of bullion affected European economic development has been the subject of much scholarly debate. In 1929 Earl Hamilton published an article entitled "American Treasure and the Rise of Capitalism." In it he argued that the massive influx of bullion in the sixteenth century was responsible for a precipitous rise in prices throughout the European continent. Because wages did not keep pace with prices, the resultant "profit inflation" proved to be the basis of the "primitive accumulation" of capital that was necessary for the development of capitalism. Although subsequent researchers have pointed out flaws in his argument, which raise doubts about the precise role of American silver in stimulating the inflation, there is no disagreement that prices experienced an unprecedented rise and that the nature of their escalation was significant. That is, agricultural prices rose faster than industrial, wages did not keep pace with inflation, and the problem took hold earlier and more acutely in the Mediterranean than it did in northern Europe. These considerations were important factors in determining the massive redistribution of wealth that was a major phenomenon of the early-modern era.[2]

Although by the 1590s most regions had begun to experience problems of one sort or another, it was not yet apparent that a serious crisis was approaching. In some regions there was the threat of overpopulation and extreme immiseration caused by the advanced fragmentation of properties, which, in turn, resulted from the system of partiable inheritance that was in place almost everywhere. Many parts of the Continent also showed indications that commerce was becoming lethargic. Yet other problems appeared more ephemeral. For example, it could be expected that the ravages of warfare, which caused substantial local hardships, would eventually be ameliorated. Moreover, many of the famines experienced during this decade seem to have resulted from unusually bad weather rather than from permanent structural weaknesses.[3]

Yet the downturn of the 1590s indeed proved to be the harbinger of what is often referred to as the general crisis of the seventeenth century. There remains considerable debate as to the nature of the crisis and the factors that caused it. Most would agree that, at best, total population remained stagnant, although there is ample evidence for absolute decline in many regions. Moreover, neither production nor commerce seems to have maintained the vibrancy of its immediate past. Although some see this downturn as having partly been determined by the Eighty Years' War between Spain and the Netherlands and the Thirty Years' War (which, in its several phases, pitted a larger number of adversaries against each other), the process of stagnation was not limited to those areas and countries that actively participated in these frequently vicious struggles. In light of this last point, the question should be raised whether Europe had once again arrived at the kind of cul-de-sac that had stymied its growth in the later thirteenth and fourteenth centuries.

It is suggested that the problems were of a different nature. Both this chapter and the next, in fact, will argue that the changes that took place in seventeenth-century Europe were greatly influenced by social considerations and that the various results were related to the outcomes of struggles between the dominant social groups in the different regions. That is, despite the gloomy economic picture that manifested itself during the seventeenth century, where social structure had been modified and increased in flexibility, the new social orders were able to adjust and even to profit from the opportunities that stagnation in other regions offered. On the other hand, as was the case in many important regions of the Mediterranean, where traditional forces resisted modification and anachronistic forms remained dominant, the adjustments required by the challenges of the seventeenth century were too demanding for the brittle regimes that remained in force.

## MEDIEVAL IBERIA

In many respects the historical experience of medieval Iberia was a unique phenomenon on the European continent. Its uniqueness stemmed from the invasions of Muslims from North Africa, who overran much of the peninsula in the eighth century. With them the Muslims brought many of the techniques, especially in the agrarian sphere, that were associated with the golden age of Islam. Thus, while much of the remainder of Europe was suffering through the painful epoch that initiated the Middle Ages, economic and social life on the peninsula remained vibrant. Nevertheless, despite an early era of toleration and accommodation, the tensions between Christians and Muslims in Iberia would continue to mount. This, in turn, led to centuries of hostility and open warfare. As important as the conflict itself was the legacy of undying enmity harbored against Muslims and Islam that became part and parcel of the Christian mentality.

The Muslim conquest of Iberia that was completed during the early years of the eighth century represented an extension of the process of the expansion of Islamic power that had swept across North Africa in the seventh century. With only a minimum amount of opposition, the conquering armies occupied the more inviting parts of the peninsula. Dominated by an Arab and Berber aristocracy, the new rulers forged an extremely progressive kingdom bound together by a centralized administration that controlled and coordinated the affairs of the provinces. Commodity production, international trade, urbanization, and higher learning were just some of the activities its leaders encouraged. Ultimately, everything was underwritten by the painstaking agricultural improvements that were imported from the Muslim world. The most important of these were the systems of irrigation, which enabled Iberia's inhabitants to produce surpluses despite the aridity of much of the terrain. Thus, Muslim Iberia flourished at a time when the rest of Europe was floundering.[4]

Nevertheless, those Christians who had taken refuge in the forbidding far north of the peninsula never accepted the notion of Muslim rule in Iberia. Their numbers increased in the ninth century when a special tax was levied on Christians living under Muslim rule. Although many Christians chose the expedient of conversion to Islam in order to avoid the tax and others complied with the additional impost, some fled north. To the religious motivation of reconquest was added the practical need to provide more space for a population that had grown too large for the inadequate mountainous regions. Finally, there was the strong desire among this largely pastoral group to secure winter pasturage for their flocks of sheep. Because this could only be obtained in the southern zones occupied by the Muslim enemy, further incentive was provided to the Christian northerners to expand southward.[5]

The *reconquista*, or reconquest, proceeded in a very irregular fashion. As new territory was added to the Christian domain, different principalities emerged. These included León, Navarre, Aragon, Catalonia, Valencia, Portugal, and Castile. Over the long centuries of the *reconquista*, however, there was as much fighting among the Christian kingdoms as there was against the Muslims. Although temporary combinations of some of the principalities were not uncommon, they were never simultaneously brought under one head. Yet, eventually, two foci of power emerged: In the east was the federation that joined the separate kingdoms of Catalonia, Valencia, and Aragon. After much trial and error, Castile established its supremacy over much of the remainder.

Despite their internal strife, however, the Christians were gradually able to make inroads against the Muslims. In this they were greatly aided by the eleventh-century split of the formerly formidable caliphate of al-Andalus into thirty independent principalities, none of which possessed the resources to provide staunch resistance to the Christian challenge. A major milestone was accomplished in 1039 when Toledo, the most important city on the peninsula, fell to Castilian forces. By the thirteenth century, all except the kingdom of Granada in the extreme south had been incorporated into the kingdom of Castile.[6]

One by-product of the jockeying for position among the Christian kingdoms was the emergence of Portugal as what has been described as the first modern nation-state in Europe. Although until the twelfth century it was nominally a province of Castile, it was isolated from the rest by a chain of mountains. Behind these mountain barriers, the dukes of Portugal ruled virtually as if they were independent. The culture that emerged featured a language distinct from that spoken by the Castilians. Finally, in 1139, Afonso Henriques declared Portugal's autonomy and successfully defended it on the battlefield. Thereafter, the major concern of the Portuguese was the liberation of its southern flank from Muslim control. The taking of Lisbon in 1148 was to be followed 102 years later by the ousting of the Muslims from the Algarve in the far south. Thus, Portugal became the first of the Iberian principalities to complete its mission against the forces of Islam.[7]

From the outset, the monarchy was comparatively strong, although for a time, like other European monarchies, its potency was tested. During the fifteenth century, a resurgent seigneurialism, abetted by centrifugal forces within the royal family itself, threatened to betray the unity that had characterized the state since its inception. Yet the independent resources of the monarchs were greater than those of the combined assets of their real and potential opponents, which made the task of restoring centralized order relatively easier than it was in other kingdoms. What was required was a strong and capable ruler. Just such a figure appeared in the person of D. João VI. Fearing the pernicious influence of the rival Braganza family, in 1483 D. João VI charged its leader with crimes against the state and had him beheaded. Other nobles were obliged to surrender their castles upon demand and to forswear private jurisdictions and warfare.[8] Although no additional attempts were made to weaken the nobility as a class and although many of their exemptions and privileges remained intact, the crown unmistakingly demonstrated its primacy. This primacy was to stamp itself on the nature of Portuguese expansion overseas.

During the period of the consolidation of the state, important developments took place in the economic and social spheres. The Portuguese functioned in an extremely difficult environment. Fully two-thirds of the land surface was said to be either too rocky, too steep, or too poor to be productive. Nevertheless, Portugal was able not only to feed itself but to export such primary products as oils, figs, raisins, fish, almonds, and cork. This achievement was largely the work of an industrious peasantry, presumably spurred by the incentive of having had their labor services commuted to fixed rents. These small-scale tenants formed the backbone of a state that was modestly prosperous as it entered the early-modern phase of European history.[9]

In many respects the history of Portugal contrasted sharply with that of medieval Castile. Whereas Portugal's transition from the Middle Ages was relatively tranquil, turbulence was the primary characteristic of medieval Castile. Founded as a frontier outpost of the primordial Christian kingdom of León, its very name was derived from the military castles that dominated its borders with Islam. As one modern scholar has suggested, throughout its history Castile was a society organized for war. Its unique class of "commoner nobles" possessed horses and armor and used them in the service of the king to combat the infidel. Militarism was so much the order of the day that towns were divided into cavalry and infantry wards.[10] Moreover, even many of its religious orders were composed of warrior monks, whose main raison d'être was to carry the fight against Islam. Stanley Payne observed that "In Castilian society, riches were commonly considered not as something one created or built . . . but as something one conquered or enjoyed because of one's status as a warrior, conqueror, or nobleman."[11] This tendency would have important ramifications with respect to the approach the Spanish would adopt in the Americas.

The monarchy in Spain ultimately became as powerful as its Portuguese counterpart, but only after a great deal of internal strife. In the early stages of Castilian development there was a strong monarchical tradition. Toward the end of the fourteenth century, however, rival contestants for the throne internationalized the struggle by soliciting aid from abroad. In the midst of foreign intervention, nobles who had been granted vast tracts of land during the reconquista took advantage of the fragmented monarchical authority; for about a century they reduced the crown to virtual impotence. In fact, for much of the fifteenth century, a state of anarchy prevailed while nobles fought among themselves with absolute disregard for the crown or country. It was not until the throne of Castile was inherited by Isabella in 1474 that the monarchy reasserted itself. Ably aided by her husband, Ferdinand V of Aragon, they singled out individual nobles to be brought under royal control. Because the nobility as a whole was unable to join together to defend its class interests, the "Catholic monarchs" were gradually able to reduce them all to submission. In this endeavor they made special use of military brotherhoods financed largely by urban contributions. Eventually, therefore, with substantial aid provided by the growing municipalities, the monarchs were able both to restore rural order and to reestablish royal supremacy over the country.[12]

In many ways it was a remarkable partnership. Although the kingdoms of Castile and Aragon remained separate, Ferdinand and Isabella coordinated policy to the extent that it is not completely inaccurate to say that the term *Spain* had a definite meaning from the time they came to power. Principally by tightening loopholes, they so successfully reorganized finances that crown revenue, which had been 885,000 reales in 1474, rose to 26,283,333 by 1504.[13] In another significant departure from the past, nobles in the administration were replaced by civilians with legal training. The new legists, who were granted exemptions and privileges similar to those of the phased-out nobility, established a bureaucratic tradition in government that was unmatched in any other European kingdom. Thereafter, the affairs of state came to be regulated by the ubiquitous *consejos* (councils) that debated all aspects of royal policy.

Nevertheless, as indicated by the policies pursued with respect to minorities, the Catholic monarchs remained firmly in control, and they were no more enlightened or tolerant than the mainstream of Spanish society. Prior to the accession of Ferdinand and Isabella, the Inquisition had been established mainly as a device for detecting deviation among former Jews who had converted to Christianity. Ultimately Isabella and Ferdinand came to decide that these "new Christians" could only be saved if they had no contact with the infectious presence of the remaining Jewish population. Thus, in 1492, an edict was promulgated ordering the expulsion of all Jews from the realm. The Catholic monarchs were no more tolerant of the Muslims who resided in the kingdom. Granada, the last surviving stronghold of Islam on the Iberian peninsula, fell to Castile in 1492. Part of the terms of surrender had included promises of religious freedom and toleration. Yet Isabella, under the influence of her confessor, Cardinal Cisneros, was persuaded to renege on her commitments. Soon it was decreed that all Muslims must either convert to Catholicism or be expelled from the country.[14]

Although it was the objective of the crown to establish royal supremacy, it did not seek to undermine completely the position of the aristocracy. Especially after the nobility remained docile during sporadic revolts against the monarchy, the crown came to perceive that the nobility was no longer a threat to royal hegemony and allowed it to continue to enjoy its favorable position. Although the often-quoted figure of 97 percent would appear to be an exaggeration, it is still accurate to say that the seigneurial class owned the vast majority of the territory. Divided among six ranks, the nobility shared virtual exemption from direct taxation. Moreover, they were practically immune to the threat of losing their landed property, as it could not be confiscated even if they fell into debt. Rather, it was decreed that only the product of such an estate could be exposed to creditors. Thus, as noted by Charles Jago, whereas there was a significant turnover of noble property in France and England, in Spain there was a powerful deterrent against the transfer of property from the nobility to other segments of society.[15]

In a relative sense, at the beginning of the sixteenth century, the peasantry was not necessarily in an unfavorable position. Its fortunes had waxed and waned over the centuries. During the early stages of the *reconquista*, terms of settlement in frontier regions had been generous, for these territories were often regarded as war zones. Over time, however, as these lands ceased to be part of the frontier, the terms on which tenures were based began to be more onerous, and something resembling a feudal tradition began to be established. Then, as a result of the depopulation caused by the plague, the terms of tenancy were eased again. By the beginning of the sixteenth century, peasants may have owned as much as 20 percent of the land. Moreover, labor services had been commuted to cash rents, which were often fixed by contract.[16]

Despite Spain's rather unfavorable environment and the turmoil that marred its history, the Spanish economy was surprisingly vibrant in the late Middle Ages. It is calculated that 62 percent of the landscape was arid. Although the Muslims had overcome this problem by extensive irrigation, the Spanish disdained this solution. Rather, they placed great emphasis on pasture, which was logical for a mobile society. Nevertheless, the country produced a sufficient quantity of cereals, oils, fish, and wine to satisfy its own needs. As the reconquest proceeded, a series of internal fairs developed to distribute the products of the various regions. Moreover, there was an extensive overseas trade. Whereas the Catalans in the east were particularly active in the Mediterranean, often audacious enough to contest Venice and the other Italian cities, the Castilians concentrated on the north. Initially wine and iron dominated exports, but by the fifteenth century the first-class wool of the merino sheep had become a lucrative source of overseas earnings. In addition, the abundance of wool enabled Castile to begin to produce and export small quantities of finished woolen cloth.[17]

## EXPANSION

In the late fifteenth century, the nations of the Iberian peninsula would suddenly and violently burst forth into the wider world. In some ways their backgrounds were similar. Both had recently developed strong monarchies. Both were reasonably prosperous as well, even though neither possessed a territory that was fertile or blessed with great natural resources. With the exception of their tendency to resort to force in dealing with the peoples they would encounter, however, there were few other similarities between the subsequent careers of the two countries. Whereas the process that would bring Portugal into direct contact with much of the wider world was the result of conscientious planning that unfolded at a deliberate pace during the course of the fifteenth century, the motivation that stimulated

Spain to seek its fortune across the ocean remains a mystery. Moreover, right from the outset, the two nations conceived of their "discoveries" in radically different ways. The Portuguese, on the one hand, placed almost exclusive emphasis on the commercial possibilities that suddenly were opened to them. The Spanish, on the other, decided to create an empire that was to be sustained by settlement from home.

Much mystery surrounds the question of Portuguese expansion. The traditional and widely accepted view is that it resulted largely from the efforts of the man history has learned to call Prince Henry the Navigator. It is said that he established a "think tank" at Sagres in the south of Portugal to which the best nautical minds were imported. Over time, the scientists gathered at Sagres perfected many techniques that would make circumnavigation of Africa possible.[18] Bailie Diffie and George Winius, however, have recently argued that much of the story is apocryphal. There is, they point out, very little documentation to support any of it. Because the entire exercise was deliberately concealed, it is impossible to determine what the Portuguese did and did not do. All that can be said with any certainty is that the Portuguese entered the fifteenth century in possession of nautical knowledge that was equivalent to that which was common in the Mediterranean world of that era, but that they ended the century with a superior naval technology. Precisely what the steps were in the process, what the Portuguese borrowed, what they invented, and who ultimately was responsible for the overall planning, however, remains a mystery.[19]

Although there was secrecy surrounding Portuguese preparations for overseas ventures, the stages of progress along the African coast that ultimately led them to Asia are well documented. One of the early successes was the rounding of and return from Cape Bojador in 1434. This overcame an important psychological barrier, for until then the Portuguese were uncertain that the techniques of sailing against the current would actually work in these conditions. The next important stage was the establishment in 1448 of a factory at Arguim, the first permanent European settlement in Africa south of the Sahara. Although there was a hiatus in exploration during the middle of the century that appears to have been caused by internal political squabbles, by the 1460s the Portuguese were again undertaking regular ventures. The Gold Coast was reached by 1471, the inviting mouth of the river Kongo by 1482, and the tip of southern Africa by 1489. Finally, in 1497, Vasco da Gama became the first European captain to circumnavigate the African continent and enter the Indian Ocean.[20]

A diverse set of motives, some stronger at different times than others, lay behind this expansion. Because it was blocked from the interior by chains of mountains, Portugal naturally faced the Atlantic. It has also been pointed out that the maritime tradition of the Portuguese long predated the birth of Prince Henry.[21] The religious factor was also important, for the Portuguese considered themselves to be at war with Islam. Henry derived much of his financial support from an anti-Muslim religious brotherhood he headed whose main purpose was to carry the fight from the Iberian peninsula into the Muslim world. The missionary tenor is also suggested by Portuguese attempts to proselytize wherever they landed in Africa.[22] It was only after they reached Asia and fully appreciated the vastness of the world and the magnitude of the task that their religious zeal became tempered by a more practical sense of reality.

In many ways the entire venture seems to have resulted from the speculative impulses of small groups of individuals. Mention of direct sailing to the Indian Ocean does not appear in any document prior to the 1460s, so it is likely, at least at the outset, that the quest for Asia was less important than the craving for immediate profit. For throughout their voyages the Portuguese seemed less concerned with discovery for the sake of knowledge than for the sake of money. In this sense, the main goal of the entire process was to find wealth in the distant unknown. Finally, it should be pointed out that this was not the effort of a nation unified in its purpose and committed to a single objective. Rather, throughout the fifteenth century, even up until the departure of da Gama, many important segments of Portuguese society remained opposed to overseas exploration.[23]

What the Portuguese attempted once they reached the Indian Ocean is staggering to the imagination. Having nothing that was of interest to the sophisticated commerce of Asia, they were obliged to rely on force. In a startling series of events that resembled a blitzkrieg, this tiny nation was temporarily able to impose itself on a vast universe. Beginning with a stunning naval victory over a combined Muslim fleet in 1509, a battle that has been referred to as one of the most important in naval history, they proceeded to dominate Asian waters.[24] From the center of operations that had been established in Goa in 1510, they launched a daring raid on Malacca in 1511.[25] With this vital strategic base in their hands, they were able to begin the erection of a series of forts and fortified factories that stretched from Sofala in southeast Africa all the way to Nagasaki in Japan. In the words of K. M. Panikkar, the era of Vasco da Gama had begun.[26]

Initially, the results of Portuguese expansion brought great relief to the royal treasury. In several places in Africa the Portuguese were able to procure slaves for use on plantations in their Atlantic islands. The coup de grace in Africa, however, was the amount of gold they obtained from the Gold Coast. Gold that before had tediously crossed the desert on the backs of camels to North Africa was now diverted southward to the coast. In 1506, 25 percent of the crown's revenue was derived from this source.[27] Once Asia had been reached, however, the gold of Guinea was obliged to take second place to the products of the Orient. Indigo, silk, ebony, and especially pepper formed part of this lucrative trade. As early as 1502, Venetian merchants in Cairo could find no pepper, the Mediterranean having seemingly been cut off from its traditional supplies of spices. How grave this must have seemed to merchants in the Mediterranean network is suggested by Bernard Lewis, who writes that "the Portuguese dealt a mortal blow to the . . . very lifeblood of the Mamluk state. . . . The Arab Near East had been outflanked."[28]

The initial success of the Portuguese was not paralleled by the Spanish. That the Spanish indeed should have established themselves overseas in 1492 was itself somewhat ironic. Unlike the Portuguese, they had no tradition of systematic exploration. In fact, even the nearby Atlantic islands had been leased to Genoese entrepreneurs for settlement. Indeed, until 1492 the series of requests from the Genoese geographer Christopher Columbus for support for his notion of sailing westward in order to find a direct route to Asia were turned down. Reasoning that God would not have concealed valuable lands, a learned council of theologians appointed to weigh the merits of his request rejected his appeal in January 1492. For reasons that are not clear, however, the Catholic monarchs reversed themselves in April and agreed to provide him with modest support. With this help, he completed the first of his four voyages to the Americas in very short order. He returned to Europe in triumph, carrying with him captive Indians to demonstrate that he had found islands off the coast of China.[29]

Columbus's discovery began the roller-coaster relationship that would always characterize Spain's dealings with the Americas. Such excitement was generated that in 1493 an expedition composed of twelve thousand men was dispatched to establish settlements in the lands Columbus had found. The Spanish crown, sensing the importance of the discoveries, soon began to whittle away at the generous privileges it initially had granted to Columbus and his heirs. Soon voyages of exploration and investigation were being undertaken throughout North and South America. Not until the sighting of the Pacific by Vasco Nuñez Balboa in 1512, however, did it become apparent to those who had not previously been convinced that this was indeed a new world of which Europe had previously been totally ignorant. Further confirmation of this startling discovery was provided by Ferdinand Magellan's crossing of the Pacific, which conclusively demonstrated the degree to which this was a world apart. Nevertheless, this new world did not live up to the expectations of those who had found it. The gold of the Caribbean Islands was soon exposed as being of extremely limited supply; the Indians upon whom the Spanish had come to depend began to die in droves. Indeed, twenty-five years after their arrival in America, the Spanish had very little to show for their endeavors. In many circles in Spain, in fact, America had come to be discounted as virtually worthless.[30]

Spanish fortunes, however, soon would experience a significant improvement. Acting brashly on rumors circulating in Cuba about a wealthy kingdom located in the interior of the continental mainland, a freebooter named Hernán Cortés led a party (which initially consisted of 509 men) into the Mexican highlands. With the aid of Indian groups eager to avenge the spoliation the Aztecs had perpetrated over the years, the Spanish were able to pacify Mesoamerica. In what often resembled a treasure hunt rather than a conquest, the Spaniards secured an unprecedented windfall of gold and silver.[31]

The events that transpired in South America were even more remarkable. In 1531 another freebooter, the illiterate Francisco Pizarro, led a force of only 168 men to challenge the Inca empire. It would be logical to assume that because of its military tradition, regimentation, and centralized control, the Inca would have found no difficulty in dealing with Pizarro's tiny party. Beset as it was, however, by internal strife and short-sighted leadership, it, too, fell to the Spaniards armed with iron and horses. For their impetuousness and audacity, the conquerors, both horsemen and foot soldiers, were amply rewarded in gold and silver.[32] The conquest of two large empires by a handful of paraprofessional Spaniards is still, as one scholar has put it, "shrouded in a curious air of unreality."[33]

Control over the Americas seemed to offer many advantages to Spain. The conquest of the remainder was achieved when covetous Spaniards ran amuck throughout the two continents in the hopes of duplicating the exploits of Cortés and Pizarro. Once this period came to an end and as additional settlers made their way to the Americas, the demand grew for products the emigrants were familiar with, such as wines, oils, grains, fruits, and livestock. These goods commanded high prices in the newly settled lands, and Spain responded by producing for export on an unprecedented scale.[34] Whereas the period of the conquest brought windfall profits to individual Spaniards and to the crown, the postconquest period would bring a regular supply of indispensable bullion. By the middle of the sixteenth century, new silver mines were being discovered in both Mexico and Peru. After the middle of the century, Zacatecas, Real del Monte, and Guanajuato in Mexico and especially Potosí in Peru (in part of what is now Bolivia) had begun to pour out their riches. According to Earl Hamilton, the average output per annum was 303,121,174 pesos from 1551 to 1560; by the last decade of the century, this figure had risen to 2,707,626,538 pesos.[35] The Spanish must surely have believed that this addition to their already prosperous and powerful kingdom could only push it toward even greater economic progress.

## DECLINE IN THE MEDITERRANEAN

At the beginning of the sixteenth century, the Mediterranean represented one of the most prosperous regions of Europe. Having thoroughly outdistanced other cities in Italy, Venice in the late fifteenth century was, as one historian described it, "a triumph. . . . Her prestige and pride stood high. . . . these were to stand out as Venice's golden years."[36] Although its success was perhaps not as gaudy as that of Venice, Portugal could also take pride in its achievements. In addition to being peaceful and relatively wealthy, it had established an overseas commercial empire unprecedented in human history. Nor were Spain's accomplishments any less impressive. Not only had it carved out a vast empire in the Americas, but from the time of the accession of young Charles V to the throne in 1517, Spain was at the center of something unique. One of his advisers went so far as to tell the king, "God has set you on the path towards a world monarchy."[37]

That is, many of the most prosperous regions of Europe had come under the rule of the Habsburg king of Spain. Scarcely a century later, however, virtually everything had changed. Overseas Portugal was everywhere on the retreat, and at home it had even lost its own independence. At the same time, Venice was reverting from its status as one of the most commercially and industrially vibrant centers of Europe to domination by a natural economy. Even Spain, arguably the most powerful nation-state in sixteenth-century Europe, had begun to traverse the path that would forever reduce it to third-rate status. That a similar fate befell each of these regions was not coincidental. For although each suffered from a multitude of problems, none was unique in this regard. What appears to have decided their destiny was that the unresolved contradictions within their respective social formations rendered them incapable of finding solutions to the dilemmas they faced.

Because of a series of unlikely accidents, in the early sixteenth century Spain emerged at the center of what, on paper, appeared to be the most powerful coalition in European history. In the process of attempting to isolate France diplomatically, Ferdinand of Aragon had constructed a complicated set of marriage alliances for his children. Yet through a bizarre string of untimely deaths arose a situation that Ferdinand could neither have anticipated nor approved. The entire inheritance fell to Charles, who, as the sole heir of Isabella of Castile, Ferdinand of Aragon, Mary of Burgundy, and Philip of the Austrian Habsburgs, found himself in control of numerous territories. In addition to the thrones of Castile, Aragon, Burgundy, the Low Countries, Austria, large parts of Italy, and the newly conquered American empire, he was also elected Holy Roman emperor.[38] Although he had been raised as a Fleming, there were a variety of reasons why Castile became the center of his imperial scheme. As a legacy of the royalist triumph engineered by his grandparents, Charles was in a relatively stronger financial position in Castile than in any of his other domains. Moreover, the Castilian army had already demonstrated itself to be the most powerful in Europe. With its large and growing population, it offered him a military potential unmatched by his other realms.[39]

The Spain over which Charles presided was expanding both industrially and agriculturally. Partly stimulated by the demand created by the settlement of the Americas, there was a tendency to turn from pasturage to cultivation. Not only was a significantly higher percentage of land being devoted to cereals, oils, and wines, but there was an increase in the use of mules for plowing, as they were twice as fast as oxen. In addition to continuing exports of wool, Spain was also developing its own textile industry. Industry was not limited to textiles, however. Shipbuilding grew in response to the demands of communication with the Indies. Similarly, necessitated by the many wars of the Habsburg monarchs, the manufacture of arms became an important area of production.[40]

Nevertheless, by the mid–sixteenth century there were already harbingers of the problems that would sap Spain of its vitality. For despite its outward grandeur, the Habsburg empire was less than the sum of its parts. Rather than capable of being mobilized for a united effort, the various elements were more likely to present vexatious, particularistic problems for their universal sovereign. For a time, American treasure masked the structural weakness in the empire. With the advantage of hindsight, however, historians have come to remarkably similar conclusions concerning the direction and priorities of the Spanish monarchs. Fernand Braudel notes that American treasure "created illusions, a false sense of prosperity."[41] J. S. Parry adds that "large as the Indies revenue was, larger still was it believed to be, but it was never enough."[42] The commentary of J. S. Elliott, however, is perhaps the most telling. "The comforting appearances brought by the American silver," he writes, "masked the beginnings of a radical change in the structure of the entire Atlantic structure."[43]

The problems of mid-sixteenth-century Spain need not have determined its destiny. Left unattended and even allowed to compound, however, they soon created a ripple effect that left no sector of the economy untouched. The main problem was the perceived responsibilities of Charles, the universal monarch. As king of Castile, he was constantly engaged in war against France to establish territorial supremacy on the Continent. As Holy Roman emperor he was responsible for defending the church against the Protestant heresy that had spread like a brushfire throughout his German territories. In this same role he was obliged to attempt to blunt the Muslim threat represented by the Ottoman advance from the East. Although the military activity that these endeavors engendered was a significant drain on the resources of the monarch, he did little to reduce his commitments. John Lynch caustically captures the essence of the problem when he observes that "peace was the only remedy Charles did not consider."[44]

It is ironic that the situation only worsened under his successors. The irony is that Philip II did not succeed to his father's Austrian possessions nor to the position of Holy Roman emperor, so his responsibilities should have been fewer. Nevertheless, although Philip acceded to the throne declaring a policy of peace, military expenditures that had been "considerable" under Charles became "quite extraordinary" under his son and successor.[45] It has been estimated that by 1587 Philip had more than one hundred thousand men in his military service. Between 1578 and 1594, the money spent on Spain's military forces tripled; between 1581 and 1595, the amount spent on armaments also tripled.[46]

The need to pay for military exploits triggered a series of vicious cycles. The Low Countries had been a fairly generous contributor to imperial finances. By the 1560s, however, they balked at the increased levies Philip demanded. Although excessive taxation was only one of a number of sources of discontent, it was a major factor behind the revolt of the Netherlands that began in the 1560s. Thus, for eighty years and at an enormous cost, Spain would unsuccessfully try to suppress this rebellion. Spain was obliged to find not only other sources of funding but also money to bring the recalcitrant provinces back under its control.[47]

By the seventeenth century other problems beset the already shaky imperial finances. At its peak during the sixteenth century, American silver provided the crown with as much as 25 percent of its revenue. After the turn of the century, however, the American mining industry would suffer a severe depression, which, in an odd twist, was stimulated by the grasping policies of the crown. By interfering in the management of the industry in the hopes of maximizing its tax revenue, the Spanish monarchy only succeeded in hastening the demise of mining.[48] After 1620, production levels, which had already begun to decrease gradually, began to fall precipitously. Production that had reached almost three billion pesos per annum in the last decade of the sixteenth century fell to a little more than one-sixth of that level by 1651. Once again, in trying to swallow everything it could, the Spanish crown had bitten off another hand that fed it.[49]

The finances of the country were not aided by other state policies. Like the impecunious everywhere, the Spanish crown resorted to borrowing. It turned to international financiers to bail it out of one jam after another. Prior to the revolt, it borrowed heavily in the Low Countries; it borrowed in Italy and Germany as well. Another device for securing revenue was the confiscation of private silver shipments arriving from America and the issuance of a bond that guaranteed the holder repayment. All of this meant that during ordinary times a good deal of government revenue was pledged to debt repayment. Even during the early years of the reign of Philip II, two-thirds of his income was mortgaged in advance. During extraordinary times the crown was obliged to declare bankruptcy. Unfortunately for Spain, however, the extraordinary became ordinary: Bankruptcy was declared in 1557, 1576, 1596, 1607, 1627, and 1647.[50] Not only were many of Spain's creditors wiped out on these occasions, but with each succeeding bankruptcy, the terms of borrowing worsened significantly.

At the beginning of the sixteenth century, much government revenue was derived from indirect taxation. As the century wore on, however, with all else failing, the crown resorted increasingly to direct taxation. Because the nobility was exempt from direct levies, the personal tax known as the *servicio* fell squarely on the shoulders of those least able to pay. David Vassberg notes that by the end of the reign of Philip II, "the peasant had been stretched to the limit."[51] This observation is more than confirmed by Henry Kamen, who argues that between 1559 and 1598, the tax burden increased by some 430 percent, whereas wages increased by only 80 percent.[52] Spain, therefore, experienced not only a price revolution but a tax revolution as well.

By the seventeenth century, agriculture had also begun to suffer. Output and yields made a sharp decline, partly because much of the better land was converted to the vine during the sixteenth century in order to take advantage of American demand. Moreover, the backward techniques of Spanish cultivation were beginning to take a toll on regions that had remained devoted to grain. The problem was exacerbated by the Spanish reliance on the mule, which was faster than the ox but could not turn over as much soil, especially harnessed to the relatively primitive Roman plow the Spanish still used. The net result was that as the moisture content of the soil was depleted, erosion ensued. Yields from the marginal lands, pressed into service in response to the American windfall began to produce drastically reduced harvests. Compounded by drought, the maintenance of the two-field system, the loss of the American market to American production, and the continuing privileges enjoyed by the guilds of shepherds, who grazed their sheep almost anywhere they chose, Spanish agriculture faced a multifaceted crisis for which there was no obvious remedy.[53]

By the seventeenth century agriculture faced a crisis of another type. This one, however, was even more the result of man and his institutions. Peasants increasingly found themselves in a vice. Agricultural yields were dropping simultaneously with grain prices. Yet the continuing tithes paid to the church, rising rents in some cases, and the onerous burdens imposed by the state all squeezed the peasantry to the point of desperation. Many chose a solution that had not been possible for their forebears of earlier centuries: to abandon the countryside rather than to pursue an existence that was continually worsening. The result was that by the end of the sixteenth century, as much as one-third of the arable was no longer being cultivated.[54]

The seventeenth century was also a period of severe demographic decline. Estimates vary, but one calculation suggests that a population of 6.7 million in 1590 had been reduced to roughly 5 million in 1683.[55] Several major and a few lesser reasons appear to have been responsible for the sharp demographic turnaround. Among the principal factors was the expulsion of the Moriscos, those of Muslim ancestry who had chosen to convert to Christianity in preference to leaving the country following the edicts promulgated by Isabella. That the action on the part of the government had little rhyme and less reason is suggested by J. S. Elliott, who notes that their major crimes were "spending too little, working too hard, and breeding too fast."[56] At any rate, as a result of the expulsions, between 1609 and 1611, 3 percent of the population was forced to leave the country. Another major factor was emigration to the Americas. Although adequate census data do not exist, Jaime Vicens Vives estimates that by the middle of the sixteenth century there were already 120 thousand Spaniards in the Indies and that the number of emigrants continued to climb.[57] The drain on Spain was enormous. Add to these two factors the intermittent reappearance of the plague, almost constant warfare, and falling birthrates and it becomes easy to understand why population decreased.

In view of all the other problems that beset Spanish society in the seventeenth century, it is not surprising that Spanish industrial production was also gravely affected. In this instance, however, Spain was affected by forces partly beyond its control. The inflation that swept across sixteenth-century Europe struck first and most severely in the southern portions of the Continent, where prices rose most rapidly. As a result the price of Spanish manufactures escalated dramatically, leading to a situation in which, according to Lynch, "inflation pushed Spain out of the international market and then even out of the domestic market."[58] The nascent textile industry, shipbuilding, mining, and metallurgy all suffered greatly. The situation deteriorated to the point where even the famous munitions manufactures of Toledo, which had been the envy of Europe in the sixteenth century, ceased production by the middle of the seventeenth.[59]

Spain also developed a serious balance of payments problem. In part, this came about because Spain had to import virtually everything, which in turn resulted partly from the poor internal communications. Road construction had been neglected and canals never undertaken, making the costs of internal transportation extremely high. Quite ironically, it was cheaper to transport goods to Seville from the Low Countries than from Old Castile. The balance of payments problem was aggravated by the failure of Spanish production. No longer just luxuries from abroad, the list of imports came to include such mundane commodities as textiles, grains, timber, and even the arms with which Spain fought its wars. With the exception of wool, Spain produced little with which to meet its payments, so the balance increasingly had to be settled in 'bullion. Although mercantilistic legislation, (dating from the era of Ferdinand and Isabella) against the export of specie remained in force, both the exemptions and the evasions allowed much of the silver that was imported into Spain to be reexported northward. A perceptive contemporary realized the dimensions of the problem when he observed that "Spain was becoming the Indies" of other countries.[60]

By the seventeenth century, not even the protected market of the Indies brought much comfort to Spain. Despite the system of convoys and closed ports that were at the center of Spain's exclusive trading system, it reaped little benefit from the transatlantic commerce. Americans of the second imperial century had long since been able to produce what they had once imported from Spain, and the goods they still needed to import could not be acquired from Spain. Thus, although it had to be channeled through Seville, a staggering percentage of the goods that legally made their way to the New World were of foreign origin. By 1691, France, Genoa, the Netherlands, the Spanish Netherlands, and England all exported more to the Americas than did Spain. In fact, Spain's share of the commerce of the Indies had shrunk to a mere 3 percent.[61] To make matters even worse, conniving settlers and enterprising foreign interlopers had developed such sophisticated networks of contraband that a significant portion of the goods that reached America were not even taxed.

The downfall of Spain was so rapid and so complete that it almost boggles the imagination. It also begs for an explanation. Although the relative poverty of the environment might be invoked in order to explain why it could not maintain its ascendancy, David Vassberg is quick and accurate in refusing to accept this as the reason. He writes that "the real problem of Castilian agriculture was not meteorological or entomological, but . . . the political and social—that is, human. The environment was not at fault. The poverty that characterized the system was the product of man-made institutions that were inefficient, and did not permit the proper utilization of existing resources."[62] Although Vassberg is speaking specifically of the failure of Castilian agriculture, his judgment has a great deal of validity for the general failure of the Spanish political economy.

In looking for an explanation for why this should have been, one can begin with the contradictions inherent in an absolutist state. Freed from accountability, Charles and the Philips who followed him pursued policies that might have satisfied some mystical imperial goals but had little relevance to the basic needs of Spain and its inhabitants. Quite the contrary, they were parasitical in the sense that they produced absolutely nothing that could benefit the nation. Rather, as the ultimate parasites, they continued to suck away at the productive base of society until it could yield no more and died. Why the contemporaries themselves were not aware of this, however, is a most interesting if unanswerable question.

The other principal culprit was the social relations of production extant in Spain as it emerged from the Middle Ages. For despite the demise of feudalism in its classic form, the country remained firmly entrenched in a world of seigneurial privilege. As many as one in ten persons enjoyed noble status, which exempted them from any significant contribution to the maintenance of the country. Stated somewhat differently, the minority that had the means to make an effective contribution to the general well-being were absolved of this responsibility. Even worse, the system of buttresses by which they reproduced their position in society guaranteed them immunity from competition. Hence there was little incentive for them to initiate improvements that might increase productivity.[63] Under these circumstances, the aristocracy was able to maintain such anachronistic attitudes as those of the nobleman who argued that "any good wretch would die of hunger before he would take up a trade."[64] Seigneurialism and its attitudes were not conducive to dealing with a rapidly changing world. It would not be until the next century that those in power would begin to question the logic inherent in this observation, but by then too much damage had already been done.

Over the course of little more than a century, Madrid not only succeeded in bringing down the productive capacity of Spain but also helped to bring about the fall of most of its erstwhile allies. Upon his accession, Charles presided over dominions that contained the most productive centers of sixteenth-century Europe. These included much of northern Italy and southern Germany. It also included Antwerp, a city unrivaled in its commercial supremacy; according to H. G. Koenigsberger and George Mosse, "perhaps no other city has ever again played such a dominant role as did Antwerp in the second quarter of the sixteenth century."[65] Nevertheless, either via destructive warfare or equally pernicious bankruptcy, Charles's successors managed to bring about the ruin of all that had glittered at the beginning of the century. "Spain did not decline alone," writes Immanuel Wallerstein, it "brought down all that had been linked to [its] accession: northern Italy, southern Germany . . . Antwerp and Portugal."[66] Although taken out of context this observation is an overstatement in that it ignores the internal dynamics that were eating away at the prosperity of the respective regions mentioned, it does suggest the extent of the fallout from the failure of the imperial policy of Spain.

Indeed, these observations are borne out by the experience of Portugal, whose decline preceded its intimate relationship with Spain. Rather, Portugal's decline stemmed from the unique but ultimately counterproductive attempt of the monarchy to monopolize the commerce not only of Portugal itself but also of its trading empire. "Never before or since," observes Bailie Diffie, "has [a government] become the entire entrepreneur of an entire imperial undertaking and thrown its whole resources into the creation of profits from a trading monopoly."[67] The gold of El Mina, the ivory of East Africa, the calicoes of India, the spices of Indonesia, and the silver of Japan were a monopoly of those trading on behalf of the crown. Inter-Asian commerce, on the other hand, was subjected to Portuguese taxation. All traders were obliged to purchase licenses and to land their goods in ports where they paid duties to Portuguese officials. Even if the system made sense on paper, however, such an undertaking demanded a military-bureaucratic system that was far beyond the resources of such a tiny nation.

By the second quarter of the sixteenth century, the system had already begun to break down. From the 1530s, European interlopers, as they were viewed by the Portuguese, became an increasingly important and menacing factor on the Gold Coast. Try as they might, the Portuguese were powerless to prevent these rivals from trading in the area, especially because they were supplied with more attractive trading goods.[68] In Asia, as well, the system of licenses soon began to break down. Indigenous merchants learned that smaller and faster ships could easily bypass the Portuguese blockade. Although many had initially been intimidated into complicity with the embargo, most learned to evade and ignore it.[69] The most serious problem of all, however, was Portugal's failure to secure control of Aden, which commanded entrance into the Red Sea. As a result, by the 1530s the Red Sea route to the Mediterranean was open again. By the 1560s, it was supplying as many spices to Europe as did the all-sea route via the Cape of Good Hope.[70]

From the outset the attempt to monopolize the spice trade of Asia proved to be an expensive proposition. Although an all-sea route ideally should have enabled lower costs, the system of forts and factories required to maintain it had just the opposite effect. Portuguese spices, which from 1508 were marketed in Antwerp, cost significantly more than those Venice had supplied in the previous century.[71] Even while high prices were sustained and before competition was renewed, the cost of the military establishment necessary to enforce the monopoly was higher than the value returned. As early as 1524, the Portuguese crown was borrowing money, pledging next years' spice harvest as collateral. By 1548, it has been noted, the need to borrow had become quite chronic and had to be undertaken on increasingly worsening terms.[72] Once the Red Sea route was opened again, the efforts of the Portuguese crown were doomed to failure. Pepper prices fell dramatically, but the overhead of maintaining the system did not decrease at all. As suggested by Anthony Disney, "the cost of the state of India to the Portuguese crown was greater than its value."[73]

The Asian fiasco did not represent a loss solely for the crown. Rather, its repercussions were felt throughout Portuguese society. One result was that population levels in Portugal began to fall well before this became a generalized phenomenon in seventeenth-century Europe. The Portugal of the sixteenth century was a country of limited human resources, and the attempt to staff an empire of global proportions represented a severe strain on these fragile reserves. In addition, on several occasions overzealous attempts to achieve policy goals or to implement other aspects of the royal will by resorting to military means resulted in disaster.[74] To this should be added the slow but steady drain on population resources that was represented by the settlement of Brazil. Ironically, whereas in the early years of the sixteenth century, every effort was made to stimulate such an emigration, by the seventeenth century, many were predicting that its continuation would spell doom for Portugal.[75] When all of these factors are taken into consideration, it becomes obvious that this tiny nation had bitten off several times more than it could chew.

Depopulation, in turn, had very negative repercussions for the economy as a whole. Prior to the sixteenth century, the country had had a largely self-sufficient, if relatively unspectacular, economy. The lure of gold and other forms of wealth, however, tempted many to desert the countryside in pursuit of the dream of making a fortune in a more promising setting. Soon much of the landscape was abandoned, as even some of the more productive soils ceased to be cultivated. Portugal was transformed from an exporter of certain types of foodstuffs into a nation that became wholly dependent on imports for its basic sustenance. Thus, just as had been the case with Spain, even the meager earnings that were generated by its overseas endeavors were transferred northward in order to satisfy daily needs.

It was a generally weakened and dispirited Portugal, then, that allowed itself to come under the control of Spain in 1580. Two years before, the religiously fanatical king, D. Sebastião, had led an unwise expedition into Morocco, from which neither he nor seven thousand of his followers returned. What is more, D. Sebastião had neglected to produce an heir to the throne. Many claimants rushed forward to present their credentials. Of the various contestants, Philip II of Spain had the strongest army, if not necessarily the most convincing genealogy, and he was able to bribe many influential Portuguese to support his candidacy. There were others who believed that being ruled by the man who was still arguably the strongest potentate in Europe would reverse the fortunes of a nation already in decline.[76] Thus, with the stipulation that Portugal would remain a separate kingdom from Spain, after only minor opposition, the country acquiesced in the accession of Philip II as king of Portugal.

The union of the two crowns, however, subsequently referred to as the period of Babylonian captivity by the Portuguese, proved a disaster for the smaller nation. Rather than gaining access to the wealth of the Spanish Indies as many had hoped, the Portuguese inherited the same enemies with which Spain was at war. At the time, Spain's main foe was the Netherlands, which was still in revolt against Spanish rule. A series of ironies connected with Portugal's linkage to Spain were to bring tragic results. Until the union of the two crowns, Dutch merchants traveled to Lisbon to purchase their spices. When Philip banned Dutch trade in Lisbon in 1594, the Dutch decided to attempt to acquire spices at their source. This meant issuing a direct challenge to the Portuguese pretensions of a monopoly of the trade of Asia. Because the Dutch had larger population resources and their shipping had so advanced that it was superior to that of Portugal, they were able to launch an all-out assault on the Portuguese empire. For more than forty years, Portuguese settlements and shipping in Asia, Africa, and South America were subjected to constant and disastrous harassment from Dutch tormentors. By the time the Portuguese had regained their independence in 1640 and negotiated a peace with the Dutch, almost all of the Asian establishment, as well as São Jorge da Mina on the Gold Coast, had been lost. The final irony is that the Spanish empire, centered as it was on *tierra firme*, the mainland, and thus being relatively immune from sea-power, hardly suffered at all, while the Portuguese empire was largely dismembered by an enemy it had inherited from Spain.[77]

Even after its release from the Babylonian captivity, Portugal continued to decline. In seeking an explanation for this phenomenon, it can be noted that the role of the Portuguese crown was different from that of its Spanish counterpart. Whereas the Spanish monarchs had erred by taxing the economy into impotence, largely in the pursuit of an illusive imperial strategy, the Portuguese monarchy was less concerned with matters of state than it was with economic considerations. Yet the Portuguese monarchy failed precisely because it tried to regulate the economy in ways that were not feasible. The one advantage that Portugal possessed at the beginning of the sixteenth century was superior shipping. Had it done what Venice had done in the the eastern Mediterranean, that is, been content with domination of the "country trade" of Asia, Portugal might have been successful. Michael Pearson notes that because of its superior shipping, "Portugal could have shared in and probably dominated the spice trade without using force, but this was not attempted."[78]

Nevertheless, there are similarities between the declining fortunes of Spain and Portugal. By the seventeenth century, there were many observers in Portugal who realized that the downward spiral could only be changed by a more effective mobilization of the country's resources. Attempts were made to increase the base of taxation, to provide government subsidies to promising undertakings, and to foment import-substitution. Yet this was almost an impossibility in a social formation that continued to be dominated by seigneurial privilege. The nobility staunchly resisted changes that did not cater to their immediate interests. Because little could be done to force their compliance, reformist efforts could not even begin to make inroads into the many ills that afflicted virtually every aspect of Portuguese society. Carl Hanson observes that "as was the case of most of Europe, Portugal's social foundations remained firmly embedded in privilege and landed property."[79] Under these circumstances it was hardly likely that effective change could have been enacted.

In the sixteenth century Portugal and Venice were the major competitors for the spice trade of Asia; it might be assumed, therefore, that as Lisbon's fortunes waned, those of Venice would improve. To a degree, but only to a limited degree, this was true. The secular trend in Venetian history during the sixteenth and seventeenth centuries was remarkably similar to those of its counterparts in the western Mediterranean. This is somewhat surprising because its social structure and attitudes were very different from those that prevailed in Spain and Portugal. For example, the Venetian standard of usury was notably different from the doctrines expounded by the church. A recent historian has commented that the Venetian usurer's attitude resembled that of a modern businessperson.[80] In fact, there are some historians who see traces of incipient capitalism in the social structure of Renaissance Venice. Nevertheless, Venetians were to prove no more capable than the other Europeans of breaking the barrier into modernity. Although the specific reasons for its failure were different from those of Spain and Portugal, it can be argued that the demise of Venice also stemmed from social considerations.

Venice had achieved complete supremacy in the eastern Mediterranean by the end of the fifteenth century. As early as the eleventh century, it had secured favorable rights in Byzantium, which allowed it to dominate the "country trade" of the region.[81] Despite papal objections, it also made significant profits from the spice trade at Alexandria. By the fifteenth century, however, it had become more than just a conveyor of goods; it had developed its own productive base to the extent that its balance of payments with the East had been reversed. So completely beaten were such rivals as Amalfi, Pisa, and Comacchio that they no longer even competed. Even Genoa, with which Venice had "fought in almost every patch of ocean crossed by trading convoys of either city" had decided to concentrate on financing the Portuguese and Spaniards rather than continuing its losing battle in the East.[82] Not even the fall of Constantinople to the Ottomans in 1453 made a significant difference. Their privileges were slightly reduced, but the Venetians continued in much the same manner as they had always done.

Although the rounding of the Cape of Good Hope by the Portuguese posed a severe challenge to Venice, it was able to make a remarkable adjustment. Rather melodramatically A. H. Lybyer states that "the beginning of the economic decay of Venice . . . dates . . . from the doubling of the Cape of Good Hope by the Portuguese." He goes on to point out that in 1502 Venetian merchants could find no pepper in Alexandria.[83] Nevertheless, the Venetians responded by diverting into production capital that was formerly used in trade. By 1569, woolen textile production, which had been only 1,306 cloths in 1516, rose to 26,549. Venetians also concentrated on naval construction, glass, metallurgy, chemicals, sugar refining, silks, mosaics, and leather.[84] By the 1560s, the pepper trade returned to its fifteenth-century peaks, seemingly providing Venice with a well-balanced mix between industry and trade. Even agriculture prospered, as those who had invested in land as a sinecure began to profit from the high price of grain that accompanied the price revolution.[85]

The return to prosperity, however, was to be a temporary phenomenon. Soon Venice was faced with competition from other Italian cities, which had begun to recover from the long series of wars fought on Italian soil between France and Spain during the first half of the sixteenth century. Toward the end of the century there was also a virtual invasion of Dutch and English cloth into the Mediterranean, which posed a severe challenge to Venetian textiles. The "new draperies," lighter in texture than those of Italian manufacture, found a ready market in the warm Mediterranean climate.[86] At the same time, another problem presented itself. Whereas the Portuguese had been inefficient in their attempts to monopolize the spice trade, their Dutch and English successors were much more effective. From the beginning of the seventeenth century, Venice was permanently cut off from Oriental spices.

Some of Venice's problems were caused by the state itself. It was administered by a grand council, which, in its militant pursuit of trading advantage, had always needed to levy significant amounts of taxation in order to maintain Venetian military superiority. During the sixteenth century, as the price revolution raised the costs of administration, the state's need for greater revenues caused it to increase taxation. Many craftsmen revolted, preferring to move where the tax burdens were not as severe. Although in order to protect industrial secrets Venice had banned emigration abroad, the exodus could not be contained. With them the emigrants took knowledge of the sophisticated techniques of Venetian manufactures that had largely been responsible for its competitive advantage. Thus, Venice lost one of the factors in its ascendancy.[87]

Still, there was a more fundamental reason for the absolute and permanent decline of the once preeminent city-state. In Venice the craft guild structure remained intact and in possession of a great deal of power.[88] This is ironic insofar as craft guilds were able to maintain their buoyancy in Venice, while they were increasingly being ruled by merchants elsewhere, solely because the Venetian economy in the late Middle Ages had been so dominated by trade that merchants had never bothered to try to bring the crafts under their control. Moreover, in the wake of the plagues of the 1570s, population had declined severely. In these conditions of labor scarcity, craftsmen were able to demand and receive much higher wages than was the case in other cities. Richard Rapp argues that whereas wages in England and Venice were roughly the same in the 1570s, by 1629 those of Venetian workers were twice as high as those of their English counterparts.[89]

Because the price of Venetian manufactures rose correspondingly sharply, the temporary victory of the worker in the struggle for the lion's share of the surplus paved the way for both the worker's own and for Venetian decline. As its commodity production lost out in the competitive market, Venetian capital was pulled out of manufacture and once again returned to the land. In the seventeenth-century environment of falling grain prices, however, Venetians did not expect to improve the land in order to emphasize its market potential. Rather, they hoped to find sinecures and the safe existence of the rentier.[90] Thus, in a rather incredible transformation, in little more than a generation Venice reverted from a vibrant industrial and commercial center to yet another economy that was unable to sustain its momentum.

## CONCLUSION

To argue that the failures of the Mediterranean were social in origin does not explain why this should have been. Nor does the lack of success, in varying degrees, of the overseas ventures of Spain, Portugal, and Venice explain why they failed at home as well. As a starting point, it should be noted that their respective social relations were developed in and were appropriate to a world that was vastly different from that of the seventeenth century. Although a myriad of changes had taken place, a few stand out as being of particular importance.

One was the emergence of the absolutist state in the early-modern period. It is possible to suggest that in the medieval world feudal rent could be reproduced precisely because there was virtually no state with which the surplus had to be shared. Moreover, the needs of the ruling class were relatively modest in comparison with the demands that the nation-state would subsequently make. Indeed, once this state became a reality, a fundamental contradiction was created. The productive base, even though it had been significantly enlarged, could not support both the parasitic state and the parasitic seigneurial elite. Perhaps the way out of the dilemma would have been for the two forces to confront each other with the winner taking all. After a period of jockeying, during which the primacy of the state was demonstrated, however, they chose accommodation rather than confrontation. In choosing this course, it is likely that the dual parasites condemned the economy to failure. So much of the surplus was siphoned off into nonproductive endeavors that the system proved incapable of reproducing itself. In essence, the host could no longer meet the demands that were made upon it.

A second major factor was the changing nature of production and the inadequacy of a strong guild structure to confront the challenges that this brought into being. One important facet of the medieval world had been its isolation and insulation. In most endeavors competition from abroad was nonexistent. Under these conditions, guilds were designed more for stability than flexibility. Indeed, by their exclusivity, guilds sought to buttress their members against competition by suppressing it at its source. The guild structure, however, was wholly inadequate for dealing with a world in which distant production became a competitive reality. As a wider range of producers sought to infiltrate a given market, innovation, cost-cutting, and the delivery of goods to an appropriate region became the principal means of success. Yet, as was the case in Venice, most guilds remained too myopic to perceive the magnitude of the transformations occurring beyond their immediate horizons. Thus, in Venice they chose to make their stand on the ground of the preservation of their high wage levels rather than seeking more realistic methods of meeting the challenges that threatened to overwhelm them.

In many respects, however, the states of the Mediterranean were not unique. Special interests that sought to gain unhindered privileges were quite common throughout the Continent. Moreover, aspects of the feudal tradition survived the age of feudalism in other parts of the Continent as well. Nor, on the surface, were the kings, nobility, and guilds of the Mediterranean vastly different in outlook from those that existed elsewhere. Yet the degree to which this region declined and became underdeveloped during the era of the general crisis of the seventeenth century was qualitatively different from other areas of western Europe. The question that immediately suggests itself is why the differentiation among countries that took place during this epoch occurred. What forces were at work in northwestern Europe that were absent in the Mediterranean?

# 5

# EUROPE IN TRANSITION: CAPITALISM

Capitalism is a term used frequently but often in different ways. In popular usage it is an imprecise notion vaguely equated with a system of free enterprise. As demonstrated by Frederick Lane in a short article entitled "Meanings of Capitalism," however, scholars are no more precise in their usage of the term. For some it involves little more than an emphasis on profit-making. Others see "capitalistic enterprise" in societies strongly motivated by commercial concerns. Still others identify it with a spirit or a world-view they believe was greatly stimulated by the Protestant Reformation and the value system it engendered.[1] When dealing with such a subjective notion, therefore, it is probably accurate to conclude that there is no single definition that will find universal acceptance.

Nevertheless, as it is used in this study the term has a specificity derived from Marx's definition of the concept: It refers to a specific mode of production that became dominant in Europe after a period of "primitive accumulation" of wealth by a relatively restricted class. Although the sources of this wealth were multiple, Marx identified "feudal rent" as the most important. This wealth was subsequently converted into capital, or, in Marx's colorful expression, given the power to breed, by its use in the process of commodity production. As opposed to having primarily a use value, this production in turn was destined for the market. As the process continued, those in possession of capital gradually obtained a monopoly of the access to the means of production.

The necessary and equally important corollary was that while ownership of the means of production was being concentrated into the hands of the few, the vast majority were being divorced from independent access to those means of production. Whether the process took place in urban or rural areas and whether it occurred in agriculture, manufacturing, or commerce, the results were the same: This new class had no means of subsistence other than the sale of its labor power and therefore came to form a proletariat. This phenomenon could only occur after the old feudal mode had begun to crumble, for, paradoxically, the potential laborer needed to have the liberty to sell his labor.

By definition, however, the system was dominated by competition and conflict. At one level there was the struggle between capital and labor, a struggle that was dominated by the desire of each class to reap maximum benefits from the process of commodity production. Ideally, the proletariat sought just compensation for the fruits of its labor. Nevertheless, as the capitalist mode of production gained in momentum, this goal became increasingly illusory: The capitalist strove for precisely the opposite result. The decisive point was turned when the capitalists arrogated to themselves a monopoly of the ownership of the means of production. Under these circumstances the workers were unable to find an alternative means of subsistence and were obliged to sell their labor power at rates determined by the capitalists. These rates were fixed at levels well below the market value commanded by the commodities they produced. It was the ability of the capitalists to appropriate this surplus value, that is, the difference between the price of the commodity he sold and the wages he paid to the producer, that provided the system with its principal dynamic.

Nevertheless, the capitalist was not only in a constant struggle to maintain his position vis-à-vis the working class, but was also engaged in a life-and-death struggle with those of his own class; as Marx put it, "one capitalist kills many." In order to survive this self-inflicted competition, the capitalist had to reinvest profits in order to guarantee that the system reproduced itself. Thus, in a perverse but pervasive manner, the logic of capitalism suggested an inbuilt dynamic that thrust it forward. Unlike previous modes of production, which emphasized privilege and stability, the capitalist mode of production as it emerged in Europe presupposed change and progress.[2]

Using this model greatly limits the number of European societies that can be said to have developed a capitalist mode of production and also suggests a time frame for its emergence. In fact it was only in northwestern Europe, in the Dutch Netherlands and England, that capitalist relations were established. Specifying exactly when this occurred is more problematical, as it raises the unanswerable question of precisely when capitalism became the dominant mode of production in the respective social formations. Nevertheless, it is not beyond reason to suggest, as does Lawrence Stone, that it was a phenomenon of the late sixteenth and early seventeenth centuries.[3] Enough time had elapsed since the beginnings of the collapse of the feudal mode of production in the fourteenth century for the differentiation among the petty producers—which Dobb sees as absolutely necessary for the emergence of capitalism—to have advanced sufficiently to result in a new class structure.[4]

It can also be said that the development of capitalism was neither planned nor accidental. On the one hand, there were no groups of visionaries who consciously worked to foment a more productive economic system. Quite the contrary, contemporaries would have been at a loss to explain the dynamics of the changes that were taking place around them. On the other hand, it was not purely accidental that capitalism developed where and when it did. Its gestation was facilitated by a number of innovations developed during the later Middle Ages. It was aided commercially by such techniques as banking, the development of a system of credits, the use of bills of exchange, and other devices mainly pioneered by the Italian city-states. In terms of productivity, the diversification and the magnification in scale of output begun in the later Middle Ages was also significant. Even more important were the social changes that erupted during the molten years that preceded the early-modern era.

Yet despite the ubiquitous nature of these phenomena, capitalism developed only in certain select regions of Europe. This happened precisely because, unlike in most parts of the Continent, the institutional development in the Netherlands and England favored its creation. The unique social framework of these regions, which arose because their historical experiences diverged from the rest of the Continent in critical ways, set them on a course that was also unique. In essence, this difference in background created syntheses that favored a series of choices that would not only logically lead in the direction of capitalism but that would also establish the means for its implementation.

## BEFORE THE DUTCH GOLDEN AGE

There are many fine studies that deal with the Netherlands in the seventeenth century, a period that is often referred to as the "golden age." This era of Dutch ascendancy is indeed a legitimate and even fascinating subject of inquiry because for a time, this tiny nation became recognized as the economic leader of Europe. What most of these studies fail to do, however, is to point out the degree to which the golden age was linked to the past. Rather, if only by omission, the tendency is to treat the Dutch Netherlands as if it had been born in a fully mature state in 1585.[5] The failure to mention, even by way of introduction, the unique past of the region is a serious flaw. For it is impossible to understand the ascendancy of the Dutch and the development of a capitalist mode of production without an appreciation of their deviant medieval heritage.

By the late Middle Ages there were a number of independent counties located in the northwest corner of continental Europe. They were spread over parts of what today are France, Luxembourg, Belgium, and the Netherlands. There were many similarities among the counties but no collective term to describe them, though on occasion, because of their nearness to sea level, they were referred to as the Low Countries. By the fifteenth century, some sense of collectivity was achieved as all were brought under the control of the dukes of Burgundy. Because this control was obtained variously by inheritance, purchase, or conquest, each of the counties had a different constitutional arrangement with the dukes. Nevertheless, with the creation of the Estates General, in which all of the counties were represented, an embryonic sense of federalism came into being.[6]

The river Meuse is often mentioned as the dividing line between the north and the south of the Low Countries. The south differed from the north in a number of ways. For example, the southern Low Countries had formed part of both the Roman and Carolingian empires. As a result, it had numerous institutions in common with regions to the south. These included a significant feudal complex whose social relations were similar to those developed elsewhere in western Europe. Moreover, during the high and late Middle Ages, the southern Low Countries formed one of the most economically developed areas of the Continent. This was especially true of the counties of Brabant and Flanders.

Its sophisticated agriculture was one way in which it differed from most of Europe. At a comparatively early date, it developed complicated rotations unknown elsewhere. The cultivation of the turnip allowed farmers to end fallow periods. It also made possible the foddering of cattle, which not only rendered pasturage viable on a scale unheard of in other parts of western Europe but contributed to maintaining the fertility of the soil. Thus, in agricultural productivity and diversity, the availability of meat, and the development of a dairy industry, the southern Low Countries excelled.[7]

The southern Low Countries also stood out for their craft production, the most important of which was cloth. Textile production on a significant scale was evident from the high Middle Ages. As elsewhere, however, the industry was profoundly affected by the demographic downturn that followed the plague. With the depression in the market for ordinary cloth, emphasis increasingly came to be placed on high-quality cloth for the relatively more buoyant luxury market. This shift was facilitated in the fifteenth century by the importation of fine merino wool from Spain. Thus, a product of the southern Low Countries was able to establish a niche for itself at home and even proceeded to conquer much of the European luxury market.[8]

Yet another way in which the southern Low Countries differed from the general western European pattern of the late Middle Ages was the degree to which urbanization developed. By the thirteenth century, there were a large number of towns throughout the region. The process continued to the extent that Henri Pirenne described the area as one that was "par excellence a country of towns."[9] Perhaps only northern Italy can be considered to have been as urbanized during this period. By and large, these were centers of craft production; in addition to textiles, they turned out furniture, chests, tapestries, enamel, jewelry, metals, copper, bronze, arms, and other crafts.[10]

Urbanization was also a major factor in the demise of the feudal mode of production. As towns increased in strength, they were able to undermine the authority of the local nobility. Sometimes this was accomplished by repurchase of their charter. Moreover, as the strength of urban militia grew, towns were able to assume full juridical power from the nobility. There were also important changes in the countryside. As a result of the postplague depression, many urbanites began investing in land. Along with them they brought new notions of tenure. Rents were converted from kind to money, and tenures changed from hereditary right to short-term leases. As early as the late fourteenth century, notes David Nicholas, "tenants actually gained all pertinent rights over the land by payment of a fee of quit-rent recognition."[11]

Trade and commerce were significantly stimulated by the dynamic nature of the economy. In the thirteenth and fourteenth centuries, Bruges became the main entrepôt in northern Europe. On the one hand, it dealt with the export of the products of the southern Low Countries. On the other, it had far-ranging linkages with many parts of Europe. As early as the thirteenth century, Scandinavians, Germans, and Poles did their business in Bruges. English wool, too, was reexported from Bruges to the rest of the Continent. Even though a variety of factors conspired to end the supremacy that Bruges enjoyed until the end of the fourteenth century, other coastal towns waiting in the wings were prepared to carry on the tradition Bruges had pioneered.[12]

Economic growth and diversification, however, took place in an environment beset by a struggle for supremacy. As was the case elsewhere in western Europe, there was conflict between merchant and craft guilds. In its early stages victory went to the merchants, who came to form an urban patriciate that not only exercised municipal control but also monopolized the wholesale trade. The entrance fees were raised to levels far beyond the capacity of craftsmen, so that merchant guilds, for all intents and purposes, became closed corporations. Craftsmen, on the other hand, never fully accepted their disenfranchisement. Between the thirteenth and the early fifteenth centuries, violence between the two groups was endemic. By the fifteenth century, indeed, the craft revolt was so successful that craftsmen obliged the merchants to allow them a share in urban government.[13]

The second important struggle was the continuing conflict waged between the towns and the countryside. In the thirteenth century, attempts were made to introduce craft production into rural areas. Under a variety of pretexts, towns interceded in the countryside in an attempt to prevent the rise of competition. Ghent, Ypres, and others launched raids into the rural areas seeking to destroy the tools of the peasants. In fact, in Flanders the principal cities divided the countryside into spheres of influence, each to be regulated by the respective urban area. Although Pirenne describes the process as "protectionism gone mad," it was to be a fairly successful tactic. For until the fifteenth century, craft production remained a virtual urban monopoly.[14]

Then a significant change occurred. Elements among the urban patriciate began to perceive that organizing rural production could be more profitable than suppressing it. Thus they began to organize rural households into an extensive system of putting out. Although the attitude of many of the towns remained hostile, the decisive change in the balance of power stemmed from the appearance of the dukes of Burgundy as arbiters in the struggle. Not only did they favor rural interests, but unlike the largely impotent counts whom they superseded, they were strong enough to protect the rural areas from urban interference. Thus, according to Dobb, the fifteenth century was an era of the "impressive revival of rural industry."[15]

Although the provinces located to the north of the river Meuse were not as developed as those of the southern Low Countries, certain processes taking place during the later Middle Ages would ultimately enable them to share in the general thrust forward. One of the ways in which they differed from the south was the institutional framework that dominated their social formation. The northern provinces had not been included in either the Roman or Carolingian empires. Partly as a result of this factor, feudal notions of social relations had never taken firm root.[16] Even though it had not been encumbered by a strong feudal tradition, however, the north had not made as much economic progress as had the south.

The main regions were the maritime provinces of Holland and Zeeland. In part because of their location, fishing became extremely important there at an early date. It was greatly facilitated by the development of the *haringbuis*, a large, oceangoing vessel capable of remaining at sea for long periods of time. The *haringbuis* allowed expeditions to travel great distances to search out the best fishing grounds as far away as the waters off of the coast of Iceland. Voyages might keep a ship away from port for as many as six to eight weeks, long sojourns made feasible because the Dutch had pioneered new techniques of curing and drying fish while still at sea, thus obviating the necessity of frequent stops in port. Once these cargoes were landed, they formed the staple of the vital exchange of salt with the Iberian peninsula and grain with the Baltic.[17]

Although agriculture had been comparatively backward, it was stimulated by the process of reclamation that gained great momentum during the Middle Ages. Because much of the territory was below sea level, there was a constant struggle against the ocean. Beginning in the middle of the twelfth century and extending well into the fourteenth, however, much land was reclaimed. This was made possible by the development of poldering, a method by which water was pumped and siphoned away, creating much new potential arable. Thereafter it was necessary to construct a vast network of dikes to prevent a return of the ocean. The Dutch were so successful that one historian has pointed out that Holland was literally a "new country."[18]

Equally important as the reclamation was the nature of the process, generally financed by counts of the region who viewed their undertakings as business ventures. Either by sale or lease they expected to make a profit from the lands they created. In turn, the principal purchasers of these lands were the urban bourgeoisie, who bought rural property not as sinecures but with the intent of making a profit by bringing them under commercial cultivation.[19] The new lands, therefore, were given over both to agriculture and to pasturage. Much of the agricultural production was geared to serving the local urban industrial areas, whereas livestock and other dairy products were destined for export.[20]

Nevertheless, even though members of the urban patriciate invested in the countryside, the dominant landholding group remained the free peasantry. Where remnants of a seigneurial class continued to exist, they were largely irrelevant to the overall structure. For example, in Holland they owned less than 10 percent of the land.[21] Within the peasantry itself the process of social differentiation had already begun. Jan de Vries argues that by 1500 capitalist relations had developed in the countryside. "Some peasants owned much of the land," he observes, while "other peasants owned nothing and found themselves economically dependent."[22]

As was the case in the south, urban dominance was maintained over the rural areas. Although the area was more backward in urbanization than the south, there were still a significant number of small towns in the north. Moreover, the northern towns were in a relatively stronger position than their southern counterparts: Because seigneurial tradition there was even weaker than in the south, there was no force capable of defending the rural areas. Thus, towns such as Dordrecht and Groningen completely subsumed their hinterlands and came to regulate a variety of rural practices. These included what could be produced, what could be marketed, and where this could take place.[23]

As the Low Countries entered the early-modern period, there was still a great deal of difference among them. As the sixteenth century progressed, however, the gap was narrowed and the distinctions blurred. Growth and development became the order of the day. It is well to remember, too, what had already preceded. De Vries appreciates the importance of the past better than most historians who have commented on the evolution of the Netherlands. He writes that "the weak seigneurial powers, the strong bonds of the free farmers . . . and the capitalistic organization of the colonization movement endowed the maritime region of the Netherlands with taxing and property rights of a modern state long before the sudden rise of Amsterdam . . . to economic supremacy."[24]

By the sixteenth century the once preeminent position of Bruges had been assumed by Antwerp. Not only did it become the major trading center in the Low Countries, but soon it outdistanced all other European cities. All the leading economic concerns of Europe transacted their business in Antwerp. German financiers based their operations there; soon after they came to dominate the spice trade of Asia, the Portuguese transferred the marketing of their pepper to this dynamic entrepôt. The Merchant Adventurers of England, as well, sold their cloth on the Antwerp market.[25] "For the first time in history," write Koenigsberger and Mosse, "there existed both a European and a world market; the economies of different parts of Europe had become interdependent and were linked through the Antwerp market . . . with the economies of large parts of the world."[26]

Despite the scale and diversity of the Antwerp market, perhaps the most important component of commerce was what merchants referred to as the "mother trade." This was the commerce with the Baltic from which large supplies of grain were obtained. Because of the price revolution in western

Europe, the cost of grain had skyrocketed. The price of grain in the Baltic, however, remained more stable. By the latter part of the sixteenth century, as many as twelve hundred ships were in regular service between the Low Countries and eastern Europe: By buying cheap in the neighboring markets of the northeast and either consuming these goods domestically or selling them at greatly marked-up prices in western Europe, the Dutch were able to reap benefits in two major ways.[27]

The "mother trade" was important in yet another way. By supplying a good deal of the basic foodstuffs for local consumption, it freed farmers to specialize in other crops. This trade was a crucial factor in enabling the kind of diversity that was developed during the sixteenth century. In addition to the familiar dairy products usually associated with the region, flax, hemp, hops, dyes, livestock, cabbage, apples, pears, plums, cherries, chestnuts, oats, barley, wheat, rye, rape, lettuce, spinach, tobacco, cauliflower, hyacinths, and tulips were among the crops that were grown commercially.[28] It was a diversity that was not approached anywhere else on the European continent.

This capacity for specialization was made possible because the Dutch converted agriculture into a science. Spurred by the incentives provided by the market, they experimented with and perfected a number of different rotations. According to de Vries, there emerged a "flexibility that defies description." Fodder crops, which played an essential role in the cycle of rotations, also allowed large herds of cattle to be kept, despite the fact that land was at a premium. These, in turn, produced sizable amounts of fertilizer that helped to maintain the vitality of the soil. De Vries again notes that the "extraordinary amounts of all sorts of fertilizer that the Flemings applied to their fields never ceased to amaze foreign observers."[29] As a result, yields continued to increase. Whereas it has been calculated that the ratio of wheat was 1:4 in the fourteenth century, by the sixteenth this had risen to 1:10.[30]

During the sixteenth century, the urban-rural struggle was renewed. Whereas during the fifteenth century, rural production had made a comeback in both the north and the south, in the sixteenth century there was a reversal of fortunes. The fifteenth century revival had been made possible by the supportive attitude of the Burgundian dukes. Once Charles V succeeded to the throne, however, the towns found a ruler with a sympathetic ear. In 1531 he promulgated the *orde op de buiten rieringe*, which forbade all rural manufacture. Although its effectiveness has been questioned, it seems certain to have had an important impact. For thereafter, as noted by Pieter Geyl, "industry outside the all powerful towns was . . . unthinkable."[31]

In the midst of the general peace, prosperity, and growth, the Low Countries soon found themselves in a revolt against Spain that had significant repercussions. As one of the most prosperous regions in Europe and one of the few areas where the Habsburg monarchs could raise taxes in almost arbitrary fashion, they had borne the brunt of the fiscal needs of their king. By 1559 there was sufficient resentment for a protest to be lodged with the new ruler, Philip II. Although he promised reform and moderation, this was not forthcoming. Quite the contrary, the impositions on the Low Countries were made even more onerous. Although there was increasing unrest during the 1560s and 1570s and the more radical elements in the region sought confrontation, it was not until the mutiny of Philip's unpaid army in 1576 and their subsequent sacking of Antwerp that the majority of Netherlanders were convinced of the necessity of joining the revolt. "What changed the situation everywhere in 1576," comments Gordon Griffeths, "was the mutiny of the Spanish army."[32] Most of the Low Countries, which had joined together in 1579 to form the Union of Utrecht, declared their independence in 1581. Although there was more militancy in southern centers such as Brussels, the south soon fell to Spanish troops; the seven northern provinces, protected from invasion by the river barriers, held out against the Spanish.[33]

One of the most important ramifications of the revolt was the demise of Antwerp and the rise to prominence of Amsterdam. Antwerp suffered greatly from the bankruptcy of the Spanish monarchy in 1576, its sacking in the same year, and finally a blockade imposed by Spain in 1585. Merchants from Antwerp flocked northward to relocate in Amsterdam. Craftsmen from the south also resettled in such cities as Leiden. "The war," writes Hermann van der Wee, "was one of the main causes of the massive emigration of tens of thousands of especially skilled laborers who, for religious, psychological, or economic reasons," deserted the south.[34]

This factor should be borne in mind, for it has sometimes been convenient to associate the progress in what became the predominantly Protestant Netherlands and the relative retardation in the Catholic Spanish Netherlands with a world-view fostered by the respective religions. One need not look that far for an explanation. In the north there was a government with progressive economic policies and a concentration of almost all the skilled labor. In the south there was an occupation by a foreign army and a government bent on taxing the economy diabolically in order to finance its own imperial policies. Therefore, people congregated in the north not because of religious considerations but because this was the region in which they were likely to be able to increase and protect their prosperity.

## THE GOLDEN AGE

Although the war with Spain did not conclude until 1648, it hardly seemed to matter to the Dutch. They were able to build on the foundations of previous centuries to create, in the words of Immanuel Wallerstein, "a cohesive agro-industrial complex" unrivaled in the rest of the world.[35] With adequate supplies of capital, much of which had been accumulated during the "profit inflation" of the sixteenth century, the range of endeavors broadened considerably. By the seventeenth century, if not before, capitalism had clearly become the dominant mode of production. Yet, as impressive as the Dutch nation became, it, too, would not be able to sustain its momentum. Almost like the proverbial hare, by 1660 it seemed to stop for a rest and then to decide that it would leave the race to the tortoise.

During the seventeenth century, agricultural output continued to expand. The expansion of production was made possible by the continuing process of reclamation, new land constantly being made available. Dutch farmers, whether they were smallholders or owners of large estates, all concentrated on market gardening to supply the cities. What made the Netherlands unique in this regard was that farmers both near and far were able to participate. Thanks to a massive system of canals that was constructed during the early seventeenth century, no area was beyond the reach of the market.[36] As a result, the Dutch farmer of the seventeenth century was able to continue and expand upon the tradition of the past.

The Dutch are often thought of as specialists in commerce, an association that obscures the extent to which the industrial sector of the Dutch economy was developed. A look at a monograph such as Violet Barbour's *Capitalism in Amsterdam* will quickly dispel that myth. For the range of undertakings was truly impressive; a very incomplete list can include ironwork, coal mining, salt manufacture, shipbuilding, sugar refining, chemical production, brewing, printing, diamond-cutting, and even the manufacture of chocolate. Various cities were known for their specialties. Leiden produced textiles, Haarlem dyed linen, and Liege manufactured arms. Glassware on a par with that of Venice was produced, and English cloth was finished in the Netherlands, Dutch craftsmen having developed a high degree of skill. They even went so far as to use windmills and other sophisticated devices in industrial production.[37]

Amsterdam emerged as the major financial capital of Europe. Taking over where Antwerp had left off, it became a center that attracted merchants from all over Europe. It was in Amsterdam that the major exchanges of currency were transacted; it developed a large number of commercial banks responsible for the financing of many important businesses. In 1609 the stock exchange of Amsterdam began operations. The Dutch were also pioneers in marine insurance, a primary consideration for a nation so concerned with maritime commerce. More so than even Antwerp in its heyday, Amsterdam took on the appearance of a distinctly modern city.[38]

By the early years of the seventeenth century, the Dutch were clearly the leaders in world commerce. Although the percentage by value of the Baltic trade decreased significantly, this resulted not from a diminution in this commerce but from the growth of other sectors. Passage through the Sound, the waterway separating Denmark from Norway and Sweden, to the markets of the East remained a crucial part of the overall pattern of exchange. Moreover, quite ironically by modern standards, although the Dutch were at war with Spain, commerce with the Iberian peninsula and thence to the Americas grew considerably in importance. By the early years of the seventeenth century, Dutch produce had invaded the Mediterranean and had begun to threaten the products of the Italian city-states. At the same time, Amsterdam became a major clearinghouse for American sugar, Swedish iron, English woolens, Venezuelan tobacco, Norwegian timber, Spanish wool, and even the Asian spices.[39]

The spice trade of Asia, in fact, became an important staple of Dutch overseas commerce. After it was determined that free competition drove up the price of pepper and other spices to the point of rendering its trade unremunerative, in 1602 the Dutch government oversaw the incorporation of the numerous concerns that had ventured into eastern waters. The Dutch East India Company, imbued with powers usually reserved for a sovereign nation, proceeded to act as if it were one. After driving the English out of Indonesia during the first years of its operations, this *staat buiten die staat* (state independent of the state) launched an all-out assault on the Portuguese trading network in Asia. Wresting control of Malacca in 1641 and Ceylon in 1658 put the final seal of destruction on the remaining bastions of the Portuguese Asian empire. Both in terms of its impact on the Netherlands and on the world in general, the Dutch East India Company's achievement was of considerable importance. Unlike the Portuguese, the Dutch were able to make their monopoly effective and to prevent most spices from reaching Europe by other means; great profits accrued to the company because of its daring Asian policies.[40]

The very success of the East India Company led to the incorporation in 1621 of the Dutch West India Company. Possessing powers similar to the older company, it was to undertake its mission in the Atlantic. Like the East India Company, it took aim directly at Iberian shipping. Its greatest success came in 1628 when Piet Heyn captured the Spanish fleet, which was returning to Europe with the year's supply of silver. Nevertheless, its most consistent prey were Luso-Brazilian vessels, of which more than three hundred were taken. The company also made attempts to foster permanent settlements. In 1624 it occupied the island of Curaçao with the express purpose of fostering illicit commerce with the Spanish mainland. In Africa in 1637 it succeeded in ousting the Portuguese from the Gold Coast. The very same year witnessed the capture of Pernambuco, the most prosperous of the Brazilian sugar-producing regions. At the time, the company was so successful that dividends of 50 percent were declared. Ultimately, however, it would not be able to duplicate the success of the East India Company. Dissipating too many of its resources on the attempt to conquer northeastern Brazil, an attempt foiled more by the Brazilians than by the Portuguese government, the West India Company was obliged to declare bankruptcy by the middle of the century.[41]

The careers of the trading companies are indicative of the flexibility that made the Dutch successful. When force was required, they were not loathe to use it. Nevertheless, they specialized in cost-cutting. No better example of this phenomenon can be found than the *fluyt*, a large, awkward, slow-moving vessel that was developed in the late sixteenth century. It was ideal, however, for the Baltic trade, as its huge carrying capacity and its small crew enabled the wholesale purchase of bulk quantities and limited the cost of their delivery. Charles Wilson observes that "Dutch expertise was alternatively regarded in the outside world as a profound mystery beyond the comprehension of less gifted operators, or as a shameless and unjustifiable exploitation of others."[42]

Part of the reason the Dutch were able to undersell their competitors stemmed from the low levels of wages commanded by the labor force. Although the countryside appeared prosperous, it should be noted that these farms belonged to the fortunate minority. Beside them stood an army of those who had not fared nearly as well. J. A. van Houtte speaks of a movement to enclose the commons, which deprived many of an independent means of existence.[43] These and other measures that squeezed out the more unfortunate members of the peasantry helped to create a sizable rural proletariat, many of whom eked out an existence as best they could.[44] Whereas rural craftsmen formed an elite among the working class, others, such as the peat diggers and the dike maintenance workers, suffered through an extremely marginal existence.[45]

The natural tendency under the circumstances of rural immiseration was to flock to the towns. Partly for this reason, the Netherlands was unique in the degree of urbanization that was achieved. It is suggested that in 1622, 56 percent of the population lived in urban areas. Most of these, however, fit into Pieter Geyl's category of a swarming proletariat.[46] In addition to the low-paid journeymen who were responsible for a good deal of the craft production, there was a significant amount of female and child labor. Barbour emphasizes how little workers in the cities were paid, but Audrey Lambert suggests that the Dutch could dominate so successfully on the high seas because they paid miserably low wages to the sailors.[47]

The entire framework of the Dutch economy was conducive to substantial capital investment. Successful farmers plowed profits back into improvements. Capital also continued to improve established industries, and there was constant experimentation with new ones. No aspect of the economy was beyond the pale of the adventurous entrepreneur. Land reclamation continued as a private enterprise, undertaken by individuals who were inspired by the profit motive. Canal construction was also a phenomenon sponsored by those who expected to earn significant dividends from their investments. Perhaps nothing is more indicative of the Dutch mentality than their efforts to foster English and French settlement in the Caribbean Islands. Perceiving that they themselves did not have the population resources to colonize these islands, Dutch entrepreneurs encouraged the English and French in the hope that they would ultimately profit by transporting products from the islands to Europe.[48]

By about the 1660s, however, the momentum that had thrust the Dutch forward during the golden age was dissipated. Although J. G. van Dillen is quick to point out that decline was neither cataclysmic nor precipitous, the indications of a downturn appear on so many fronts that it is impossible to deny its existence.[49] There is evidence of a reduced trade with the Baltic and a decline in the fishing industry. Both land values and agricultural prices decreased. Population levels first became stagnant and then began to diminish.[50] The essence of the problem is captured by Ralph Davis who notes that "by the middle of the eighteenth century the Dutch played only a small part in the Atlantic economy. . . . Like the Italians, Germans, and Spanish before them, they had dropped out of the race for economic leadership of Europe."[51]

Although the reasons for the decline of the Netherlands are not as clear-cut as for the failure of their Mediterranean predecessors, several important factors suggest themselves. Increasingly during the seventeenth century, the Dutch came to face competition from their neighbors. For example, England, Scotland, Denmark, and Norway all made impressive strides forward in the fishing industry. Similarly, their competitors, especially the English and the French, began to adopt protectionist measures designed explicitly to counteract Dutch ascendancy. Between 1651 and 1672, largely at the behest of the London merchant community, the English Parliament passed a series of acts whose main purpose was to eliminate the Dutch as carriers of English commerce. Although three wars would be fought between the two countries before the issue was resolved, the Navigation Acts achieved their purpose. "As one nation after another devised its own measures against the Dutch," observes Charles Wilson, "it became clear how perilously exposed they were to reprisals."[52]

The Dutch can also be seen to have been victims of the general crisis of the seventeenth century. Partly because wages in the Netherlands were so low and partly because of the relatively small population, the domestic market was limited. C. R. Boxer notes that "many Dutch industries . . . had expanded far beyond the demand of the home market."[53] Their continuing success, therefore, was linked to their ability to continue selling abroad. In an environment of protectionism and a general depression throughout Europe, however, exports could not continue at their peak levels, despite Dutch efficiency. In this regard, the Netherlands can be seen as having been a major victim of the seventeenth-century crisis.

Tendencies within Dutch social structure may also have militated against sustained success. Inheritance was partable, so both landed and industrial property was continually fragmented. This, in turn, reversed the trend toward the accumulation of capital. The strength of the urban guilds also contributed to what Braudel referred to as "petty capitalism."[54] On the one hand, there was no large-scale accumulation derived from the organization of rural households. On the other, within the towns themselves, guild restrictions kept production small-scale in both operation and outlook.[55]

Thus, although the Dutch flirted with the transition into modernity, they ultimately withdrew from the brink. In looking at the Netherlands, Dobb makes the powerful observation that "the launching of a country on the road towards capitalism is no guarantee that it will complete the journey."[56] The rhetorical question has been raised whether the world economy of the seventeenth and eighteenth centuries could have sustained two hegemonic capitalist social formations.[57] It has also been suggested that for a variety of reasons, England was better suited to assume the role of leadership than was the Netherlands. Dutch entrepreneurs sensed this intuitively. Eschewing loyalty to the flag, capital was increasingly withdrawn from domestic endeavors in the republic and invested in the economy of its erstwhile adversary.

## ENGLAND IN TRANSITION

As late as the early-modern period, England was a relatively backward country. It is surprising, then, that it was the one to make the great leap forward. Even Henry VIII described himself as a "small king in the corner of Europe."[58] If one had observed it in the later Middle Ages, one's surprise would be even greater, as it exhibited few of the traits that were common in the more advanced regions of Europe. Yet that it was able to make the strides that it did is particularly instructive. For what was different about England was neither its technology nor its economic base. Rather, its uniqueness stemmed from a conjuncture of forces that would bring about radical social change. And precisely these changes paved the way for its subsequent development.

The England of the late Middle Ages was a comparatively undeveloped country. Not only was its population relatively small, but it was one of the least urbanized areas in Europe. Because of its fertile soils and adequate rainfall, however, its agricultural sector, although not spectacular, was fairly prosperous. In the postplague crisis, however, in the pursuit of a viable export, much of the arable was turned over to the grazing of sheep. Either in the form of raw wool, but increasingly marketed as unfinished woolen cloth, these exports through the entrepôt of Bruges provided the only significant foreign-exchange earnings for an otherwise largely self-sufficent land.[59]

By the fifteenth century, most of the countryside was cultivated by tenants. Yet the terms of their tenancy varied greatly. According to Leslie Clarkson, the land was "cultivated by an army of tenants differing greatly from one another in the nature of their tenures, size of holdings, and wealth." The fortunate few were the freeholders who possessed virtual title to their land. Next in the hierarchy were those who had contracts that guaranteed them long-term fixed rents. Others, however, might have leases of varying duration, which often meant that upon the expiration of their contracts their rents could be raised or, worse, they could be evicted. Even further down on the scale were the tenants-at-will, cottagers with access either only to small plots of land or the commons, and a variety of lumpen elements who led a hand-to-mouth existence.[60] Moreover, it is important to note, as does Robert Brenner, that the rebellions of the fourteenth century had helped to hasten the demise of many aspects of the feudal regime, but the English peasantry had not gained as much security as had their French counterparts. Whereas the latter had obtained fixed rents and guarantees against eviction, the English peasants were thrust into a highly competitive world.[61]

The fifteenth century also witnessed a decline in the power of the nobility, spurred by the internecine struggle known as the War of the Roses. The minority and incompetence of Henry VI led the country into disorder and precipitated the extralegal assumption of control by local factions, oftentimes punctuated by vicious civil war. By the time an acceptable compromise candidate had been agreed upon in 1485 and Henry Tudor ascended the throne as Henry VII, fully half of the peerage had succumbed to the carnage that had accompanied the struggles for power and influence.[62] One of Henry's first decrees banned private armies and warfare, though aristocratic militarism was already becoming anachronistic in England as elsewhere in Europe. "Now that small arms had been invented," writes Lawrence Stone, "strength, courage, and skill on horseback were no longer any protection against an ignominious death. . . . War was no fun anymore."[63] Equally important as the demise of the nobility as a military force were the changes in status that had overcome the peerage as a class. For unlike their Continental counterparts, their rank no longer absolved them from taxation and accountability. Specifically, when confronted with debt, their estates were not immune from confiscation.

The social structure of England as it moved into the sixteenth century was extremely complex and fluid. Stone views it as having had a broad base of the very poor, most of whom were peasants, although there was a growing number of at least equally poor urban dwellers. Superimposed on this platform he identifies a narrow tower, composed in ascending order of yeomen, gentry, squires, and peers of the realm. Wealth, as opposed to status, increasingly was becoming a gauge of an individual's position in society. Remaining true to its traditional agrarian values, however, English society was easier to categorize according to the possession of landed property than other considerations. Just where others, the upwardly mobile but landless elements, fit into the hierarchy was more difficult to determine. For example, to some, wealthy merchants were an inferior sort of gentleman; and where artisans, the clergy, smaller merchants, professionals, and administrative officials were to be placed in the social order was open to debate.[64]

Although unique in many ways, sixteenth-century England was soon caught up in a number of the same processes that affected the rest of Europe. Far removed though England was from the Mediterranean, the price revolution was as pervasive and perplexing in England as on the Continent. Between 1500 and 1640, the price of agricultural produce rose anywhere from 400 to 650 percent. Population also grew rapidly. Estimated by some as being about 2.4 million in 1475, by 1640 it is believed to have risen to approximately 5 million. This in turn stimulated urbanization. At the beginning of the period, London was the only city worthy of the name. Although London's population continued to rise by leaps and bounds and it far outdistanced all other towns in terms of numbers of inhabitants, many new towns arose during the sixteenth and seventeenth centuries. Such names as Nottingham, Worcester, Birmingham, Bristol, Norwich, and Coventry would become discernible on the maps of the age.[65]

Agriculture also underwent a significant change during the sixteenth century. At the beginning of the era, the common-field system was still firmly entrenched. Over time there had evolved a system by which villagers cultivated their own strips, but only after rotations had been agreed upon so that the harvested land could be used for common pasturage. One new tendency, however, was the practice of up-and-down husbandry. With its greater emphasis on cattle, the new system involved cultivation on one part of the holding while the other was used for rearing cattle. The two subsequently would be rotated, with the land used for pasture becoming particularly productive when turned with a plow because of the large amounts of fertilizer that had accrued. The other tendency was a return to sheepherding, which after a temporary slump regained its attractiveness.[66]

The new emphasis on pastoral endeavors required important adjustments in the countryside. Neither sheepherding nor up-and-down husbandry was viable in the context of the common-field system. What was needed were consolidated holdings. This need, then, led to the dual phenomena Joan Thirsk described as enclosing and engrossing. Whereas enclosing basically involved no more than the elimination of the commons, engrossing meant the construction of larger, consolidated holdings.[67] These processes proved to be attractive to landlords, for by offering consolidated blocks of land they could attract tenants who were able to pay the highest rents.

Diversification in industrial activity was another new departure of the sixteenth and the seventeenth centuries. Considering how limited production had been in the past, the range of new undertakings was impressive. Iron-working, brewing, and shipbuilding led the way, but refining, printing, and the production of glass, copper, brass, alum, and salt also became prominent. Coal mining was a crucial component in fueling the change; with a critically decreasing supply of wood, coal was an essential ingredient in the process of production. In this light, it was particularly fortunate that large supplies were available in the northeast of the country. Output, which was estimated at 51,000 tons in 1551, skyrocketed to 1.28 million tons in 1690.[68] Initially these increases were made possible by borrowing techniques from the Germans. By the middle of the seventeenth century, however, English technology had come first to parallel and then to surpass that of its erstwhile teachers.

This change in the patterns of production was dependent on the domestic market, which in turn was possible because of the relative ease of internal communications. Unlike many of the new nation-states of early-modern Europe, England had no internal tariff barriers. Thus overland trade was not suppressed by the additional burden of vexatious local exactions. Yet because the road system was inadequate for the task of moving large quantities of goods, water transport became crucial. Although there was no canal construction to rival that of the Netherlands, England was blessed by more than seven hundred miles of navigable waterways. In addition, it benefited by being a small island: No part of the country was more than seventy miles from the sea. Indeed, the coastwise trade, especially the ability to transport coal, was a primary ingredient in England's development. So, too, were improvements in ship design, which over time meant that vessels grew in size yet the number of sailors required to run them was greatly reduced.[69]

Nevertheless, despite its impressive industrial diversification, England's exports remained confined almost exclusively to textiles. Between the late fifteenth and the early years of the seventeenth century, the amount of cloth shipped abroad increased significantly. In fact, textile export reached its peak in 1614. English textiles, however, remained of a relatively inferior sort. It was shipped to Antwerp and subsequently to Amsterdam in an unfinished state. There the Flemings dyed it and then resold the finished product throughout the European continent.[70]

The predominance of cloth in English exports, however, did not signify that attempts were not being made to diversify. On the contrary, the sixteenth century witnessed attempts to open new areas to English commerce. In order to accomplish this, new companies were formed to investigate the possibilities beyond Antwerp. In addition to the Eastland Company, which was chartered to operate in the Baltic, as their names suggest, the Russia Company, the Turkey Company, the Venice Company, the Levant Company, and the East India Company carried English commerce far beyond the northwest corner of Europe. Although it was still in its infancy during the early years of the seventeenth century, the colonial trade with the Caribbean and the North American mainland seemed to present another commercial opportunity.

Even more significant than the economic changes that accompanied the inception of the early-modern era were the unprecedented upheavals that led to a radical restructuring of the social order. Perhaps at no other time in European history or in no other country was social mobility, both upward and downward, as pronounced as it was in England during the sixteenth and seventeenth centuries. The Catholic church was one of the institutions that suffered because of these tendencies. Its problems resulted largely from the rupture with Rome that Henry VIII engineered. Once the break occurred, England lost not only the advantages of an official church but also much of its monastic lands through confiscation by the crown. Its successor, the Church of England, also faced problems: It lacked the wealth previously associated with the church and, moreover, underwent an identity crisis. Although when he created his new church Henry had envisaged little change in doctrine, the opening left by the break with Rome allowed the entry of many precepts associated with Protestantism into Anglican orthodoxy. Thus the Church of England came to suffer from being in the center. On the one hand, its revisionism went too far for those who wanted to repair relations with the Vatican; on the other, it did not satisfy those who wanted to do away with bishops and be guided by independent judgment based on the Bible.[71]

The monarchy also suffered a decline in its fortunes. Although it might have appeared that the house of the Tudors emerged from the War of the

Roses in a strong position, such an assumption would be deceiving. Indeed, the nobility had been weakened, but the crown still had few independent means of securing revenue. For a time the parsimony of Henry VII disguised the contradictions inherent in a situation in which a monarchy had greatly expanded obligations but a revenue-raising power still geared to the needs of the feudal age. Indeed, that Henry left nearly a million pounds in the treasury is truly exceptional.[72] His achievement was all the more remarkable because during normal times the monarch could only depend on customs revenues, certain anachronistic feudal dues, and the revenue from his estates. It could only institute new taxation, however, with the consent of Parliament. As this usually required the crown to make important concessions, monarchs considered it an unpopular choice.

Thus, throughout the sixteenth and seventeenth centuries, the crown found itself in financial difficulties. Its responsibilities were increasing at a time when inflation greatly multiplied the costs of its duties. Yet much of its revenue was derived from fixed sources of income, whose value was being diminished by the rise in prices. Although confiscation of church lands provided a temporary windfall, kings and queens still found it difficult to balance income and expenditure. One of the few independent options on which the crown could depend was the sale of its private estates, an expedient to which it resorted with increasing frequency. Whereas in 1561 it still owned 9.5 percent of the land mass of England, by 1641 this figure had been pared to a mere 2 percent.[73]

The plight of many nobles was no more encouraging. How successful they were in confronting the challenges posed by the price revolution often depended on the nature of their lease arrangements with their tenants. Where leases were short-term agreements, a lord might survive by rack-renting. Where they were confronted by long-term leases and fixed rents, however, the nobility faced a crisis. During times of inflation, it was difficult to survive on a fixed income. This was especially true for a class accustomed and expected to consume conspicuously. For many, breaking old habits did not come easily, even though the times had changed.[74]

The more desperate tried a variety of novel solutions. Some engaged in speculative commerce, even though that option should have been beneath their dignity. Others sought their fortunes at court, hoping to obtain a perquisite that might see them through. More so than was the case anywhere else in Europe, the more visionary turned to production as a way out of their dilemma, the fortunate few who had mineral deposits on their estates turning to mining. For those who were unable to make the transition demanded by the new conditions, however, the one means of survival was to sell at least part of the family estate. Thus, although many peers of the realm remained in a strong position in the seventeenth century, the peerage as a class had grown much weaker.[75]

Yet another group whose fortunes often declined during this period was the category that can be referred to as the "second sons." England was unique in the degree to which the rules of inheritance followed the precepts of primogeniture. Whereas the first son inherited virtually everything, the remaining sons were usually left with a small annuity hardly sufficient for their survival. Their relative success or failure often depended on their creativity. The professions, the clergy, or the army might provide a viable alternative. For others, the situation might demand a more drastic solution, such as emigration to the colonies to make a completely new start. Although many voices continued to be raised against a system that institutionalized the pauperization of so many of its well-born elements, little relief was to be forthcoming.[76]

No group, however, suffered more than the poor peasants. Faced with improving landlords who were interested in consolidating estates, those without fixed tenures were often obliged to abandon their lands. As the process of enclosure gained momentum, those who had depended on access to the commons as the margin of survival were similarly displaced. Thus, the dual processes of enclosure and engrossing led to significant rural immiseration. Some migrated to urban areas in the hopes of finding a way to improve their lot. The rest remained in the countryside, where they came to form the backbone of a constantly growing rural proletariat. Not only did this class increase numerically, but the widespread unemployment it encountered caused great fears of massive rural unrest.[77]

While a broad spectrum of the English social order experienced downward mobility, the group that benefited most from the decline of the others was the gentry. Over time these commoners who emerged from the ranks of the peasantry had been able to aggregate property. By taking advantage of the ills that beset other members of the peasantry, they converted themselves into the most dynamic force in England. By the sixteenth and seventeenth centuries, they were buying up not only small peasant holdings, but lands of the crown, the church, and the nobility as well.[78] They came to form the most important landowning group in the country, having gained title to as much as 50 percent of the arable by the beginning of the seventeenth century. With farms usually exceeding two hundred acres, these newly ascended gentlemen used wage labor to produce agricultural commodities for the market. In essence what had taken place was the emergence of the capitalist farmer in the "really revolutionary way." Agriculture, according to Marx, came to be "dominated by capitalists who differ from [other capitalists] only in the manner in which their capital and the wage labor they set in motion . . . are invested."[79]

Another group that rose to prominence was the merchants. Because overseas commerce was dominated by foreigners throughout the Middle Ages, it was not until the sixteenth century that English merchants were able to wrest control of their own trade. The normal vehicle for this process was the regulated company. At one extreme it might be a loose association such as the Merchant Adventurers, which had more than thirty-five hundred members. At the other extreme was the Turkey Company, whose membership was limited to twelve individuals. Increasingly, however, these entrenched interests turned to joint-stock ventures such as the East India Company, which was founded in 1600. By and large these "old merchants" were based in and around London. They often used their connections with the crown, the court, and the privy council to secure special concessions. Thus, they formed an elite whose ranks were often difficult for others to breach.[80]

Nevertheless, increasingly complaints were being raised against the dominance the "old merchants" enjoyed. Often those who complained the loudest were supplicants from the "outer ports," which in those times meant everywhere but London. They were upset about such unfair advantages as the restrictions on the export of cloth. They were equally concerned about the division of the world into zones monopolized by privileged companies. Their protests, indeed, did not go unheeded. In 1606, for example, Parliament passed legislation that guaranteed free trade with Spain, Portugal, and France. Similarly, in 1622 the outports were granted additional rights in terms of cloth exports.[81] Still, these "new merchants" would not be satisfied as long as what they perceived to be lucrative possibilities were being denied to them.

The clothier was another force that assumed prominence during this era. His forte was the coordination of rural household production through the system of putting out. It was possible to organize on a scale unheard of elsewhere in Europe because there was little opposition from urban-based guilds. Guilds in England were relatively weaker than in other countries in part because historically there had been only limited urbanization, which meant that towns were too weak to mount campaigns to suppress rural production. Over time, despite efforts to reverse the trend, urban influence in the countryside actually diminished. This was even true of London, whose guilds failed in their attempt to restrict production in the environs of the city.[82]

Freed from the interference of towns, the clothier was able to organize production on a large scale. He distributed the wool to the rural household and sometimes provided the machinery for its conversion into cloth. He then paid a small fee for the finished product. The rural worker was at a disadvantage. Usually the family was in desperate need of additional income, yet it produced on such a limited scale that to attempt to market the cloth would not have been worth the effort-price. Thus the clothier was able to pay wages much lower even than those an urban journeyman received. Many clothiers coordinated the production of hundreds of rural workers and were able to accumulate capital on a large scale. In the process clothiers provided the vital linkage between the manufacture of cloth and its availability for marketing abroad.[83]

As the scale of production increased, the amounts of capital invested in industry grew enormously. Such enterprises as ironworks, breweries, and shipyards demanded economies of scale. Stone notes that the mines at Newcastle were the first "really large-scale bulk producing industry in the western world."[84] Although it cannot always be determined where this capital came from, there is evidence that by the seventeenth century some investors had become full-time specialists.[85] Two observations by Dobb seem particularly appropriate. The new undertakings transformed techniques "as to require capital beyond the means of ordinary craftsmen." Furthermore, "this subordination of production to capital and the appearance of this class relationship between capitalist and producer is to be regarded as the crucial watershed between the old mode of production and the new."[86]

As Dobb suggests, the social order had changed dramatically. The vast majority still made their living directly or indirectly from agriculture. Yet the early-modern era had witnessed the emergence of groups that, although numerically still small, had hardly existed during the Middle Ages. In this regard, the gentry was particularly important. For nowhere else in Europe had there ever arisen a group that had acquired so much land without the benefit of privilege, descent, or military aggrandizement. As Stone suggests, the rise of the professionals was only slightly less remarkable, for they had come to exercise a great deal of influence in the new society. When to these categories are added the merchants, capitalist clothiers, the increasingly important manufacturers who were also emerging from the category of small-scale artisans "in the really revolutionary way," and a variety of others who derived their livelihood from sources unrelated to the traditional economy, the extent to which England had economically exited from the Middle Ages becomes apparent.[87] What is more important is that, in combination, these elements possessed a unique potential for challenging forces that might try to resurrect the past.

Thus England in the second quarter of the seventeenth century was radically different from the England that entered the early-modern phase. The structures of both industry and agriculture were in the process of transformation. Yet change was taking place within the framework of an economic environment that was becoming increasingly difficult. For much of Europe was experiencing the downward cycle marked by the seventeenth-century crisis, a crisis exacerbated during the first half of the century by the dislocations caused by the Thirty Years' War.

In England the difficulties of the times were exemplified by the prolonged depression in the cloth industry that dated from the middle of the second decade. Although it first became apparent in the aftermath of Alderman Cockayne's ill-fated scheme to dye cloth at home before marketing it in Europe, which led to the loss of much of England's trade, it soon became obvious that the crisis was caused by more than an aberration of policy. Rather, the competition from new sources and changing tastes represented a more fundamental restructuring of European patterns of demand and supply. England was fortunate in that it eventually found salvation in the so-called new draperies, a lighter cloth that soon discovered a waiting market in the Mediterranean. What was equally important, perhaps underscored by the waxing and waning fortunes of the textile industry, was the growing awareness that the world was changing and that adjustment was needed.[88] The question that remained to be answered was whether England possessed the flexibility to achieve these ends.

## THE STRUGGLE FOR CONTROL OF ENGLAND

Already numerous examples have been presented of social formations that achieved great progress but were unable to maintain their dynamism. Because all ultimately succumbed to one or another contradiction that was inherent in their respective social relations, it would be surprising if England did not also possess a threat to its continuing progress. Indeed, England was no different from other social formations insofar as there were forces at work whose logic would have been to slow down and even arrest its development. In fact, even during its march toward modernity, there were enemies nipping at its heels. Ironically, had the English crown been allowed to have its own way, it, like rulers in other parts of the world, would have blunted and in all probability destroyed the progress that had grown up around it. Thus, not until 1660, with the confirmation of the limitations of the English crown, was it assured that this would be the country that would complete the journey.

Relations between the English crown and its parliaments were determined both by circumstances and the personality of a given ruler. Although their powers had been limited at least since King John had been forced to sign the Magna Carta and King Edward had acquiesced in parliamentary control of royal finances, English monarchs continued to be fascinated by the Continental tendency toward autocracy. Most especially admired the almost unfettered dominance exhibited by the kings of France. It has been observed that Henry VIII was a natural autocrat but that his conflict with Rome required him to be more conciliatory than might otherwise have been the case. Elizabeth, as well, found the idea of autocracy attractive. She, however, was shrewd enough to shy away when confrontation appeared likely. By the time of the advent of the Stuarts, however, the tenor and temper of the monarchs would change. Unlike his predecessors, James, who was fond of delivering lectures on the divine right of kings, became increasingly confrontational in his dealings with Parliament.[89]

The bind that the would-be autocrats found themselves in was caused by the fiscal restraints under which they functioned. Unable to levy ordinary taxes without the approval of Parliament, the monarchs sought other solutions, some of which were of doubtful legality. The creation of monopolies was one of the ways in which parliamentary control over royal finances could be circumvented. By granting monopoly privileges to an individual or a group and garnering a fee in exchange, the monarch was legally able to replenish the royal coffers. Elizabeth, for example, chose this course when she granted the twelve members of the Turkey Company their exclusive privileges. Even though they repaid her with a loan that was subsequently converted into a gift, she modified her policy on the granting of monopolies when it seemed as if this course would lead to hostile relations with Parliament. The Stuarts, however, knew no restraint. During their reigns the number of such concessions multiplied. By the time of Charles I, no fewer than seven hundred monopolies had been granted.

Although some of these were of only minor significance, others involved more important sectors of the economy.[90]

In their attempts to raise revenue, the Stuarts, however, did not limit themselves to selling monopolies. Rather, they began to market a wide range of privileges. In return for subsidies, they tried to increase the powers of the guilds. Public offices were put up for auction, and new peerages were available for those who could afford them. Charles even went so far as to attempt to levy new taxes without consulting Parliament. These were usually cloaked under the guise of the invocation of the monarch's powers of national defense. Although his courts, not surprisingly, upheld his right to levy these exactions, the public increasingly came to suspect that his revenue collection was nothing more than a disguised form of taxation. In assessing this policy, Christopher Hill notes that "the fiscal benefit to the crown was considerable, but it could not compare with the injury done to the consumer and industry."[91] Charles Wilson, however, pinpoints a more fundamental problem when he observes that significant segments of public opinion were being alienated for "absurdly small yields of tax."[92]

After Charles succeeded his father in 1625, relations between Parliament and the crown reached their nadir. Elizabeth had experienced problems over specific issues, but there had been a mutual understanding of the nature of the constitution that both sides respected. James, unpopular for many other reasons, would have liked to alter the constitution in favor of increased monarchical power, but ultimately he did little more than talk about his desires. Charles, on the other hand, showed himself willing to stretch his interpretations of the constitution to limits unacceptable to most members. Parliament became convinced that a staunch stand was needed in order to rein in the sovereign.[93] Charles, in turn, became so exasperated over Parliament's seeming attempt to stymie him at every juncture that in 1629 he decided to rule without it. For the next eleven years he tried to steer the course of state without having to rely on his oftentimes adversarial parliamentarians.

How long he might have succeeded and how much harm he might have done to the English economy will never be known, for his foolhardiness ultimately obliged him to convene Parliament again in 1640. Considering that so many major issues were festering in the country during these years, it is ironic that the crisis was to be caused by a relatively minor issue: In a characteristically impetuous moment, Charles decided to impose a new Bible on the staunchly Presbyterian Scots. Equally characteristic was that it was as much the manner in which the attempt was made as the Bible itself that provoked anger and subsequently rebellion. When his resources proved inadequate to the task of independently quelling the rebellion, he was faced with an unpleasant decision. He either had to risk an ignominious defeat or to reassemble Parliament to seek the funds needed to bring the Scottish fiasco under control. In the interim since he had last met with Parliament, however, much water had passed under the bridge. He could be assured that Scotland would not be the only item on the agenda.[94]

The Parliament that was reconvened in 1640 differed in many respects from its predecessors. Indicating the degree to which royal policy had become a concern, the elections were bitterly contested. Although the parliamentarians who were returned largely represented the gentry, their principal concerns were with gaining concessions to assure that the constitution functioned as it had in the past and to obtain guarantees that the monarch could not overstep these boundaries. To this end they wanted to abolish what they considered such illegal taxes as those represented by ship money (taxes traditionally paid by the ports that were now imposed on the whole country) and the arbitrary raising of customs duties. Their program also included triennial parliaments to ensure that monarchs did not try to rule arbitrarily. Nevertheless, Charles remained intransigent and chose to dissolve Parliament rather than make concessions. This, unfortunately, only added fuel to the smoldering fire, for the new Parliament returned the same representatives, only in a much more hostile mood.[95] By 1642 all communication had broken down. Although almost everyone professed to want to avoid a confrontation, the die was cast. The contradictions that had grown during the early-modern era could not be resolved, and the English Civil War became inevitable.

Recent scholarship has begun to show how complex a phenomenon the Civil War really was. Stone has concluded that none of the polarities such as feudal-bourgeoisie, rich-poor, employer-employee, and rising-declining that dominated the literature of an earlier generation seem to have much relevance. Nevertheless, it is not overstepping the mark to suggest that a broad-based coalition, most of it opposed to royal economic and religious policies, came into being. Nevertheless, in 1642 few would have envisaged that the king would lose his head or that England would first become a republic and then a dictatorship under Oliver Cromwell, who was an unknown and innocuous figure at the beginning of the war. Nor would they have believed that Puritanism would become the official religion, that the Church of England would be dismantled, or that the House of Lords would be abolished and the lands of peers confiscated. Had most perceived in 1642 that the democratic ideas of the Levellers would come to the fore, there probably would not have been an English Civil War. Yet before a compromise that returned England to normalcy was reached, all of the foregoing had transpired.[96]

After 1660, when the monarchy was restored, everything seemed to return to normal. The traditional institutions were restored to the extent that almost everything fell neatly into the places they had occupied before. The king, albeit a different one, returned to the throne. The established church was reestablished. Not only were the peers of the realm restored to their elevated status, but most of them recovered the lands that had been confiscated during the most revolutionary phase of the war. Textbooks such as the popular *History of the Modern World* emphasize this return to normalcy. R. R. Palmer and Joel Colton write that "everything was supposed to be as it had been in 1640."[97]

Nevertheless, it is crucial to understand that what was restored was the form of 1640, not the substance. For the England of the post–Civil War period was a different creature indeed from its predecessor. As Stone explains, "Many things were restored at the restoration, but it is surely significant that among those that were not were feudal tenures, restraints upon enclosing of land, such monopolies and economic controls as did not suit the convenience of influential interest groups, and a foreign policy that gave little weight to commercial objectives."[98] In essence, although it is impossible to demonstrate that the Civil War was bourgeois in origin, it can be said that it was definitely bourgeois in outcome. England had produced a class capable of withstanding those who would succumb to the temptation of misusing extant gains at the expense of future growth. It is in this light that one should understand Hill's judgment that "the destruction of the royal bureaucracy in 1640–41 can be regarded as the most decisive single event in the whole of British History."[99]

The gentry won a number of victories as a result of the defeat of the monarchy. In 1656 the last vestiges of feudal obligations were swept away. Prior to the Civil War there had been a ban on the export of grain, largely because the monarchy feared the consequences of a serious famine should too much grain be shipped abroad. After the war, however, grain exports not only were permitted but provided with government subsidies as well. Similarly, the monarchy had been the staunchest opponent of enclosure, concerned as it was about the unrest that might be caused by rural unemployment. Significantly, the last anti-enclosure bill was introduced into Parliament in 1656 and was defeated on its second reading. Thereafter, there would be little official interference in the process of enclosure.[100]

Commercial interests—or, more specifically, the new merchants—also won a series of triumphs. One of their notable successes was the abolition of monopolistic trading concerns. Although special exceptions were granted to concerns such as the East India Company whose dealings in distant lands obliged them to maintain infrastructures that involved significant cost overheads, the ax fell heavily on regulated companies such as the Merchant Adventurers and the Eastland Company. The new merchants were also successful in having implemented an aggressive foreign policy, which, although it would lead to three wars with the Dutch, ultimately would bring commercial superiority to England. J. E. Farnell notes that "it was the non-company, interloping, free-merchant par excellence who supported" the Navigation Act of 1651, which can be seen as the inauguration of the new policy.[101]

After the restoration, the government increasingly sought to use mercantilistic legislation to promote production. Numerous laws were passed to aid English industry. These usually took the form of prohibiting the import of a given commodity so as to provide its English counterpart with a monopoly of the domestic market. For example, in 1678, in order to stimulate new forms of cloth production, a ban was placed on the import of French silks and linens. Similarly, the Mines Royal Act of 1689 halted the import of foreign copper.[102] Although the legislation taken as a whole did not produce spectacular results, it is indicative of the changed climate following the Civil War. It demonstrated that, insofar as the economy was to be managed in the future, it was to be done so in the interests of the productive sector rather than to suit the needs of opportunistic and parasitic elements. In essence, rather than searching for ways in which to manipulate economic growth for the benefit of the government, the role of the post–Civil War bureaucracy became supportive of commerce and manufacturing interests. Quite ironically, thereafter merchants and manufacturers were to constitute an undertaxed segment of the population.[103]

There were also important changes of a structural nature. In fact, for all intents and purposes the last traces of feudal tenures were abolished after the Civil War. This was given concrete expression by the dismantling of the Court of Wards, which previously had been entrusted with enforcing feudal obligations.[104] Landed-property ownership assumed the absolute characteristics that partly defined the capitalist mode of production.

Despite the triumph and consolidation of capitalist relations of production, post–Civil War England exhibited few dramatic changes. D. C. Coleman cautions against singing its praises too loudly, for it remained "pre-industrialized, pre-mechanized and predominantly agricultural."[105] England also was not immune from many of the side effects caused by the continuing general crisis of the seventeenth century. During the middle of the century, the population seems to have leveled off. In agriculture, despite some hard-pressed yeomen and a few visionaries who began experimenting with new rotations and crops, the improving farmer remained distinctly in the minority. Moreover, although yields continued to increase, they did not do so dramatically. The same general trends were to be observed in the manufacturing sector, even those that had received preferential treatment from the government. Thus, as late as the 1690s, the country was still experiencing periods of depression.[106]

Nevertheless, some of the more significant changes cannot be quantified. Despite the ongoing economic doldrums of the second half of the seventeenth century, the mood became distinctly optimistic. This in itself represented a departure from the static medieval notions of limited growth potential that had constrained European society. The new attitude was exemplified by the haste with which men turned to joint-stock enterprise. For example, in 1671, when the Royal African Company appealed for a subscription, it was immediately oversubscribed.[107]

Thus, the most important changes of the immediate post–Civil War period were structural and ideological. With agricultural prices no longer soaring, land became less attractive as an investment. Therefore, the number of enclosures and the level of transfers of landed property decreased significantly. At the same time, with the end of most of the restrictions on commercial activity, investment in commerce became a more appealing proposition. Capital, which previously had sought out other endeavors, now began to flow into trade. This would pave the way for the tremendous surge of commercial activity that would dominate the eighteenth century. More important than the areas of investment, however, was the level of investment. C. H. George observes that by the end of the seventeenth century, the levels of saving and investment in England had reached those of a developed society.[108] These were the changes that would enable England to assume primacy in the world economy that was taking shape. Had the events of the seventeenth century taken another course, it is unlikely that these trends would have been possible.

# 6

# PERIPHERIES IN
# THE WORLD ECONOMY

Just as there are many meanings of capitalism, so too there are multiple usages of the term *periphery*. In some cases, the word appears to be nearly synonymous with the world beyond Europe. Such a connotation, for example, appears in the work of André Gunder Frank, who refers to the "periphery in Asia, Africa and Latin America." To this list, he adds Siberia, North America, and the Caribbean. A similar approach is taken by Patrick O'Brien, whose periphery is only marginally less extensive than Frank's. He includes Latin America, the Caribbean, Africa, Asia, and the U.S. South in this category. Peter Kriedte is even vaguer: He uses the terms *periphery*, *underdeveloped*, and *colonial world* almost interchangeably. Moreover, he confuses the issue further by noting that the Mediterranean slipped into a position "halfway towards the periphery," whereas North America somehow mysteriously managed to escape from it.[1]

Another approach has been to see the periphery in spatial terms. In this context various regions are assigned to the periphery because of their distance from what is perceived to be the center of the world economy. Braudel is the principal proponent of this line of reasoning. In his schema there have been many world economies, each of which revolved around a dominant city. Radiating from these core regions, he argues, there was "a fairly developed middle zone and a vast periphery."[2] Bruce McGowan also sees the spatial relationship as being a crucial factor in the interaction between western Europe and other areas of the world. He suggests that the principal dynamic in this articulation is that as Europe developed, it began to specialize in commodities that paid higher rents. Commodities that paid lesser rents, in contrast, were "pushed out toward the periphery."[3]

The most complete formulation of the notion of the periphery is presented in the volumes of Immanuel Wallerstein. His is not only more complete but also more discriminating than that of other historians. He states that "the periphery of the world economy is that geographical sector of it wherein production is primarily of lower-ranking goods but which is an integral part of the overall system of the division of labor, because the commodities involved are only for daily use." With this as the basis for his categorization, he defines the periphery as comprising the Baltic region and the Americas, including colonial Spanish America. At the same time, Africa and Asia are seen as being external to the world economy, as they did not produce "lower-ranking goods."[4]

Largely because the term *periphery*, as it is used in the literature, is so vague as to be almost meaningless, in this study an attempt is made to provide it with a specificity that not only reflects the reality of the world during the era of merchant capital but also demonstrates how peripheries were the creation of the incipient first world economy. In this sense the term is applied to territories that underwent similar transformations and came to share certain characteristics. In this understanding, the periphery came to comprise eastern Europe, Brazil, the Caribbean Islands, and western Africa.

These were social formations that developed intensive trading relations with the capitalist regions of northwestern Europe. One factor that made this possible was that the peripheries were spatially situated in such a position to give them easy access to their markets. Although, as was the case of Africa, for example, the connection with the capitalist economies could be indirect, the peripheries nevertheless supplied commodities that greatly benefited the more advanced sector. In the process, however, the social relations of production in the peripheries were transformed.

One important factor hastening the transformations was that the economy merchant capital was creating served as a magnet to other regions of the world. That is, the new demand patterns that it elicited provided opportunities to those who could satisfy the needs of western Europe, which involved a whole range of different commodities. These included staples for daily consumption as well as more exotic products. Especially with regard to the latter, tropical and subtropical areas enjoyed the advantage of being able to supply goods that could not be produced in Europe.

Yet there were impediments to the smooth functioning of exchange relations. One aspect of the problem arose because production in the capitalist economies took on a new and different character from what had preceded. Commodity production combined capital, skilled labor, and labor time, so by definition exports possessed a high intrinsic value. Production in the incipient peripheries, differed insofar as it sometimes involved little capital, rarely contained significant amounts of skill, and often involved heavy inputs of labor. The result was that the finished product had a lower value than that produced in the capitalist economy.[5]

There was one way of striking a balance between the two spheres. If the costs of labor in the potential periphery could be significantly reduced, the principal obstacle to exchange would be circumvented. Thus, those who would organize production in the peripheries resorted to the expedient of extra-economic coercion. Because they were able to marshal their resources efficiently and effectively before a corporate sense of resistance could be mobilized among the potential ground-level producers, what would become the peripheral ruling classes were able to impose either slavery or serfdom on the labor force. In essence, this drastic expedient was necessary because the system could not have functioned if the labor power of the worker were treated as a marketable commodity under free-market conditions.

Spatial considerations were important in determining the locations of the peripheries. They usually produced bulk commodities, making the cost of transport crucial. That is, if the equation that made exchange relations possible was to be maintained, peripheries had to be located within easy reach of their market. It was not accidental, for example, that northeastern Brazil and the Caribbean came to be included in the periphery, as they were fairly accessible to Europe. There were other regions in the Western Hemisphere, however, which, although they enjoyed similar tropical climates, did not become part of the periphery precisely because they were too far removed from Europe to maintain the trade equation.

Although peripheries sometimes emerged in colonial territories, there was no direct correlation between the one and the other. Peripheries emerged in different colonies, but they were not the products of colonial planners. Rather, as was the case with Brazil, for example, peripheralization resulted from a process of trial and error initiated and undertaken by the inhabitants themselves. One of the principal dynamics of the process was not dissimilar to what transpired in the capitalist world, insofar as it involved cutthroat competition and a high rate of attrition among the would-be organizers of production. Peripheralization was a rational response to the objective conditions that came into being along with the development of capitalism.

Peripheralization became a key process in the growth of the world economy. Territories that previously had contributed virtually nothing to international exchange were transformed during the era of merchant capital into zones of significant growth. Within the peripheries themselves, however, the benefits of this growth were limited to a very narrow strata of society. The emergence of the peripheries was equally beneficial to certain elements in European society. This was especially true of the merchant capitalist, who was able to reap considerable profits from the redistribution of goods that originated in the periphery. Thus, although the two regions differed substantially in their structure and composition, each contained segments that had good reason to be wedded to the system.

## EASTERN EUROPE

For a number of reasons it is difficult to make generalizations about eastern Europe. For even excluding Muscovite Russia, the history of the lands to the east of the river Elbe, traditionally considered to be the dividing line between East and West, was very complicated. Whereas in the West during the early-modern period there was a tendency toward the consolidation of the nation-state and monarchies, no similar trend was experienced in the East. On the contrary, it remained a region of innumerable separate polities. What was happening at any given time in one area need not have taken place in neighboring regions. The early-modern period was also a turbulent era marred by warfare, religious strife, and foreign interventions.[6] Nevertheless, one widely applicable truth is that many regions of eastern Europe developed intensive trading relations with the West. A second theme that can be applied to much of the area is what is often referred to as the rise of the second serfdom during the early-modern era. The two, it should be noted, were intimately related to each other.

The periphery in eastern Europe emerged in a region that was extremely decentralized. The political plight of the region, however, was not preordained. In fact, in the early-modern period, Poland could lay claim to being the largest social formation in Europe, including as it did parts of Prussia, the Baltic regions of Lithuania and Livonia, and even the Ukraine within its domains. Even during the seventeenth century, when it was increasingly being attacked from all directions, Poland seemed to hold its own. Nevertheless, Poland's most dangerous enemy was growing from within the body politic. Exacerbating the situation was the parliamentary procedure that required unanimity of delegates before any action could be taken. That forty-eight of the fifty-five legislative sessions after 1652 were destroyed by vetoes reflected the impotence of central institutions. It also reflected the socioeconomic regime that had come to dominate a vast region. Rewarding only a small minority, the new political economy that was linked with the growth of the first world economy was to have disastrous consequences for the region as a whole.[7]

Just as the development of capitalism in the West arose in regions that had a deviant past, so, too, can it be said that the uniqueness of the experience of eastern Europe was critical in influencing the course of its history. Whereas by the twelfth and thirteenth centuries, population levels had increased and land was becoming scarce in the West, land was still abundant and population densities low in the East. This, in turn, stimulated an eastward colonization movement that resulted from a compatibility of interests: Eastern lords wanted to increase the number of tenants on their estates; therefore, they began to recruit potential settlers from the Germanies. And because land shortages were being experienced throughout the Germanic-speaking world, it was a fertile field for the recruitment of colonists.[8]

The colonization movement had a significant impact on the patterns of land tenure in the East. To attract settlers, lords had to offer favorable terms to the Germans. Among these were free tenancies and fixed rents. The new arrangements with the Germans also had a decisive influence on the nature of tenure relations with the indigenous population. Until that time there had been a multitude of tenures, some of which even approached the status of slavery. However their arrangements might have differed in detail, a unifying theme was that most peasants were bound to the soil by law. Once the landlords began to realize that a relaxation in the regime could increase the number of tenants on their estates, however, the same privileges came to be extended to the indigenous peasantry. Thus, by the fourteenth century, the Eastern peasant had become relatively freer than his Western counterpart.[9]

During the fourteenth and early fifteenth centuries, the trends in the East continued to be different from those of the West. One significant factor was the comparatively small impact of the plague in the East. Because northeastern Europe was furthest removed from the center of diffusion of the pandemic, it did not suffer the same disastrous decimation as occurred elsewhere. Thus, while contraction was the dominant theme in the West, expansion of population and settlement continued to be the principal tendencies in the East. For the first time virgin forests were being felled. Moreover, as population grew, marginal land was reclaimed and brought into production.[10]

This period also witnessed a steady and continuous growth in trade with the West. The East exported a variety of primary products such as timber, potash, hemp, and copper. The most important, however, were rye and wheat. Just how significant the growth was is demonstrated by the increases in exports from the port of Danzig. Karl von Loewe suggests that whereas the annual average of grain exports in the late fifteenth century was only eighteen thousand tons, by the mid-sixteenth century that figure had risen to sixty-five thousand tons per annum. It was not, however, until the early seventeenth century, when exports reached two hundred thousand tons a year, that the maximum output was reached.[11]

From the outset, commerce was dominated by foreigners. During the ascendancy of the Hansa, Germans played a significant role. During the sixteenth and seventeenth centuries, however, they were overtaken by the Dutch, who came to dominate the traffic. By the middle of the sixteenth century, more than sixteen hundred ships were in regular service between the Netherlands and the Baltic. Although by 1620 the number of Dutch bottoms that crossed the Sound had been reduced to four hundred, this represented no diminution in the volume of trade. Rather, by that date the Dutch had perfected the *fluyt*. Designed specifically for the Baltic trade, these vessels of over two hundred tons established an economy of scale with which few could compete. By the seventeenth century, the English had also become intensely interested in trade with the Baltic.[12]

At its eastern end, commerce involved a number of termini and a wide variety of imports. It has been calculated that second through fifth places in terms of relative importance of the ports of eastern Europe were occupied respectively by Riga, Revel, Windau, and Konigsberg. The port of Danzig, however, greatly overshadowed the others. Through these ports eastern Europe imported both necessities and luxuries. In the former category should be placed the herring and salt provided by the Dutch. In the latter there were the high-quality silk and wines that were used and consumed by the Eastern nobility. From the point of view of the Eastern lords, however, the most important consideration was the ability of Westerners to pay for their exports in bullion. By the seventeenth century, the Dutch were being joined by the English in the waters of the Baltic. Although this was representative of England's increasing commercial activity, it did not signal a conflict situation; at this stage the respective traders of each nation sought different products.[13]

It is paradoxical that the period of the most significant growth in exports was also a period of economic downturn. Although population in the East had continued to increase steadily during the late Middle Ages, compared with the West its density remained relatively low. By the early-modern era, although there are disagreements among scholars as to when it actually began, stagnation and even decline in the number of inhabitants was clearly in evidence. This tendency was only exacerbated by a number of disastrous seventeenth-century wars that culminated in the devastating Swedish invasion of Poland in 1675. Known popularly as "the deluge," this event caused a severe drop in population levels.[14] In addition to the effects of demographic reverses, production was hampered by other factors. Yields of grain per acre at first stagnated and then began a continuous decline. One result of these general trends was that as early as the end of the fifteenth century, the income of the lordly class had begun to fall.[15] In light of the overall patterns, they came to feel threatened and to search for an alternative system that would enable them to continue to prosper.

Even before trade with the West had reached its pinnacle, Eastern landlords had begun to react against the decline in their incomes. In the face of stagnant population levels, they increasingly imposed a system that came to be called *Grundherrschaft* on the peasantry. In essence, at a time when peasants in western Europe were winning their freedom, their counterparts in the East were losing theirs. The first step was the passage of laws that forbade the free movement of peasants. Having bound the peasants to the soil, the lords subsequently began to break other contractual agreements. The most important of these was the abrogation of contracts that fixed rents. Jerome Blum notes that higher rents were imposed in Bohemia, Silesia, Brandenburg, Poland, Prussia, and Lithuania.[16]

Nevertheless, in response to the opportunities that trade with the West was coming to offer, by the sixteenth century, Eastern lords were turning to *Gutherrschaft*. As opposed to *Grundherrschaft*, which stressed the increase in rent, *Gutherrschaft* emphasized cultivation of the demesne under the supervision of the lord. The first step in this process was engrossing land in order to enlarge the demesne. This involved the lords in a number of legal and not so legal activities. Purchase, reclamation, enclosure of the commons, and, toward the later stages of the process, the outright expropriation of peasant lands were the devices to which they resorted. Soon vast tracts of land were in their possession. It is estimated that in Poland the lords came to control 25 percent of the arable; in Lithuania they owned as much as 50 percent.[17] In Bohemia, because of the expulsion of the Protestant lords and the disruptions of the Thirty Years' War, the lordly share may have been even larger. William Wright observes that "the new lords who arrived following the Habsburg victories in Bohemia and the redistribution of estates and titles often found vast tracts of deserted land adjacent to their own. To the already generous grants [they] added even more by seizure of untended, previously serf-held acreage."[18]

By the seventeenth century, throughout eastern Europe social relations had been transformed into a feudal system the likes of which had not been seen in the West since at least the twelfth century. Everywhere emphasis was on the demesne and production for export. Hermann Kellenbenz demonstrates its growth in Denmark, eastern Schleswig, Holstein, and Mecklenburg; others speak of its prevalence in Lithuania. It was in Poland, however, that it seems to have become most pervasive.[19] While lords throughout eastern Europe were increasing the size of the demesne, they were also reintroducing and continuously raising labor services due from the peasantry. For example, in Mecklenburg, labor dues were raised from a few days a year in the fifteenth century, to one day a week in 1550, and finally to three days a week in 1660. The process was almost identical in Lithuania and Bohemia. Nowhere, however, was labor service as prominent as in Poland, where, at least in certain parts, four to six days a week were demanded. Keeping in mind that in Silesia, Moravia, Croatia, and other regions lords often had access to the labor of hundreds of villages, one can perceive how enormous the level of exploitation became.[20]

It was a reciprocal process by which their wealth and power increased. It stemmed partly from their ability to pass legislation that blatantly favored their interests as a class. In many respects they were in a stronger position than their counterparts in the medieval West. For whereas the latter theoretically held title to their holdings as a benefice bestowed upon them by the king, the Eastern lords gained freehold tenure without reference to the monarchy. They also came to exercise complete legal jurisdiction over the peasantry, which had no recourse to a higher authority. The interests of the lords became so dominant that in certain areas they were even exempted from paying import and export duties.[21]

The total victory of the lords can be attributed to their functioning in an environment where those who, as a class or an interest group, might otherwise have opposed them were completely impotent. Considering the trends in the West, it is difficult to understand why monarchical power in eastern Europe did not increase in the early-modern period. Yet the fact is that kingship in the East saw the erosion of much of what had been its limited authority during the earlier age. This is perhaps more understandable in Bohemia and Poland, where the nobles elected the king, who thus remained little more than a tool of the nobility. Nevertheless, the phenomenon also occurred in regions where the latent potential for the development of royal authority would appear to have been stronger. One problem was that constant warfare often kept monarchs in debt. As a result their needs for loans were so great that they were obliged to make concessions that meant virtual abdication of their authority.[22]

Nor could merchants, towns, craftsmen, or peasants counteract the ascendancy of the nobility. At an early date the nobility recognized the merchant class as a potential rival. Therefore, they passed legislation that bestowed favors on foreigners to the detriment of the indigenous merchants. Thus, during the late Middle Ages Danes, Germans, and Italians dominated, and in the early-modern period the Dutch and the English.[23] Towns were in no better position to oppose, for urbanization had proceeded slowly and most towns remained firmly under seigneurial jurisdiction. Similarly, the colonial nature of trade, that is, the import of Western manufacture in exchange for eastern European raw materials, helped to destroy the crafts of the region. Nor did the peasantry, which elsewhere developed a threatening militancy, present a signficant obstacle to aristocratic domination. Not without opposition, Robert Brenner has argued that because many were recent immigrants, the peasants lacked the social cohesion of their Western counterparts and hence were incapable of effective organization and resistance to the seigneurial offensive. Whatever the reason, while the Germanic world was wracked by massive peasant upheavals, the Eastern peasantry accepted its plight almost passively.[24]

It is easier to describe the evolution of the second serfdom than to explain why this specific form should have arisen. The answer, however, would appear to be related not only to the existence of trade but also, and more specifically, to the nature of production. That trade was important can be demonstrated in that demesne production with servile labor was much more prominent in those regions that had relatively easy access to the market.[25] Another consideration is just how high the costs of production were. With yields as low as 1:3, inadequate fertilizer, the absence of livestock, and primitive rotations, only by a tremendous increase in labor inputs could a surplus have been produced. Had this labor been remunerated, there would have been no surplus value for expropriation by the organizers of production. Laszlo Mikkai captures at least the spirit of the argument when he notes that "in the final analysis, the basic reason for the appearance of Gutherrschaft . . . was the change that took place in the market structure. . . . This export trade could not be handled . . . without forcing neo-serfdom on the producer."[26]

Support for this contention can also be marshaled by looking at those regions where *Gutherrschaft* did not develop. It has been shown that within eastern Europe, the second serfdom was hardly known in areas far removed from the market. Moreover, where cattle and timber were mainstays of the economy, it also did not become prominent,[27] as exemplified by Norway, which became England's principal supplier of timber. Because the timber industry involved workers with specialized skills, at a time when the second serfdom was making its appearance in neighboring regions, small proprietors continued to be the dominant force in Norway.[28]

Finally, in looking at the Balkans, one encounters additional evidence of the two trends. Early in the sixteenth century, there appear to have been tendencies both in the direction of the export of wheat to the West and an incipient movement toward the institutionalization of servile relations of production. From the 1560s, however, fear of famine caused rulers to ban the export of grains. Thereafter, emphasis in production for the overseas market came to be dominated by cattle in certain parts of Hungary, wool in Serbia, and hides in Bulgaria. The drift toward coerced labor was aborted at roughly the same time that these commodities came to dominate the trade with the West. The absence of a second serfdom, then, must be related to the fact that what the peasants produced required low inputs of labor relative to the return the goods commanded.[29]

The transformation of eastern Europe that resulted from its intensified relations with merchant capital in the West had both internal and external ramifications. One was the enormous disparity in wealth that accompanied it. It has been calculated that seigneurial income tripled between 1650 and 1700. At the same time that peasant immiseration was becoming more pronounced, a noble named Boris Ostrogski enjoyed a revenue larger than that of the Polish state.[30] With the exception of the port towns, which in essence were extensions of the world economy, urbanization actually decreased. Denied a domestic market, craft production dwindled even further. Thus, it is easy to suggest that the underdevelopment of the region was intimately linked to its involvement with external commerce. How important a factor Eastern retardation was in promoting Western advance is open to question. Certainly, it was of some importance in enabling the Dutch to specialize as they did in agriculture. Marion Malowist has argued that "it is difficult to envisage the rapid economic development of Holland, and partly also in England . . . without the constant deliveries of Eastern European grain, flax [and] hemp."[31] Nevertheless, although there is some basis for this judgment, it must also be borne in mind that the Baltic connection was only one component of a worldwide system in the process of being erected.

## THE PLANTATION ECONOMIES

This era also witnessed the growth of the plantation economy in the region that has been referred to as the "Near Atlantic" because of its proximity to Europe. With its tentative beginnings in the sixteenth century, its growth during the seventeenth, and its flowering in the eighteenth century, the plantation economy was unique. Never before in human history had people from one continent transformed parts of another with the intention of producing for the homeland they had left behind. Whereas the immigrants into eastern Europe maintained few contacts with the world they abandoned, those who crossed the Atlantic did so with every intention of remaining linked to the world they left. The plantation sector was different from eastern Europe in other ways, as well. The lands to the east of the Elbe supplied commodities the West preferred not to produce, whereas the plantation economy specialized in crops that Europe was incapable of cultivating. As Richard Sheridan notes, this ability to exploit a different ecological zone provided the West with a unique windfall.[32] Yet the plantation economies also shared similarities with eastern Europe. For they, too, placed primary emphasis on commodities that demanded high labor inputs relative to the price they were able to command on the world market. Therefore, in order to participate in the world economy the organizers of production in the "Near Atlantic" also had to resort to extra-economic coercion in order to make their commodities viable.

Although Brazil was the first territory to be converted into one that was largely dependent on plantations, the transition was gradual. It is believed that the discovery of Brazil in 1500 by Pedro Cabral was accidental, insofar as his ship appears to have been destined for Asia and inadvertently touched Brazil when the vessel strayed too far westward into the Atlantic. The promontory of northeastern Brazil was located in the half of the world the pope had graciously designated as belonging to Portugal in the Treaty of Tordesillas in 1494, so Brazil was immediately claimed in the name of the crown.[33]

Nevertheless, it was to be almost a century before significant growth would take place in Brazil. Officially, the government was too committed to its African and Asian ventures to be able to devote much attention to Brazil, and its citizens preferred the possibilities of enriching themselves in the Eastern trade to the drudgery and uncertainty of pioneering a tropical wilderness. Although a formal administration was established in 1549 in order to forestall the pretensions of other countries, another generation passed before the conditions favored Brazilian settlement. By that time Portugal was not only losing ground in the East, but many Portuguese were disenchanted when Philip II of Spain assumed the crown in 1580. Because Brazilian sugar had begun to demonstrate its viability, under the changed circumstances emigration increased significantly. So great was the reversal in the trend that by the seventeenth century cries of anguish were being raised in Portugal to the effect that if emigration were not halted, the kingdom would fall into ruin.[34]

Until the end of the seventeenth century, Portuguese expansion into the interior was a gradual process. For most of the seventeenth century, settlement remained within fifty miles of the coast for two reasons: The crown wanted settlement to be as dense as possible in order to be able to defend the territory better, and Indians made the penetration of the *mato* (dense vegetation) a dangerous undertaking. Lisbon's concern with defense was not mere paranoia. At various times French and English interlopers sought to establish a foothold in different parts of the territory. The most serious threat, however, came from the Dutch West India Company, which actually seized control of Pernambuco for a number of years. It was only after the Dutch were forced to evacuate that challenges to Portuguese hegemony ceased.[35]

There were, however, two exceptions to the general pattern of settlement restricted to the coast. In the sixteenth century, cattlemen began penetrating the *coatinga* that bordered the banks of the São Francisco River. Simultaneously, in the south, rugged frontiersmen known as Paulistas conducted slave raids on the Indians of the southern plateau. In the process, they forced Spanish missionaries who had established villages to retreat further into the interior. During the second half of the seventeenth century, the crown began to sponsor a series of explorations throughout the region in the hope of finding mineral wealth that might relieve the beleaguered treasury. Ironically, only a few years after officially sponsored expeditions were discontinued, gold was found in what came to be known as Minas Gerais.[36] The subsequent discovery of gold in Goiás and Mato Grosso also helped to bring about a demographic revolution in Brazil. In the hopes of getting rich quickly, many Brazilians abandoned the coastal zones for a chance to make their fortunes in the Brazilian hinterland.

The economy of Brazil that developed as the colony expanded was never based exclusively on one crop. The earliest staple was brazilwood, which produced a dye that was used in textile production. It was initially obtained by barter with the Indians. At the outset, the terms of trade were favorable to the Portuguese, for the local population was fascinated by the exotic items brought by the Iberians. When the novelty wore off, however, and the Indians became disinterested in the trade, the frustrated Portuguese began to enslave them. Thus, from an early date, a prominent feature of the export of brazilwood was the coercion that accompanied it.[37]

Brazilwood was soon surpassed in importance by other endeavors. Tobacco was the crop most consistent in its growth and expansion. It possessed several qualities that made it an attractive proposition. First of all, it could be grown on relatively poorer soils than could sugar. Second, it did not require significant amounts of either capital or labor, so that virtually anyone could engage in its production. As a result, the tobacco industry continued to expand. For example, the number of rolls exported from Bahia rose from twenty thousand in 1720 to eighty thousand by the mid-eighteenth century. Even the lower grades found a ready market in Africa, so tobacco at times even challenged sugar for primacy in terms of its earning power as a Brazilian export. Rae Flory suggests that in Bahia, "the district of Cachoeira . . . [became] one of the richest tobacco growing regions in the world."[38]

Despite the consistency of tobacco, it was never able to rise above second place in importance as one of Brazil's exports. During the first fifty years of the eighteenth century, minerals took primacy. In addition to gold, diamonds were discovered, and in combination the two revolutionized Brazil. Nevertheless, because wholesale smuggling was rampant throughout the era, it is likely that no one will ever come close to quantifying how much wealth was produced. Some idea of the magnitude, however, is suggested in that during the long reign of D. João V (1706-1750) in Portugal, he never once was obliged to call on the Cortes for funds. That is, the royal fifth of mineral production to which the crown was entitled was sufficient to satisfy the needs of his administration. Manuel Cardozo estimates "that for every person who brought his gold to the mint, 20 others disposed of it elsewhere"; it can only be concluded, then, that vast amounts of treasure were clandestinely filtered into the world economy.[39] By 1750, however, the boom suddenly came to an end and yields began to decline in alarming proportions. Thus, almost as suddenly as it had begun, the mineral revolution—and with it Brazil's golden age—came to an end.

Although brazilwood, tobacco, and minerals, as well as cattle ranching, played a significant part in the economic growth of Brazil, sugar was the most important of its exports. Yet sugar too, experienced cycles of prosperity and depression. Beginning in the late sixteenth century, its cultivation was centered in Pernambuco and Bahia. By the early seventeenth century, the rich soils of the northeast enabled Brazil to become the world's largest producer. Although Brazilian production continued to increase, by the eighteenth century the industry underwent a prolonged series of difficulties. As the number of competitive producers multiplied, the once buoyant prices of the seventeenth century began to stagnate. There is disagreement as to precisely when and to what degree West Indian competition affected prices, but it is certain that sugar production in eighteenth-century Brazil no longer represented the bonanza that it had at an earlier date.[40]

Falling prices and hence falling profit margins had an impact on the nature of production. The seventeenth-century sugar estate was organized in a highly complex fashion. It was dominated by the *senhor do engenho*, the owner of the mill. He was usually an individual who in the sixteenth century had been able by quasi-legal means to aggregate vast tracts of land. Because most of his capital was usually tied up in sugar mills, the actual cultivation of the cane was dominated by the *lavradores de cana*. This was an exclusively white group, whose members usually owned between seven and fifteen slaves apiece. In addition to the slaves who were responsible for the production of sugar, the estate housed a variety of workers, some of whom were free men. They performed tasks such as carpentry, cattle- and sheepherding, woodcutting, and whatever else was needed on the plantation. In its self-sufficiency the sugar estate in many respects resembled a medieval manor.[41]

The sugar estate also resembled a medieval manor in that there usually were a variety of tenure arrangements. Some *lavradores* were full-scale tenants who were obliged both to pay rent and to process their sugar at the mill of the *senhor*. Others enjoyed a great deal more freedom. Nevertheless, it appears to have been common for the *senhor* to take 50 percent of his tenants' crops in fees, and there are cases in which the tariff was as high as 80 percent. That the *lavradores* could pay such high rents, still afford to purchase slaves, and continue to make profits, suggests that the profit margin in the marketing of sugar was extremely high.[42]

By the eighteenth century, however, there were significant changes in the organization of production. The *lavradores* abandoned sugar en masse. On the one hand, they were pulled away by the attractions of the goldfields. On the other, they were pushed out because of falling profit margins, which became more chronic after the early decades of the eighteenth century. Increasingly, therefore, production was left to the *senhores*, who were the only group capable of establishing the economies of scale necessary to continue production under the changed circumstances. For example, in

Sergipe, whereas in 1669 their production accounted for only 38 percent of the total, by 1700 their share had risen to 84 percent of the harvest.[43] This was possible because they alone had access to the credit that was essential to continue functioning during times of constriction and because they resorted to a more intensive use of labor, diverting the work force from nonessential tasks into concentration on the production of sugar.

After more than a century of constant use the soil of the northeast was beginning to protest by producing diminishing yields, making it necessary to extract the maximum labor potential from the work force. Mortality rates rose to the extent that slave imports from Africa quadrupled during the eighteenth century, although there was no corresponding increase in output. As the price of a slave was relatively modest compared to the value that his labor could return under conditions of maximum coercion, it was more profitable to replace the labor force than to reproduce it.[44]

One of the reasons Brazilian sugar production began to experience difficulties was that from the later part of the seventeenth century it was faced with increasing competition from Caribbean islands that were being brought into production. For much of the sixteenth century, the Caribbean had remained a preserve of Spain. Yet it was almost totally neglected by the metropolis. After a disappointing period of feverish combing of the region in search of profit soon after it had been discovered, the Spanish satisfied themselves with settlements on Hispaniola, Cuba, and Puerto Rico. Aside from the catastrophic demise of the Indian population, little was achieved. Ironically, partly because it was able to satisfy its own needs from other sources, Spain never fully appreciated the full potential of sugar as a commodity that could be reexported. In fact, rather than seeking to maximize production, the dominant trend in government policy was to attempt to limit the number of producers in order to protect the growers in the already established sector.[45]

From the latter half of the sixteenth century, the Caribbean was to become internationalized. At first, this took the form mainly of piracy and privateering as French, English, and Dutch freebooters sought to prey on Spanish wealth. For the Spanish, the situation deteriorated considerably after the Dutch West India Company began to deal in more organized violence. Rather than confronting this threat, Spain moved and removed populations and abandoned many small settlements. Because its major concern was to protect the treasure fleet, it tacitly surrendered the pretense of dominating the islands. In the words of Kenneth Andrews, they chose "to protect what was most valuable rather than what was most vulnerable."[46]

Over the course of the next century and a half there would be intense activity in the region as a number of different European countries established settlements. This was made possible largely because of the Dutch. In the incipient stages of colonization, the fleet of the West India Company protected the islands from reprisals from the Spanish. In some instances the Dutch even taught the art of sugar cultivation to the newly arrived settlers. In the hope of being able to dominate the carrying trade, they even went so far as to finance some of these operations. During the seventeenth century, English settlements were planted on Barbados, Nevis, Antigua, Montserrat, and Jamaica; in the eighteenth they added Dominica, Grenada, Saint Vincent, and Tobago. The French, in the meantime, contented themselves with Saint Croix, Martinique, Guadeloupe, and San Domingue, which was carved out of the western third of the island of Hispaniola. The Dutch, who were sorely disappointed when the protectionist measures adopted by the governments of their former pupils denied them a role in the carrying trade, occupied Guyana and Curaçao. Nevertheless, only after many years did Spain, which was restricted to Santo Domingo, Cuba, and Puerto Rico, grudgingly accept an obvious fait accompli.[47]

The early settlers came from a wide range of backgrounds. A very few arrived with capital that they preferred to transfer from its European uses to the potentially more profitable undertakings in the Caribbean. The majority fit the category of poor to middling and were often sponsored by companies that paid their transportation and initial subsistence costs. The logic of the system was that the company would ultimately profit from its indebted producers by marketing their goods in Europe. Many, both English and French, went as indentured servants, agreeing to be virtual slaves for a period of years in return for the hope of becoming an independent freeholder once the contract had expired. At other times the English government resorted to deportation, sending criminals and equally undesirable royalists to meet their destinies in the tropics.[48]

During the early period, small- to medium holdings came to predominate. From the outset, some islands were settled by a large number of smallholders, who were almost completely devoid of capital. As a result they engaged in either subsistence or petty cash-crop production. At the other end of the spectrum were the islands where large land grants were made. Although the individuals who received these grants were usually much better off than the smallholders, they often did not have sufficient resources to produce sugar. Therefore, they turned to tobacco, which, however, was not particularly suited to extensive cultivation. The result was that these estates tended to become subdivided into more manageable allotments. Richard Pares notes that "the average plantation, at first, got smaller. The big grants could not be worked profitably as tobacco plantations and began to split into fragments."[49]

Whatever their original circumstances, there were many who could not sustain their holdings. Some who had engaged in partnerships with merchants were never able to overcome the initial debt. The environment could also be fickle. Richard Dunn notes that "careless management, a tropical storm, an endemic disease, a slave revolt, or a French attack [against a British possession] could wipe a farmer out overnight."[50] For those who had turned to sugar, the early eighteenth century proved a time of special vicissitudes. During periods when the price of sugar plummeted on the world market, the margin for error decreased enormously. As a result, a large number of farmers were obliged to abandon their holdings.

Still there were those whose fortunes were exactly the reverse. Their success may have stemmed from good management. Good luck may have played an equally large role, as an individual who borrowed in a season when prices were high and yields were good might be left with enough to repay his debt, save enough to have a buffer against a bad year, and even have sufficient capital for expansion. Pares notes that "at a date which varied from colony to colony, the process [of fragmentation] was reversed and small plantations began to be aggregated into large ones."[51]

The individuals who became successful planters usually rose from the ranks of production. That is, they were descendants of smallholders who "by a combination of skill, drive and luck," as Dunn says, were able to take advantage of the plight of those who had been neither skillful, driven, nor lucky. Insofar as it paralleled the differentiation among the peasantry that occurred in England, the process has been referred to as "tropical enclosure."[52] It also resembled the English situation in that it paved the way for economies of scale and more efficient production. The two processes, however, differed in the important respect that whereas in England engrossing was an important stepping-stone in the march toward capitalism, in the Caribbean it led in the opposite direction.

The consolidation of estates led to the creation of a class of wealthy planters. Neither the *grands blancs* of the French Caribbean nor their English counterparts were thought of highly in their metropolises. Their ostentatious displays of wealth, their nouveau status, and their rustic crudeness in circles of *haute culture* made them the butt of jokes. The derision with which they were viewed, however, should not obscure that they were almost always men of considerable talent. At one and the same time they had to be knowledgeable agriculturalists, possess the technical skills to operate a mill, manage a complex business, oversee a large labor force, and exercise the skill of a merchant in conducting their business operations. The successful operation of a plantation was no easy task.[53]

The evolution of the plantation was a gradual process. At the outset most farmers were satisfied with mere survival and therefore were content with growing food crops for subsistence. Once they established a base, they would supplement staples with a cash crop. Tobacco, which has been described as a beginner's crop, was a favorite because it required little skill, a small labor force, limited capital, and no expensive machinery. Those who prospered in this way might subsequently attempt to diversify. Indigo, cocoa, and ginger were among the other crops that were grown. No matter what might be grown along the way, however, all aspired to convert to sugar.[54]

There were both obstacles and advantages to the cultivation of sugar. The main obstacle was that it not only required expensive equipment but also demanded a large labor force to handle the cane's complicated cycle. Therefore, not until a planter had accumulated enough capital could he turn to sugar. Once the conversion had been made, however, the benefits could be great. Whereas the demand for a product like ginger was relatively inelastic, eighteenth-century Europe continually discovered new uses for sugar. Thus, although the price was not sustained at the dizzying levels of the halcyon days of the seventeenth century, it remained fairly buoyant considering the degree to which worldwide production increased. Moreover, of all the crops grown on tropical plantations, it returned the highest price per acre and the highest yield per worker. Therefore, as Pares pointed out, "every great planter turned to sugar sooner or later and, having turned to it, he hardly ever turned back to anything else."[55]

In fact, the tendency was for estates to be converted from extensive agriculture to intensive monoculture. The first step in the process was for most other cash crops to be abandoned so that concentration could be focused exclusively on sugar. During this stage, part of the estate continued to be devoted to food crops to feed its labor force. Soon, however, a planter usually came to perceive that land was too valuable to waste on the cultivation of food, and the entire estate was planted with sugar. It was more economical to import food from North America, Bermuda, or Ireland than to produce it locally and thereby decrease the acreage planted in cane. Thus the plantation was converted into a factory whose only activities were the growing, harvesting, processing, and shipping of sugar.[56]

Indeed, sugar was the estate crop that best achieved an economy of scale. Although significant capital was required to begin production, this investment was justified by market demand. Moreover, because of the intensive use of labor, the returns on this particular branch of investment were particularly high. For sugar, unlike many other estate crops, demanded the year-round employment of the labor force. Weeding, thinning, hoe-plowing, and replanting were required in addition to planting the fields. Once the crop had been harvested, it had to be rolled, boiled, clarified, cooled, dried, cured, and packed.[57]

Just how profitable sugar planting was has been the subject of considerable debate. Several years ago Richard Sheridan published an article in which he emphasized that great fortunes were made in sugar planting. Others reached a different conclusion, even going so far as to suggest that Britain would have been better off had there been no Caribbean possessions. Between these two extremes has emerged a compromise position that argues that there were boom periods when great fortunes were made and depressions when many of those fortunes were lost. In essence, sugar cultivation proved very profitable for some of its growers but not for all. When the median between the two was calculated, J. R. Ward concluded "that sugar planting was profitable throughout the years of slavery," but that these profits "seem similar to other areas of endeavor."[58]

Some of the general trends that emerged in the Caribbean can be discerned by looking at individual islands, such as Barbados. Settled by the English in 1624, it possessed the natural advantages of not being threatened by hurricanes, low elevation, and relatively fertile soils. Equally important, because it was located in the southeastern Caribbean and thus far removed from the highways and byways traveled by the Spaniards, it was also less prone to Spanish reprisals. Although subsistence production marked its early years, sugar began to be grown in the 1640s. The timing could not have been better: The gestation of sugar production corresponded with an era when the Dutch attempt at conquest in Brazil severely reduced the output of the Brazilian planter. Because the other islands had not begun to produce sugar, Barbados enjoyed a period of unfettered boom. "The rise of the Barbados planter class," writes Richard Dunn, "was intoxicating. Virginia might be the Old Dominion . . . but Barbados was something more tangible: the richest colony in English America."[59]

The career of Barbados provides several examples of how fortunes could wax and wane in the Caribbean. The demographic statistics speak volumes about the process of tropical enclosure. In 1645, out of a total white population of 40 thousand, 11,200 were landowners. By 1667, shortly after the boom in sugar, the number of landowners had been reduced to 745. Moreover, by 1745, the number of whites had been reduced to twelve thousand, the shortage of land having obliged a great number to emigrate to North America. The figures of the African slave population are equally instructive. Whereas there were only six thousand in 1645, the total had risen to forty-six thousand by 1685.[60]

The conversion to a heavy dependence on slave labor, however, did not assure Barbados of maintaining its ascendancy. On the contrary, its early start meant that its soils lost their fertility more rapidly than the islands that began production at a later date. As a result, it became necessary to invest in expensive inputs of fertilizer in order to maintain the land's productivity. Thus, although the literature sometimes overstates the degree of decline that overtook the island, its productive capacity was soon surpassed by a large number of other islands.[61]

For indeed, by the eighteenth century, the Caribbean came to experience a virtual sugar explosion. The number of islands that were brought into production multiplied dramatically. English planters became more active on such islands as Antigua, Nevis, Montserrat, Dominica, Saint Vincent, and Grenada, while their French counterparts expanded operations in Martinique and Guadeloupe. Even the Dutch in Suriname intensified their interest in sugar. Not only did the number of islands in production increase, but the output of each usually grew significantly. For example, Martinique, which had produced 115 cwt of sugar in 1715, increased the total to 410 by 1753.[62]

In the British sphere, however, the most important island came to be Jamaica. Although it was the largest British possession in the Caribbean, its growth had been arrested for many years. Its use as a base from which pirates attacked Spanish shipping proved inimical to settled cultivation. Once the policy decision was taken to suppress piracy, however, the way was cleared for its rapid growth. The number of plantations increased from 57 in 1673 to 775 in 1774. In the process Jamaica became the single largest producer in the British Caribbean. Contrary to popular opinion, although it is sometimes suggested that Jamaican production had peaked by the middle of the eighteenth century, a more accurate assessment is that the growth rate may have decelerated but that there was continuing expansion during the remainder of the century. By Caribbean standards it had an ample supply of land, so it was possible to bring new soil into cultivation once the older land began to tire. As late as the 1790s, Jamaica was passing through what has been described as its "second childhood," a phenomenon that enabled it to retain its preeminent position in the British sphere.[63]

Nevertheless, the most remarkable story in the Caribbean was the one that unfolded in the French territory of San Domingue. Although this colony on the western third of the island of Hispaniola did not receive official recognition from Spain until 1697, it soon began a meteoric period of economic growth notable for the size, diversity, and quality of its output. By 1720 it had already surpassed Jamaica to become the largest single producer of sugar in the West Indies. Thereafter, its production expanded by leaps and bounds. Sugar totals rose from 135 cwt in 1714, to 848 in 1742, to 1,252 in 1767; by 1783 it also produced 1 million lbs. of indigo and 2 million of cotton. The growth of coffee production was equally astounding. It proceeded so rapidly, in fact, that by 1790 Haiti accounted for 60 percent of the world's production. So fantastic, indeed, was the production of Haiti that it came to produce more than the entire British Caribbean. Not only were the totals impressive, but so, too, was the quality. Its sugar, tobacco, coffee, cotton, and indigo were reputed to be the best in the world. Moreover, yields per acre were much higher than elsewhere. If all of the preceding were not enough, as an encore, it doubled its production again between the end of the war in 1783 and 1789.[64] C.L.R. James aptly describes the situation when he notes that "on no portion of the globe did its surface . . . yield so much wealth as the colony of San Domingue."[65]

The wealth of San Domingue and the more modest Caribbean islands, however, could only have been produced by coerced labor. In this regard, San Domingue represented the most extreme example of a general phenomenon. For production could only increase as the number and percentage of nonremunerated producers increased. San Domingue may have been an aberration insofar as it imported 40 thousand blacks in 1787 alone, leaving it with a ratio of 24 thousand whites to 408 thousand blacks, but the trend was evident elsewhere.[66] Although attempts were made in Jamaica to maintain a maximum white:black ratio of 1:10, by the mid-eighteenth century, this, too, had risen to 1:20.

Just how pervasive the phenomenon was, however, can be gleaned from the breakdown provided by Philip Curtin of the number of slaves imported into each of the islands. The statistics with respect to slaves reflected that, under the conditions that prevailed in the plantation economy, the enslaved could not reproduce themselves, making it necessary to continue to escalate the levels of importation. Around 1770, there were more than one million slaves toiling on the plantations of the Caribbean and Brazil. Most of them had been born in Africa and transported to the New World. This was because of the preponderance of males over females and the low rates of fertility among those women who did survive. For survival, indeed, was difficult in an insalubrious environment of constant, arduous work from morning to night. In fact, the perceived economic wisdom of the day was that it was more profitable to work a slave to death and import another than to try to encourage longevity. Thus, in the late eighteenth century, the system seemed to be heavily dependent on the continuation of the slave trade.[67]

Nevertheless, neither as individuals nor as groups did the enslaved population passively accept the inevitability of remaining in bondage. Where possible, they adopted the strategy of desertion. In some instances groups of escapees waged guerrilla warfare against the plantation they had deserted. At times their numbers swelled to the extent that established communities with regularized institutions and elected officials were created.[68] Although few plots that envisaged the overthrow of the system have been unearthed, it is probable that some of the more enlightened slaves dreamt of the day when the conditions would be ripe for the overthrow of the slave regime.

By definition, therefore, the system could only be maintained by what by modern standards were hideous amounts of force. Among the numerous examples of barbaric practices that were used was the feeding of human flesh to dogs who were trained to track down escapees, so as to ensure that an apprehended fugitive would be mutilated to the extent that others would be dissuaded from escaping. Corporal punishment, including mutilations, dismemberment, breaking on the rack, and even disembowelment were standard practices.[69] These extreme measures were resorted to because the dominant segments of plantation society felt themselves under siege. All members of that establishment were empowered to engage in the armed defense of the status quo. As the ratio of unfree to free began to widen, in the more prosperous regions, full-time professionals were hired to police most facets of the slave regime.[70]

Although the free population of the Caribbean demonstrated a unity with respect to suppression of the nonfree population, there were many sources of dissension among the dominant classes. Because the interests of merchants and planters were usually different, they often sought to achieve different goals. Similarly, the interests of the planters often collided with those of the middle-class elements in plantation society. Even among the planters, however, there were cleavages based upon the crop that was grown and also between the permanent residents and the absentees. The metropolitan government, the ultimate arbiter of these disputes, was always likely to make decisions that created dissatisfaction in one camp or the other. The problems appear to have been more severe in the French islands than in the English. In fact, because they believed Paris was unresponsive to their needs, some planters even considered transferring their allegiance to England.[71]

## FUELING THE PLANTATION ECONOMY

Western Africa was the key to the development of the American plantation systems. For without the millions of people who were transported across the Atlantic, sugar cultivation on a significant scale could never have taken place. It is, therefore, obvious why the Brazilian and Caribbean planters participated in a system that brought them such profits. The African component of the equation, on the other hand, is more difficult to understand. This is especially true because, until recently, this crucial factor in world history has received very little scholarly attention. In the past decade, however, much new information has come to light. Among the many hypotheses that can now be suggested is that Western Africa, too, should be classified as part of the periphery in that, for reasons similar to those in the other territories, a slave mode of production became dominant there.

One of the most widely debated issues is the number of Africans who were landed in the New World. Until the publication of Curtin's *Atlantic Slave Trade: A Census* in 1969, wild guesses of as many as fifty million could be encountered. Reconstructing as carefully as he could, Curtin arrived at a total of just over eleven million who reached the Western Hemisphere. In 1976, however, J. E. Inikori suggested a modification. Believing that Curtin's totals were too low by 40 percent, he argued that the figure should be adjusted to 15.4 million. Some subsequent researchers have tended to support Inikori, but others still believe that Curtin's numbers are closer to being accurate.[72] It is impossible for the nonspecialist to make a reasonable judgment in such intricate matters; what is more important than establishing an absolute figure is to suggest the range of probability that is being discussed.

Prior to the nineteenth century, almost all of the slaves who arrived in the New World came from West and West-Central Africa. Over time, West Africa, that is from Senegal to the Cameroons, was the source of between roughly 55 and 60 percent of the slaves, most of whom after the seventeenth century found their way to the Caribbean. Within West Africa, during the more than three centuries of intensive trading, there was a gradual shift eastward in emphasis, so that by the end of the eighteenth century, the Niger Delta was the single most important supplier. In comparison, West-Central Africa, which extended from the Cameroons in the north to the port of Benguela in the south, supplied approximately 35 to 40 percent of the total. Although the Portuguese-controlled ports of Luanda and Benguela accounted for the majority of exports during the seventeenth century, by the eighteenth century the number of points of embarkation had increased significantly, as had traders from other nations, whom the Portuguese considered interlopers. In contrast to those from West Africa, however, the majority of slaves exported from West-Central Africa were transported to Brazil.[73]

Although Europeans transported the Africans to the Americas, they usually were not involved in the process of capture. There were a few exceptions to this general trend, but they were relatively unimportant. For example, early in the fifteenth century, as the Portuguese were wending their way down the western coast of Africa, they frequently engaged in kidnapping. Nevertheless, they soon discovered that captives were readily available for purchase without having to run the risks involved in raiding. The other major exception occurred in Angola. In 1575, the Portuguese crown granted Angola to Paulo Dias de Novaes as a *donatorio* (grant) provided, of course, that he could conquer the territory. There thus began fifty years of desultory warfare, the major spoils of which, from the European point of view, were the Africans who were captured in the process. Still, just as had been the case in West Africa, the Portuguese discovered during lulls in the fighting that slaves remained available for purchase. Therefore, by the early 1620s, their direct involvement virtually came to a halt, except when a newly arrived governor felt that he had sufficient force at his command to risk going to war.[74]

Following the lead of the Portuguese, traders from different European nations began to venture to Africa. Within a relatively short period they developed a variety of methods of transacting their business. By the seventeenth century, increasing numbers of Dutch and French slavers had become prominent in many regions along the coast. In most areas they remained aboard ship while their factors negotiated the transfer of cargos. In some regions, however, Europeans constructed permanent buildings where they aggregated captives until the arrival of ships to transport them across the Atlantic. On the Gold Coast, where inter-European competition was fiercest, some of these structures were formidable. By and large, elsewhere European edifices were rather makeshift in nature. Aware that they were incapable of defense against local populations, Europeans realized that they were in Africa on the sufferance of the indigenous people. In some instances, in fact, the European trader was treated as a client who was both protected and supplied by an African sponsor.[75]

Although the rulers of many African social formations would have liked to preserve the slave trade as a state monopoly, they were rarely able to achieve this goal. At various times and in various places attempts were made to enforce regulations that reserved the export of human beings to official circles. Nevertheless, despite the states' ability to promulgate legislation favorable to themselves and their access to prisoners of war, the means of acquiring captives were so numerous and the ways of evading detection so easy that states rarely succeeded in preventing other agents from participation. As early as the beginning of the sixteenth century, for example, the king of the Kongo complained to his "ally," the king of Portugal, that Portuguese traders were dealing directly with his "vassals" and thus undermining his authority.[76] Similarly, the king of Dahomey, a small and extremely centralized state, was unable to maintain his monopoly. In fact, it has been estimated that the exports from the private sector exceeded those of the king.[77] Not even in Angola, where both the agents of the Portuguese crown and the king of the state of Kasanje had a mutual interest in maintaining a monopoly, was their policy feasible, for each side also contained individuals who were willing and able to run the blockade.[78]

In most areas attempts at monopoly were not even considered. Rather, the dominant tenor of the times was the extreme competitiveness and the variety of ways in which it was practiced. On the Upper Guinea Coast, for example, African "hosts" competed with each other to acquire European "guests" whom they would supply and protect. Similarly, on the Gold Coast, numerous coastal towns vied with each other both to control access to the interior and to attract European clients.[79] Perhaps the most elaborate and most competitive system, however, was to be found in the Niger Delta, which by the eighteenth century had earned the title "queen of the slave trade." A number of city-states competed with each other in order to attract customers. Within the respective towns themselves there was intense rivalry. In Bonny, for example, the traditional social structure was challenged by a new system of canoe-houses, trading organizations that owned a number of canoes and had armed retainers used in procuring slaves. The rivalries that developed among the various houses were often so intense that open hostilities among them were not uncommon.[80]

As the trade continued to grow, great distances came to be involved. During the first century, it is to be presumed that most slaves were acquired in coastal regions. As demand expanded, new areas of acquisition, located farther in the interior, were sought out. Thus, northern Nigeria, which seemingly was not involved in the earlier stages, became a major source of slaves. The secular trend, however, is best exemplified by the case of Angola. During the seventeenth and early eighteenth centuries, the kingdom of Kasanje was directly responsible for procuring large numbers of slaves. By the latter half of the eighteenth century, as the sources around it began to dry up, Kasanje was converted from a producer of captives into an entrepôt that transshipped people supplied by other groups who lived farther in the interior.[81] The supply networks became so vast that market towns and other staging points came to extend from the coast to the distant hinterland.

Although slaves were obtained in a variety of ways, violence of one sort or another was usually involved in their acquisition. There were exceptions, however, even to this general rule. Occasionally people were enslaved for having committed crimes. There is also evidence of groups faced with famine who voluntarily surrendered themselves into slavery in preference to confronting the threat of starvation.[82] Nevertheless, the vast majority were produced by a combination of warfare, slave raiding, or kidnapping. In fact, the distinction between warfare and slave raiding tended to become blurred over time; in many instances, the objective of warfare was the capture of victims to enslave. In many parts of the continent, this led to the growth of the phenomenon of warlordism, that is, the creation of private armies whose principal function was raiding and entrapping often defenseless communities.[83]

Because the violence that accompanied the slave trade so adversely affected the quality of life in such a large part of the African continent, the question why there should have been a slave trade at all and why it reached such proportions begs for an answer. In the past liberal apologists developed what they called the gun/slave-cycle model, which basically suggested that Africans unwittingly became involved in a vicious circle. According to this hypothesis, guns were considered by many groups to be necessary as a means of self-defense against neighbors who might otherwise take advantage of the inability of an individual group to defend itself. Europeans, the argument continued, seized upon this climate of fear and were able to impose a form of blackmail. By refusing to sell guns for any commodity other than slaves, they obliged groups that otherwise might have abstained from participating in the trade to become actively involved. Thus virtually all peoples of western Africa became entrapped in a vicious cycle.[84]

Unfortunately, as seductive as the thesis is in suggesting a rational explanation for the reasons people acted in a seemingly irrational manner, it cannot stand up to the challenge of empirical evidence. For it can be demonstrated that there were groups who participated in the export of slaves without the prior acquisition of firearms and others who neither possessed firearms nor participated in the slave trade but were not subject to the kind of tyranny that the hypothesis proposes for those who sought to escape from the supposedly inescapable trap.

Another explanation for growth of the slave trade is that, whereas many disapproved, in the absence of centralized institutions sufficiently powerful to bring about order from the prevailing chaos, the slave trade developed a dynamic of its own that could not be controlled. Afonso, king of the Kongo in the early sixteenth century, and Agaja, ruler of Dahomey in the beginning of the next century, have been cited as monarchs who opposed the trade but were unsuccessful in their attempts to bring it to a halt.

A closer reading of the few documents that record their sentiments, however, suggests that it was not the slave trade per se that they opposed, but certain specifics that surrounded its organization. In the case of the king of the Kongo, it appears that he objected to the lack of control of the trade. In essence, he complained that the wrong people were being enslaved. Similarly, when Agaja refused to sell slaves to certain groups of Europeans, it was not, as has been suggested, because he was loathe to sell slaves. Rather, it stemmed from the more mundane consideration that most European traders refused to deal in gold.[85] Thus, although it may be true that there was an absence of strong state systems that might have imposed an interdiction on the slave trade, there is, as yet, no evidence to suggest that there was a body of opinion in high places that was particularly offended by the commerce in human beings.

It would seem, however, that in searching for the reasons for the genesis of the slave trade one need not conjure up scenarios of innocent African societies being entrapped by a nefarious outside world. To be sure, the totality of this "odious commerce" was monstrous, but it was a monster with which certain elements in the social formation elected to live. As suggested many years ago by Walter Rodney, an increasingly powerful strata of society that profited enormously from the existence of the slave trade was able to ensure its growth and perpetuation.[86] They were no more sensitive to the plight of the victimized and the victims than were the lords of eastern Europe or the plantation owners of the Western world. In this regard, chiefs, warlords, traders, and many other elements most closely connected with the rewards of the trade acted no differently from other dominant classes. More recent studies, several of them quantitative in nature, confirm these sentiments. Warfare, which was once ruled by political considerations, increasingly was perverted so that it came to have the primarily economic end of securing captives. It was the means by which an enterprising strata of society enriched itself and ensured its domination.[87]

Nevertheless, that certain elements within the social formation perceived the potential profitability of a slave trade does not explain why this was a uniquely African phenomenon. Several years ago J. D. Fage argued that the growth of the African slave trade was related to the fact that both slavery and a slave trade existed in Africa prior to the arrival of Europeans. It was relatively easy, therefore, to make the transition from an intra-African trade to an external commerce in human beings.[88] The weakness of his argument is that slavery existed at one time or another in most parts of the world, yet no other region became involved in a long-distance slave trade of such proportions. If the prior existence was indeed a likely "launching pad," one would expect most regions of the world to have been involved in an intercontinental slave trade.

Arguments have also been put forth that Africans were enslaved because of certain inherent characteristics they possessed. The negative side of this racist approach is that Africans were viewed as being innately inferior and thus ripe for being made into slaves. In this regard scholars from different disciplines have produced a great deal of evidence to demonstrate that anti-African prejudice predated the growth of the slave trade. In answering this thesis, it should be noted, among other considerations, that Europeans did not insist upon Africans to perform their labor. Rather, they were quite willing to and tried to enslave Indians and even other Europeans. That these forms of coerced labor did not take hold was not because of the racial world-view of the slaveholder but because under many conditions Indians died too quickly to be of much value and sufficient numbers of Europeans were not available at an acceptable cost/return ratio. On the other hand, the positive side of the racist interpretation suggests that Africans were extremely suitable to the task: They came from tropical climates, were seasoned cultivators, and, in some cases, even brought mining skills with them.

Nevertheless, even though there may be much truth in the notion of the suitability of Africans to American conditions, this argument, as well as others, misses a very simple but fundamental point. Africa was converted into a supplier of labor because of the conjuncture of demand in the Western Hemisphere with the fact that it was the only area capable of supplying that demand at an acceptable cost. The economic problem was one of delivery, and Africa, like other areas in the periphery, was located within easy reach of its potential market. In this respect, distance was even more important, as the nature of the slave trade was such that, in order to achieve an economy of scale in the delivery of labor, it was necessary to pack cargos virtually to maximum capacity. Under these conditions, however, mortality increased by geometric proportions the longer a voyage lasted. To have imported labor from any area more distant than western Africa would have been impossible because of the costs that would have been involved. It is not coincidental that East Africans, although they, too, should have been despised if race were the crucial variable, did not become a part of the Atlantic slave trade until the nineteenth century. By then, the inflation in the prices of slaves that resulted from its official abolition made the higher mortality rates occasioned by the longer delivery time economically acceptable.[89]

As in other regions of the periphery, the ruling classes in Africa were those who profited. The bizarre sight of African chiefs wearing red velvet jackets in the tropical forests has created the myth of slaves being exchanged for worthless trinkets. Nothing could be further from the truth. Although some luxury items that were ascribed a much higher value in Africa than in Europe because of their novelty and scarcity were imported, the commodities Africans received were often valuable in terms of the needs of the local economy. Inikori estimates that at least twenty million firearms were imported into western Africa between 1750 and 1807. Although traditional wisdom has often suggested that these guns were of an inferior quality, Inikori points out that, under conditions of intense competition, European traders were obliged to provide high-quality merchandise or be left empty-handed. In addition to textiles, which included the finest calico from India, and Brazilian tobacco, Africans imported iron and copper, both of which were in short supply in the forest regions of western Africa. Moreover, with demand in the Americas increasing more rapidly than the ability of Africa to meet the supply, the terms of trade came to favor the African producer at the expense of his Western trading partner.[90]

Although the terms of trade came to favor Africa, it was the organizers of production who reaped the benefits. Because so little is known about West African societies prior to the era of the slave trade and also because societies differed radically from each other, care must be exercised in making generalizations. Yet it seems safe to suggest that even where status differences had been pronounced, there was little in a material sense that had separated one segment of society from another. This situation was dramatically altered by the slave trade. At one extreme were the kings, nobles, warlords, and incipient merchants who expropriated almost all of the wealth that was imported. At the other extreme were the commoners, who, at best, continued to live a largely subsistence existence. Very few if any of the material gains of the era trickled down to them. They were often obliged to live in a climate of fear, never knowing if lowly status or some other factor might someday condemn them to slavery as well.

Just as there was differentiation within groups, the era witnessed changes in fortune among societies. The more successful were those who were able to unify into some form of state organization. Inikori notes that throughout western Africa there was a proliferation of small states during the era. Roger Anstey adds that "the peoples who profitted from the slave trade were those whose political institutions were of themselves or by adaptation appropriate to it."[91] By extension, those who suffered were those who could not make the transition. Anstey continues that "small segmentary societies were usually the losers." In this regard, for example, it has been shown that the Chokwe of Angola, a people whose hunting, gathering, and fishing life-style militated against state formation, were particularly hard-hit victims of the trade.[92]

In many instances, social organization was radically transformed. The variety of adaptations was enormous. Citing just a few, one can begin with the Gold Coast, where formerly sleepy fishing villages were converted into active city-states. In the Niger Delta, the canoe-house system of Bonny came to subsume the traditional structure, which continued in existence for a time, bent in the wake of competition, and finally broke under the weight of the changed circumstances. Similarly, the kingdom of Kasanje became an aberration, based upon an elaboration of its extremely complicated kinship system and its ties to the slave trade.[93] Finally, mention should be made of the Aro of eastern Nigeria. Although initially they were viewed by the Igbo communities they served as having special religious powers that could heal disputes among communities, the seductiveness of the slave trade converted them into ruthless purveyors of the traffic. They bastardized traditional understandings, used their judicial powers to condemn many into slavery, and backed up their arbitrary decisions by a mercenary army paid for with their newly acquired wealth.[94]

No change that occurred during the era of the slave trade was more important than the introduction of a slave mode of production into African social formations. It would appear that various forms of servile status had existed from antiquity, but under "domestic slavery" the distinction between "master" and "slave" did not involve great differences with respect to the work that each performed or in terms of social exclusivity. During the era of the overseas trade, as large numbers of foreigners were added to the community, the distinctions became more profound. It has been suggested that in the Ivory Coast, for example, there was an "introduction of slave type relations of production into social formations dominated until then by the kin-based mode of production."[95] In some regions, as many as 50 percent of the population were slaves, who came to be viewed as factors of production in ways that had never previously prevailed. Plantations, producing surpluses to feed those who were engaged exclusively in one facet or another of the overseas trade, became the order of the day, and "slavery was transformed and slave societies emerged."[96] Whereas once manumission and assimilation appeared the logical outcomes of servile status, the sheer numbers of outsiders who became part and parcel of the new order meant that this option was no longer viable for the host society. Quite the contrary, as essential factors of production, slaves deteriorated to the status of chattel.

In answering the question of why a slave mode of production and hence the peripheralization of Africa should have taken place, it should be observed that, despite seeming differences, Africa shared crucial similarities with the other social formations of the periphery. Although its principal commodity was human beings, the cost of supplying these individuals was extremely high. As Patrick Manning notes, "as prospective captives learned to protect themselves better and as middlemen and toll collectors imposed themselves on the process of delivery," the costs of the trade rose considerably.[97] Stating the problem somewhat differently, because so much domestic energy was tied up in the acquisition of slaves, but because the profits garnered were marginal relative to the labor time required to obtain them, the contradiction could only be solved by resorting to unremunerated labor. No one states the problem better than do Jan Hogendorn and Henry Gemery, who observe that the costs of the slave trade "included social, political, and psychological disruptions and specifically the costs of organized defense, or armed patrols and scouts. . . . When the imposed social costs are added to the economic costs, it becomes impossible to conceive of an alternative export which might have carried a higher real cost than slaves."[98]

Precisely what the impact of these changes were on Africa is a contentious issue. One area of disagreement is its effect on demography. Many have come to the conclusion that the decline was not nearly as great as a look at the statistics might originally suggest. Population loss was partially offset by the introduction of more nutritious American crops and by the preponderance of males exported. Under the prevailing polygynous social system, females were left in Africa to reproduce and population did not decline as radically as it might have under other circumstances.

Accepting these arguments in part, Inikori nonetheless projects that the population would have been significantly higher had there been no slave trade. It is his belief that increases in population are a major factor in obliging human societies to adapt and change; he concludes, then, that the demographic stagnation was partially responsible for the general stagnation on the continent.[99] Others interpret basically the same evidence in a radically different light. They question the ability of the environment, under the technological constraints that existed during this era, to have supported higher population densities.[100] By logical extension, this position might suggest that the slave trade may actually have saved Africa from a Malthusian crisis such as was experienced elsewhere.

There are those who emphasize as well the themes of dependency and underdevelopment. Although the process varied greatly from region to region, imported goods often had a deleterious impact on domestic manufacture. Certainly, West African society developed a taste for imported goods. According to G. I. Jones, "the general trend of the import trade was . . . to convert former luxuries into necessities . . . and to make the people . . . dependent on the overseas trade for a large range of necessities that they had formerly produced themselves or gone without."[101] Domestic cloth production, for example, was a handicraft industry that suffered in many regions. Partly as a result of this dependence on imports, it has been suggested, underdevelopment was hastened and facilitated. Inikori is one who sees a direct correlation between the growth of the slave trade and the retardation of the continent. He observes that "the huge gap in economic development between black Africa and the other major regions of the world is discernible in the descriptions . . . of the nineteenth century [provided by European observers]. Yet no such gap is discernible in the observations of Arab and European visitors in the first half of the second millennium."[102]

## CONCLUSION

Thus, by the eighteenth century, the category of periphery was complete. It consisted of territories that were located sufficiently close to their markets so that their commodities could bear the tariff of transport. These lands produced such commodities despite what should have been excessive labor costs. In each instance, the ruling classes resolved this dilemma by expropriating the surplus of the producer. It was, however, a world that was very skewed. The very many worked under onerous conditions so that a very few could reap the benefits. Unbeknownst to those who profited from the system, they were ultimately condemning their respective regions to backwardness. Tacitly, nevertheless, the system was approved of not only by those who were its immediate beneficiaries, but also by the world of merchant capital that was able to circulate the commodities it received on extremely favorable terms. That the market potential of the peripheries remained as undeveloped as the territories themselves had not yet arisen as a problem that disturbed capitalism. This, in turn, came about because capitalism had not yet passed from its mercantile to its industrial phase.

# 7
# DEPENDENCIES IN
# THE WORLD ECONOMY

As the development of the world economy progressed, there also came into being a separate category that is referred to as dependencies. Those that are of particular relevance are Ireland, Spanish America, and the mainland colonies of Great Britain. Although there were great differences among them and their respective histories, they had enough in common to be classified together and to merit designation as a separate category. One determinant of this status was that, unlike peripheries, which could function as independent entities, by definition dependencies were under colonial domination. What distinguished dependent colonies from peripheral colonies was that in dependencies servile relations became less important as the territories matured. This resulted from radical difference in the nature of commodity production in the two spheres. In the dependencies, the finished products often had a higher intrinsic value because significant amounts of skill were required to produce them. This was true of such undertakings as mining, textile manufacture, logging, hunting, and fishing. In other areas of commodity production, such as the cultivation of grain and tobacco and the herding of animals, the labor input relative to the value produced was relatively low. In either case the result was that labor costs represented a smaller percentage of the total product in the dependencies than in the peripheries. Therefore, there was enough surplus value created by commodity production to enable the payment of wages and to negate the necessity of resorting to extra-economic coercion.

Dependencies also differed from peripheries insofar as a great deal of tension clouded their relationships with their respective metropolises. The urge toward colonization initially may have been prompted by a number of motives. At the outset in some instances colonies were viewed as useful because they provided the home country either with a safety valve to relieve it of excess population or a dumping ground for religious or political dissenters. They might also be considered to have a strategic value that in one way or another would prove beneficial to the interests of the metropolis. As stated by Jean-Baptiste Colbert, who is often depicted as the architect of French mercantilism, "colonies are founded by and for the mother country."[1]

These mercantilistic views of European statesmen, which were in conflict with the interests of their colonists, were bound to create tension. Unlike peripheries, whose growth was founded upon their ability to complement the needs of Europe, dependencies did not necessarily fit into the same mold. Sometimes the climate and the soil conditions of the dependency resembled that of the metropolis, thus making it likely that they would duplicate one another in their respective produce. Similarly, the basic needs of the colonists would be virtually the same as the citizens of the metropolis. Quite understandably, the settlers would seek to satisfy these needs either by manufacturing the goods themselves, where possible, or seeking them in the most desirable markets. Both self-sufficiency and duplication, however, were anathema to orthodox imperial thinking. Therefore, the logic of imperial legislation led in the direction of ensuring that the colonies would remain dependent on the metropole for imports and that colonial produce would not compete with that of the home country. The colonists were viewed as little better than stepchildren whose interests merited scant consideration; their colonial masters saw no theoretical inconsistency in imposing on them the strictest regulations.

Yet these same statesmen usually found that what was theoretically desirable could rarely be put into practice. One obvious contradiction was that if the earning power of the colonists was too severely restricted, they could not afford to import from the metropole. A second set of considerations involved the maintenance of supremacy and questions of defense. A policy that was too draconian was likely to sow seeds of rebellion. Moreover, intervention by foreign powers always posed a danger. Only two solutions for these dilemmas presented themselves. On the one hand, the colonial power could maintain a sufficient amount of metropolitan force in the colony to suppress potential uprisings or to parry the threats of would-be interlopers. The problem with this solution was that it was likely to be so expensive that it would seriously negate any benefits that derived from possessing the colony. The more logical alternative was to mollify colonial hostility to the extent that it would not be driven into rebellion or to make common cause with a foreign power.

Thus a number of variables formed part of the complex situation that defined the dependencies. At one level was the degree to which a given metropolitan power felt compelled to make concessions to its colonies. Where these were sufficiently liberal they interacted with the nature of commodity production to generate a situation in which development, as well as growth, was possible. For, as the dominant tendency was in the direction of a nonservile labor force, there came into existence the possibility of economic diversification and the creation of a market economy. Therefore, unlike the peripheries, where servile relations of production precluded evolution in the direction of development, dependencies were not condemned to a similar fate.

## IRELAND

Of the three dependencies, Ireland was most affected by its status. "Through its effective subjugation of Ireland," writes Colm Regan, "the English state . . . ensured that developments on the two islands would be inseparably linked."[2] Two factors were instrumental in determining the nature of this relationship. One was the proximity of Ireland, which made it relatively easy for England to exercise its military domination. This proximity, in turn, made England wary of Ireland as a potential base from which a foreign power might launch an invasion. The second was that because of the similar topography and climate of the two islands, England feared Ireland as a potential competitor. Therefore, it was deemed necessary to impose a vast array of legislation designed to minimize Ireland's ability to compete with its metropole. As a result, during the seventeenth and eighteenth centuries, both the social and economic structures of the island were changed radically. Nevertheless, in terms of productivity, by the end of the eighteenth century, Ireland was considerably wealthier than it had ever been.

There were many distinctive features about the Irish Middle Ages. Dating from the Norman conquest of the twelfth century, many parts of the island were introduced to a rigorous regime. The peasant could be "bought and sold with the manor . . . [was] subject to heavy manorial services and tributes in kind . . . [and was] denied a legal interest in the soil."[3] Nevertheless, by the fourteenth century, Anglo-Norman control had diminished significantly and the feudal system itself had begun to disintegrate. Thereafter the island lapsed into a period of anarchy during which it has been said that it was ungoverned and ungovernable. This period was partly responsible for the economic backwardness of Ireland. While material techniques were being improved elsewhere, primitive methods of production remained in force in Ireland, which was a relatively underdeveloped part of a relatively undeveloped Europe.[4]

During the sixteenth century, hostile relations between England and Ireland once again became intense. Although English suzerainty over Ireland had never been renounced, its own internal difficulties had obliged England to abdicate its authority in practice if not in theory. With the restoration of central authority under the Tudors, England once again turned its attention to Ireland. As he had done in England, Henry VIII, who assumed the title of King of Ireland, dismantled the established Catholic church. He proceeded to found, as the official religion, the Church of Ireland, which was modeled on the church he created in England. Both the religious issue and the colonial nature of English rule led to endemic rebellion during the Tudor era. The Tudors, whose administration in Ireland was extremely inept, responded with harsh repression. While their armies lived off of the land, they often tried to starve the populace into submission.[5]

Toward the end of the century, full-scale rebellion against the crown broke out. In 1590 the Gaelic Irish, seeking to take advantage of England's heavy commitments elsewhere, staged what became known as the Ulster rebellion. It would not be until 1603 that James I successfully brought the uprising to an end. Significantly, he received a great deal of support from the "Old English," that is, those who were the descendants of the Norman conquerors of a bygone era. As opposed to the Gaelic Irish, who maintained an ultramontagne viewpoint, the Old English, while retaining their belief in Roman Catholicism, remained loyal to the English monarchy. That crown, however, fearing that a Catholic Ireland might one day be used as a base by a hostile Catholic monarch, decided to import large numbers of lowland Scots. These sturdy Presbyterians, it was thought, would provide a bulwark against the pretensions of Catholicism.

Rather than resolving the problem, the English action exacerbated it and in the process created strange bedfellows. The anti-Catholic legislation that London promulgated was imposed not only on the Gaelic community but on the Old English as well. Thus the English drove the former loyalists into the camp of the opposition. When civil war broke out in England in the 1640s, Irish Catholics revolted both because of existing legislation and because of their fear that a victory by the Protestant forces that dominated the parliamentary cause would bring additional repression. Quite paradoxically, they found an ally in Charles, who was so desperate for funds and supporters that he agreed to reinstate Catholicism as the official religion in Ireland once he was restored to the throne. These hopes, however, were dashed in 1652 when Oliver Cromwell at the head of parliamentary forces brutally suppressed the Irish attempt at liberation.[6]

The final resolution of the destiny of Ireland, however, would not be decided until the last decade of the seventeenth century. Once again the island would find itself enmeshed in English politics. When the "Glorious Revolution" forced James II to flee to Ireland, he sought out Catholic support. He promised to redress their grievances if they embraced his cause. Although they indeed rallied to his side, their hopes were once again dashed by the crushing defeat suffered at the Battle of the Boyne River in 1690. James Beckett observes that the Protestant victory "meant that in future the Protestant minority would rule in Ireland. The power of the Roman Catholic nobility and gentry . . . was now to be overthrown."[7] James Godwin shows how decisive the changes were to be with his apt analogy that the Treaty of Limerick, which ended the conflict, "marked the end of Old Ireland as completely as Appomattox meant the end of the Old South."[8]

The cycle of Catholic revolts had economic underpinnings, as well as those of a religious, social, and political nature. For with each defeat, the Catholics lost more land. During the Elizabethan rebellions, the lands of those killed in the revolts were forfeited. This policy was followed by James I, who confiscated Catholic lands to make way for his Scottish settlers. Similarly, one of the incentives Cromwell provided was that his victorious troops were to be given ample land to resettle in Ireland. A contemporary summed up the problem when he suggested that "there must be new discoveries of a new Ireland for the old will not serve to satisfy" the demands that were being made on it.[9] One solution to the problem, although it was not particularly satisfactory to the indigenous population, was a dramatic reduction in the amount of land owned by Catholics. Already down to 60 percent in 1641, it diminished to 22 percent in 1699, 14 percent in 1703, and finally reached a low point of 5 percent in 1776.[10]

Although when inverted the figures for decreasing Catholic landownership demonstrate the increases in Protestant holdings, they do not indicate the changing structure of landownership. For not only did Protestant possessions continue to increase, they also tended to become concentrated in fewer hands. For example, when many of Cromwell's disbanded soldiers chose either not to settle in Ireland or proved incapable of making the land work, they sold out to speculators, who, in turn, sold consolidated holdings to the English gentry. Although some of the purchasers relocated to Ireland, many chose the life of an absentee landlord and lived off their rents. Patrick O'Farrell captures the bitter irony of the situation when he notes that "the Irish occupants lived in a land they no longer owned and the English owners owned a land in which they did not live."[11]

Irish Catholics not only lost their land but suffered from the double contradiction that was imposed upon indigenous populations in a dependency. Eager to placate the Protestant settlers, England allowed them to reduce the Catholics to second-class citizens. With respect to internal Irish affairs, London watched passively while the exclusively Protestant Irish Parliament passed reams of anti-Catholic legislation. Just one year after the Battle of the Boyne, for example, it was decided that Catholics could no longer sit in Parliament. In 1727 they were denied the vote. Subsequently, Catholics not only were prohibited from buying land but were condemned to the ownership of short-term leases. Discrimination reached the point where they were banned from entering the professions and even denied the opportunity to obtain an education.[12]

On the other hand, London was in no way passive with respect to issues that affected its own interests. The second contradiction, therefore, was that, though the Anglo-Irish were political allies, their economic progress was viewed from Whitehall with some trepidation. As a result, London passed legislation designed to reduce the threat of competition. Although cattle had been Ireland's most lucrative export, in 1667 cattle shipments to England were banned. In 1699, to diminish competition with one of England's major industries, the export of woolen cloth was completely forbidden, and raw wool could only be sold to England. With respect to manufacture, countless undertakings, some as petty as the prohibition on the production of glass, were forbidden. At the same time, tariffs were maintained at extremely low levels to ensure that English goods could circulate freely. Moreover, Ireland was unique insofar as it was the only territory ruled by Great Britain that was denied the right of free circulation of its goods within the empire.[13]

Despite the discriminatory legislation, the Irish economy grew significantly during the eighteenth century. This was largely the result of certain loopholes intentionally left in the Navigation Acts. Ireland, for example, was permitted to send provisions to the West Indies. Consequently, the exports of beef, pork, and butter to the sugar-producing islands increased tremendously. So, too, did the export of linen. Not perceiving it as a threat to any vested interest in England, London allowed the growth of what became a significant Irish linen industry. The growth in the economy is demonstrated by the increase in the value of trade from £63,000 in 1700 to £226,000 in 1776. At the same, time exports quadrupled and imports trebled.[14] All of which led Beckett to conclude that "compared with its own past, Ireland was much richer than it had been."[15]

In the midst of the growth of the eighteenth century, there were additional structural changes in the Irish landscape. Dating from the year 1757, England again agreed to allow the import of Irish cattle. This reversal of policy, occasioned by the changing structure of agrarian production in England, had a significant impact in Ireland, where landlords sought to convert to pasture. Between 1750 and 1780, an additional million acres were converted from tillage to grazing. This conversion, however, involved the rearrangement of the Irish plantation. To make the most efficient use of the land, landlords not only sought to engross their holdings but also to create consolidated estates.[16]

The victims of the new trends were the Irish peasants. Having been denied the right of primogeniture and obliged to accept short-term leases, many found that their rents were constantly being increased. A significant portion could not meet the new demands and were evicted. This is a prime example of the difference between a dependency and a periphery: In the latter, with labor power at a premium, the logic of the system is to bind the worker to the soil. In Ireland, where cattle made extensive use not of labor but of land, the logic of the system was the eviction of the peasant. Those tenants who clung tenaciously to their holdings did so despite their being charged rents on the basis of the value of the land if it were given over to pasture.[17] Under these circumstances, peasant immiseration was enormous. Their very survival had come to depend on the amazing nutritional qualities of the potato, only a few cultivated acres of which could provide a large family with all that it could eat. Most of the Irish peasantry ate nothing else.[18]

The social distribution of the surplus product was extremely skewed. Almost all of the spoils of the Irish plantation were consumed by the Anglo-Irish gentry. David Large notes that "it is striking to observe how very little of the rent collected from an Irish estate found its way back to it for improvements."[19] What is more, much of Ireland's wealth was diverted toward England. Among the factors responsible for this situation were shipping charges, the pension list, and the unfavorable balance of payments between the two countries. Most of all, however, the drain resulted from the direct repatriation of Irish rents to England.[20]

The Ireland that had emerged by the late eighteenth century had been changed fundamentally. Viewed from the perspective of London, it represented a textbook case of the manipulation of a colony by its metropolis. Although on the surface it was richer than it had been, its increasing wealth disguised the distortions that had been created. More importantly, Ireland was unable to pursue ends that might have proved most beneficial. In assessing the situation, Francis James noted that "British mercantile restrictions kept Ireland from realizing her full potential and probably warped her development."[21] That is, in fact, what the English presence was designed to do. Regan neatly summed up the problem when he wrote that "the Irish economy was first dismantled and then rebuilt to suit the needs of England."[22]

When the question why processes developed as they did is raised, England's desire to make Ireland into a dependency should be seen as the prime mover. Religion played such a prominent role that it is easy to confuse its impact. The fundamental struggle between England and Ireland was not one of religion. Had it been, measures would have been taken to convert the defeated populace. What took place, on the contrary, was not an attempt at proselytization but an effort to maintain the status quo. Beckett argues forcibly that "in this long struggle religion had determined the side on which a man stood, but the struggle had been one for land and power." He continues with the observation that the main intent of the English had been to "make sure that [Catholics] were kept in a position of social, economic, and political inferiority."[23] In this way England and its Anglo-Irish allies were able to take maximum advantage of the possibilities inherent in the situation.

## TRANSITION IN SPANISH AMERICA

Ideally, Spain would have liked to dominate its colonies as thoroughly as England manipulated Ireland. To this end, it, too, issued laws designed to regulate Spanish America in ways that would benefit the metropole. Yet it was easier to promulgate discriminatory legislation than to enforce it. Spanish America spanned all of South America, a significant portion of North America, and parts of the Caribbean; its sheer size militated against effective regulation. Moreover, whereas only the Irish Sea separated England from its dependency, a vast ocean stood between Spain and its colonies. There were also powerful incentives against attempting to enforce the law too rigorously, as often the most influential members of colonial society were the most guilty of evading the law. If only intuitively, Spain understood that the loyalty to be gained from leaving loopholes open was worth more than the benefits that would have been attained by closing them.[24] As a result, the practice of empire was very different from the theory—so much so, in fact, that after tenuous beginnings, Spanish America was able to develop a dynamic of its own, which differed radically from the course that was imposed on Ireland.

By the middle of the sixteenth century, Spanish America had developed certain characteristics that would remain prominent features of colonial life. The period immediately following the conquests of Mexico and Peru was dominated by fortune seeking. Would-be conquistadores fanned out throughout the continent hoping to duplicate the feats of Cortés and Pizarro. When eventually it became obvious that no new El Dorados existed, most drifted back either to Mexico, Peru, or Spain itself. Those who remained in America generally had to satisfy themselves with more modest incomes than they had envisaged in their lofty dreams. Thus, while Mexico and Peru became the dual foci of Spanish America, the rest was almost completely ignored. Although he is writing specifically about Venezuela, Roland Hussey's comments are equally applicable to the other neglected parts of the empire. "Once the chaos of the conquest period subsided," he notes, "little more was heard of it in the general history for nearly two centuries. It received few colonists and less attention from Spain."[25]

As it was to do throughout the colonial period, mining centered in Mexico and Peru dominated the economy of Spanish America. Although much gold was plundered during the conquest of the Aztecs and the Incas, little more was to be forthcoming. In essence the gold that had been uncovered represented the hoard of centuries rather than the existence of significant additional deposits. Although gold was mined throughout the colonial era in New Granada, its mines and alluvial streams ranked a distant third behind those of Peru and Mexico in terms of the value of their output. In Peru and Mexico, however, the overwhelming emphasis was on silver. In Mexico most of the mines were located in the arid north, many hundreds of miles to the north of the capital. In Peru, where the silver output was even larger, mines were to be found throughout, even though Peruvian production was dominated by Potosí, a seemingly inexhaustible supplier that was located at eleven thousand feet above sea level in the barren altiplano.[26]

The structure of Spanish American society that developed during this era was strongly influenced by the demographic catastrophe that befell the Amerindian population following the conquest. The statistics provided by Borah and Cook depict the bone-chilling extent of the tragedy. They suggest that the Indian population of the Central Valley of Mexico, which stood at approximately 25 million at the time of conquest, was reduced to 1.9 million by 1580 and that it continued to decline until it finally leveled off in the mid-seventeenth century. One might be tempted to disbelieve such startling statistics and to label them fanciful if the phenomenon had been reported only in Mesoamerica. Yet similar conclusions are reached by researchers working in other areas. For Peru, for example, Noble David Cook calculates that by 1580 a preconquest population of nine million had fallen to one million. Although statistical data for New Granada remain less adequate, it has been suggested that the rate of mortality was even greater. Nowhere was the phenomenon more pervasive than in the Caribbean, whose preconquest population of many millions was, for all intents and purposes, completely annihilated.[27]

Several factors contributed to this unique human tragedy. Although the decimation of the population from which they made their living would have been the last thing that the Spanish wanted, directly and indirectly they bore responsibility. In many respects, however, it was an unwitting contribution. In the Caribbean, for example, most Spaniards were unaware that the Indian was unaccustomed to the regimentation that was imposed by the harsh labor demands and the psychological impact of the conquest, which robbed many of the will to continue to exist. Nor did they realize that by denying protein to the Indian population they were doing irreparable damage to Indian health. Overwork, despair, and changes in diet, however, could in no way equal the ravages of epidemic disease. For the Spanish brought with them previously unknown maladies. Smallpox and pneumonia, to name just two, were illnesses alien to the Americas and for which not even a partial immunity had been acquired. Disease spread like brushfire, smallpox reaching the Andean plateau several years before the first conquistador had ventured inland from the coast.[28]

The massive Indian mortality contributed to the process of Spaniards' establishing themselves in the countryside. Although the initial European conquerors demonstrated a strong preference for urban living, two factors associated with the demise of the Indian population altered the situation. When the settlers could no longer subsist from the diminishing Indian tributes, it became necessary to engage directly in production. Second, land increasingly became available. Where entire Indian communities died, it could simply be confiscated. Another way of acquiring land was via purchase. Although imperial legislation stipulated that most Indian land was communal and hence inviolable, the Indians became so financially troubled by the exigencies imposed by crown and settler that there was no other way of meeting the demands made upon them. Thus, in spite of the law, they agreed to alienate their lands to a Spanish population that was equally willing to ignore the legal technicalities of the situation. Often the settlers went beyond the nuances of legality and simply seized the lands of downtrodden and defenseless villagers. Indeed, it has been suggested that this was the most prevalent means of land acquisition. The tradition arose that those who were found guilty of illegally expropriating Indian lands were condemned to a punishment no more severe than the payment of a fine. There were thus few disincentives to dissuade the Spanish settler from adopting this course of action.[29]

The land was put to a variety of uses. In the tropical lowlands, plantations were established. Although some of their produce was shipped to Europe, more was consumed in the colonies themselves. As is indicated by François Chevalier's statement to the effect that plantations and other forms of "intensively cultivated lands were like tiny islands scattered here and there," plantations were comparatively less important than they were elsewhere in the Americas and were responsible for only a fraction of total output.[30] The *huertas* were more indicative of the normal pattern. Medium-sized farms that grew up in the environs of the urban areas, their principal function was to supply the towns with wheat, maize, and dairy products. Meat for the market was generally produced on *estancias*, which were sprawling cattle ranches located in the more distant countryside. Because the sheep and cattle that were imported from Europe multiplied very rapidly on the virgin pasture of the Americas, animals became so plentiful that soon cattle came to be valued more for their hides than for their contribution to the Spanish diet.[31]

The most intriguing form of landholding, however, was the unique estate known as the hacienda. How haciendas came into being and whence came the *hacenderos* who ran them is a subject that has been much debated. Nevertheless, it can be stated categorically that some reached enormous proportions. One in Chile is reputed to have occupied a valley that was seventy miles long by forty miles wide. Although in the sixteenth century the hacienda had a market orientation, much of the estate was left completely uncultivated. One rationale that has been presented for the engrossing of such vast tracts of land without making intensive use of it is that in this way the number of potential competitors was significantly reduced. Another factor that stands out concerning the hacienda is its flexibility. It became institutionalized throughout Spanish America and was able to survive despite the vicissitudes that might be experienced by other sectors in the colonial world.[32]

Throughout the sixteenth and early seventeenth centuries, the question of labor remained fundamental to the colonial economy. The early conquistadores established the system known as *encomienda*. Groups of Indians, who were assigned to individual Spaniards, were obliged to pay tribute to their *encomenderos*. Although these grants conferred no title to land, as is evidenced by the allotment of Hernán Cortés, which consisted of the services of twenty-three thousand adult males, an *encomienda* could prove to be quite lucrative. The Spanish crown, however, was never happy with the system, both because of its desire to protect its Indian wards and also because it concentrated too much wealth and power in the hands of the settlers. The crown was also influenced by the polemics emanating from certain elements in the church that petitioned to have the system abolished because of the great abuses practiced by the *encomenderos*.

After years of vacillation, in 1542 the crown promulgated the New Laws. This legislation was designed to eliminate the harshest aspects of the system and to diminish the influence of the *encomenderos*. The policymakers, however, underestimated the degree to which the settlers were wedded to their brand of neofeudalism. Although the New Laws were greeted with hostility in all parts of the Americas, in Peru, where the viceroy foolishly tried to implement them without modification, there was a full-scale rebellion launched by some of the most prominent conquistadores. Although the crown was obliged to make significant compromises in order to temper settler hostility, the issue was resolved not because of a trial of strength between the two sides but because of massive Indian mortality, which so reduced the number of Indians who were required to perform *encomienda* service that the *encomenderos* could no longer live in the fashion to which they aspired. Thus, although the institution lingered longer in some areas than in others, for all intents and purposes *encomienda* ceased to be a major factor in most regions before the end of the sixteenth century. What was of more lasting importance, however, was that determined settler opposition warned the crown to be wary of imposing extremely unpopular legislation.[33]

The crown also established a system that in most regions was known as *repartimiento*, although in Peru the traditional Inca term of *mita* continued in force. Essentially, it was a system of forced labor, whose worst effects were hardly mitigated by the crown's stated policy that it was to be performed in the public interest. All Indians, except certain nobles and those assigned in *encomienda*, were subject to conscription. Thus, at all times a portion of almost every community would find itself serving one Spanish interest or another. How the system functioned varied significantly among the regions. At one extreme, an individual might only be called on to perform one week of work. At the other, there was the hated *mita* of Potosí, which required the worker to remain for as long as a year and to perform the most arduous tasks. As the agency responsible for the allotment of labor, however, the crown increasingly found itself hard-pressed to satisfy the multiple requests for laborers. Both public and private interests sought government help in supplying labor in an environment of extreme shortage. By the first few decades of the seventeenth century, as the number of petitioners continued to increase while the labor supply decreased, the system in most areas became so unmanageable that it, too, was allowed to die a natural death.[34]

Yet another means of procuring labor was through the institution of debt peonage. For most Indians, the burdens of colonial society were enormous. Where a facsimile of community life continued to prevail, an Indian remained responsible for the age-old dues associated with the maintenance of the traditional social fabric yet was also obligated to pay tribute either to an *encomendero* or directly to the crown. In many cases, because of the inadequacy of census data and because the tribute was imposed on the community as a whole, an individual might also be obliged to make up the deficit that was left because of the death of neighbors. Performing virtually unremunerated *repartimiento* labor only added to an Indian's woes. Many tried to get out of this intolerable system by contracting a debt with a *patron*, which meant that they were bound to his estate until the debt was paid. Thus, just as Chinese and European peasants had recommended themselves to a powerful lord during times of distress, Indian peasants sought out a *señor* who could shield them from the worst rigors of colonial society. Although it was once thought that these poor villagers had been entrapped by unscrupulous landowners, Charles Gibson notes that, at least during the later sixteenth and seventeenth centuries, "the accumulation . . . of other pressures upon Indian society had rendered . . . coercion unnecessary. . . . The objective of workers was not to escape but to enlarge indebtedness."[35]

In view of what may be called the general labor crisis, one might think that the Spanish would have turned to the wholesale importation of African slaves. Indeed, significant numbers of slaves were imported. These were usually concentrated in coastal Peru, New Granada, the Caribbean coast of South America, Hispaniola, and parts of the Mexican lowlands.[36] Nevertheless, when the vastness of Spanish America is taken into consideration, the numbers imported were very small in comparison with those brought to Brazil or the Caribbean.

Part of the problem stemmed from the ambivalence of the Spanish crown. Although, on the one hand, it wanted to protect its Indian wards from being overexploited, on the other, it feared the impact of having large numbers of African slaves in the midst of its colonies. Therefore, through the *asiento* agreements that it bestowed upon various suppliers, the number of slaves that it agreed to have imported was always limited by a quota. A seemingly more important, though rarely mentioned, factor was the inappropriateness of African slavery in the Spanish American situation. With the exception of the placer mining in the tropics of New Granada, Africans could not be used in mining because most of the silver deposits were located in cool to frigid climates; experimentation showed that they died in droves when exposed to these unfamiliar rigors. Throughout most of the rest of Spanish America, slavery as an institution proved equally inappropriate, for the commodities that they would have produced did not demand a sufficient labor input to justify their expense.

Despite problems in securing labor, the economy that evolved during the sixteenth and early seventeenth centuries was basically a prosperous one. Although a large number of commodities, both necessities and luxuries, were imported, the silver bonanza was able to finance them with little difficulty. Increasingly, however, Spanish Americans themselves came to produce more of the goods that were needed domestically. The stigma that was attached to manual labor in Spain was much less evident in America. In his study of Peru, James Lockhart notes that the American of Spanish descent performed a wide variety of menial tasks, and D. A. Brading observes that "the Spaniard resident in America [became] a type of man that did not exist in Spain itself."[37]

Production was buoyed by a vibrant domestic market. Even though much of the countryside was settled during the latter part of the sixteenth century, many Spaniards preferred to spend part or all of their time in towns. As a result, Spanish America was the most urbanized of the colonial territories. Towns and cities, in turn, consumed the produce of the rural areas. Mining regions also attracted goods from distant places. In Mexico the mines were located mainly in the arid north, meaning virtually everything had to be imported from the central and southern zones. Similarly, in Peru barren Potosí, with its one hundred thousand inhabitants, had to be supplied by a tortuous ascent from the coast.[38]

By the third decade of the seventeenth century, however, a depression that was to last throughout most of the remainder of the century had become pervasive throughout Spanish America. The prime mover in the downturn was a drastic decrease in the amount of silver that was mined.

Although the slump arrived earlier in Mexico than in Peru, by midcentury output had fallen everywhere. The severity of the crisis is demonstrated by E. J. Hamilton's figures, which show that production in the decade 1651–1660 was only one-sixth of what it had been between 1591 and 1600.[39] As severe contraction set in in the mining sector, the shortage of bullion and the depression in the market adversely affected many endeavors. This was especially true of agriculture, which in many areas ceased to have a commercial orientation. According to P. J. Bakewell, "haciendas during the mining decline became self-sufficient units" that had only marginal contact with the outside world. Both overseas and regional trade also decreased greatly. This was especially true of the more remote regions, which virtually lost contact with Europe.[40]

An older view blamed the depression on the decline in the Indian population and the resultant labor shortage, but more recent research suggests that the Spanish government's policies were largely at fault. Speaking principally about Mexico, Woodrow Borah blamed "the precipitate and sustained decrease in the Indian population" for a decrease in the supply of labor to the mines and hence a decline in productivity.[41] Although it is true that many endeavors were adversely affected by shortages of labor, Brading notes that the mines in Mexico never employed more than eleven thousand workers at any given time. Thus, in light of the relatively small labor requirements, he concludes that the population decline was unlikely to have caused the crisis.

Rather, he contends that the crisis was related to the problem of the supply of mercury, an agent that was essential in the amalgamation process for producing silver. The crown had insisted that the distribution of mercury be maintained as a royal monopoly, partly because it provided a fairly accurate barometer of how much silver was being extracted from the mines. A given quantity of mercury would produce a fixed amount of silver, allowing the government to demand its royal fifth on the basis of the amount of mercury it advanced. The crown continued to supply mercury, often on credit, even to marginal producers. Because of its obsessive concern with maximizing the number of producers, the government did not discriminate between those who were likely to repay and those who were more of a risk. When those who worked marginal claims increasingly became unable to repay their debts to the mercury miners, many of the latter were driven out of business.[42]

Mercury supplies were at the core of the problem in Peru as well. In this case, however, the cause of the difficulties can be traced to the *asiento* that had been granted for the exploitation of the Huancavelica mercury deposits. Over time, the guild that operated the mines had not reinvested its profits in improvements, so that when machinery began to deteriorate at the same time that deeper-level mining was necessary, it could no longer satisfy the demands of the silver miners.[43] The decline in Peru, nevertheless, arrived somewhat later and was never quite as severe as it was in Mexico, where the Spanish government, through its efforts to increase the output of silver by supplying all and sundry with mercury, had achieved just the opposite result.

The policies of the Spanish government with respect to other areas of the economy were no more enlightened. In order to ensure that it received its proper share of tax revenue, it insisted on an archaic system of trade, which decreed that Seville was the only port in Spain that could trade with the Indies and that only Vera Cruz and Porto Bello in the Americas could ship goods directly to Europe. Not only did a system of limiting the number of ports have damaging effects on commerce, it has been argued that the Spanish government did not even choose the best ports. Yet, strongly influenced by the merchant communities of Seville and Lima, both of which had a vested interest in the maintenance of the status quo, the government clung tenaciously to its outdated system. Although everyone suffered from the higher costs that were engendered, the main victims were regions such as Central America, which were far removed from the points of entry and exit and hence impeded from participation in the transatlantic economy.[44]

Within America itself, the rules were no less vexatious. Some intracolonial trade was permitted; commerce between other colonies was prohibited. Similarly, seemingly with little rhyme and even less reason, the government interfered with production. For example, whereas it decreed that Mexican sugar could not be exported to Europe, it completely banned the growing of coffee in New Granada and tobacco in Venezuela. An assessment is provided by Clarence Haring, who notes that "Spanish policies toward colonial industries lacked the clearly defined outlines one associates with . . . mercantilistic ideas. . . . Indeed it is difficult to discover any characteristic policy at all, unless it be one of blind opportunism."[45]

The depression was also likely to have been fed by the taxation policy of the crown. For if the crown showed any ingenuity at all, it was in the realm of inventing ways of raising revenue. It not only charged high import and export duties but imposed taxes on the transshipment of goods. The royal fifth, a 20 percent impost on silver and gold production, was another principal source of revenue. In addition, there were taxes on agriculture, sales, and special levies to pay for the warships that accompanied the annual treasure fleet from the Americas to Spain. Via the mechanism of *asientos*, the government sold contracts that provided the bearer with monopoly privileges in such endeavors as the supply of slaves, the mining of mercury, and a myriad of lesser undertakings. It also began to sell documents that legalized or pardoned a variety of illegal acts. Even most public offices were put up for auction to the highest bidder.[46] Although the crown often justified some of its revenue-raising measures on the basis that they were temporary expedients that were necessary for addressing specific problems, these impositions were rarely rescinded. "Once the impecunious Spanish crown discovered a means of raising money," writes Murdo MacLeod, "it could seldom afford to give it up until the source was milked dry."[47]

Despite government policies that in retrospect seem to have been destined to inhibit growth, by the end of the seventeenth century, there was an economic upturn that would last for more than a century. Once again the mining sector played the role of the prime mover. The revival was based partly on the discovery of new mines and partly on a resolution of the thorny question of mercury supply. Several factors about eighteenth-century growth, however, distinguished it from the prosperity of the sixteenth century. Whereas in the sixteenth century Spanish America was virtually synonymous with Mexico and Peru, by the eighteenth century growth was experienced throughout the region. Perhaps more importantly, the political economy was changing in ways that suggested the possibility of a breakthrough toward a developed society.

The mining industry of the eighteenth century differed in many ways from that of the previous era. Especially in Mexico, a number of new mines were discovered. Thus, whereas Peru had previously been the leading producer, the pendulum swung heavily in the favor of Mexico. In fact, the mine fields of Guanajuato alone came to produce as much as all of South America. Production levels soared to the extent that they far surpassed the peaks of sixteenth-century production. The increase in output was based partly on improvements in technique, which allowed mining at deeper levels than had previously been the case.[48]

The increase in output was also the result of a change in the system of supplying mercury. During the second half of the seventeenth century, merchants began to purchase mercury clandestinely. Unlike the crown, which had attempted to supply everyone, the merchants dealt only with those who were likely to repay, that is, those who worked the better claims. As silver production began to increase, merchants were more able to function in the open. Eventually, the government, which was benefiting from higher tax revenues, gave legal sanction to their operations. The paradox of the situation was that in order to maximize production the government had advanced mercury on credit, which ultimately led to a reduction in output. The merchants, on the other hand, in order to maximize profit, dealt with only those whose claims merited confidence. This, in turn, led to a tremendous increase in output.[49]

Both agriculture and craft production benefited from the ripple effect of the mining boom. Bakewell notes that haciendas "re-emerged in their commercial form once an upturn had been reached."[50] Brading estimates that in Mexico alone there were 4,945 haciendas that produced for the market.[51] The process was accompanied by significant increases in land values, which sometimes jumped by as much as 300 percent. Landowners profited by being able to raise rents precipitously. Growth in agriculture was mirrored in nonagrarian sectors as well. Although a wide variety of crafts came to be practiced, textile production was overwhelmingly the most important. Depending upon the region, wool, linen, cotton, leather, and even silk were manufactured. Especially in Mexico and Ecuador, production often took place in *obrajes*, workshops sometimes located in large buildings that housed many workers.[52]

Production for the market was aided by the trends in demography. In most regions the Indian population began to recover after the middle of the seventeenth century. There was also a large increase in the white population. Whereas it is estimated that there were 650 thousand people of full Spanish descent in 1650, toward the late 1700s, the number had risen to more than 3 million. The largest jump, however, was within the group that has been referred to as "Homo Americanus," the dazzling array of mixtures among Indian, white, and African that occurred over the centuries. By the end of the eighteenth century, it is estimated that almost fourteen million people were actively involved in the American economy.[53]

Whereas growth had once been limited to Mexico and Peru, by the eighteenth century most regions in Spanish America developed the production of commodities for export. For example, Chile began to export hides, wine, wheat, copper, and textiles. Although still in its embryonic stages of growth, Argentina produced hides and salt meat. Taking advantage of its tropical lowlands, Venezuela produced tobacco, cocoa, indigo, and cotton, while its neighbor, New Granada, continued to export gold. Central America, which had been an economic backwater through the centuries, joined in the general trend by growing indigo and manufacturing cochineal. Even Cuba, for centuries part of the forgotten Caribbean, was converted from subsistence ranching into a producer of tobacco and sugar. Thus virtually all of the Americas came to participate in a growing regional economy.[54]

The term *regional economy* is appropriate because despite Spanish attempts at manipulation, intra-American trade continued to grow, while the proportion of American goods destined for Europe decreased. The general phenomenon is evidenced by the continued increase in the sales tax, which was imposed on goods made and sold in America, and the simultaneous decline in the customs revenue, derived from goods imported from Europe. A sampling of Venezuelan exports illustrates the changes that were taking place. In the last decade of the seventeenth century, while it exported two million reales worth of cocoa to Spain, it sent seventeen million to Mexico. Peru as well imported most of its manufactures from Mexico and paid for them in wine, silver, and mercury. Increasingly, bullion was retained in the colonies to be invested in American development rather than being remitted to Europe. John Lynch summed up the situation when he wrote that "living more for itself, America gave less to Spain. . . . The American economies . . . were developing and disengaging themselves from their primitive dependence on the mother country. This was the first emancipation of Spanish America."[55]

By the eighteenth century, because of American growth and Spain's restrictive policies, smuggling had virtually become a way of life. This was equally true of the prohibited intercolonial trade as it was of the more odious, from the point of view of the Spanish government, contraband with foreigners. Although the very nature of illicit commerce renders it unquantifiable, it should be noted that all sources agree that it reached significant proportions. The Dutch island of Curaçao served mainly as a base for trading with northern South America. By midcentury, French ships were doubling Cape Horn to engage in contraband trade with Chile. The English, however, were more ubiquitous. Jamaica was used as a base from which to deal with Central America and Mexico. They also used their Brazilian connection in order to infiltrate the Rio de La Plata and hence to tap the silver of Upper Peru. Moreover, the *asiento* of the slave trade that England won in 1715 gave it legal entry into Spanish ports, which it then proceeded to use for illegal trade. All of this, of course, was done with the connivance and complicity of Spanish settlers and local officials. The resort to smuggling has been described as being "almost universal."[56]

By the eighteenth century, the structure of the organization of trade had changed considerably. Not only had intra-American and clandestine commerce taken on great significance, but preeminence in the transatlantic trade had been assumed by American-based merchants. In its earliest phases, merchants in Seville, who were often backed by Genoese capital, had dominated the transatlantic connection; the only sphere in which American-based traders reigned supreme was the frequently lucrative trade via Manila to the East. As time passed, however, they were able to garner larger and larger shares of the European trade as well. Although the social norms of the day dictated that only Spaniards born in Spain could enter the merchant community, they were rooted firmly in America and their primary links were with the American, as opposed to the Spanish, economy.[57]

In fact, by the eighteenth century, this merchant capital had become heavily involved in American production. This phenomenon pervaded the economy of virtually every region. For example, the merchants of Lima, Santiago, Caracas, and Guatemala City took part in the dominant industries of their respective colonies.[58] Merchant capital became engaged in a wide range of endeavors, both in agriculture and industry. Nowhere, however, was it more prominent and more successful than in mining. Referring to the Mexican situation, John Lynch notes how "the profits from mining were largely escaping the control of the [mine owners] themselves, with the result that they had insufficient margin for reinvestment at a time when operations were posing new problems." It was the merchants of Mexico City who stepped into the breach by providing the necessary funds. As a result, they were able to lay claim to the lion's share of the profits.[59]

Urban-based merchants also dominated rural trade and organized rural production. In an ironic twist, their agents were the very government officials who were appointed to administer the rural areas. So lucrative were the spoils that those who obtained the position of *corregidor* often purchased the office by paying several times the salary it yielded. Yet once they were installed, they were in an ideal position to act as intermediaries between the merchants and the rural inhabitants. Because their office enabled them to prevent competitors from having any contact with the rural population, they enjoyed both monopolistic and monopsonic privileges. Speaking of Peru, Karen Spalding notes that the *corregidores* "commissioned cloth which they marketed with urban based merchants. . . . They [also] had a monopoly on the sale of wine, mules, and other goods."[60]

By the eighteenth century, most forms of coerced labor had been superseded by either wage labor or free tenancies. Increasingly, however, both workers and tenants came to be dominated by the interests of merchant capital. In most areas *encomienda* and *repartimiento* no longer existed. Although slavery as an institution survived, it had become even less important than in the past. In lieu of physical coercion, the most advanced regions depended on a free labor force. For example, by the later stages of the century, the region known as the *bajío* (lowlands) had become the most economically advanced part of Mexico. It was calculated that 59 percent of the noncommunal Indian population were classified as workers.[61] In Chile, to provide another example, most of the population were categorized as *inquilinos* (tenants). These were tenants who were subjected to ever-increasing rents by their landlords. In Ecuador, production was dominated by *obrajes*, whose free workers received only a very small remuneration for their labor. Once again, however, the mining sector provided the prototype of the trends of the day. Traditionally workers in Mexican mines had been entitled to a *partido*, that is, a profit-sharing arrangement that guaranteed them part of the ore that was mined. During the eighteenth century, the mine owners were able to eliminate the *partido* and thereby to reduce the workers to full-scale proletarians.[62] Similarly, in Peru, where free and coerced labor existed side by side, increasing amounts of labor were being demanded, whereas remuneration was being reduced. Enrique Tandeter goes so far as to argue that "the very survival of the [mining] industry depended upon the reproduction" of increasingly inequitable surplus extraction.[63]

Throughout the eighteenth century, merchant capital not only expanded the scope and range of its activities but also engaged in improvements in the productive capacity of the economy. Mexican agricultural output increased because capital was used in improving farms and in land reclamation. In Peru it was used to construct new irrigation systems. Mining, however, was the most important endeavor in which capital was used to finance an increase in the productive base. Having established its superiority over labor and hence its profit margin, capital felt free to invest in the future. The digging of deeper shafts and the large-scale reclamation of flooded mines were just two of the ways in which capital sought to increase yields.[64]

The growth of the eighteenth century may have led some historians to a premature optimism. Bakewell refers to the Mexican economy as being "plainly of a capitalist nature."[65] Similarly, Lynch speaks of "the agrarian capitalism of Peru."[66] Nevertheless, although great strides were made during the era, there still remained obstacles to completing the journey toward full-scale development. One problem was that of partiable inheritance, which meant that capital was fractionalized with the passage of each generation. Brading notes that "a prolific wife was almost a guarantee that a family would lose its estate."[67] In theory, this problem could have been circumvented by resorting to the device of entail, which guaranteed that a property would not be subdivided. This right could be extended only to properties that were not mortgaged, however, so the vast majority of

American states did not qualify. The situation was exacerbated in that in most instances the mortgages were held by the church, which was a very liberal lender. As long as interest payments were made on the outstanding debt, it ignored that little headway was made with the principal.[68] Thus, although most *hacenderos* who were located within easy reach of the market continued to increase their output and to improve their estates, there were many for whom neither the market nor the threat of eviction served as a stimulus to improve productivity.

Thus, as Spanish America progressed through the eighteenth century, it found itself at a crossroads. In many respects it had overcome impediments of being a dependency. Not only was the economy growing, but it was being improved by the investment of merchant capital in production. The working force, as well, was being modernized insofar as it became attuned to wage labor. Finally, the colonies were becoming more self-sufficient, while Spain was becoming increasingly irrelevant. All of this had been accomplished despite Spanish policies that aspired to arrest colonial development. Yet there were no guarantees that Spanish America would continue to grow. For as long as it remained a dependency, it did not necessarily control its own destiny.

## THE NORTH AMERICAN MAINLAND

The mainland colonies of British North America constituted the third of the dependencies to be considered. Although there were similarities between their growth and development and that of Spanish America, there were also important differences. Both experienced rapid growth during the eighteenth century, but the English colonies could produce nothing to match the importance of silver. Moreover, because much of its climate was similar to that of Europe, it could not cultivate the exotic plant forms that were readily in demand. On the other hand, hindsight teaches that it was almost ideally located. It was close enough to Europe to make communication relatively easy, but at the same time it was sufficiently distant so that it did not pose a threat to the principal endeavors of the metropole. In fact, its location benefited the whole imperial scheme, for it was able to supply the Caribbean with the necessities that could not have borne the tariff of transportation from Europe. As a result, albeit in a much less spectacular fashion than Spanish America, the mainland colonies were also able to make significant strides during the eighteenth century. As in Spanish America, these strides were made largely by a labor force that was free from coercion.

The English crown perceived the settlement of that part of the Americas that the Spanish and Portuguese had ignored as being in the best interests of many groups in England. The vast continent, the English believed, could provide many raw materials that were in short supply at home. Timber, especially, was coveted, as it was essential for a nation intensely interested in expanding the merchant marine. The colonies were also viewed as a safety valve. Presiding over a rapidly growing population, the English crown, like many others, had begun to fear some sort of Malthusian crisis. Colonies, it felt, could act as a useful outlet for the excess population that might arise at some time in the future.[69]

There were others who concurred in the beneficial aspects of colonization. Since Henry VIII's break with Rome, the religious issue smoldered as a potential source of conflict. On the one hand, those who remained loyal to the Roman Catholic church faced a good deal of discrimination. On the other, those who chose to dissent in a more thorough fashion than the Anglicans were viewed with equal disdain. Allowing them to establish refuges across the ocean was considered an ideal solution to the problem insofar as it made suppression at home less likely to be a necessity and at the same time offered the possibility of removing the cancer to a location where its harm would be minimized. Just as they did with respect to the Caribbean, merchants also had an interest in sponsoring colonization. They formed companies that aided the settlers to establish themselves; the hope was that ultimately the merchant community would profit by transporting the goods that these settlers produced.

One of the outstanding characteristics of the colonial era was the rapid growth in population. Although the initial settlers experienced great hardship, once the environment had been conquered, the numbers of colonists increased rapidly. In 1660 there were still fewer than one hundred thousand settlers. A century later the numbers had swelled to more than one million. Yet immigration was a significant source of growth only during the first generation, as the deceleration of population growth in England, which became evident by the second half of the seventeenth century, reduced the incentive for emigration. Thereafter, population growth would result from natural increase. The birthrates in the American colonies came to be significantly higher than those in Europe, whereas the death rates were as much as 50 percent lower.[70]

Some of the early immigrants went to the North American colonies as indentured servants. In return for their passage, they agreed to work for a master for a period of time. Although the length of the contracts varied in accordance with the qualifications of the person who was to become a servant, the conditions under which he labored were often onerous. Without a long-term interest in the servant, the master sought to extract as much labor as possible during the period of servitude. Nevertheless, indentured servitude in the mainland colonies remained much more important than in the West Indies. For, unlike the islands, North America offered ample land and a fresh start for those who completed their contracts.[71]

By the end of the seventeenth century, the phenomenon of indenture was dying out and being replaced by slavery. This was partly the result of the inelastic supply of potential indentured laborers, which meant their cost tended to increase along with demand. At the same time, as English participation in the growing slave trade became more intensive, involuntary black labor became more readily available. Under these circumstances, the cost of a slave was only two to three times that of a servant and was therefore a more economically rational investment. Whereas the master was entitled to the labor of a servant only for a limited period, slaves and their children were his in perpetuity. In the American context ownership of the progeny was particularly important: Partly because of the less demanding climate and less rigorous commodity production, it was the only territory in the Western Hemisphere where the slave population grew by natural increase. In 1690 slaves constituted 8 percent of the population; by 1770 the percentage had increased to 21 percent. Rather than significantly higher levels of importation, the growth can be attributed to the high birthrate that was maintained among the slave population.[72]

During the eighteenth century, agricultural output increased tremendously, although agricultural techniques were not refined in the same ways that were being perfected elsewhere. This growth came about in part because it was an overwhelmingly agrarian society in which fewer than 10 percent of the population was engaged either in trade, skilled labor, or the professions.[73] It also resulted from an expansion in the number of producers. Per capita output, however, did not rise, largely because the methods of the American farmer were wasteful and unscientific. While his European counterparts had come to practice intensive forms of cultivation, the American still resorted to extensive agriculture. Blessed with seemingly endless supplies of land, the American farmer had little incentive to adopt more sophisticated methods. As Thomas Jefferson put it, it was cheaper to buy an acre of new land than to manure an old one.[74]

There were significant regional variations, however, both in what was produced and the methods used to produce it. In the northern and middle colonies, the emphasis was on cereals such as wheat, corn, and rye. There was also a heavy emphasis on pastoral endeavors. Both were usually produced on the family farm, which averaged about one hundred acres and was worked by the owner/occupier, who can truly be described as a yeoman. Only infrequently would the farmer resort to hiring labor for a specific task such as helping with the harvest.[75] Although there were family farms in the south as well, plantations played a larger role in agricultural development. In general plantations were estates of more than five hundred acres, which were worked by gangs of twenty or more slaves. The American plantation, however, differed from those of the West Indies. Although they specialized in one cash crop, they also produced their own food. Because land was not as precious as it was in the Caribbean, there was less need for intensive monoculture.[76]

Nevertheless, within the south itself there was regional specialization. In the upper south, that is, Virginia and Maryland, tobacco was the major estate crop. Output grew steadily, if not dramatically. From the humble beginnings of 119 thousand lbs. in 1620, it rose to 36 million in 1700, and had reached 100 million lbs. by 1776.[77] South Carolina, for its part, produced both rice and indigo, crops that ideally complemented each other. Rice was grown on the coast, indigo in the hills. Moreover, they had different planting and harvesting cycles, so the same slaves could be used to produce both crops. Thus, as a result of the ability to exploit slave labor to the fullest, it is no wonder that South Carolina was the only one of the American colonies where slaves outnumbered free men.[78]

Although each of the colonies was a separate entity, by the eighteenth century a broad similarity had developed in the way they were regulated. Initially each enjoyed an unprecedented amount of freedom from England, the charters under which they had been founded granting great latitude to their proprietors. There was such mismanagement in many of the colonies during the first two generations, however, that many of the colonists revolted. Ironically, in their search for more equitable treatment, they sought and obtained a greater degree of royal control, which after 1688 was generally regarded as being synonymous with Parliament.[79] Nevertheless, Parliament was often more concerned with weightier issues and too busy to enact legislation dealing with the colonies. In the absence of direction from London, the colonies were able to pass their own laws, which went into effect unless they were vetoed by the board of trade, the Privy Council, or the governor. In assessing the colonial relationship, Duncan Innes concludes that "what distinguishes England from other colonial powers was not her arbitrary subjection of their interests to her own but the very much greater latitude of action she allowed her colonists to enjoy."[80]

Overseas trade, however, was one area in which the colonies were not allowed to regulate their own affairs. Rather, the trade of the colonies, like other parts of the British imperial system, was regulated by the Navigation Acts. Passed between 1650 and 1673, these acts sought to maintain a tight trading system in which England occupied the central position. Among the most important stipulations was that specific items referred to as the "enumerated goods," such as sugar, tobacco, rice, cotton, indigo, wool, naval stores, and furs, could only be sent from the colonies to England or to another part of the empire. Similarly, with a few exceptions, the colonies could only import directly from Britain. In essence, this meant that almost any interaction between the colonies and continental Europe had to be funneled through England. Moreover, all goods within the imperial system had to be transported in British-owned ships.[81]

Differences of opinion arise over the impact of the Navigation Acts on colonial development. Those who see them as having been prejudicial to colonial growth argue that the colonists were denied freedom of action. Had they been able to sell their wares in markets of their own choosing, they could have received significantly better prices. As it was, runs the argument, the colonists were preyed upon by British merchants, who, by their intervention, diminished the profits of the producer. The hardest hit by the Navigation Acts were the southerners, whose plantation-produced commodities would naturally have enjoyed a wider market than would have been the case of the farm-produced goods of the north.[82]

Admitting of some deleterious effects of the Navigation Acts, others stress that their positive aspects outweighed their negative. First of all, the colonists benefited from the protected British market, which discriminated against the produce of potential competitors. As was true in the case of indigo, the Navigation Acts also provided bounties for the cultivation of certain commodities that were in short supply in England. Moreover, as part of the general imperial scheme, they not only enjoyed the protection of the British navy but could also take advantage of a broad definition of *British*, in which they themselves were included. Thus, colonial shipping was given a considerable stimulus. Finally, because they were allowed to trade with all parts of the empire, their location gave them a significant advantage in the trade with the West Indies. When all of these factors are weighed, it is argued that the Navigation Acts did not impose the onerous shackles earlier generations of historians have described.[83]

A balance sheet drawn up to assess the Navigation Acts and other British legislation might conclude that in some ways growth was stifled but that most obstacles were minimal. A modern calculation, for example, suggests that growth would only have been between 1 and 3 percent higher had there been no Navigation Acts.[84] There was other legislation, however, that was clearly more discriminatory in intent. Nevertheless, the crucial questions involve how important and how effective it was. For example, the Hat Act of 1732, which prohibited colonial manufacture of fur hats, could only have affected an infinitesimal number of people. The Molasses Act of 1731, which sought to prohibit trade with the French West Indies, was potentially more damaging. But because it was also potentially more inflammatory, local officials made little attempt to enforce it, thus demonstrating the type of compromise that was sometimes necessary for a colonial power to make in dealing with a dependency. New Englanders continued to trade with the French islands because, in the words of Stuart Bruchey, they "had grown up doing the things they found profitable, whatever British laws had been."[85]

A similar ambivalence marked the British attitude toward colonial manufacture. Some, such as shipbuilding, was actually encouraged. Despite higher labor costs, the abundance of raw materials made colonial production cheaper. As a result, more than one-third of the ships in the British merchant marine were built in America. Similarly, England encouraged the production of raw iron. In an era of intense competition in Europe, the English were more worried about their dependence on Sweden for iron than they were about the development of this colonial endeavor. In other areas, however, the laws were stringent, especially if the manufacture was competitive with an industry in the metropole. Nevertheless, it has been pointed out that even in these instances, little was done to suppress colonial production as long as no attempts were made to export the goods.[86]

Despite British laxity in enforcing regulations, the economy of America in the eighteenth century was of a distinctly colonial nature. Essentially it exported food and raw materials and imported manufactures. The northern and middle colonies exported bread, flour, wheat, salt, pork, beef, and dried fish to both the British and French West Indies. Because these goods were not enumerated in the Navigation Acts, they were also able to be exported directly to the Mediterranean.[87] The south, on the other hand, exported its rice, tobacco, and indigo directly to England. As time passed, both the northern and southern colonies became an increasingly important factor to the metropole. By 1772 they consumed 37 percent of English exports, most of which consisted of metal goods and textiles. Although the balance of trade distinctly favored the British, remittances from the West Indies and the Mediterranean helped to redress the imbalance. The most important source of foreign earnings, however, was derived from shipping and insurance, which proved to be sufficient to offset most of the deficit.[88]

Despite the colonial nature of the structure of the American economy, as it emerged in the second half of the eighteenth century, it had assumed a character that has been described as "truly advanced."[89] This, in turn, stemmed in large part from the fertility and abundance of its land. The average American farm could produce more than the average European farm simply because it was larger. The abundance of land and the fact that almost anyone who so desired could become a yeoman farmer mitigated against the large-scale creation of depressed classes.[90] Land, however, was just one component of an array of previously untapped resources that contributed to American growth. Because these resources could be brought to the market without undue coercion, a situation evolved in which, according to Edwin Perkins, "by the mid-eighteenth century, the typical white inhabitant of the mainland colonies was . . . enjoying the highest standard of living in the contemporary world."[91]

The outcomes of the experience of the mainland colonies and of Ireland, at least if viewed in the context of the mid-eighteenth century, were very different. This disparity might appear surprising, for it has been pointed out that British mercantilists viewed the American colonists with as much skepticism as they viewed their Irish counterparts. Yet North America was not dismantled and rebuilt to suit the needs of England. The crucial difference was what Gary Walton and James Shepherd refer to as "the natural tariff of distance."[92] Although some of the products of North America and England were similar, they were not competitive. The colonies were not in a position to invade English markets, making draconian suppression unnecessary. Quite the contrary, North America not only provided a crucial market for England but also allowed the West Indies to concentrate exclusively on sugar.

Nevertheless, what the North American colonies would become in future was still open to doubt. The absence of legal status distinctions for the majority of the population, the nature of the ownership of landed property, and a myriad of institutions inherited from England suggest that it might be referred to as protocapitalistic. It was also a social formation in which the vast majority performed uncoerced labor. By the late eighteenth century, the importance of white indentured servitude had become infinitesimal. Although the labor of black slaves was considerably more important than it had been in the seventeenth century, blacks formed a majority of the labor force only in South Carolina. This tendency is particularly instructive in that slavery was legal throughout the colonies yet appears to have been deemed an inappropriate form of labor organization for the endeavors most Americans practiced. Thus, as was the case with the other dependencies, the growth of the economy did not result in a movement toward servile relations of production.

On the other hand, there were few concrete indications that would suggest that these colonies would continue the journey. Little capital was employed in production and there were few signs of the creation of a proletariat. Moreover, slavery as a dominant mode of production had not emerged largely because no commodity appropriate to its exigencies had been discovered. Yet there were no guarantees that one would not be found in the future and no certainty about what the ramifications would be if one were encountered. Finally, it should be noted that North America was still a dependency of Great Britain. Although relations had been harmonious by and large, there was nothing to ensure that England would continue to conceive of its own interests as being best served by making the kinds of compromises and concessions that had facilitated economic growth and maintained colonial loyalty.

## CONCLUSION

Despite many successes in fomenting growth in the dependencies, by the second half of the eighteenth century, the colonial powers must have viewed their achievement with ambivalence. For example, whereas Spain could applaud the ending of the seventeenth-century depression in the Americas, it must have been less than enthusiastic that little of the resultant growth proved beneficial to it. Similarly, neither Spain nor England could have been comforted by the ease with which their colonists ignored imperial legislation. When the colonies had been founded, it had rather simplistically been assumed that their growth would follow a blueprint that was vaguely engraved in the minds of imperial thinkers. Yet experience had shown that it was easier to legislate than to regulate. This, in turn, raised the perplexing question of just how much colonial growth was desirable. By the middle of the eighteenth century, in fact, many imperial planners had begun to believe that the dividing line between the creation of successful colonies and the growth of ungrateful and potentially insubordinate underlings had already been transgressed.

# 8

# THE COLONIAL POWERS AND
# THE WORLD ECONOMY
# IN THE EIGHTEENTH CENTURY

By the eighteenth century, European participation in the world economy had expanded greatly both in terms of its volume and its intricacy. Although some of the growth stemmed from improvements in technology, most of it can be attributed to attitudinal changes. Vainglorious monarchs still enjoyed pomp, ceremony, duplicity, and warfare, but increasingly they came to understand that these luxuries had to be paid for and that a strong economic base provided the best means of achieving their goals. More so than their parasitical predecessors, they realized that the goose should be induced to lay a few fertilized eggs before it was slain.

Planners, however, still functioned in a milieu dominated by a mercantilistic mentality that suggested that the wealth of the world was relatively inelastic. Therefore, they believed that the improvement of one nation's position could only be achieved at the expense of another. This attitude guaranteed that the age would be one of intensive competition. In fact, the desire to gain economic advantage came to be viewed with such importance that increasingly vague dynastic aspirations became a much less important cause of warfare than material considerations. Moreover, rather than being confined to Europe itself, Europeans fought each other for commercial supremacy in the four corners of the globe.

During this era the nation-states of western Europe paid greater attention to commerce and development. Nowhere was this more true than in England. Freed by the Civil War and the Glorious Revolution from anachronistic parasiticism and functioning within the framework of full capitalist relations of production, this small and unimpressive island was able to move forward in unprecedented ways. By the end of the seventeenth century, it had clearly wrested predominance from the Dutch. During the eighteenth it would establish a trading nexus that linked almost all parts of the globe. It did not, however, have the field completely to itself. Rather, throughout the eighteenth century, the French would offer competition wherever and whenever it was feasible. Moreover, even the Iberian nations were awakened from their lethargy and sought to modernize so that they, too, could compete.


## ENGLAND AND WORLD TRADE

The eighteenth century witnessed the emergence of England as an economic superpower. Prior to 1640, English commerce was still relatively modest. It consisted mostly of the export of woolens to the Netherlands, where they were finished by the technologically superior Dutch. Even at the end of the Civil War, overseas trade still constituted a small portion of the national income. Nevertheless, as suggested by W. A. Minchinton, who refers to the restoration "as marking the economic exit from medievalism," the aftermath of the Civil War saw the establishment of a framework that would contribute to growth.[1] Production in England would increase significantly as it emerged from the doldrums of the seventeenth century. This, in turn, would facilitate its development as a trading nation.

During the late seventeenth and eighteenth centuries, English agriculture continued to improve. Making use of techniques pioneered by the Dutch, English farmers harvested more bountiful yields. Specifically, there was a greater emphasis on fodder crops such as turnips and clover, which were used to feed an ever-expanding number of domestic animals. The manure that these beasts produced, in turn, brought about a tremendous increase in the fertility of the land. Farmers thus were able to switch their attention from heavy clay soils to the more easily managed lighter soils. The result was extremely important: Whereas in the past England had at times had to import grain, it became a country that consistently exported to the Continent.[2]

Increased efficiency was a major factor in making possible the export of grain. Consolidated holdings could be worked more effectively, promoting the enclosure of many of the remaining open fields. Farmers were so aware that these holdings could be worked more profitably that they were willing to double the rent that they usually paid. This only hastened the procedure. During the eighteenth century, however, parliamentary enclosure remained fairly infrequent, and most arrangements were arrived at by what was termed agreement, although a large element of intimidation directed at the smallholder was always likely to be present. The complementary process of engrossing also contributed to the trends of the day. Low grain prices meant that many farmers did not have an adequate margin for survival. In combination with periodic outbreaks of animal disease, killing winters, and harvest failures, many were forced to the wall. Thus, there was a continuation of the process whereby smallholdings were swallowed up by the larger and more efficient farmers.[3]

Although the low price of basic foodstuffs adversely affected the smaller farmers, it proved beneficial to some segments of society. The relative abundance of grain meant that the price of a loaf of bread decreased significantly. Therefore the average worker was obliged to spend less on subsistence than his counterparts in most regions of the Continent. Although by modern standards it might seem negligible, the English worker had a disposable income that could be used to make other purchases in the marketplace.[4] Thus, insofar as the domestic market remained buoyant and ready to serve English manufacture, England avoided the overdependence on foreign markets that had produced the crisis for Dutch industry.

The English economy was also able to survive the potentially crippling South Sea Company bubble scandal of 1720. In the period after the restoration, joint-stock activity became extremely popular. It provided the means for large-scale undertakings in such areas as banking, insurance, water supply, and canals. Yet this expanding form of economic enterprise was almost completely unregulated. It was in this environment that in 1711 the South Sea Company received a charter granting it possession of the *asiento* to supply slaves to Spanish America and also conferring other trading privileges. In many circles it was believed that this was the most important concession that was obtained as a result of the War of Spanish Succession.[5]

Many of the directors hastened to invest in the company on this basis, but publicly they declared their interest in taking over the national debt from the Bank of England. It has been observed that, privately, from the outset the scheme was little more than a sham by which the directors hoped to manipulate an artificially inflated stock. Indeed, during the first half of 1720 the price of the stock soared; then it came to be perceived as extremely overvalued, and panic ensued when doubts surfaced about the potential of the South American trade. The bubble burst even more rapidly than it had been inflated, and many investors were wiped out as stock quotations fell dramatically. Nevertheless, although there were serious ephemeral dislocations in the aftermath, the incident was not without its beneficial aspects. Thereafter, joint-stock enterprise would be much more closely monitored. Moreover, the ministry of Robert Walpole, which was swept into power as a result of the scandal, took the important step of ensuring that the government itself would set aside funds to pay the interest on the national debt. Hence by guaranteeing that there would be no duplication of the debt repudiation practiced by the Stuarts, the British government firmly established its credit.[6]

The restructuring of other aspects of England's commercial institutions provided additional incentives to the growth of foreign trade. Prior to the Civil War, the Stuarts, especially, had sought to make money by selling monopoly privileges to private individuals and companies. In essence the world had been divided into spheres of influence in which monopoly rights had been sold by the English monarchy. Victory in the Civil War, however, allowed the "new merchants," those who wanted trade to be open to all and sundry, the chance to have their policies adopted. Although it did not happen overnight, the charters of such bodies as the Eastland and Levant companies—with the major exception of the East India Company—were revoked. Trade was opened to all. Thereafter, privilege would no longer determine who was successful and who was not. This new factor, in addition to the decreasing land values, made commerce a more attractive proposition than it had previously been.[7]

At first, trade with northwestern Europe gained in importance. During the early years of the seventeeenth century, English trade with the Low Countries decreased. One factor was the closing of Antwerp, traditionally the port to which English woolens had been shipped. A second was the disastrous Cockayne project, which had envisaged the finishing of cloth in England before it was exported. Unfortunately, while the English were unsuccessfully attempting to find the means to carry out their designs, Dutch production filled the void that had been created. Although the English were slow to recover their markets in the Low Countries even after the Cockayne experiment had been abandoned, they were able to make up their losses by finding new markets in France and Germany. Their woolens were exchanged for French wines and German linens. Just how long this commerce with France remained vibrant is open to debate. It has been argued that it continued at a high level at least until the end of the reign of James II. Nevertheless, by the eighteenth century, if not earlier, France adopted more stringent mercantilistic policies that stressed self-sufficiency. The tariff barriers that were erected severely limited the scope of English export activity. Still, thanks to a revived trade with the Netherlands and the continuing vitality of the German connection, these two regions in northwestern Europe occupied first and second place as importers of English goods.[8]

The English also made a strong move into Scandinavia and the Baltic. Although they had had some contact with the region in the sixteenth century and their involvement grew during the seventeenth, not until the eighteenth century did the English surpass the Dutch as the primary traders in the region. By this time, however, they no longer needed grain but sought out other raw materials. With Poland unable to supply what was needed, the English looked elsewhere. In Norway they found ample supplies of timber to be used in ship construction. Sweden, on the other hand, provided the precious iron that was in such short supply at home. Despite the tariff barriers these Scandinavian countries erected against English produce, especially woolens, the demand for English coal, tobacco, and other colonial products compensated for the losses it suffered in other commodities.[9] English capital also came to be invested in the putting out of linen in several different regions. Thus, insofar as it provided not only uses for merchant capital but also commodities that were in short supply at home, the trade of northern and northeastern Europe was an important link in the overall pattern of economic growth.[10]

English commerce with the Mediterranean also increased dramatically from the second quarter of the seventeenth century. It was aided on the one hand by the precipitous decline of the Italian clothing industry and on the other by the fortuitous development in England of worsteds, a material in whose manufacture the people of East Anglia, Norfolk, and Devon came to be quite expert. Not only, however, did English cloth become dominant in Italy; for a time during the late seventeenth and early eighteenth centuries, it became the "undisputed leader" in the Balkans and in Egypt as well.[11]

English trade with Spain also grew considerably during this period. In addition to the legal exchanges of goods, this commerce was based on more furtive and clandestine dealings. As a result of military defeats, Spain was obliged to sign commercial treaties that gave English merchants special privileges in the Spanish market. This was especially important in that it opened up a legal trade from Cadiz to the vast market of the Spanish Indies. England's position in the Spanish market was strengthened even more in 1713, when it obtained by treaty the *asiento* for supplying slaves to the Spanish colonies. Once they gained legal entry to Spanish American ports, the English began to abuse their privileges by dealing in goods they were legally forbidden from selling by the Spanish government. Other English traders were more blatant in ignoring Spanish regulations. Some operated out of Jamaica; others concentrated on the Rio de La Plata. Although the volume of the clandestine trade probably will never be known, it should be pointed out that traders were paid mostly in silver, a precious metal that helped to finance other transactions.[12]

English commerce with Portugal, however, was twice as large as that with Spain. During the seventeenth century, England gained a foothold in the Portuguese market by signing treaties in 1642 and 1654. In exchange for guaranteeing Portugal's independence from Spain, the English gained significant privileges. Their favorable position was further advanced by the Methuen Treaty of 1703, which reduced the duties on English goods in exchange for a reduction on the rates charged to Portuguese wines. As a result many English merchants relocated in Lisbon, where they came to constitute what was known as the "English Factory." By the early eighteenth century, there were no fewer than fifty English firms that based their operations in the Portuguese capital. This solid foundation proved particularly advantageous to the English. With the value of English manufactured goods far exceeding that of Portuguese wines, England always enjoyed a favorable balance of trade.[13]

Although the Portuguese market itself was helpful, the access that the Lisbon base provided to Brazil was probably of greater significance. Because English merchants were able to compete on a parity basis with their Portuguese counterparts, they found themselves in a propitious spot. Better capitalized and with access to superior goods, they came to dominate the Brazilian trade. Moreover, the English also became predominant in the shipping of goods between Portugal and Brazil. The timing of the English rise to ascendancy in the Luso-Brazilian nexus was extremely important, for it corresponded with the growth of the Brazilian mining industry. The English demanded that their account be settled in gold, which meant that a significant portion of all the gold mined in Brazil ultimately found its way to England. It has been estimated that as much as 75 percent of Brazilian gold ended up in England and that the drain on Portugal was no less than two million pounds sterling annually. Just how important this commerce was is suggested by Harold Fisher, who argues that "without the growth of this trade, without the expansion of Brazilian gold output on which so much else turned, English commerce, finance, and industrial advance would have been even slower."[14]

Another major development of the late seventeenth and eighteenth centuries was the growth of commerce with Asia. The vehicle for this increasing trade was the East India Company, a monopolistic concern founded in 1600 that survived despite the vocal anticompany lobby. One component of this lobby was composed of the "new merchants," who wanted to gain access to India. They argued that since trade with other areas of the world had been thrown open to all comers, its value had multiplied. Their position, therefore, was that the government should rescind the charter of the East India Company. Others who opposed the continuation of the charter based their objections on soundly mercantilistic principles. Because India neither needed nor desired any commodity produced in Europe, the East India Company had to settle its account in bullion. This segment of the opposition concluded that the resultant drain of bullion was a severe threat to the economic well-being of the nation. Therefore they demanded the special privileges be revoked.[15]

The company, however, was even more convincing in defense of its position. By its very nature, it argued, the trade with Asia demanded a high overhead in terms of the factories that were needed to prosecute the trade. It would have been unfair to allow others to benefit from the infrastructure built and maintained by the company. Responding to the bullion drain argument, the company admitted that the Asian trade could only be primed by exporting silver but pointed out that much of what was obtained in Asia was subsequently reexported to Europe, where it ultimately was sold for even larger amounts of bullion. Thus, it concluded that both the monopoly and the trade were beneficial to England. Although Parliament often came close to making alterations in its charter, the East India Company was able to hold on to its monopoly.[16]

The East India Company of the seventeenth century, nevertheless, was a rather unimposing entity. With little capital at its disposal, it was unable to compete with its Dutch counterpart and thus was obliged to retreat from the Spice Islands. It had to content itself with the less appealing trade of India, where it constructed factories in Surat, Madras, Bengal, and Bombay. Unlike the Dutch East India Company, which imposed itself on Indonesia, the English company resided in India on the sufferance of local princes. English agents went out of their way to avoid disputes, refused to participate in local squabbles, and even, on occasion, accepted insults without retaliation. Speaking of company policy, Lucy Sutherland observed that "compromise rather than conflict and a determination to avoid political controversy are obvious in all the actions of the early years" in India.[17]

The operations of the company were multifaceted. One aspect of its activities was the prosecution of the "country trade" of Asia. That is, the East India Company involved itself heavily in the intra-Asian commerce. The basic guiding principle was the very simple one of buying cheap and selling dear. With various commodities ascribed different values throughout Asian ports, it was easy to make a profit. For example, the company might purchase silk where it was relatively inexpensive and abundant and sell it where it was scarce and costly. In this regard, its superior shipping proved to be an important asset. Part of the profit from these ventures might then be used to finance the operation again and another part employed in financing a different undertaking. Although the whole process initially had to be set in motion by making purchases with silver, the profits were considerably higher than the initial investment.[18]

Some of the goods procured in Asia ultimately found their way to Europe. Silk, cotton, tea, indigo, dyes, spices, and muslins were among the most important. Over time, however, the relative importance of these commodities would be altered significantly. The trade to Europe was initially dominated by spices, especially pepper. Although the demand for pepper remained fairly static, the late seventeenth century witnessed a great increase in the demand for calicoes. This fine cotton cloth was so popular in England that it came to pose a threat to the woolen textile industry, which successfully lobbied to have the sale of calico banned in England. After 1720 all textiles from Bengal had to be reexported. Most found their way to the Continent, although some formed part of the trade with Africa. By the middle of the century, calicoes were replaced by tea as the most important commodity the company handled. It not only changed the drinking habits of a nation but proved to be extremely lucrative to the concern that imported it.[19]

By the middle of the eighteenth century, the East India Company was a far different institution from the humble entity that had begun operations 150 years earlier. In England it had become the largest business concern. In India its establishments were being transformed from the "fenceless factories" of the seventeenth century into fortresses. Although the company justified its action by claiming that the new fortifications would protect it from French attack, the truth would seem to lie elsewhere. According to Pamela Nightingale, "fortification was not a defensive measure to protect Bengal from the French, but the result of new commercial demands." Specifically, independent trade from Bengal was seriously competing with the company's trade in other parts of the country. In assessing policy options, it was decided that the control of the trade of Bengal was essential for the economic well-being of the company.[20]

The year 1757 was a watershed in the history of the East India Company. Fortification had been encouraged by the crumbling of the once vibrant Mughal empire under the combined assaults of Hindu revivalists and fresh invasions from the north. That the Mughal empire was incapable of mounting sufficient force to deal with the East India Company was proved when its agent, the nawab of Bengal, unsuccessfully tried to dismantle the company's fortifications. The victory of the English in the resultant Battle of Plassey paved the way for the subsequent takeover of the entire country. Marx described the situation: "The power of the Great Mughul was broken by the Mughul viceroys. The power of the Mughul viceroys was broken by the Marattas. The power of the Marattas was broken by the Afghans and while all were struggling against all, the British rushed in."[21]

The victory of the East India Company allowed it to demand concessions that ultimately would enable it to change the entire structure of its operations. One provision of the settlement was that its agents were granted the right of free trade in Bengal. With no tariffs to pay, it was able to undercut local merchants, who still were obliged to contribute significant amounts to the public purse. The company also gained the right of farming the taxes of Bengal. What followed was nothing short of a looting of the public treasury. Before the worst of the abuses had been corrected, many company agents returned to England very wealthy. Of even greater significance was that the revenues of the company increased to such a degree that bullion no longer needed to be shipped from Europe. Thus the profitability of the company was greatly enhanced.[22]

While these changes were taking place in India, the East India Company was expanding its operations in China. Although since their accession to power in the mid-seventeenth century, the Manchu successors of the Ming dynasty continued to maintain an isolationist policy, they allowed merchants in the port of Canton to conduct a strictly regulated foreign commerce. The two most important commodities that the East India Company exported were silk and tea. As had been the case in India, the English produced nothing that the Chinese wanted and had to settle their account in silver. It was significant and portentous, however, that one of the fruits of the English victory in India was winning the monopoly of the opium trade of Bengal. Gradually the company would be able to convert this into a staple in the China trade that would ultimately reverse its balance of payments and obviate the necessity of paying in silver.[23]

The success of the English in Asia was duplicated in Africa. Whereas it has been noted that English slaving was virtually nonexistent during most of the seventeenth century, by the eighteenth their participation had become quite intense. The annual exports rose from five thousand at the beginning of the century to twenty-five thousand in the 1740s to almost forty-five thousand by the latter part of the century. This total made the English the largest suppliers of slaves to the Americas. Most of the slaves were sent to the British Caribbean Islands, where they were paid for in bills of exchange drawn upon London, not in sugar or molasses, as is sometimes suggested.[24] After 1715, because of England's possession of the *asiento*, other slaves were shipped to the Spanish Indies. Moreover, in addition to supplying the rather limited needs of Spanish America, between 1748 and 1777 English traders were able to dominate the more significant market of the French West Indies.[25]

Whereas the trade of Asia was dominated by the East India Company, no single organization maintained a similar position in the slave trade.

Originally, monopoly privileges were extended to the Royal Africa Company. Although the company tried to justify and defend its monopoly on the grounds that it, like the East India Company, had a significant overhead to maintain in the form of factories, its arguments fell on deaf ears. Not only did the government decree that others could participate, it added insult to injury by requiring the company to provide protection to private traders within the very walls of its factories. Soon the private traders came to be much more important than the company, which was dissolved in 1750.[26] Although popular mythology suggests that those engaged in this "odious commerce" reaped huge fortunes from their unwholesome business, this would appear to be an exaggeration. Certainly, on occasion, vast fortunes were made in a very short time. Yet the secular trends suggest that most profits fell into the range of 10 percent, which was similar to those of most other trading activities.[27]

Although English commercial ascendancy was a global phenomenon, the most important component continued to be the imperial system. The members of the system were England, Scotland (after 1707), the West Indies, the mainland colonies, and Canada (after 1763). Each possessed certain rights and duties as specified in the Navigation Acts. Ireland, too, was part of the system, albeit as the member that was most discriminated against. Although they provided the colonies with certain advantages, the Navigation Acts imposed restrictions upon them that did not apply to England. Thus buttressed by the advantages provided by this legislation, England maintained its closest economic contacts within the perimeters of this exclusive system.

For most of the latter half of the seventeenth century and the early eighteenth century, England viewed its Caribbean possessions as the most important component of the empire. Because of the Navigation Acts, England was guaranteed a supply of sugar that was often lower in cost than the price of sugar on the world market. The increase in the number of Caribbean Islands in the production of sugar in the eighteenth century posed no problems, the demand proving to be very elastic. The ways in which sugar could be used seemed to multiply as rapidly as the supply. Nevertheless, the importance of the West Indies began to decrease even though the amount of sugar sent to Britain continued to grow. Numerically dominated by unremunerated coerced laborers, the islands elicited an inflexible demand for commodities from abroad. Even though the system of intensive monoculture determined that foodstuffs be imported, England was located too far away to qualify as the principal supplier. Thus, by the second half of the eighteenth century, the West Indies commanded a much smaller percentage of the value of British trade than it had done at the beginning.[28]

The primacy once enjoyed by the West Indies was assumed during the eighteenth century by the mainland colonies. Once viewed as very poor relations of the Caribbean Islands, they emerged as a less glittering but more substantial partner. As their populations continued to grow and prosper, so, too, did the demand they elicited. Trapped as they were by the Navigation Acts, they provided a captive market for England. The mainland colonies came to be viewed as more valuable than the Caribbean for another reason as well. Whereas the Caribbean produced little other than sugar, the mainland provided indigo, iron, sea-island cotton, tobacco, and timber, which when aggregated provided much more valuable inputs into the English economy than a mere foodstuff.[29]

Canada and Ireland remained junior partners in the imperial scheme. Canada, which was only acquired in 1763, possessed much land but few people. Although its fur trade was profitable, the country as yet produced little of substance. Ireland, on the other hand, had been molded into niches that, if not crucial to England, were at least useful. Once the Irish woolen industry had been destroyed, more and more emphasis was placed on linens. It was an industry that grew so quickly that by 1768, 67 percent of Irish imports into England consisted of linens, which, in turn, made England less dependent on Holland and Germany. Moreover, after 1757 the numbers of cattle imported from Ireland increased greatly. In addition to benefiting from the imports of cattle and linen, England also profited from its exports to Ireland: Virtually devoid of industry, Ireland was obliged to import almost everything.[30]

English trade not only grew during the eighteenth century, but its character changed significantly. One notable tendency was the decrease in the importance of wool. Whereas it had been the only major export at the end of the Civil War, by 1701 cloth composed just 47 percent of the total. Once trade with the wider world became more important, reexports came to constitute a primary component of English commerce. Colonial sugar, furs, rice, and tobacco from the Americas joined with Asian tea, calicoes, and silks to form the main commodities in these transactions. The most significant secular tendency, however, was the increasing percentage of manufactures that dominated overseas trade. It was not only manufacture in and of itself that was important. Rather, it was the diversity of manufacture, which meant that the economy was no longer dependent on one staple.[31]

The expansion of trade had a broad impact on England. The transactions that were involved helped to convert London into the major financial center of Europe. There was some borrowing based on institutions pioneered by the Dutch, but there were also new departures, such as the creation of the Bank of England and the institutionalization of the public debt. Central banking was supplemented by the growth of a network of regional banks. Shipping was another area in which England forged ahead. During this era especially the tradition of maritime supremacy for which England would remain famous for two centuries was evolved. Along with shipping, many new ports came to play leading roles. At the end of the Civil War London was the only port worthy of mention; by the middle of the eighteenth century, however, Bristol, Newcastle, Plymouth, and, in particular, Liverpool had risen to prominence.[32]

Trade, in conjunction with various factors, helped to transform England in a number of ways. Industry diversified as such endeavors as the production of brass, copper, glass, paper, and a myriad of others began to grow. Part of this diversification stemmed from the need, for example, to refashion Swedish iron and refine West Indian sugar. This, in turn, created employment possibilities where there otherwise would have been none. Increasingly, this employment was generated in urban areas. For, in addition to port cities, industrial centers such as Leeds, Birmingham, Sheffield, Nottingham, and Manchester began to play an important role in the English economy. The eighteenth century indeed presented ample testimony that England was continuing the journey toward capitalism.[33]

England's domination of world commerce during the first three quarters of the eighteenth century was unprecedented. Although the Dutch had established an extensive trading network in the 1600s, it had never been as truly global as the system forged by English merchants. The Netherlanders had never gained direct access to Spanish or Portuguese America, nor had the seventeenth-century slave trade been the big business that it would become in the eighteenth century. Moreover, the Netherlands was too small to develop an extensive colonial empire of its own. England's commerce, on the other hand, not only had firm European roots but also extended to virtually every corner of the globe. It was an achievement that was unprecedented but certainly not one that was unnoticed by contemporaries.

## COLONIAL EUROPE TRIES TO NARROW THE GAP

The nation-states of western Europe did not abandon the field to England. Rather, what they hoped to accomplish, at the very least, was to cut into the sizable lead that England had established. It was sometimes perceived that reform at home was an a priori condition of being able to compete. Thus ministers of state promulgated legislation and devised programs whose goals were the economic betterment of their respective countries. Usually state funds were used in order to implement the programs. How successful they were depends on one's point of view. The economies of France, Spain, and Portugal grew much more rapidly during the eighteenth century than they had in the seventeenth. Nevertheless, the gap between them and Great Britain continued to widen, for their respective rates of growth did not keep pace with the English.

Of the three nation-states, France presents the greatest enigma. On the one hand, it was the largest country in Europe and the second leading economic power. Every European monarch envied the long reign of Louis XIV, who ruled between 1643 and 1715, and would have dearly loved to be able to say, as he did, L'Etat c'est moi. Moreover, France never suffered through a period of decline as did its Iberian neighbors. On the other hand, it remained relatively backward in both production and economic organization. The paradoxes presented by France led Wallerstein to refer to it as "neither fish nor fowl."[34] That is, it duplicated neither the dynamism of England nor the decay of Spain and Portugal.

One advantage that France enjoyed was a relatively fertile landscape. Unlike that of its Iberian neighbors, whose lands were plagued by aridity, the soil of France remained relatively productive. Thus, despite outdated agricultural techniques, the country was usually self-sufficient in basic necessities. During good periods, it was even able to export foodstuffs. Similarly, it was well endowed with raw materials. The result was that France never fell victim to some of the ills that constantly beset Spain and Portugal.

France also benefited in a number of ways from its colonial trades. In San Domingue it possessed the most productive territory on earth. The insatiable demand for slaves emanating from the Caribbean led French slavers to import more than one million blacks into the islands during the eighteenth century.[35] Further, the bounty provided by its West Indian islands enabled France to reexport large amounts of tropical produce to southern Europe and the Levant. Reexports, in fact, constituted one-half of all French exports.[36] The colonial trades also had a significant impact on other aspects of the French economy. Especially for southern France, supplying the islands became big business. Ports such as Nantes, which specialized in outfitting slavers, and Bordeaux, which provisioned the islands, were converted into thriving centers of activity. The colonial trade also stimulated French shipping, which was both enlarged and modernized.[37]

In addition to reexporting colonial produce, France exported staples of its own. Many regions of the country were concerned with viticulture. They not only produced unique and high-quality wines but produced them in large quantities, thus gaining an advantage in most competitive markets. France also enjoyed an edge in the manufacture of certain high-quality textiles. Although it could not compete with England in the production of day-to-day cloth, its silks were uncontested, especially in southern Europe and the Middle East. François Crouzet demonstrates, therefore, that French growth throughout the eighteenth century was consistent and that, although it lagged behind England in most areas, there were some in which France predominated.[38]

In many ways the state sought to promote this growth and to enact policies designed to improve the economy. This was especially true during the tenures of Cardinal Richelieu (1624–1642) and Jean-Baptiste Colbert (1661–1683) as first minister. They were true mercantilists in that they believed in bullionism and tariff manipulation. They also believed in state subsidization of various projects that would make the economy grow. Sheperd Clough and Charles Cole argue that "no where else was so vigorous an effort made on such a large scale to put into practice mercantilist ideas. In no other country was the attempt [made] to apply at one and the same time all the mercantilist theories."[39]

Under Colbert, for example, a strong attempt was made to develop French industry. State capital was used to sponsor a variety of new manufactures. Realizing, however, that French craftsmen were inadequate for the task of undertaking the high-quality production he envisaged, Colbert expended large sums on the importation of highly skilled but high-priced Venetians. Aware that French textiles could not compete against their English rivals even in the domestic market, Colbert considerably raised tariffs on manufactured imports. At the same time, the duties charged on raw materials were greatly reduced. Under these policies, the state hoped, French industrial production would grow and ultimately become competitive with that of England.[40]

Improving communication, both internally and externally, was deemed as a prerequisite for economic development. Although its size, both in terms of land mass and population, helped France become a big power, it often proved to be a hindrance in terms of the basic transportation of goods and services. Colbert not only sought to improve on the rudimentary road network but also delved into the question of the construction of canals. Communication was also hindered by the many ways France remained medieval. Although it was united under the strong monarchy, it still contained numerous internal tariff barriers that Colbert tried to rationalize. With respect to external matters, it was his firm belief that the Dutch and English enjoyed their position of ascendancy because of naval strength. He was so convincing in his arguments that Louis agreed to make sizable contributions to naval development. The result was that by the end of the seventeenth century, French ship designs had become technologically more advanced than those of either of its rivals.[41]

The French state was also heavily involved in sponsoring overseas endeavors. In 1664 it was responsible for the founding of the French East India Company, which was chartered on the model of its Dutch counterpart. Heavily subsidized by the state, by the eighteenth century it had a larger number of stations in India, if not a larger operation, than the English company. The French state also sponsored colonization. To increase its tropical produce it secured title to San Domingue in 1697; it settled Canada with an eye to enhancing temperate produce. The state also went to great lengths to secure the *asiento* to supply the Spanish Indies with slaves. In 1702 this aggressiveness paid off when the contract was awarded to France.[42]

Despite what by contemporary standards was a massive infusion of capital by the state into the economy, however, the returns failed to justify the expenditure. With the very important exception of the benefits brought by the acquisition of San Domingue, government intervention in the economy did not produce a radical transformation. During the eighteenth century, for example, industrial output rose, but certainly not in a fashion commensurate with the way in which the pump had been primed. The great strides in the naval revival, as well, proved ephemeral. Even less success was encountered in resolving the difficulties of internal communications as they were so enormous that the resources of the state were totally inadequate even to make a dent in the problem. Finally, after a promising beginning, the East India Company became defunct in 1761.[43]

Why did a country with a large population, fertile territory, and a government dedicated to the task prove incapable of transforming itself? Although it has been suggested that France suffered from ills that were not of its own making, there would seem to be more fundamental reasons for its failures. Certainly, it does appear to have been particularly hard-hit by the seventeenth-century crisis. It is also true that the devastating Thirty Years' War must have had a significantly depressive impact. Yet one wonders if these factors were as crucial as Crouzet implies when he writes that "it was during this 'tragic' post-1630 seventeenth century that France was clearly outdistanced by England and . . . she was never able to catch up."[44] It would appear more worthwhile to look at the social bases of French retardation. For quite clearly it was the attitude of citizens aggregated as social classes rather than a business cycle or a devastating war that ultimately determined the fate of France.

For although there were degrees of social change in many spheres, there were also more obstacles to contend with than the progressive forces could overcome. For example, in his campaign to rationalize internal communication, Colbert had a degree of success in uniting a large part of the north into a customs union that came to be known as the Five Farms. Elsewhere, however, medieval rights and customs were used to resist the removal of internal obstacles to development. Thus, man-made barriers determined that France remained a congeries of different regions, each possessing anachronistic privileges. Similarly, the spurt forward in naval development that was followed by a quick withdrawal from the brink also resulted from human considerations. Louis XIV was willing to invest heavily only until he realized that powerful elements within the landed aristocracy, who derived no discernible benefit from a strong navy, objected to the nation's resources being spent on such folly. Seeing that the weight of important opinion was against him, Louis withdrew the subsidies and naval development languished.[45]

The king's susceptibility to pressure suggests the degree to which France remained firmly entrenched in seigneurial privilege. Outwardly there might be the façade of the absolute monarchy and the king might think of himself and the state as one. Yet despite the glitter of Versailles as a symbol of the strength of the centralized state, traditionalism was still alive and well. On the political level, especially after the death of the Sun King, various elements in the nobility formed a sometimes vocal opposition. With respect to financial matters, however, there was a continuing struggle between a monarchy desperate to tap the resources of the nobles and an aristocracy that was equally determined to resist the erosion of the privileges that exempted them from most taxation.[46] Thus, eighteenth-century France failed to make the transition to a modern bureaucratic state. "In the time of Louis XIV," writes Eugene Asher, "France was much more feudal and much less regimented than many observers have been willing to admit. Power in the provinces was exercised . . . by entrenched families . . . who manipulated provincial affairs."[47]

Despite its intransigence with respect to taxation, some members of the heterogeneous collection of people who made up the nobility were forward-looking in their attitude toward economic and commercial matters. During the eighteenth century many became deeply involved in international trade.

Others were interested in innovation and invention. In some instances their ventures were even undertaken jointly with partners who were members of the bourgeoisie. Their activities, in fact, persuaded one student of the period to refer to them as capitalists, businesspeople, and entrepreneurs. Nevertheless, this same student is forced to admit that these pioneers not only constituted a distinct minority among the nobility but also that their contribution to economic growth remained extremely modest.[48]

Unlike their English counterparts, French peasants were unable to produce a dynamic class that was capable of challenging the aristocracy of privilege. So many factors contributed to this situation that it is virtually impossible to ascribe relative importance to individual phenomena. One may start with the absence of primogeniture and the resultant extrafragmentation of holdings that prevented most of the peasants from even considering participation in the market economy. It should also be noted that many occupied their land either on terms of sharecropping (*métayage*) or short-term leases. Neither tenure provided an incentive for reinvestment and improvement. This last point, however, is probably moot, as the financial burdens to which they were subjected left them without the resources to improve their holdings had they been able to overcome their conservative and subsistence-oriented mentality. Thus, rather than thrusting forward as a dynamic element that could have served as a dissolvent of the extant social relations, the French peasantry symbolized the general resistance to change.[49]

That the French peasantry proved so incapable of fomenting change was both because of its political impotence as a class and because its main ally was a wolf dressed in sheep's clothing. If peasant militancy can be credited with initiating the process that would undermine the solidarity of the feudal oligarchy and thus hasten the demise of the feudal mode of production, it was royal paternalism that guaranteed the liberation of the countryside. Yet altruism played no role in influencing the monarchy to protect the peasant against a seigneurial reaction. Rather, as long as a free peasantry capable of being taxed was essential to the crown, it was self-interest alone that motivated French kings. This was especially important when the results of Bourbon attempts to impose direct taxation on the nobility remained indecisive. As a result, as the exigencies of the monarchy grew by geometric proportions in order to meet the requirements of the early-modern state, so, too, did the necessity to increase the taxes imposed on the peasants. Catharina Lis and Hugo Soly describe the causes and effects that monarchical policy brought into being: The "protection of small peasant proprietors by the French monarchy with an eye on fiscal interests led to agrarian stagnation. . . . In order to recover the steeply rising costs of its foreign and internal policies, the absolutist state proceeded to squeeze the poor unmercifully."[50]

In terms of developmental possibilities, the French aristocracy could not have, even had it wanted to, pioneered agricultural development. Whereas their English counterparts had access to sufficient land and were obliged to be competitive because of the absence of buttresses against failure, the French aristocracy had neither the same opportunities nor incentives. Peasants in France could resist eviction, so the aristocracy could not gain land needed to experiment with large-scale, market-oriented production. Thus, they were condemned to be nothing more than rentiers of fragmented holdings. The one class with enough revenue to invest in improvements in agriculture, therefore, was unable to attempt it, even had it been so inclined.[51]

The social structure that so impeded French economic development shared much in common with that of Spain. Both countries, despite their modern monarchical traditions, were solidly rooted in seigneurial privilege. Yet, especially in the seventeenth century, their paths diverged significantly. France could be described as a country whose wealth "lay . . . in the . . . combination of a fertile and varied land [and] a large population. . . . This was a strong but still traditional economy."[52] The land of Spain, on the other hand, was varied, but it certainly could not be described as fertile or heavily settled. Moreover, rather than possessing a strong but still traditional economy, it suffered almost total collapse in the 1600s. By the end of the century, however, the Spanish were coming to accept notions that the French had arrived at somewhat earlier. They became convinced that modernity, progress, and economic development would only be achieved with the aid of a strong interventionist state.

At the beginning of the eighteenth century, there was a change in the dynastic line that presided over the Spanish monarchy. As part of the compromise to end the war that was fought over the disputed Spanish succession, the many contestants in the struggle agreed to allow a grandson of Louis XIV to ascend the throne of Spain, as long as the two Bourbon houses remained separate. Under Philip V and his successors, the Spanish Bourbons attempted to infuse a new sense of dynamism into a nation that had languished under their Habsburg predecessors. However geneticists ultimately conclude the debate about inbreeding, heredity, and genetic decay, it is fair to say that the closely knit Habsburg monarchs of the seventeenth century became increasingly incompetent. Considering all of the ills that beset the country during this era of decay, perhaps not even pure genius would have been able to resolve them. The incompetence and lethargy of the later Habsburgs, however, severely aggravated the already critical situation. Philip V, though, was prepared to address rather than ignore the country's ills. In the words of Richard Herr, "the road to economic self-sufficiency and equality with north European powers was clearly long and hard, but along this road the Bourbon Ministers optimistically determined to lead Spain."[53]

In many respects, Bourbon policy in Spain was more ambitious and enlightened than it was in France. One of Philip's first tasks was putting to rest many anachronisms of the medieval past. For example, he was able to take advantage of the war that brought him his throne and the rebellion in Aragon that challenged it, to suppress provincial autonomy. Instead of separate kingdoms obeying different sets of laws, Spain as an entity and a reality can be said to date from his accession. He also addressed outdated ideas by passing decrees such as the one that stated that one could work with one's own hands and still be regarded as a decent person. Similarly, Philip tried to remove the stigma that had been attached to commercial endeavors. Where he and his successors differed most from the French monarchs was in the realm of challenging the nobility. Although it was a long drawn-out process, toward the end of the century, the crown won the right to impose certain sorts of direct taxation on this previously exempt group.[54]

One of the problems the Spanish Bourbons faced was that of the low level of internal commerce. In the mid-seventeenth century, it had been more expensive to transport goods from Old to New Castile than from the Netherlands to Seville. To remedy this situation, a significant program of road construction was undertaken. Another problem was that, like France, Spain was still bedeviled by medieval customs barriers that severely affected internal trade. Whereas in France the monarchy achieved only limited success, in Spain the crown was able to abolish all impediments to internal communications. Finally, in order to facilitate the transfer of goods, the sales tax was greatly reduced. Although the results of these new policies fell far short of spectacular gains, there was a significant increase in internal transactions.[55]

Charles III (1759-1788) attempted to promote agricultural growth. He was convinced that a strong peasantry formed the backbone of a strong state. Partly for this reason and partly because of the falling price of wool, the privileges traditionally extended to the Mesta were revoked. Instead of sheep being grazed over large parts of the potential arable, lands were fenced off and made available to peasant cultivators. The results, once again, were only partially successful. Although the jump in the production of wheat, corn, and rye greatly decreased Spanish dependence on foreign sources, the profits did not accrue to the producers. Rather, it was the landed aristocrats who were able to "wax fat and strong" as they increased rents to coincide with the increases in productivity.[56]

Industry, as well, was not neglected. Rather later than elsewhere, most guild restrictions were brought to an end. The state also began to play a more active role. It sponsored model factories in a number of endeavors, hoping to stimulate others into emulation. In order to ensure that these enterprises got off the ground, they imported skilled foreign workers to act both as producers and instructors. One of its most successful policies was the prohibition in 1771 of the importation of cotton textiles. As a result, the textile industry, especially in the Basque country, Catalonia, and Valencia, experienced a boom.[57]

Although Spain's revival was successful to a degree, it was not as far-reaching as the changes that were experienced in Portugal. An index of Spain's success is provided by certain trade statistics: Whereas goods of Spanish origin constituted only 12 percent of Spanish American imports in 1700, by 1784 this figure had risen to 45 percent. Moreover, at home, the country became much more self-sufficient, needing to import less from the outside world. Yet the gap that separated Spanish and English production continued to widen. Although Portugal began from equally humble beginnings, it was able to achieve many of the goals that eluded the Spanish. In fact, by the latter part of the eighteenth century, Portugal had succeeded in reversing its balance of payments with England.

By the late seventeenth century, Portugal faced a serious crisis. It had become accustomed to importing virtually everything. This included not only manufactures but basic foodstuffs such as grain and codfish. As long as Brazilian reexports were in demand, the system remained viable, if unhealthy. As the seventeenth century progressed, however, increasing competition to Brazilian produce was encountered from the British and French Caribbean Islands. Both the crown and the country were thrust into a desperate situation. Sugar prices dropped dramatically, and traditional markets were beginning to disappear.

It was in this milieu that the reform-minded Conde d'Ericeira (1675–1690) was appointed first minister. Sometimes referred to as the Portuguese Colbert, he had an acute awareness of the need to industrialize and the sacrifice this would demand. His basic philosophy was to begin a policy of import-substitution. To this end he raised tariffs on many imports and enacted sumptuary legislation against luxuries. He encouraged manufactures in those areas where the raw materials could be provided locally. With the aid of state subsidies, the manufacture of iron, silks, woolens, and various enterprises based on raw materials obtained from the agricultural sector were begun.[58]

Despite Ericeira's attempts to inject mercantilist-inspired planning into the sagging Portuguese economy, a variety of factors conspired to doom his plans. One of the most basic was that his industries produced low-quality merchandise and produced it in insufficient quantities. Second, he was always opposed by the numerous, entrenched aristocracy, which had to acquiesce in the policies of change only as long as the crisis continued. When Brazilian gold brought renewed prosperity, however, these elements emerged from the closet in full opposition. The Methuen Treaty of 1703 sounded the death knell for the attempt to modernize Portuguese manufactures. S. Sideri writes that the "Methuen treaty had a disastrous effect on infant Portuguese manufactures. Woolen imports quadrupled and domestic industry was almost totally eliminated."[59]

It would not be until the appointment in 1750 of the Marques de Pombal as first minister of D. José I (1750–1777) that reform would again be considered. During the long reign of the previous monarch, D. João V, the tax revenue derived from imposts on Brazilian gold filled the coffers of the state to the extent that the king never had to call on the Cortes to meet his financial needs. Nevertheless, as an astute observer of political economy, Pombal believed that, despite the appearances of prosperity, Portugal was more of a slave to England than it had ever been to Spain, even during the period of the Babylonian captivity. Although he realized that there were positive aspects to the English alliance, he sought to achieve parity with rather than subservience to his so-called ally. Like Spanish ministers, however, he was bound by a series of irrevocable treaties, which provided the English with so many advantages that it seemed difficult to undo the damage that had already been done.[60]

The treaties did contain a loophole Pombal hoped to use to manipulate the situation to Portuguese advantage. Although they guaranteed the English the same rights as Portuguese citizens, they were silent on the right of the Portuguese state to institute monopolies. Thus Pombal conceived the uncanny idea of state-run monopolies as the vehicle for his escape from dependence. The grand scheme envisaged the investment of Portuguese capital in state bonds. These funds, in turn, would be used to develop monopolistic concerns. Technically, these plans did not discriminate against foreigners, for they were able to participate in the same way as Portuguese citizens. That this participation was to be minimal did not trouble the marques at all.[61]

Pombal concocted a variety of projects in this mode that were designed to advance Portuguese industry with the use of Portuguese capital. The coordinating body was the *junta do comercio*, which was to be responsible for the distribution of state subsidies. Because shipbuilding was one industry in which he believed the Portuguese could compete, large subsidies were designated for this purpose. Luxury trades such as jewelry, china, and silk manufacture also were viewed as having potential. Counting on the difference between wage scales in Portugal and the more advanced economies, he was even willing to invest in and compete with woolen and cotton textiles. All told, seventy-one major new enterprises were founded with the aid of state capital.[62]

The control of commerce was another of Pombal's concerns. Most of Portuguese trade, both within Europe and across the ocean, had fallen into English hands; the problem, then, was how to reverse the situation. Once again monopoly was the solution. The marketing of Portuguese wine, previously dominated by the English, was delegated to a body known as the Upper Douro Company. In the transatlantic sphere, he created the Companhia do Grão Pará e Maranhão, which was given a monopoly of slave imports and charged with beginning the cultivation of rice and cotton in those large provinces. In the decaying sugar sector, he created the Companhia de Pernambuco, which, in return for a monopoly of many categories of imports, was to be obliged to use the profits to revive and modernize the still declining Brazilian sugar industry.[63]

The most novel aspect of Pombaline policy, however, was his attitude toward Brazil. He perceived that its ultimate dependence on England was detrimental to the Luso-Brazilian connection. Although one of the main tenets of colonial orthodoxy demanded that colonies be prohibited from manufacture so that they had to depend on the metropole, Pombal realized the folly of this argument in the Luso-Brazilian situation. As long as Portugal could not supply a variety of goods needed in Brazil, it was far better, he thought, that the Brazilians should supply themselves than to remain dependent on Europe, which, in this case, meant England. Therefore, the restrictions on colonial manufacture, especially those that were supplied from England, were lifted. Thus, in the second half of the eighteenth century, Brazil, albeit haltingly, began to attempt to supply many of its own needs.[64]

The Pombaline legacy is a complicated subject. During his period in office, his policies brought only limited improvements. This, however, can at least partially be explained in that his initiatives were undertaken during the extremely depressed period that accompanied the precipitous decline in Brazilian gold production after 1750. In the medium term, he can be considered to have been much more successful. By the 1790s, when a variety of factors had conspired to make Brazil vibrant again, much had changed. Import-substitution proved successful. Neither Brazil nor Portugal needed to import from England on any significant scale. Both, in fact, developed favorable balances of trade with England and continental Europe. An almost final assessment is provided by Sideri, who observes that "as a result of Pombal's efforts and due also to the favorable international situation . . . the necessary conditions for a basic change had been fulfilled."[65]

Nevertheless, the colonial powers of western Europe, including Portugal, failed in their attempt to narrow the gap between themselves and England. They failed despite their governments' attempts to promote economic development in a variety of policies that might be summed up by the word *mercantilism*. It has been argued that the problem was social in origin. Although the nation-state was capable of consolidating large amounts of capital for use in specific endeavors and modernizing such undertakings as textile manufacture and shipbuilding, in and of itself it proved incapable of eliminating the parasitic classes that stunted economic growth. Rival nations failed to perceive that England's decisive advantage derived from the victory of the bourgeoisie. Until and unless England's competitors were able to duplicate this feat by diminishing the influence and power of nonproductive elements within the social formation, their efforts were doomed.

In opposition, it might be argued that the case of Portugal suggests that there were other ways of modernizing an economy. Indeed it was exceptional. What happened in this instance appears to have been that one man, the Marques de Pombal, for a time was able to suppress the regressive elements in Portuguese society. For a time, therefore, there appeared to be real economic advance. Nevertheless, Pombaline progress was so detested by most of the upper echelon in Portugal that he was dismissed as soon as his mentor, D. José, died. In his absence, the traditionally privileged elements were able to reassert their influence and undermine much of what he had accomplished. This reassertion of the feudal mentality, coupled with other factors, would determine that Portuguese progress was only a façade. Within a short period after the fall of Pombal, Portugal's manufacturing sector would revert to impotence and the country would return to its dependence on imports from abroad. The rapid demise of the attempt to modernize reflected that the social bases of Portugal remained ensconced in the past.

## RIVALRY

By the eighteenth century, competition among the nations of western Europe was not limited to tariff manipulation. Rather, there was a significant increase in warfare among these countries. Eighteenth-century wars, however, differed notably from the conflicts that had been common in the past. Previously, dynastic considerations or religious strife had been the principal bones of contention, as monarchs had sought either to sway the balance of power in their favor or to enforce spiritual conformity. As the seventeenth century progressed, priorities began to change. Although warfare continued to be a primary instrument of policy, its goals were radically altered. Instead of being consumed by the issues that had excited earlier generations, statesmen became dominated by their concerns with industry, commerce, and colonies.

Not only did objectives undergo a radical transformation but so, too, did the conduct of military actions. Fortunately for most European inhabitants, military operations assumed a civilized character to the extent that the citizenry of the combatants no longer bore the brunt of the often drawn-out struggles. The result was that, at least in some spheres, production was increased as the needs of national armies elicited a demand that society, in general, was more than willing to supply. Of even greater importance, however, was that wars ceased to be land-based and confined to Europe. Rather, they came to be truly global in orientation, with the seas assuming at least as large a role as the land. In essence, it was deemed necessary to fight the battle for economic advantage in Europe and on the continents of Africa, Asia, and the Americas as well.

In many respects the series of wars fought between the English and the Dutch in the third quarter of the seventeenth century suggests the transition between the old and the new causes of warfare. Partly as a result of the Civil War, a conflict itself more than tinged with religious concerns, there emerged a new and aggressive segment among the mercantile classes of England. Many of the problems the nation faced, they argued, stemmed from the supremacy the Dutch enjoyed in the commercial sphere. They hastened to add that the privileged position of their rivals had been attained by less than scrupulous means. The Navigation Acts of 1651 and 1660 were designed expressly to address this problem.[66]

For many, however, a more direct solution was deemed both necessary and desirable. Although Cromwell continued to cling to a more traditional world-view, believing that the Protestant Dutch were England's natural allies and that Catholic Spain remained the principal enemy, the mercantile community pressed for an all-out assault on the "lusty, fat, two-legged cheese-worm" who inhabited the republic across the Channel. Comforted by a tremendous increase in naval strength that had transpired by the time of the restoration, the English sought to wrest from the Dutch by military means what they could not achieve by peaceful competition. These pressures resulted in three wars against the Dutch, the last of which was fought, ironically enough, in alliance with Louis XIV of France. In the sense that only the first war, with its harvest of many prizes and the cession of New York, brought much in the way of tangible results, the wars in and of themselves cannot be credited with seriously damaging the Dutch economy. Yet the aggressiveness they nurtured, which increasingly was to become a facet of English overseas endeavors, must be seen as a primary factor in accelerating the commercial growth of England at the expense of its rival.[67]

By the eighteenth century, as exemplified by the changing nature of the relationship between England and the Netherlands, the foci of rival alliances would change significantly, largely because the principal objectives of warfare also changed. England and France came to form the cornerstones of two blocs that contested supremacy not only in Europe but also in virtually every corner of the world. Throughout the second half of the seventeenth century, most of the territorial ambitions of Louis XIV were thwarted by a series of ephemeral coalitions usually organized by the Dutch. As opinion in England began to lose its virulently anti-Dutch content and especially because of the policies of the extremely unpopular James II, the way was paved for the extension of an invitation to William of Orange to assume the throne of England. As both the principal opponent of the pretensions of the Sun King and the husband of Mary, James's senior child, William was ideally placed to cement a unity between the two countries that so many other considerations seemed to encourage.

Thereafter, dating from the War of the League of Augsburg, which raged between 1688 and 1697, the two came to be so closely associated that the expression *maritime powers* became synonymous with their alliance. Denoting how radically circumstances had changed, this more or less permanent coalition came to include Portugal, which for many years had been the principal target of Dutch aggression. Simultaneously, while England dominated this grouping, France also found itself allied with what previously would have seemed an unlikely partner. This was Spain, a country with which the French had fought for more than two centuries. Yet partly as a result of Spain's perception that it suffered from England's economic imperialism and its fears that England coveted unbridled access to its colonies, Spain became more inclined toward France. The alliance was made all the more natural when the two countries came to be ruled by collateral branches of the Bourbon family. As a result, throughout the century, when quarrels among the powers arose, the two nations combined in what were called "family compacts," which fought against the English-backed grouping.[68] At various times, Sweden, Bavaria, Austria, and Prussia were induced to join one of the two alliances. Nevertheless, although Continental issues were of importance, the most consistent point of contention was overseas trade and the struggle to dominate it.

The War of Spanish Succession was the first major conflict of the eighteenth century. When Charles II, the last Habsburg ruler of Spain, died without an heir, the claims of Philip d'Anjou, the grandson of Louis XIV, were put forward. Although the English and the Dutch were wary, they were willing to acquiesce in his accession as long as the crowns of Spain and France remained separate. They also insisted that France should gain no undue advantage from the new arrangement. When, however, in 1702, the *asiento* for the Spanish slave trade was given to a French company, thus violating the understanding reached among the parties, there was a renewal of the alliances that had fought the War of the League of Augsburg. All parties agreed that the search for commercial advantage constituted the basic reason for the conflict. Louis himself offered the opinion that "the main goal of the present war is colonial commerce and the wealth it produces."

The English alliances not only proved successful in the War of Spanish Succession but also in the War of Austrian Succession (1739–1748) and the crucial Seven Years' War (1756–1763). In the War of Austrian Succession, despite some French victories in India, British naval superiority so dominated the Atlantic sphere that the French economy was seriously damaged and the government was obliged to seek peace. Ironically, however, Britain's own financial plight obliged it to accept a settlement that did not necessarily reflect the military situation. Thus, with the important exception of Prussia's acquisition of Silesia, the long war produced no significant exchanges of territory or alterations in the balance of power.[69]

In fact, it was little more than a prelude to the Seven Years' War, which also combined the objectives of Continental nations with the more important aspirations of the colonial powers to acquire advantages in the overseas. Pitting Russia, Austria, Sweden, and France against England and Prussia, the war was remarkable in that it was fought in the Caribbean, the North American mainland, and India, as well as on the European continent. In fact, fully two years before warfare spread to Europe, the French and Indian War, as it was known in America, had already broken out, thus reflecting how colonial affairs had grown in importance. Eventually, in 1761, Spain was convinced to join a new "family compact" with France and thus also entered the war, once again hoping to abrogate its treaty obligations with England. Nevertheless, British naval strength proved decisive. By 1763 Britain's rivals were obliged to accept defeat and come to a settlement.

Several factors about the war are worthy of mention. The British concentrated mainly on the Western Hemisphere and India; in the European theater they were content to subsidize the armies of their Prussian ally. What is astonishing is that with England's financial backing, Prussia, with a population of some 3.5 million, was able to defeat the forces of France, Austria, and Russia, which had a combined total of 70 million inhabitants. That England was able to achieve this end was the result of the modernity of its economic and social systems, which made it much more capable of underwriting the costs of war than France. To a small degree, this was because England had a broader tax base to tap. Even more important, however, was the system of public borrowing that enabled it to "spend on war out of all proportion to its tax revenues."[70] Nevertheless, in the sense that all parties had to borrow to finance their war efforts, neither side was able to afford the war. This was especially true of France, whose finances were so dislocated because of the war that recovery would depend on an extended period of peace.[71]

France was indeed the big loser. England returned most of the Caribbean Islands it had captured, but it retained possession of Canada, thus, for the time being, bringing to an end France's career as a colonial power on the North American mainland. Moreover, it was ousted from India as well, the French East India Company unable to compete with the superior forces of its English rival. Spain also suffered losses. In order to regain Havana, which had fallen to England in 1762, it had to surrender Florida. Nevertheless, as significant as the gains achieved by England were, many felt that they were not commensurate with the magnitude of the military victory. More importantly, the results of the war were not decisive. As J. S. Parry and Philip Sherlock noted, "for the French, the resumption of war was certain. It awaited only financial recovery and a suitable opportunity."[72]

In the process of preparing for the struggle that everyone knew was coming, European ministers became aware that their colonies could prove to be their Achilles' heel. As they began to assess the situation, they became alarmed. Colonial defenses almost everywhere were inadequate. Moreover, they were shocked at the degree of independence and freedom of action that had become commonplace in their colonies. As a result, according to Parry, "all the metropolitan governments set to work after the peace [of 1763] . . . to strengthen colonial defenses . . . to tighten colonial administration . . . [and] to encourage and to expand colonial productivity and trade."[73]

England had won the war, but it had involved considerable expenses for the British treasury. One reason was that during the conflict it had been obliged to subsidize some of its allies. As a result, the national debt, which had stood at £70 million in 1756, rose to £130 million in 1763. English ministers knew that much of the outlay had been for defense of the colonies. They also saw that in future it would be necessary to have a permanent military force in America. It was their considered opinion that at least some of these expenditures should be defrayed by the colonies themselves. The reasoning, in part, was that the colonists had a much lighter tax burden than their English cousins and so could afford to pay for their own protection.[74]

The attempt to implement the new policy triggered a colonial reaction that London could not tolerate. In order to make the colonies more secure, Parliament forbade further settlement in the west. It also passed legislation designed to raise revenue to pay for the troops who were to defend the colonies. Because the measures were unprecedented, the colonists concluded that they were unconstitutional. In order to demonstrate their opposition, they organized boycotts and other forms of resistance. Viewed from the perspective of Parliament, this challenge could not go unanswered. The issue, indeed, brought to the fore the validity of colonial dependencies. George III, recently ascended to the throne and anxious to resurrect the authority that his immediate predecessors had allowed to slip through their hands, was most concerned. He was worried that they would try to "cast off the constitutional dependency on the mother country."[75] Neither he nor his cabinet was willing to acquiesce in such an outcome.

Similarly, ministers in Madrid began to reassess the relationship with their colonies. They were alarmed at the political and economic independence that had been allowed to develop, especially the degree of self-sufficiency that the colonies enjoyed. In order to reverse the situation, it was decided to implement a policy known as *comercio libre* (free trade). The plan envisaged a drastic reduction in import and export duties and the opening of a great number of ports that had previously been closed. Among the many purposes of the legislation was to increase the amount of goods imported from Europe. The rationale was that colonial manufactures were of such an inferior quality that if the price of European goods were placed on a parity cost basis, they would soon undermine domestic production. Charles III justified the policy by stating that "the security of the Americas must be measured by the state of their dependence on the metropolis, and this dependence is founded on their need for consumer goods. The day they can supply all their needs themselves, their dependence will be voluntary."[76]

Ministers in Lisbon were independently coming to similar conclusions with respect to Portugal's relationship with Brazil as had their English and Spanish counterparts concerning their own colonies. There had always been a significant undercurrent of opposition to Pombal's policy of encouraging colonial manufacture. After he fell from power in 1777, discussions began about the advisability of reversing his policies. Eventually, it was decided that his monopolistic companies should be abolished and other aspects of his legislation dismantled. The policy that was implemented not only decreed that there would be no new manufactures but also demanded the destruction of those that already existed. By 1788 a comprehensive plan for the complete regulation of every aspect of colonial economic life had been drafted. As justification for the draconian legislation, Martinho de Melo e Castro, the first minister of state, defended his stance by noting that "workshops and manufactures would make the inhabitants [of Brazil] totally independent of the metropolis."[77]

Thus, as indicated by the statements emanating from Lisbon, Madrid, and London, the degree to which colonies had been allowed to develop a dynamic of their own came to be a major source of concern. Although at first glance it might seem remarkable that such similar opinions would emerge in different places within a relatively limited time span, it becomes less surprising when one realizes that each country functioned in an environment that was both competitive and sensitive to international pressures. On the one hand, these forces had obliged governments to become more involved with domestic economic policies; under these circumstances, it was logical that these same concerns would be applied to the colonies. On the other, the eighteenth century had shown that overseas enterprises were not immune from attack by enemies. Quite the contrary, that Louisiana, Florida, Canada, and various Caribbean Islands had changed hands and other territories had been occupied during the Seven Years' War was ample proof of how exposed overseas possessions really were.

## CONCLUSION

In many respects, the eighteenth century was notable for the vigor exuded by the colonizing nations of western Europe. It was also an epoch of remarkable myopia. Although much energy was expended, both with respect to reforming their own economies and contesting the position of others, few recognized the real sources of potential strength. As the century entered its final quarter, there were few indications that in-depth perception was improving. For in their haste to remedy weaknesses in their own imperial spheres, the colonial powers would sometimes forget that their real strength was derived from compromises that had made the systems functional. As was widely predicted in Europe, war did indeed break out again. Yet before it did, tensions had been raised within the various imperial systems that had upset the delicate balance upon which they had been based. The attempt to protect the colonies against perceived enemies would, ironically, awaken latent hostilities that were much more potent than the dangers against which the colonial powers sought to fortify themselves. By the time the next series of wars was concluded, changes of a more permanent nature had occurred.

# 9

# REVOLUTION

Although the first three quarters of the eighteenth century were marked by intensive competition, there were few fundamental changes in either the balance of power, the structure of empires, or the organization of production. In the last quarter of the century, however, the world economy was radically restructured. Partly as a result of the overzealous attempts of European powers to tighten control over their imperial systems, previously docile colonies rose in arms against their respective metropoles. As an outgrowth of a century of attempting to improve their own fortunes by weakening their adversaries', the nations of Europe, with almost suicidal blindness, rushed to feed the fires of revolt in the colonies of their rivals. Unlike previous hostilities, the series of wars that erupted in 1776 and did not abate until well into the nineteenth century left in their wake a vastly different world. By the time they concluded, most of the colonial world had ceased to exist in its previous form. Moreover, in part because of the shuffling that had taken place, the power balance in Europe itself was irrevocably altered. These momentous structural changes ushered in along with the nineteenth century in turn obliged nations to rethink policies and doctrines that had long been held sacrosanct. In fact, the age of revolution would serve as a bridge between an antiquated system and a new and more dynamic world economy.

## CHALLENGING THE OLD ORDER

One of the dominant characteristics of the fifty years that spanned the turn of the eighteenth century was the phenomenon of revolution. It is notable that in the Atlantic sphere, after centuries of relative tranquillity, the colonies of England, France, Spain, and Portugal rose up against their metropoles. What is especially amazing is how pervasive the attempt to end colonial bondage became. On the surface, it might appear that vibrant dependencies such as Spanish America and the British mainland would have been the likeliest candidates to sever their connections with Europe. After all, it was apparent that their respective home governments were bent upon restricting and rechanneling their growth. Peripheries, such as Haiti and Brazil, in contrast, would have seemed less likely to follow a similar course. Prior to their respective revolts, each not only had enjoyed a period of extreme prosperity, but the generation of this wealth had proved mutually beneficial to colony and metropole alike.

Upon closer scrutiny, then, the factors that triggered the various revolts were complex and often seemingly contradictory. In some cases, for example, the desire to preserve as much of the status quo in times portentous of upheaval was a more powerful motive to revolt than the desire to institute change. Yet, however disparate the catalysts and the motivations of the actors themselves, it would be a mistake to view these movements in isolation. For each, in one way or another, resulted from adjustments that were being made in the structure of the world economy. Moreover, despite their separation in time and space, there were important ideological, social, and political linkages among them.

Although tension between Britain and its mainland colonies appeared minimal, there were those who were not surprised that North America was the first region in the colonial world to attempt to liberate itself from European control. Included among the factors that might have suggested a continuing amicable relationship between the two was the virtual absence of overt hostilities during the colonial era. Whereas in the seventeenth century war and rebellion were constant reminders of the contradictions that dominated the Anglo-Irish relationship, nary a shot had been necessary to maintain the ties between England and America. Moreover, British legislation with respect to the thirteen colonies clearly lacked the draconian content that was applied to Ireland. In fact, even where it was intended to be discriminatory, the absence of a bureaucracy capable of regulating colonial affairs or the presence of prudent governors who preferred not to arouse the ire of the colonists usually meant that the harshest aspects of British policy were mediated to the extent that the colonist regarded imperial legislation as little more than a nuisance.

Shrewder observers, however, could foresee that, despite benign appearances, a collision course seemed likely. For example, as early as the 1730s, John Ashley published a volume in which he predicted that the mainland colonies would separate from England because of the competitive nature of their respective products.[1] And despite the absence of overt hostilities, many urban merchants, as well as indebted planters in Virginia and Maryland, were disenchanted by the restrictions of the colonial system. On the other side of the ocean, even before the end of the Seven Years' War, questions were being raised about the loyalty of the colonists and whether it could be maintained.[2] Nevertheless, prior to the end of the war in 1763, there was little to suggest that the bases of the imperial system would be seriously challenged. Rather, it would not be until after the cessation of hostilities, when Britain would reassess its priorities, that the latent contradictions inherent in this metropolis-dependency relationship would manifest themselves.

Despite England's overwhelming victory in the Seven Years' War, many prominent statesmen in London became convinced that basic changes needed to be made with respect to the mainland colonies. The war had been tremendously successful insofar as France had been eliminated from both Canada and India, though in order to pacify Spain, France ceded the vast Louisiana Territory to its unfortunate ally. Moreover, the war exposed the vulnerability of the possessions of the French and the Spanish in the Caribbean.

It was widely believed that the basic administrative framework for regulating colonial affairs needed reform. Prior to the war, few statesmen in England considered colonial issues worthy of parliamentary concern. In this climate, the colonials had been able to regulate much of their own affairs. Equally annoying to the British mentality that emerged after 1763 was that the colonists often ignored legislation when it served their best interests to do so. For example, the Molasses Act of 1733 had been intended to regulate commerce with the French West Indies. But the colonists chose to ignore it, and the administration lacked a staff capable of even a token patrolling of the coasts. As late as the 1760s, therefore, the customs duties collected from the excises on this commerce were virtually nonexistent.[3]

To put an end to this lax state of affairs, several means suggested themselves to the British government. As a starter, the number of bureaucrats was to be increased to the extent that effective measures of regulation and enforcement could proceed. Although rarely stated explicitly, the administration would also be able to avail itself of the quartered troops when emergency police powers were required. Perhaps most important of all was that Parliament was to take a much more active role in the regulation of colonial affairs. From the perspective of Whitehall, the scheme was not so much harsh legislation as rules that had to be complied with so that the broader imperial network would be made more secure and coherent.[4]

Indeed, after 1763 a new tenor could be perceived in England's attitude toward the colonies. The striking down of the Currency Act presaged the changes that would be enforced: Several colonies sought to mediate their indebtedness by passing legislation to authorize the issue of paper currency. They were both surprised and disappointed when, in a fashion uncharacteristic of past performance, Parliament intervened by promulgating an edict that prohibited the issuing of paper money in any of the colonies to the south of New England. The cancellation of the Currency Act not only represented England's decision to oversee colonial affairs more thoroughly but also instituted a period when England would seize the initiative in shaping the direction of future policy. There was increased regulation of the use of natural resources, intracolonial trade, and local American manufacture. Migration to the west of the Appalachians was also summarily banned in 1763. One year later, Parliament promulgated the Plantation Act, which sought to regularize trade with the French West Indies, and gave every indication that the new law would be enforced. The British government demonstrated, indeed, that it intended to do more than simply talk about imperial reform.[5]

The new spate of legislation was indicative of imperial thinking and also suggestive of some of its shortcomings. From the point of view of London, it was fair because it sought no more than to make the Americans shoulder their own burdens. Where the new policies were suspect, however, was at their source. George III, who had assumed office in 1762, entrusted much of his government to friends, who, in their brief sojourns in office had little time to study the complexities of the issues that were raised. Although they spent more time on colonial questions than had their predecessors, they devoted little or no attention to colonial opinion. In this regard, the colonists were at a distinct disadvantage, as they possessed few on-the-spot lobbyists to influence ministerial decisions. As one member suggested, just how little thought went into colonial legislation is indicated in that the Stamp Act aroused less debate than an uncontroversial turnpike bill.[6] In essence, what was fair and just was to be determined exclusively in London without prior consultation with the colonists or consideration of how the measures would be received. An underlying assumption, though rarely voiced in its crudest form, was that colonists were duty-bound to accept whatever London dictated.[7]

On most issues the colonists profoundly disagreed with the imperial viewpoint. In theory few denied that England had the right to regulate commerce, although in practice many believed that it was their de facto privilege to circumvent such proscriptions whenever possible. Yet their reading of history and constitutionality differed radically from the English government's interpretation. Because the French threat had been removed, the colonists questioned the necessity of stationing a permanent force in America. Not only did they dislike the inconvenience and expense of supporting the redcoats, they also questioned the right of Parliament to regulate the affairs of the colonies and especially to raise revenue taxes.

The matter first came to a head over the Stamp Act of 1765, a piece of legislation that was blatantly designed to raise revenue. The colonists responded with riots, a gathering of delegates from various colonies to discuss the means of noncompliance, and, most importantly, a boycott on English goods. According to Edmund Morgan, it is important to remember that the colonists "wanted, as yet, no more freedom than they had enjoyed in the past. But they wanted no less, either."[8] To the extent that British merchants put enough pressure on London to have the act revoked, the movement was a success. Still, London was apparently not prepared to allow the issue to die a quiet and natural death: On the heels of the repeal of the Stamp Act, Parliament passed the Declaratory Act, which boldly stated its right to levy any legislation of its choice.

As time progressed, the gulf between the imperial and the colonial viewpoints would widen and their respective positions would harden to the extent that conflict seemed inevitable. Undeterred by the opposition that the Stamp Act precipitated and convinced that the colonies should pay for themselves, Parliament passed a series of laws that came to be known as the Townshend Acts, which charged import duties on a wide variety of commodities. The purpose was to raise enough revenue to defray the costs of administration. As was to be expected, the colonists responded with campaigns of nonconsumption and nonimportation. Although resistance was widespread, it was in Boston that it approached its most threatening level. In fact, angry mobs became so unruly that in October 1768, British troops opened fire on a crowd. The death toll of five people in this so-called Boston Massacre was far less important than that this was the first time there was evidence that a British army used its muscle not to defend the colonists from a common enemy but to uphold the rights of the metropole against dissident Americans.

Once again the offending pieces of legislation were repealed, although their cancellation had little to do with the events in Boston. Rather, the boycott had been so successful that the legislation came to be perceived as counterproductive. Yet, in the meantime, the rival positions were becoming increasingly polarized. Although thoughts of independence had once been confined to a tiny minority, as the controversies continued to mount, the influence of the radicals similarly began to increase.[9] To many more Americans, virtually any legislation passed in England was considered an infringement on their constitutional rights; to the British, to tolerate colonial impudence was viewed as nothing short of abandoning sovereignty.

Given the extent to which each side saw the same phenomena in completely different ways, it is not surprising that the conflict came to a head. More intriguing is that between 1770 and 1773, although the situation remained tense, little overt conflict took place. Then, again with the wider imperial schema in mind, the British government granted to the East India Company a monopoly on tea imports into the colonies. Especially as the price of tea was to be lowered, London, demonstrating that it had learned little from the events of the recent past, felt justified in instituting this new policy. To the colonists, especially the merchants, who had always been wary of such initiatives, the specter of an imperial government that could by fiat arbitrarily cause ruin to members of, or even the entire, commercial sector could not be tolerated. The broader community was becoming politicized, asking, if merchants could suffer such discrimination, what was to prevent similar enactments on other forms of property, including their own homes.[10]

Again resistance was widespread, but again it was in Boston, where a group of activists went beyond the traditional policy of nonconsumption and dumped tea into the harbor, that opposition was most concentrated. This time the gauntlet had definitely been thrown down. George III was particularly offended. Moreover, whereas previously there had always been voices of conciliation and compromise in cabinet circles, now the government unanimously agreed that effective steps were needed to suppress colonial opposition. In addition to a number of other punitive measures, the new edicts stated that Boston Harbor was to remain closed until the tea was paid for. Nevertheless, if Britain expected these actions mysteriously to subdue the colonists, it was sadly mistaken. All Britain succeeded in doing was to broaden the base of the opposition and change its goals. As Cecilia Kenyon noted, the "resistance to the Stamp Act . . . had . . . been motivated by a desire to maintain their rights as Englishmen. Independence was a last resort, a means to secure these rights as men, and as Americans."[11]

The struggle that was to erupt between Great Britain and its colonies in 1776 was to be profoundly affected by long-standing rivalries in the world economy. Had it remained purely a parochial affair between a colonial power that believed it was exercising its rightful authority and a disenchanted group of colonists who felt that they were suffering from an arbitrary abuse of power, the outcome might have been different. For neither side particularly distinguished itself in the art of warfare. Both the British and their mercenary employees proved incompetent on the battlefield; the American cause, for its part, would have been facilitated had the revolt been as truly popular as its publicists proclaimed it to be. In fact, as the war dragged on, enthusiasm rapidly waned, troops deserted, and the supplies necessary to sustain the effort dwindled.[12] At some points, historians have suggested, the movement commanded the support of no more than one-third of the population.

The crucial watershed, however, occurred in October 1777, when the army of the revolution forced the surrender of General John Burgoyne at Saratoga. It was with this victory that the French, still reeling from the humiliation of the defeat in the Seven Years' War, decided that the "suitable opportunity" had arrived and that it was realistic to support the American cause. By striking at the heart of the British imperial system, France hoped to repay its rival for a century of continuous defeat.[13] In the following year, Spain was again enticed to join in an anti-English alliance, to be followed in 1780 by the Dutch. Despite being motivated by opportunism, support from European allies, especially on the high seas, was decisive. By 1781 the defeat of Cornwallis at Yorktown, coupled with other reverses the British suffered at the hands of their European opponents (who accounted themselves in a superior fashion to their past performances), convinced the British that the likelihood of reconquering the colonies was illusory. As a result, in 1783 they signed a treaty that has been described as "the greatest victory in the annals of American diplomacy."[14] It also put a seal on the first major breach in the old colonial system.

It is one of the cruel ironies of modern history that the dismemberment of the British empire, for which France was principally responsible, should have brought little joy to the victor. This lone victory, which produced temporary exhilaration after a century of failure and humiliation, was to result in the demise of the ancien régime. For although France had found a suitable opportunity, it had yet to experience financial recovery. When it entered the war, the treasury was characteristically empty. Yet the temptation of inflicting a decisive wound to its long-standing enemy was too great to resist. As a result, France borrowed at high rates to finance both its military operations and its aid to the rebels. What was more important was that in 1786 the country entered one of the most severe economic downturns of the century, at precisely the time that repayment of the loans came due. After a number of ministers, few of whom had much financial expertise, unsuccessfully attempted to rectify the situation, it became apparent just how grave the crisis was. Nothing short of a radical reconstruction of French society, it came to be perceived, could possibly solve problems of such magnitude. Thus, the events that would culminate in the French Revolution were intimately related to the American Revolution. In fact, Georges Lefebvre goes so far as to suggest that "the revolt of the English colonies may in fact be considered the principal direct cause of the French Revolution."[15]

The American Revolution also influenced events in France in a more indirect way. Although the obvious initial motivation of France's involvement in the American war for independence was to take revenge on England for past defeats, over time the French people developed a great deal of sympathy for the American cause. Moreover, at a time when French institutions began to appear increasingly anachronistic and ossified, the American experience seemed to suggest that fundamental change indeed was possible. William Doyle, in fact, believes that the American Revolution was much more powerful than the Enlightenment in molding the mindset that was bent upon dismantling the ancien régime.[16]

Although the impact of the American war and the ideology identified with the movement can be considered the main catalysts of the French Revolution, prior to the outbreak of the upheaval, few could have envisaged the course that it would take. The crisis was precipitated in 1788 by the resistance of the *parlements*, the elite corporations that had the power to delay the implementation of royal edicts. In the words of Theda Skocpol, their refusal to approve the measures concocted by the ministers of Louis XVI "opened the door to the revolution."[17]

The *parlements* believed the crisis was so grave that it could only be resolved by a reconvening of the Estates General, an institution consisting of delegates elected to represent the three segments of which French society was legally composed. This body had not met since 1614 and was little more than an historical precedent, yet many people blindly believed that it was the panacea that would remedy the situation. Louis XVI apparently placed so much faith in its innate powers to cure the ills bedeviling French society that he neither put forward a plan for national regeneration nor even sponsored a slate of candidates that might represent a government position once the Estates convened in 1789. Instead, rather naively, the king, along with many of his subjects, seemed to believe that the Estates would somehow find a way to create a simpler, healthier, and more virtuous society.[18]

When the Estates convened in 1789 there was still little hint of the crisis that would explode. It has been noted that the delegates were elected by a liberal franchise that extended the privilege of voting to a remarkably large number of people. Although those who were chosen to sit in the Estates General were elected to represent different classes, seemingly few ideological barriers separated them. For example, 87 percent of those elected to represent the Third Estate were members of the proprietary bourgeoisie. As such, they shared much in common with the delegates who represented the nobility, many of whom originated from among the lower provincial orders. Both could agree on the desirability of a constitutional monarchy. They also disliked the increasing centralization that had become state policy dating from the era of Louis XIV. Moreover, reflecting the ideology of the Enlightenment, they believed in the notion of careers open to talent.[19]

Despite the modest objectives espoused by the majority of the delegates, France soon experienced an unprecedented spate of liberal reforms. Although the promulgation of the new decrees was preceded by a complicated series of events, ultimately the main stimulus came from lower-class militancy. In Paris economic hardship and rumors of aristocratic plots incited the masses to rise up and threaten the existing order. These sansculottes, consisting mostly of artisans, shopkeepers, and journeymen, resisted the troops of the king and thereby preserved the sphere of independent action for the Third Estate. The capture of the Bastille on 14 July 1789 represented the crowning achievement of the Parisian revolution.[20]

Violence also erupted in the countryside. Evidence suggests that, especially during the second half of the eighteenth century, poor peasants became more numerous and even more destitute. They were equally hard-hit by the depressed conditions of the later 1780s and had mistakenly assumed that the grievances that they had been invited to enunciate in *cahiers* (memorials) submitted to the Estates General would automatically be rectified. Taking their cue from events in the capital, peasants throughout the country refused to pay taxes, tithes, and even their feudal dues. Demonstrating that these were not symbolic acts in response to a specific set of circumstances, but an attempt to overthrow the old order, the peasants seized and burned the documents that legalized their subjugation.[21]

It was in this environment of both urban and rural unrest that the National Assembly acted. Even members of the upper nobility joined in the revolutionary vote that abolished the last vestiges of feudalism. Soon venal office, a bulwark of the ancien régime and its parasites, was similarly done away with. The culmination of the reforms was achieved in August, when the National Assembly promulgated the Declaration of the Rights of Man. Calling for equality before the law and defining sovereign power as residing in the nation, this document purported to enact an irreversible break with the past. Thus, within a few months, the moderate reformers of 1789 seemed to have staged a revolution. As noted by George Taylor, the "revolutionary mentality was created by the crisis."[22]

The sansculottes were soon called upon to defend the revolution again. Although a constitution including the Declaration of the Rights of Man had been promulgated, it also distinguished between those with property and those who were propertyless. Moreover, the Legislative Assembly the constitution called into being offered very little to the masses. As a result, in 1791 those who had risen two years earlier to save the National Assembly now turned on its less liberal descendant. Spearheaded by provincials who arrived in the capital singing the *Marseillaise*, the revolutionary anthem of the contingent from Marseilles, they demanded a new constitution. Thus, a new legislative body known as the Convention came into being. Elected by universal suffrage, it proceeded to enact much of the program demanded by the lower classes.[23]

In the next few years, however, France was to undergo a bewildering series of changes that would have important repercussions both domestically and internationally. Intraclass rivalries and the absence of ideological cohesion caused the revolution to deteriorate to the extent that it served the interests of virtually no one and its excesses caused widespread disenchantment. In the process the king was executed and much of the nobility was obliged to flee abroad, where it was successful in capitalizing on the threat to the existing order that it claimed was posed by revolutionary France. Partly because of the revulsion caused by the decapitation of Louis XVI and partly because France had pledged to support republican movements throughout the Continent, soon most of Europe had declared war on the isolated republic. Despite the overwhelming odds it faced, however, by raising a truly popular army of 750 thousand men, France was able to neutralize the coalition that sought to undo the revolution.[24]

In 1798, after a brief interlude of peace, France fared badly when confronted by a new coalition of European states. The military reverses enabled a young general named Napoleon to stage a coup d'état. Domestically, he was able to reimpose many of the ideals of 1789 that had fallen victim to the ideological backlash that had accompanied the overthrow of the Jacobins. Internationally, his war effort was so successful that he suffered few military reverses, even though Spain alone did not join in the alliance against France. By 1807 he dominated the Continent to the extent that almost all of his erstwhile enemies were converted into allies. Only England, secure behind the barrier of the Channel, remained at war with France.[25]

One of Napoleon's principal goals was to make France economically competitive with England. Despite the territorial losses of the later stages of the eighteenth century, he believed that it was possible to resurrect a colonial empire in America. To this end, the reconquest of Haiti, which had been able to become virtually independent during the years of revolutionary turmoil, was critical. Martinique, Guadeloupe, Florida, Guyana, and Louisiana were to play subordinate roles in the new French overseas empire. Moreover, in order to achieve his goals, Napoleon considered the reintroduction of slavery to be absolutely essential. Such plans came to nought, however, when the expeditionary force sent to reconquer Haiti succumbed partly to disease and partly to the ire of the war-weary populace, who were able to summon up one last-gasp effort to ensure that bondage would not again become a way of life. Renewed warfare in Europe and the threat that the expansionist United States would pose in future to French pretensions convinced Napoleon that his American vision was untenable and goaded him into hastily disposing of the extensive Louisiana Territory to the fledgling American nation.[26]

Closer to home he envisaged a more direct assault on England. He believed that England's main strengths were derived from its trade and industry. Because by 1806 he had already won the allegiance of most of Europe, he was emboldened to issue the Berlin Decree, which effectively sought to close the harbors of Europe to English goods. To enforce what came to be known as the "continental system," his forces invaded Portugal in 1807, treacherously overthrew the government of Spain in 1808, and subsequently occupied the coastlands of the Netherlands and Germany in an attempt to seal the Continent hermetically against English produce. This policy was intended to foment French industry, which, in the absence of English competition, was expected to flourish. Additionally, the loss of markets and the resultant inflation was intended to drain England's "economic blood."[27]

The impact of the French Revolution and the Napoleonic Wars on both Europe and the wider world was enormous. With the economic assault on England falling short of achieving its desired ends and the alliance that constituted the French "imperium" breaking down in the face of incipient nationalism, the tide turned against Napoleon. By 1815 France caved in under the weight that it could no longer sustain. Yet the events that transpired in France between 1789 and 1815 would serve as catalysts to social and political movements in several regions of the world that had previously remained fairly tranquil.

Both the French and American revolutions profoundly influenced developments in Ireland, where each movement had a significant, albeit a very different, impact. From the outset of the American troubles, the Irish took a great deal of interest in the affairs of its sibling colony. On the one hand, this concern was stimulated by the recent emigration of many Irishmen across the Atlantic. On the other, because Ireland suffered from even greater disabilities than the thirteen colonies, events in America were viewed somewhat as a test case for the future of Ireland. Therefore, as the revolution unfolded, events were reported with the same avidity as if they were happening in Ireland. In addition to eliciting sentiments that were truly sympathetic toward the colonial cause, the Irish seemed to revel in the embarrassment that the revolution heaped on the British government.[28]

The American Revolution occurred at a juncture when the political climate in Ireland was undergoing significant change. Although Ireland possessed its own Parliament, English precedent, as defined in Poynings Law of 1494, so restricted its initiative as to render the Irish Parliament little more than a rubber stamp. To make matters worse, it was presided over by a lord chancellor who was appointed from London. Not only was the executive not responsible to Parliament, he was able to manipulate it via the mechanism of individuals who were referred to as "undertakers." These were members who, via perquisites, bribes, or officeholding, could be relied upon to provide the government with a majority on virtually any issue. By the middle of the eighteenth century, however, an independent group began to emerge that often opposed measures put forward by the government. Increasingly, the Patriots, as they came to be called, enunciated the aspirations and grievances of the vast majority that had no representation in Parliament. Among their goals were the securing of the definition of Ireland as a separate kingdom from Great Britain, a relaxation of the disabilities suffered by Catholics and Presbyterians, and freedom from England's trade restrictions.[29]

It was in this environment of increasing assertiveness that the conflict in America was to have an impact. An embargo arbitrarily imposed by the British government on Irish exports to America caused severe economic hardship and raised awareness of yet another injustice. Many Irish were already disenchanted that Irish troops paid for by the Irish treasury had been dispatched to America. The entire complexion of the situation, however, changed when France entered the war against Britain. For it raised the specter of French invasion of an Ireland denuded of troops, with no possibility of protection by an overly committed metropole. Almost spontaneously there grew up a volunteer movement whose avowed purpose was to defend the country against the possibility of foreign invasion. By autumn 1778 there were forty thousand of these paramilitary irregulars.

The growth of the volunteer movement, as well as other considerations, convinced London that appeasement was in order. Nevertheless, although Lord North sought to provide relief in the form of relaxed trading restrictions, commercial interests in England mounted such a staunch opposition that the government was forced to back down. This latest of a long series of rebukes, however, was directed at an Ireland that was no longer passive. Following the American precedent, the Irish organized a boycott against the importation of English goods. Moreover, with the undisguised support of the volunteers, the Patriots increased their demands in the Irish Parliament. In view of the dire nature of the circumstances, the British were obliged to make concessions that a few years earlier would have been unthinkable. Freedom of trade, relaxation of Catholic disabilities, the enfranchisement of the Presbyterians, and the complete independence of the Irish Parliament were the fruits of the Irish movement.[30] As Reginald Coupland observed, the American movement "had given Ireland not only the lead but her chance of following it." He added that the "American war was the Irish harvest."[31]

Remarkable as the reforms were in the Irish context, they fell far short of providing the means for the creation of an equitable society. In an environment of increasing expectations, it was certain that unless these defects were remedied there would be additional problems. Although Britain had retained a dominating influence over Irish affairs, it made no effort to enlarge the scope of participation. Thus, as a result of the selective system of choosing parliamentarians, that body was dominated by representatives of the Anglican gentry, who were a minority of the members of the established church, which was a minority of the Protestant population, which, in turn, was a minority of the population of Ireland. Rather than representing any fundamental changes in outlook toward Ireland, the British reforms had been enacted under duress, and it was unlikely that magnanimity would be demonstrated when circumstances began to return toward normalcy.

Indeed, soon after attaining parliamentary independence, disenfranchised Irish of all persuasions began to petition for parliamentary reform. Yet the requests were met with a resounding no by the legislators, who were loathe to vote themselves out of existence. Moreover, although majority sentiment favored Catholic emancipation, Parliament remained steadfast in its refusal.[32]

In the sphere of Anglo-Irish relations, prospects were no brighter. Although Henry Grattan, the Patriot leader, and William Pitt, then British prime minister, believed that a treaty of equality between the two would cement an alliance, it was once again torpedoed by the British Parliament. This environment spawned the formation of the United Irishmen, a group that increasingly came to feel that relief would never be forthcoming from either the Irish Parliament or the British government. Their only hope, they believed, was support from revolutionary France. Under increasing repression at home and receiving little more than sympathy from France, in 1798 they mounted a futile revolt. Despite the rebellion's abject failure, both the Irish gentry and the British government were aware that any French initiative in Ireland would be greeted with great enthusiasm. As a result, in order to forestall what was widely perceived as change of a threatening nature, in 1800 both agreed to the union of the two countries.[33]

The French Revolution had an even greater impact on the colony of Haiti. Despite the enormous prosperity that had been accelerating throughout the eighteenth century, tension between the colony and France had also been building. Although relatively few in number, the productive sector of the colonial economy was dominated by a group often referred to as the *grands blancs*, the white planter aristocracy that produced the sugar, coffee, cotton, and other commodities for which San Domingue had become famous. Nevertheless, they were not without their grievances against the system. Just as had been the case in the British colonies, after the Seven Years' War legislation of Haiti in some respects had been liberalized but was also much more strictly enforced. This only served to emphasize to the *grands blancs* their often overstated view that they had much less influence on colonial policy than did their British counterparts.[34]

The French planters also disliked the *exclusif*, the trade policy that required all colonial goods to be landed in France before being reexported. Whereas the British planters, who once had also complained about the Navigation Acts, had come to realize the advantages that they derived from a protected market, the French planters justifiably recognized the degree to which the *exclusif* ate into their profits. Since their production costs were lower and their products superior, the French planters could have dominated much of the European market more completely if there had been no mercantilistic interference. As the system functioned, however, much of what would have accrued to the producer under conditions of free trade was appropriated by the French mercantile class. Exacerbating the situation, as seen through the eyes of the planters, was that they were increasingly falling into debt to that very merchant class they accused of being favored by the imperial system. If one common aspiration among the planters could be identified in 1789, it was desire to escape from debt.[35]

Although they were dominant in economic and social affairs, the planters constituted only one segment of a complex society. Those whites who performed the more mundane aspects of everyday life were referred to as the *petits blancs*. They chafed under a social system that they believed relegated them to a position of second-class citizens. Again, if the *petits blancs* shared one aspiration in 1789, it was to improve their lot. Although they were extremely concerned with their own social mobility, they were equally obsessed with making certain that the growing number of mulattoes in Haitian society would be denied a similar opportunity. Not only had the numbers of free mulattoes risen sharply during the eighteenth century, but many had been able to accumulate significant amounts of property. Although some had become successful slave-owning planters, legal barriers against their participation in society were constantly being raised. As a group, what they most desired in 1789 was admission to full-scale participation in society that they considered to be commensurate with their economic status.[36]

Finally, there was the huge slave population, whose numbers were being swelled with each passing year. In 1788, for example, no fewer than forty thousand were landed in San Domingue. Although their goals were the most difficult to ascertain, it has been suggested that most probably wanted little more than an amelioration of their wretched status, which though theoretically protected by the Code Noire of 1685, was thoroughly degraded by their owners' desires for quick profits.

The social situation, however, was even more complex than portrayed in this simple schema. Europeans ridiculed Creoles, sugar planters looked down on those who grew coffee and cotton, the planter class as a whole despised those who earned wages, new barriers had arisen between white and colored, and even the Creole and domestic slaves felt themselves to be far superior to those who worked the fields. "This high degree of segmentation," writes David Geggus, "was to express itself in the ruthlessly shifting alliances of the revolution."[37]

As the French Revolution proceeded, the aspirations of the various social categories created the strangest bedfellows. When word first reached San Domingue of the events of the summer of 1789 in Paris, bickering began among the whites, even though all could find something that they approved of in the revolution. By 1791, with revolutionary France finding itself incapable of imposing order on the situation and the two groups, the *grands* and *petits blancs*, still parrying over their respective positions vis-à-vis the revolution, a massive slave revolt broke out. Although the island remained in limbo for a time, as the revolution in France moved toward the left, significant changes unfolded in the way various interest groups perceived the revolution and the future of Haiti.[38]

Soon revolutionary France found itself at war with a great part of Europe, including England and Spain. Spain, which was particularly upset over the regicide of Louis XVI, the distant cousin of Charles IV, previously had done what in more normal times would have been considered the unthinkable by supplying arms from Santo Domingo to the slaves in Haiti. With the declaration of war, Spain joined Britain in an open assault on France's most important colonial possession. Because the foreign forces held out the hope of the ultimate defeat of France and the abolition of slavery, they were joined by the slave armies, which François-Dominique Toussaint-Louverture was transforming from a rabble of undifferentiated field hands into an effective fighting force. To this already unlikely combination of forces was soon to be added the weight of the French planters, who had become alarmed at the excesses of the French Revolution, especially what appeared to them to be its assault on property and privilege. They came to hope that sovereignty over the territory would be transferred to Great Britain. Thus, the British and the Spanish, enemies during most of modern European history, were joined in alliance by revolting slaves and former slaveholders in one of the most unlikely partnerships imaginable.[39]

The rival camp also included factions that, under more normal circumstances, probably would have been at each other's throats. From the outset, revolutionary France had the support of the *petits blancs*, who saw in the movement the means for their own advancement. In May 1792, when Paris promulgated a document that guaranteed the legal equality of mulattoes, this influential group also pledged its support to France. Although relations between *petits blancs* and mulattoes remained suspect, after many false starts, the two groups agreed to make common cause in defense of the revolution. The most important addition to the French cause, however, was the defection of the slave armies from the English side to that of France. When the Jacobins abolished slavery, Toussaint-Louverture decided that the most likely way of guaranteeing the liberty of his followers was to cast his lot with the revolution.[40] Thus, groups who prior to the revolution felt nothing but disdain for one another found themselves supporting the same cause, even if there was little coordination among them.

Although the military aspects of the conflict were as complex as the diplomatic, over time Toussaint-Louverture came not only to dominate the battlefields but also to restore a semblance of order to what had become an extremely chaotic situation. In 1795 Spain, thoroughly beaten in Europe, sued for peace and agreed to cede its share of the island of Hispaniola to France. Two years later, after five years of suffering heavy casualties and having spent large sums of money without much to show for their efforts, the English also withdrew. With the departure of the European forces, the erstwhile allies, Toussaint-Louverture at the head of the black armies and André Rigaud, the leader of the mulattoes, were left to confront each other, the stakes being nothing less than control of the island.[41]

Soon after he won this test of strength, Toussaint-Louverture addressed himself to the task of resurrecting the country. In many instances property was restored to its former owners, racial tensions were suppressed, and the work force was obliged to return to the fields, albeit for wages. By 1802, despite the horrendous casualties and the vast amount of property damage that the war years had created, a surprising amount of normalcy had been returned. That this remarkable achievement was almost single-handedly the work of Toussaint-Louverture was suggested by an American contemporary, who observed that he should be "considered as a phenomenon which every century does not produce."[42]

Because Napoleon intervened and undid much of what had been accomplished, what might have transpired in San Domingue had Toussaint-Louverture been allowed to finish his appointed task can only be conjectured. Initially, the French plan succeeded to the extent that a cowed population that watched passively while Toussaint-Louverture was imprisoned and exiled to France seemed willing to submit to a reimposition of French rule. Yet, when it became apparent that the French intended to reimpose slavery as well, the revolutionary adrenalin began to flow again and, in combination with the toll taken on the French soldiery by the disease-ridden environment, popular resistance ensured that the island would not return to its previous colonial status. By the time the renewed insurrection had succeeded in 1804, sixty thousand French troops had been lost. So, too, had the jewel of the French empire.[43]

The tumultuous events that took place in Haiti probably had a restraining influence on Creole opposition to the reforms that Spain imposed on its American colonies. Inadvertently, by destabilizing the situation on Hispaniola, the Spanish may unconsciously have helped to secure control of their own empire. For in contributing to the unleashing of the kind of slave revolt that all colonial whites had dreaded, Spain obliged the Creole minority within its own colonies to think seriously about the consequences of setting off a social revolution among the nonwhite majority. This sense of uneasiness was exacerbated by the knowledge that at the time revolts of the castes were quite common. In Peru, for example, where there were more than fifty Indian insurrections, the problem was endemic. The most famous of these was the revolt of Tupac Amaru, during which a large part of southern Peru came under the control of the insurgents. The rebels were concerned over increased taxation and the continuation of their second-class status.[44]

In 1781 similar grievances caused a mixture of poor whites and members of the castes to stage what came to be known as the Comunero rebellion in New Granada. Subsequently, in neighboring Venezuela, blacks and mulattoes rose up against the system. Although none of these movements declared independence as its goal and each appealed to the Creole sector to make common cause, their ethnic composition and their leveling tendencies were deeply disturbing to the colonial elite. These proclivities, together with the specter of the racial anarchy that had taken hold in Haiti, made most Creoles wary of any activity that might contribute to a general social upheaval.[45]

With the prevailing mood of reluctance to upset the social order among the Creoles, the Bourbon policies of the eighteenth century were greeted with much less opposition than were the reforms instituted by other colonial powers. This acceptance also came about because the Spanish government was more flexible and cautious in implementing its policies. One of the most significant departures from the past was the inauguration of the intendant system. Developed in France, subsequently adopted in Spain, and finally transferred to the colonies, it created both a middle-level administration that previously had been lacking and also transferred many financial responsibilities, such as tax collection, from the hands of the governor to those of the intendants. Thus, more so than ever before, the Spanish bureaucracy permeated through the length and breadth of the colonial territories. It is important to note, however, that the system was tried first only in one viceroyalty, and only after its viability had been established was it extended to the others.[46]

In addition to putting in place a more efficient bureaucracy, Spain also created militias designed to shore up colonial defenses in the event of the renewal of warfare. Unlike the situation in the British colonies, where the attempts to strengthen the defensive capabilities caused a great deal of disaffection, in Spanish America the creation of these new military units was greeted with enthusiasm, for they provided an outlet for Creoles who had complained bitterly about the absence of opportunities in the colonial administration.[47]

The most important of the Bourbon reforms, however, was the policy of *comercio libre*. Rather than being imposed in the arbitrary fashion that the British had used, the Spanish introduced these important changes gradually, over a period of twenty years. Moreover, Spanish ministers both consulted colonial opinion and made compromises to ensure that opposition would be mooted.[48] Eventually, however, by lowering duties on goods entering and leaving the colonies and also increasing the number of ports both in Spain and America that could legitimately engage in commerce, the government effected a major restructuring of colonial trade. Although one of the chief aims of *comercio libre* was the undermining of colonial industry, most colonists preferred to ignore the long-term implications of the policy and were satisfied with the great expansion in lower-cost consumer goods that became available.[49] *Comercio libre* and the other Bourbon reforms of the late eighteenth century were so successful that R. A. Humphreys and John Lynch concluded that "the empire, at the time of the death of Charles III in 1788, had never been better governed, nor had its peoples ever enjoyed a greater prosperity or well-being."[50] Lynch succinctly added that the "Bourbons reconquered America."[51]

That there was little overt opposition to Bourbon reforms did not mean that the Creole population did not feel a strong sense of injustice. On the contrary, virtually every segment of Creole society could point to at least one aspect of the colonial regime it deemed offensive. In some cases, the grievances were localized. This, for example, was the situation in Peru. Once the cornerstone of the imperial system, it suffered in the late eighteenth century from the opening of the competitive port of Buenos Aires and the transfer of Upper Peru, with its silver mines, to the newly created viceroyalty of the Rio de La Plata. In the words of John Fisher, Peru emerged as "the major casualty" of Bourbon administrative reforms.[52]

Other grievances, however, were more generalized. Those who depended on cottage industry to supplement their incomes were adversely affected by the influx of cheap European manufactures, which for the first time penetrated even the most remote regions. Whatever their economic status, taxpayers, who found it more difficult to avoid payment in the face of the improved bureaucracy, also were not pleased with the new circumstances. Perhaps the most pervasive complaint articulated by the Creole middle classes, however, was that most bureaucratic positions continued to be almost exclusively the prerogative of peninsulares, that is, Spaniards born in Spain. Hugh Hamill calculated that of the 772 individuals who occupied the positions of viceroy and governor general during the colonial era, only 18 were Creoles. Moreover, by the eighteenth century, even the middle levels of the administration were being staffed by peninsulares.[53]

Nevertheless, not even the prolonged period of warfare that began in Europe in 1792 was enough to cause unrest in the colonies. For although Spain was at war, first against revolutionary France and then as the ally of Napoleon, its involvement in the European theater had both positive and negative repercussions for the colonies. Because communication with Europe was virtually severed for long periods, imports decreased significantly. Thus, during the war years, colonial manufacture was spared the worst effects of comercio libre.[54]

Still, Spain desperately needed funds to finance the war and turned to the Spanish American church, one of the few institutions in the Hispanic world that possessed sufficient capital to rescue the government. The forced loans demanded of the church, however, were to have a profoundly negative impact on the colonies. With much of its wealth dispersed in mortgages, in order to meet the government's requisition, the church was obliged to call in its loans. Thus marginal American estates went to auction at a time when the very surfeit of these properties on the market extremely depressed their value. According to Jan Bazant, for example, the "redemption threatened to become a wholesale expropriation of Mexican landowners."[55] Yet, in and of itself, not even this arbitrary action on the part of the government fanned the flames of revolution.

Ultimately, a combination of accumulated grievances associated with Spanish reforms, French policy decisions, and the speed of events triggered revolutions in Spanish America. When Napoleon, in order to ensure the success of his continental system, forced the abdication of Charles IV and replaced him with his own brother, Joseph Bonaparte, he created an unforeseen dilemma. Most Spaniards refused to accept the coup d'état and proceeded to establish juntas to rule in the name of the exiled king.[56] These events brought about a unique situation in the Americas. Legally, the Indies were the possessions of the Spanish crown and not the nation; the question arose, therefore, where authority resided in the absence of the monarch. Denying the right of the Spanish juntas to assume sovereignty, Americans, both *peninsulares* and Creoles, began to establish juntas of their own. Although they initially received approval from the series of different institutions that claimed to rule Spain during the absence of the king and although the colonial juntas pronounced that they were ruling in the name of the deposed monarch, the aggrieved elements in society and the more radical members of the body politic, many of whom drew their inspiration from the American Revolution, increasingly moved the juntas in the direction of independence. By 1814, with the important exceptions of Mexico and Peru, most of America was ruling itself without reference to Spain.[57]

Just how weak the independence movement was, however, was demonstrated by the relative ease with which the restored monarchy was able to reassert its control. Following the French evacuation of Spain, Ferdinand VII assumed power. He immediately undertook the task of reestablishing control of the colonies. In Venezuela and Colombia, where some of the most violent conflicts had taken place, by 1815 the patriot forces were defeated and Simón Bolívar, the leader of the rebellion, was forced to flee into exile. In Chile factional disputes among the Creoles made the reconquest from Peru a relatively simple affair. Only the Rio de La Plata remained in the hands of patriot forces, although their liberal leaders had so alienated virtually all segments of opinion that a coherent movement had ceased to exist. In fact, even the radicals of Buenos Aires were willing to surrender to the royalist forces encamped across the river in the Banda Oriental if certain guarantees against reprisals were negotiated.[58]

That the dormant and expiring revolution was to be rekindled and ultimately to prove successful can be attributed almost exclusively to the policies of Ferdinand VII. Described by Stanley Payne as "the basest king in Spanish history," he did not possess the slightest awareness of the notions of reward, compromise, or conciliation.[59] For example, although the reestablishment of royalist authority in Gran Colombia was due largely to the efforts of colored *llaneros* (plainsmen), who, after having been disdained by the Creole revolutionaries, had switched their allegiance to the other side, Ferdinand saw no reason to reward them for their efforts by removing the legal disabilities under which they lived. In Chile his representatives arbitrarily took reprisals on any and all who were in the slightest way suspected of antiroyalist sentiments.[60]

Buenos Aires never surrendered partially because of the Chilean experience. Although the leadership was ready to capitulate, the refusal of Ferdinand's officers to accept anything but total and unconditional surrender convinced them that they had nothing to lose by staying in the field. Therefore, the movement in the Rio de La Plata remained a focus of the revolution that soon developed new allies as Ferdinand's autocratic rule caused defections throughout the Americas. Eventually, many who once had been among his staunchest supporters were obliged to abandon his cause in dismay. It would not be until 1826 that the last royalist resistance would be stamped out, but opposition to Ferdinand had provided the main unifying element in the wars of liberation.[61]

Eighteen years had elapsed before the revolution was successfully completed. Those who carried it to fruition were able to agree on just a few
basic issues. In addition to their opposition to Ferdinand, most retained a
healthy distrust of the castes, the majority of whom were not welcomed
as co-conspirators in the independence struggle. Most could agree, as well,
that the radical formulations of such liberals as Bernardino Rivadavia and
Bernardo O'Higgins contained too many dangerous departures from tradition
to be trusted.[62] Beyond this, however, there was little in the way of ideology
to give coherence to the independence movement. In essence, the revolution
can be characterized as having been negative, insofar as many who joined,
especially during its later stages, did so precisely because they were fearful
of change.

This was true of Mexico, as well, even though its road to independence
differed significantly from that of the other regions. Largely stemming from
their fears of a massive caste revolt such as the one spearheaded by the
Creole priest Miguel Hidalgo in 1810, Mexican Creoles remained firmly in
the royalist camp until 1821. Then, fearful that a Spain that was temporarily
in turmoil could no longer guarantee their security, the Creoles staged
their own coup d'état against Spanish rule. The preservation of the social
order, both in Mexico and elsewhere, had provided a stronger incentive
for revolution than notions of what subsequently would be established;
Spanish Americans would have to confront that issue in the future.[63]

The French invasion of the Iberian peninsula, which provided the catalyst
for the revolution in Spanish America, occurred at a time when Luso-
Brazilian relations were also very much in limbo. Although Portugal, like
the other colonial powers, had sought to reimpose dependency on its colony,
its efforts had been thwarted by local opposition. In 1788 a conspiracy
with the goal of independence, a reaction against the new Portuguese
policies, was discovered in Minas Gerais. Fearing widespread disaffection,
the government decided to shelve much of its projected draconian legislation.[64]
Nevertheless, considering the great disparity in size and wealth that existed
between Portugal and its colony, it is possible that Brazilians might have
been more militant had not the specter of what had transpired in Haiti
loomed large in their minds, becoming even more vivid when a mulatto
conspiracy erupted in Bahia in 1797, boldly demanding equality and obviously
taking its inspiration from the Haitian revolution.[65] Perched on top of the
world's largest slave population, Brazilians were understandably reluctant
to initiate any activities that might have caused unrest among the nonwhites.
Thus, there came to be an uneasy truce in which the Portuguese, fearful
that they could not suppress a colonial revolution, took few initiatives,
while the Brazilians, equally fearful of igniting the powder keg of a slave
insurrection, also trod warily.

As was the case for Spain, Napoleon's invasion provided the stimulus
that would unbalance the tenuous relations between metropole and colony
and set in motion the march toward independence. With ample forewarning
of the advance of the French, the Portuguese court was able to evacuate

to Brazil. Just as the absence of a monarch in Spain had caused an unprecedented constitutional crisis, so the arrival of the Portuguese royal family in Brazil created a unique situation. With the Portuguese court in residence in Rio de Janeiro, the status of Brazil was raised from that of colony to the exalted rank of co-kingdom. With this elevation, much of the legislation that had given Brazil its colonial character was abolished and it began to enjoy rights and privileges similar to those of Portugal.[66]

In light of the new circumstances, it began to appear that an often mulled but never seriously proposed solution to the contradiction of the Luso-Brazilian connection could be effected. In the past, some observers had suggested the transfer of the capital from Lisbon to Rio. Although this policy must have appealed to previous monarchs, it had been too radical to consider implementing. Once circumstances had dictated such a move, however, King D. João VI, as he became upon his mother's death, believed that he could take advantage of the enforced transfer without having to confront a hostile public opinion in Portugal. That this is what he had in mind is indicated by his remaining in Brazil long after the war in Europe had been concluded and French troops had become a distant memory in the Iberian peninsula. Further confirmation that the transition was intended to be permanent is suggested by the large amounts of capital that were invested in Brazil by members of the royal entourage.[67]

The separation that was to occur between Portugal and Brazil was to be more the work of the metropolis than the colony. Even prior to the elevation of Brazil to the status of co-kingdom, few Brazilians advocated complete independence. Although there was a wide range of opinion with respect to the range of ills that needed to be addressed, as noted by Caio Prado Junior, few critics carried their convictions to revolutionary extremes.[68] Nevertheless, many elements in Portugal became disenchanted not only with the continued absence of the king in Rio de Janeiro but also with the restructure, which no longer greatly favored the metropole. Eventually, so much pressure was applied that D. João was obliged to return to Lisbon. Before he departed from Rio, however, he left instructions with his son, D. Pedro, whom he left behind, that should an attempt be made by the Portuguese to reimpose a colonial relationship, independence should be declared. When the Cortes proceeded to unveil a plan that represented an undisguised attempt to reestablish an unequal relationship, D. Pedro became the focal point of an independence movement that quickly and virtually without bloodshed severed its ties with Portugal.[69]

Thus, by the end of the first quarter of the nineteenth century, the political map of the Western Hemisphere scarcely resembled that of the previous century. With few exceptions, most former colonial territories had gained their independence. Britain, France, Spain, and Portugal, then, had all lost their most valuable possessions and would be called upon to make adjustments. The newly independent countries seemed to have the opportunity to shape their destinies and thus to prosper. In the past, many colonials had complained, sometimes vociferously, that their progress had been stunted by the policies of their respective metropoles. Nevertheless, although most former colonies were probably only vaguely aware of what was happening elsewhere, theirs had not been the only revolutions of significance. On the contrary, another revolution was also unfolding. It would have a profound impact on the destinies not only of the former colonies but of most of the rest of the world as well.

## THE INDUSTRIAL REVOLUTION IN BRITAIN

While the colonial revolutions were under way, what has been referred to as the industrial revolution was gaining momentum in England. Although this term, popularized by Arnold Toynbee, won general acceptance during the nineteenth century, more recent scholars have raised many questions about the phenomenon. In fact, it is one of the most controversial issues debated among students of economic history. Therefore, in the context of the present study, it will be necessary to address such basic questions as whether the term *revolution* accurately portrays what transpired in eighteenth- and nineteenth-century England, and, if justified, when, how, and why it occurred. Such an investigation will, in turn, examine not only the changes that took place in the productive base of English society but also the fundamental ways in which the English came to reconsider economic issues.

One qualification that has been suggested is that because the term *revolution* carries with it the idea of a sharp departure from the past, it is inappropriate. Rather, many scholars emphasize that the industrialization of the eighteenth century was built upon improvements that were perfected over time. George Unwin, for example, cautions that it had been "going on for two centuries, and had been in preparation for two centuries before that."[70] Similarly, J. U. Nef points out that the stocking frame, a very complicated device containing over two thousand parts, was developed in the sixteenth century. Moreover, the same century witnessed improvements in such diverse areas as tinning, clockmaking, jewelry manufacture, wind-powered saw mills, and silk-throwing machines.[71] Others note that serious experimentation with steam had begun in the seventeenth century and that the Newcomen steam engine had been developed as early as 1708. H. Heaton, therefore, concludes that the "seventeenth century saw more technical problems than it was able to solve, but it was far from being devoid of inventive minds."[72]

Others object to the term *industrial revolution* because it connotes that the transformations were instituted suddenly and pervasively throughout the manufacturing sector. With respect to the speed with which the new departures were enacted, it has been observed that changes in the nature of production were introduced only gradually. T. S. Ashton, for example, argues that the industrial revolution "had to wait until the idea of progress . . . spread from the minds of the few to the many. . . . In the period 1700–1760 Britain experienced no revolution."[73] Not only do the critics emphasize how slowly these innovations were implemented, but they also point out how limited was the range of endeavors to which mechanization was applied. During the first half of the nineteenth century, they argue, most areas of manufacture continued to produce in virtually the same fashion as they had always done. Thus, for a variety of reasons some historians conclude that the notion of an industrial revolution is extremely misleading.[74]

The majority of scholars, however, although they understand and by and large accept the qualifications suggested by the critics, still believe that the term is justified. One factor they sometimes invoke in support of their position is that the level of investment in late eighteenth-century England reached the threshold most modern economists identify as a prerequisite for a developed economy. Whereas in 1760, 6.5 percent of the national income was being invested, by the 1830s fully 11 percent was committed to investment.[75] Moreover, the defenders of the term *industrial revolution* point to the ratio of population relative to production. Population did grow rapidly during the eighteenth century, but production increased at an even faster rate. The revolutionary significance of this trend is suggested by Phyllis Deane who notes that "nothing of this kind had ever happened before, in England or elsewhere."[76] Her synthesis, making a slight concession to the opponents, concludes that "there was evolutionary change that gained revolutionary momentum."[77]

Although various schools of thought may differ as to the appropriateness of the concept of an industrial revolution, most are in general agreement as to the changes that overtook eighteenth- and nineteenth-century England. David Landes captures the phenomenon in its broadest outline when he refers to it as "the breakthrough from an agrarian handicraft economy to one dominated by industry and manufacture."[78] More specifically, it involved the introduction of power machinery into production on a large scale. Suddenly, a task over which a craftsman would have labored for a long period could be accomplished very quickly by relatively unskilled labor. In fact, significantly, the work could now be done by women and children. Even they could turn out a standardized product that was far superior to that of the finest craftsman. At the same time output increased by leaps and bounds, the per unit costs of industrially produced goods was drastically reduced.

The harnessing of the energy provided by steam was one of the most important departures of the era. Although Newcomen's steam engine made its appearance in 1708, it was not until 1769, when James Watt perfected his engine, that the full ramifications of the possibilities offered by steam could be realized. Steam power was much more reliable than either water or wind, as it was not dependent on the vagaries of the elements. Moreover, unlike the other forms of inanimate power, steam could be deployed virtually anywhere. By the nineteenth century, the amount of energy available to English industry had risen tremendously. So, too, had the ways in which it could be used. It had become instrumental in such diverse places as blast furnaces, breweries, paper mills, and printing offices.[79]

Steam was combined with a number of other innovations to revolutionize the production of cotton textiles. The water frame and the spinning jenny, which became prominent after 1770, were one hundred times as efficient as the spinning wheel. Weaving, which had been greatly improved by the invention of the flying shuttle in 1723, was completely revamped in 1785, when Edmund Cartwright's power loom applied steam to the process. The bottleneck effect created by the new machinery, which, in essence, would have meant that the ability to produce cotton cloth would have far outstripped the supply of the raw material, was mediated by another, rather simple invention. This was the cotton gin, an implement that, by making it possible easily to separate the seed from the flower, allowed the cultivation of more productive varieties of cotton.

The way was thus prepared for a dramatic turnabout in the English textile industry. With the import of Indian textiles into England prohibited in the early eighteenth century, English cotton manufacturers were able to take advantage of a relatively new market. Although cotton production would not surpass wool until 1825, its output expanded by geometric proportions. An indication of its growth is provided by the statistics for the importation of raw cotton into England. From 2.5 million lbs. in 1760, it rose to 22 million in 1787, and reached 336 million by 1837. The number of power looms also increased dramatically, rising from 2,400 in 1813 to 250,000 in 1850. Along with the growth in output, there was an enormous decrease in costs. By the early nineteenth century, the cost of yarn had been reduced to one-twentieth of what it had been during the eighteenth century. Moreover, by 1850 cotton cloth sold for one-quarter of its 1815 price.[80]

In other areas steam, metallurgy, mining, and transport acted reciprocally to enhance output tremendously. Because charcoal supplies were inadequate for the growing number of steam engines, the output of coal had to be expanded. In this sense, steam solved its own problem in that it could be used in pumping engines, which, by enabling very deep levels of mining, greatly increased the coal supply. Greater supplies of coal, in turn, were needed in metallurgy, as the improved blast furnaces could not function efficiently with charcoal. Thus, when Cork's puddling process was perfected in the 1780s, the English were able not only to produce a more malleable iron, but greatly to increase its output. Between 1788 and 1806 production quadrupled, a dramatic turnabout: Whereas in 1780 England produced less iron than France, by 1848 it had doubled the output of the entire world. One of the major uses for these increased supplies of iron was in rail construction, which experienced a boom, especially between 1830 and 1848. Along with the improvement in steam locomotives, it became feasible to transport heavy loads of coal and iron in ways that would have been uneconomical earlier.[81] Deane emphasizes that the reciprocal process aided in the transformation of England from a "world built of wood to one that was fashioned out of iron."[82]

Although the statistics for growth underline the dynamic nature of change evident by the nineteenth century, there is no consensus on the date of its eighteenth-century origins. Deane suggests that the 1740s marked the crucial watershed between the old and the new. It was then, she argues, that for the first time production began to grow faster than population.[83] Others are more inclined to date the takeoff into sustained economic growth to the 1780s. Eric Hobsbawm, for example, sees in that decade the period at which "all the relevant statistical indices took that sudden sharp, almost vertical turn upwards which marks the take-off."[84] The confusion, however, may lie in that not everyone has posed the question in the same terms. Sidney Pollard and David Crossley provide a seemingly acceptable compromise. They agree that the acceleration of population growth, innovation, and investment took place in the earlier part of the century but that it was only toward the end of the century that these were translated into increased production.[85]

The question how the industrial revolution was financed and, more particularly, the role played by the earnings generated by overseas trade has also been the subject of some controversy. Recently, certain historians have suggested that the connection between England's overseas trade and the industrial revolution was minimal.[86] Others have emphasized that the question is not as important as it was once thought to be, for it is now generally agreed that most endeavors did not demand large amounts of capital investment. Even Marx, though he listed the colonial system and overseas trade as important sources of primitive accumulation, stopped short of according primacy to them. The overwhelming importance Eric Williams attributed to the slave-sugar cycle in the financing of industrialization is obviously an overstatement; nevertheless, a large share of the earnings of English commerce did find its way into productive investments. The case for the connection between the world economy and the industrial revolution is perhaps best stated by Ralph Davis, who observed that "overseas trade . . . helped to create the base without which the industrial take-off might not have proceeded so fast."[87]

An even more contentious issue is why there was an industrial revolution. In fact, there are almost as many opinions with respect to the prime mover as there are scholars who address the problem. Walt Rostow suggests that it was the logical outgrowth of the scientific revolution, which changed the way men thought and created "a new mentality [that] was required to yield the groups of inventors and entrepreneurs who actually created the low-cost curves that define technically the Industrial Revolution."[88] Others debate whether an increase in supply or the growth of demand was crucial. R. M. Hartwell believes that mechanization so increased supplies that the reduced costs created a demand out of a vacuum.[89] Deane, on the other hand, argues that the agricultural revolution, by providing cheaper food, in conjunction with rising wages, provided the necessary disposable income to stimulate an increase in supply.[90]

Others, however, point to the growth of international trade as the catalyst. For example, Dobb doubts the "few pence" that the factory proletariat had to spare were capable of underwriting the transformation that took place. Rather, he identifies the export trade, which showed a "quite remarkable increase" as having been of critical importance.[91] The same point is made by Hobsbawm, who believes that overseas demand was the essential factor in stimulating the industrial revolution. "Our industrial economy," he observes, "grew out of our commerce . . . especially our commerce with the underdeveloped world." Furthermore, he adds that the access that Britain gained to the world market in the eighteenth century was the "greatest triumph ever achieved by any state."[92]

Yet none of the foregoing opinions is in basic conflict with the notion that the industrial revolution was the logical outgrowth of the dual phenomena of the development of capitalism and the creation of a world economy. Certainly, the breakthrough from a mind-set that saw output, productivity, and profits as being relatively static to one that believed that innovation could be rewarded with increased productivity and profit was a logical by-product of the new capitalist mentality. Moreover, the stepped-up productivity of which Hartwell speaks can be associated with the more efficient use of capital and labor that was evident in England. The question of wages, demand, and overseas markets may also be easily resolved: During the first half of the eighteenth century, wages, especially those for skilled labor, tended to be high, which would have provided a domestic stimulus to the beginnings of industrialization. As mechanization proceeded and the amount of requisite skills was diminished, wages slumped severely and hence would have reduced the importance of demand arising from the domestic market. By this time, however, the overseas market was growing in significance. It was in this regard that the world economy was particularly important. This would appear to be confirmed by Hobsbawm's observation that industries more closely associated with exports grew much more rapidly during the eighteenth century than those geared to the domestic market.[93]

Although the impact of the industrial revolution on England is also the subject of much controversy, certain changes fundamental in restructuring its relations with the world appear to be fairly clear-cut.[94] Power machinery, because of its need to concentrate the work force, led to production within factories. Similarly, because rural production could not compete with that of urban-based industries, rural dwellers could no longer supplement their agricultural incomes by handicraft production. Therefore, not so much because of the process of enclosure but because, as J. D. Chambers notes, "a proletariat was coming into being by the natural increase of the peasant population," many of the hard-pressed rural population began to gravitate toward the towns. Chambers concludes that in the age of the railway there was "a wholesale evacuation from the countryside."[95] Urbanization proceeded to the extent that by 1831, 25 percent of the population lived in urban areas. Although population continued to grow in the well-established cities, often the migrants swelled the ranks of the new industrial towns, many of which had been little more than villages a century earlier.[96]

Just as the emergence of the bourgeoisie in the sixteenth and seventeenth centuries upset the extant social order, so, too, did the industrial revolution create new categories for which there was no obvious niche in nineteenth-century English society. This process was intimately related to the phenomenon of the new urbanization. In these new towns the positions of wealth and influence were occupied by the incipient industrial bourgeoisie, the factory-owners who were often derisively called "chimney aristocrats." As a group they were deeply concerned with what they perceived to be a government that was unresponsive to their needs. Yet because there had been no change in the structure of Parliament since the Glorious Revolution, the new urban areas over which they presided were completely unrepresented.

At the other extreme, there was the equally new industrial proletariat, which was crowded into cities that grew much faster than the amenities necessary to accommodate them. Equally disenfranchised, they generally bridled under the harsh conditions they suffered. According to Pollard and Crossley, the people "were genuinely deploring the passing of the old bases of their existence, the family in its old form . . . , the land, the local associations, the old skills and identification with job or product, [and] the established social balance."[97] In making this assessment, however, they were only echoing E. P. Thompson, who had observed that "by 1840 most people were 'better off' than their forerunners had been 50 years before, . . . but they had suffered and continued to suffer this slight improvement as a catastrophic experience."[98]

Many, under these circumstances, believed that only an effort to make Parliament more representative would avert trouble. Parliament at the beginning of the fourth decade of the nineteenth century was a strange mixture of unevenly allocated seats. Although most seats were the prerogative of either counties or boroughs, especially in the latter, there was nothing resembling a uniform size, franchise qualification, or even method of election. Some, indeed, were so-called rotten boroughs, which represented no one. It has been pointed out, for example, that the borough of Dunwich continued to be represented even though most of it had long since eroded into the North Sea. There were also nomination boroughs, the most absurd of which was the Scottish borough, where an individual nominated and seconded himself, and then proceeded to win the election one to nil. In this environment seats could often be purchased; wealthy West Indian planters thus were able to constitute a force in Parliament all out of proportion with their numbers. For those who were disenfranchised, the situation was an affront and a reminder of their impotence.[99]

As Michael Brock caustically observed, "scholars can debate about whether the worker was better off [under industrialization]: about the discontent that the new conditions generated there can be no doubt at all."[100] The working class was in a surly and hostile mood; the year 1830 witnessed working-class uprisings in many parts of Europe. In England the situation seemed potentially even more dangerous because the disenfranchised and disenchanted chimney aristocrats seemed willing to fan the flames of working-class discontent.[101]

Although the uncertain social backdrop must always be borne in mind, the major impulse toward the reform of Parliament emanated from a completely different source. In 1829, fearing that a revolt was imminent in Ireland, Prime Minister Robert Peel secured the passage of a bill that conferred equality upon Catholics. His Tory opponents were infuriated not only because of the act but also because his majority was obtained only with the aid of completely unrepresentative seats. Paradoxically, they suddenly became champions of parliamentary reform, largely because they felt that a Parliament that represented English opinion would soon overturn Catholic emancipation. Thus, by 1832, the forces in favor of parliamentary reform, albeit for diverse reasons, were strong enough to carry the day.[102]

The Reform Bill, which was secured only with great difficulty, was not the revolutionary document many had hoped for. By doing away with the rotten boroughs and reallocating many other seats, it did make Parliament more representative of the various regions of England, especially the industrial towns. Yet it did nothing for the working classes. The property qualification for the franchise remained extremely high, the bill appearing to be "a device calculated to join the middle and upper classes to government, and to leave [the worker] . . . as a sort of machine to work according to the pleasure of government."[103]

Nevertheless, the working class did not rise in arms. Whether this can be attributed to the slight improvement in the conditions of the working classes in the 1830s is less important than that the Reform Bill was a singular triumph for the industrial bourgeoisie. They had gained representation primarily through the threat of potential working-class militancy. Yet in a cunning fashion they were able to manipulate the process so as to ensure that the proletariat would reap none of the fruits of the reform.[104]

With the forces in Parliament realigned, the way was cleared for major changes in the structure of English trade. Because industrialization gave them a competitive advantage, the new forces were concerned with removing all barriers to free trade. One special target was the Corn Laws. Enacted in 1815, largely at the behest of the landowning classes, they imposed a prohibitive duty on the import of grain. Thus, the price of a loaf of bread was artificially raised. Partly because some of them wanted to reduce, or at least restrain, wages, middle-class businessmen formed the Anti–Corn Law League in 1838. Although the campaign was often acrimonious, by 1846 Parliament was induced to repeal the Corn Laws and thus allow foreign grain into England. In the same year, it passed both the Sugar Duties Act, which removed all tariffs on foreign-grown sugar, and a law that abolished all duties on the import of cotton. Three years later Parliament repealed the Navigation Acts. Symbolically, the repeal put the seal on the end of an era, for the Navigation Acts had formed the cornerstone on which British commercial supremacy had been built. With them the last vestige of the old Britain passed into history, and the way was cleared for the triumph of the new.[105]

Freed of all restraint, Britain's trade with the world continued to grow. Yet the structure of English commerce changed radically. Whereas prior to the industrial revolution consumables such as tea, sugar, and spices had dominated imports, by the nineteenth century the new staples were items such as raw cotton, palm oil, guano, and a variety of other raw materials designed either to aid in the process of production or to be refashioned into finished goods. Although English agriculture during the age of "high farming" continued to improve, both the increase in the population and the flight from the countryside meant that England could no longer feed itself. The country increasingly came to depend on the imports of foreign foodstuffs. Just how important this became is suggested by Ralph Davis, who notes that "dependence rose to the point where starvation rather than inconvenience became the alternative."[106]

There were other ways in which the needs of industrial Britain differed. During the age that was dominated by commercial capital, a great deal of emphasis was placed on the movement of tropical goods from one site to another. With its increased productive capacity, however, Britain became more concerned with exports of its own manufactures. In this respect, cotton textiles were particularly important. During the first half of the nineteenth century, the increase in the export of cotton cloth was tremendous. Yet because the productive capacity of England's industries continued to accelerate, England was obliged to concentrate on the search for new markets. Thus, the priorities that came to dominate Britain's relationship with the wider world were changed by the process of industrialization.

## CONCLUSION

By the early stages of the nineteenth century, then, the first world economy was threatened with extinction. That most colonies in the Western Hemisphere had become independent, indeed, indicated that a crossroads had been reached. What the significance for the former colonies or their former metropolises would be was as yet undetermined. The French Revolution, which had been so instrumental in the general phenomenon of upheaval, would also leave important legacies for the future of Europe. Not the least of these was the restructuring of the social and legal framework of a continent whose map had also been redrawn. The combination of these changes, in concert with the maturation of the industrial revolution, would spell doom for the first world economy. For new productive forces would be unleashed, which, in turn, would create new class relations both in Europe and in a new world economy.

# 10

# RETROSPECT
# AND PROSPECT

## RETROSPECT

This study has sought to ask a number of relevant questions concerning the relationship between Europe and the remainder of the world. One important issue was why the wider world was unable to sustain the momentum it once generated and maintain the lead over Europe it once enjoyed in a number of endeavors. It began with a topical survey of the achievements and deficiencies demonstrated by the wider world during the early-modern era. The next three chapters dealt with changes in medieval and early-modern Europe, again with the intent of identifying crucial factors in the development of development. Beyond these considerations, it was deemed necessary to focus on the secondary expansion of Europe and how it created new economic and social structures in different parts of the world. After a brief period of flowering, however, this first world economy was to be supplanted by a new world economy that was based on capitalism of a different nature. In essence, what transpired gave credence to Marx's observation that every mode of production was pregnant with its successor.

The very first issue of importance was the agricultural revolution and its flowering in the wider world. In large parts of the Americas, Africa, and Asia, agriculture was developed to the extent that it became extremely productive. Staples such as wheat, rice, and maize came to form the cornerstones of what were often extremely diverse and varied agrarian complexes. The production of surpluses, in turn, was made possible by significant combinations of innovation and labor input. Thus, many regions in the wider world evolved a well-developed agriculture many centuries before this phenomenon would occur in Europe.

It was then necessary to demonstrate how the surpluses of food enabled societies in the wider world to excel in a variety of ways, for example, in such endeavors as the fabrication of sophisticated metallurgy and high-quality textiles in the productive sphere. Artistic and architectural wonders ranged from huge pyramids to a wide variety of delicately fashioned miniature carvings. There were also significant breakthroughs in scientific knowledge and technological innovation. All of these undertakings significantly predated comparable achievements in Europe.

Although the historiography of the wider world is often characterized as having been traditional and static in outlook, this study has demonstrated that nothing was further from the truth. In fact, many of the traits exhibited by these regions can be categorized as distinctly modern. For example, in many areas huge urban centers emerged, often housing workers who were completely divorced both from rural society and the means of production. Output on the scale that was achieved also presupposed large amounts of capital in production and an institutional framework capable of marshaling these resources. These and a multitude of other characteristics were similar to ones that eventually became prevalent in those regions of Europe that would make the breakthrough into modernity.

Yet because no region in the wider world made a similar transition, the question why the momentum was not maintained needed to be raised. It was possible to isolate a number of factors that militated against continued progress. Although in many regions modern sectors devoted to production were emerging, there remained nonproductive elements that were able to divert potential capital away from production and to convert it into "mere money." The modern sectors did not develop rapidly enough to be able to defend their own interests; almost everywhere they succumbed to the parasites that surrounded them. This phenomenon was so commonplace as to merit the observation that there were many more ways of subverting development than of fomenting it.

The history of medieval Europe provided additional support for the contention that achieving development did not represent an obvious set of choices. It showed that although progress in Europe during the Middle Ages was modest, there was a noticeable quantitative expansion. Yet this growth was to be decisively stunted. Population grew so much faster than productive capacity that by the fourteenth century most of the continent had become incapable of feeding itself. Thus, a famished Europe suffered a mortality rate of as much as 40 percent when the plague struck between 1348 and 1350. It appeared that three centuries of painstaking progress were wiped out overnight.

Ironically, however, the Black Death represented an opening rather than a cul-de-sac for European society. For it provided space and precious time in which Europeans could regroup. Given this reprieve, during the late fourteenth and the fifteenth centuries, the European resurgence was able to incorporate qualitative as well as quantitative growth. In the technological sphere, Europe could absorb inventions and innovations that diffused from other continents to aid significantly in material growth. Important social and political changes also restructured and reinvigorated the context in which progress could be made. It should be pointed out that these changes did not result from problem-solving efforts by planners who had insight into the needs of European society. Rather, they were the logical outcomes of thousands of mini class struggles that, when aggregated at certain junctures, helped to set Europe apart from the remainder of the world.

Paradoxically, by increasing Europe's needs, material growth acted as a stimulant to intercontinental trade and overseas expansion. Partly because of their southern locations, Portugal, Spain, and Venice, each in its own way, pioneered this movement. Especially in its colonizing aspects, the dispersal of Europeans abroad was novel and unprecedented. For a time, their enterprise was munificently rewarded. Nevertheless, by the seventeenth century, each of these early expansionists had begun to experience chronic problems. What is particularly instructive is that the reasons for their failures were remarkably similar to the obstacles that the wider world had been unable to overcome. Once again, as was demonstrated, neither wealth nor trade in and of itself was capable of radically transforming society.

The career of the Netherlands also proved to be instructive. During the sixteenth and seventeenth centuries, it, too, became a commercial power. Nevertheless, its agricultural and industrial base continued to grow as well. In fact, during the seventeenth century, while most of Europe was experiencing a prolonged depression, the Dutch were enjoying their golden age.

This indicated that the degree of differentiation among European regions was increasing. The search for the reasons why this should have been led to the observation that the Low Countries had a deviant medieval past. Specifically, the nonexistence or the early demise of the feudal tradition had freed labor power, facilitated the accumulation of capital, and helped to create a productive system that was qualitatively different from anything that preceded it. Yet, as Dobb noted, somewhere along the way the Dutch faltered and failed to complete the journey along the road that led to capitalism: In the eighteenth century, therefore, the Dutch preferred to invest capital in England rather than to use the funds at home.

As is indicated by the Dutch capitulation, by the second half of the seventeenth century, England had emerged as the dominant force in the ascendancy of merchant capital. Superficially this would appear to have been a most unlikely result. For when compared to other parts of Europe, much less to a region like the Arab empire during its heyday, England was uninspiring. Neither in agriculture, commerce, industry, nor technology did it produce any major innovations, nor was it particularly productive. Nevertheless, not unlike the early mammals who first evolved among creatures who were swifter, larger, and more powerful, this insignificant island was undergoing structural changes that would ultimately be of the utmost importance. In England the feudal tradition came to an end earlier and more completely than elsewhere in Europe. Moreover, the legal framework in which this took place encouraged the creation and agglomeration of private property. This was to lead to social change, as Marx noted, in the "really revolutionary" way.

Indeed, it was the English Civil War that confirmed that change in the revolutionary way was not to be undermined. During the sixteenth and seventeenth centuries, England emerged both politically and economically as a force in European affairs. As had often happened elsewhere, English monarchs believed that their political adventures should be financed by the productive sector. What distinguished the social process in England from that which transpired elsewhere was that royal parasitism was effectively challenged. The phenomenon unique to England was the creation of a class capable of defending its productive relations. Thus, by the later stages of the seventeenth century, with commercial ventures promising the best returns on investment, merchant capital was freed to pursue its goals without fear of subversion.

One of the main outlets for merchant capital was in transporting goods from abroad to satisfy the demands of a growing European market. Merchants were not the only group to recognize the potential of the age. Others also realized that various regions could produce goods that were in demand, but under an economic regime the cost of production and transport would have been prohibitive. This was the same dilemma that had handicapped the ancient world and limited its long-distance trade to luxury items. Nevertheless, the new organizers of production overcame the impediment by resorting to extra-economic coercion and thereby denying compensation to the direct producer for the fruits of the labor performed. Thus, what have been labeled the peripheries came into being in widely disparate regions. One important characteristic they shared was that production could only be undertaken as long as the labor force remained unfree. Another consideration was that under normal circumstances it was in the interest of the organizers of production to maintain the status quo, both at home and in their commercial relations.

Although some of the peripheries arose in colonial territories, not all colonies fit into this category. Others were classified as dependencies because of what they produced and how they produced it. For in the dependencies, the cost of production relative to the value of the finished commodity was considerably lower than in the peripheries. As a result, it would have been economically unsound to employ extra-economic coercion. For example, where labor time represented only a fraction of the total value of a particular commodity, it would have been unproductive to use slave labor, for the cost of its reproduction would have greatly exceeded the value it generated. Thus, even where coerced labor was deemed necessary during the early stages of colonization, over time the tendency was for its importance to diminish. A second trait of the dependency, unlike the periphery, whose output always complemented that of the core, was that its production could often be competitive. This might have steered dependencies and metropolises on a collision course.

By the eighteenth century peripheries and dependencies had come to form part of a rapidly expanding global commerce. Increasingly, this trade came to be dominated by England. Although other European countries contested this supremacy, the gap between them and Britain continued to grow. The English attained success despite a lack of superior natural advantages and even though its adversaries adopted mercantilistic practices that represented artificial attempts to reverse the trends. These competitors had failed to perceive that it was the English social system that was decisive. As long as Britain's rivals were unable to eliminate privilege and the nonproductive elements from the upper echelons of their societies, they had no chance of reversing the odds.

Nevertheless, England's adversaries continued to draw the wrong conclusions. Their frustration impelled them to adopt warfare as a mechanism of achieving what they had failed to attain by peaceful means. Ironically, however, the disparity between the respective social relations that had contributed to the lack of success among the competitors during peacetime would determine that they would be no more successful on the battlefield. For although many indices, such as comparative population resources, would seem to have favored its opponents, England's institutional framework enabled it to gain access to such superior capital resources that it was literally able to finance victory.

Although England was more capable of raising adequate funds than were its adversaries, like its counterparts, it found difficulty in meeting its obligations. It has been observed that Europeans simply could not afford the escalating costs of eighteenth-century warfare. Yet they continually went to war anyway. After the Seven Years' War, however, the constantly mounting debts loomed as a serious problem. Unfortunately, the solutions Europeans chose triggered reactions that were more ominous than the dangers they were designed to forestall. The British decision to impose new taxes on the colonies would lead to a revolt of mainland North America. The French decision to support the revolt would lead to bankruptcy that would initiate the French Revolution. In combination, the legacy of the two revolutions was to produce a sort of domino effect that set off revolutions in Ireland, Haiti, Spanish America, and Brazil.

The pattern of revolution as it unfolded, however, did not conform to a simplistic model of peripheries' remaining loyal to the system and dependencies' desperately seeking to escape. Although without other complications these tendencies may have held sway, so many other variables came into play that the decisions reached in each region represented the outcomes of localized struggles at specific points in time. Thus, among the peripheries, the British Caribbean remained loyal whereas Brazil very reluctantly severed its ties with Portugal and Haiti experienced a violent social upheaval. There was no more uniformity in the reactions and outcomes in the dependencies. For both Ireland and North America, the goal was independence, but only the latter succeeded. In Spanish America, on the other hand, despite the impotence of the metropole, internal cleavages meant that eighteen years would elapse before independence was attained.

These revolutions coincided with the less dramatic evolution of the industrial revolution in England. For modern historians and contemporaries, as well, the greatly increased productivity associated with mechanization captured the imagination. Nevertheless, the change in the productive relations was even more significant. For the circulation associated with industrial capital was very different from that required by merchant capital. To achieve and finalize the necessary objective conditions would take yet another revolution. Less dramatic than the series of revolutions dating back to 1642, the peaceful revolution of 1832 that was ushered in by the Reform Bill was nevertheless of utmost importance. For it enthroned the interests of industrial capital and paved the way for the restructuring of a new world economy.

## PROSPECT

In the aftermath of the age of revolution, radical readjustments had to be made. Because England, at the core of the world economy, had changed both its productive base and its priorities, its demands on the wider world were to be different from those of the past. Because of the more advanced nature of their economies, the former dependencies would have appeared to be more flexible and hence in a better position to adjust. The peripheries, on the other hand, beset by low levels of productivity and a large labor force that seemed difficult to transform appeared to be on the verge of a crisis.

In fact, despite their distinguishing characteristics, the responses of the two categories to the changing world situation were remarkably diverse. These, however, were not the only regions that faced new challenges. As a by-product of industrialization, regions that had previously remained external to the world economy increasingly were to be confronted with similar problems. Finally, in Europe itself, both the former colonial powers and other nations would undergo transformations. Some countries were able to find the path that would lead them to modernity; others languished much as they had done in the past.

The United States of America, the name adopted by the former mainland colonies when they ratified the Constitution in 1789, became the most successful of the former colonial territories, but only after considerable difficulties. Starting from a base in which the majority enjoyed a fairly substantial standard of living, its prospects appeared to be bright. Nevertheless, severing the ties with Britain was at first a mixed blessing. The years immediately following the cutting of the umbilical cord raised the question of how an effective government could be created in an atmosphere in which many of the states were reluctant to surrender their freedom of action. Although the period of the Articles of Confederation was not without its achievement, the inadequacies of the confederal solution persuaded most Americans to agree to a convention that would draft a new constitution.[1]

The new nation also had to make adjustments in the sphere of overseas commerce. Whereas it was now free to trade with any country of its choosing, for a time, at least, it lost access to the British West Indies and the protected market of England itself. For the English, the new situation was not nearly as disruptive. Still one of the few vibrant markets for

American produce, the British were able to retain low tariffs on goods they needed yet raise those on items that were potentially competitive with their own. Along the way something unprecedented and startling happened. In the decade after the ratification of the Constitution, the value of British trade with its former colonies more than trebled, much to England's advantage. This, in turn, caused virtually everyone in England to reassess the nature of the colonial system, and, more specifically, to question the value of colonial possessions. Because it now appeared that the economic advantages commonly associated with colonies could be obtained without the inconveniences of colonial rule, for almost a century the new orthodoxy in British imperial circles argued against seeking new colonial acquisitions and even came to favor dissociating England from some of those it already possessed.[2]

After a period of uncertainty, the United States made significant progress. At first, however, torn as it was between the disciples of Jefferson, who envisaged a basically rural and agrarian society, and those of Hamilton, who believed that it was the duty of the government to foment economic growth, there was a lack of consensus on the direction the country should take. Yet, as confidence grew, even the Jeffersonians lost some of their fears of government-sponsored developmental projects. The key factors in the subsequent economic growth were the abundance of land, made possible by the generous terms that the Treaty of Paris had provided with respect to western territories, and the availability of transportation. Whether via canal, the steamboat, or the railroad, the virgin lands of the west were connected with eastern and southern markets.

In a perverse manner, the continuing availability of land for virtually all who were willing to bring it into cultivation contributed to substantial mechanization of the economy: Labor remained in short supply, making its costs almost prohibitive. The incentive to mechanize, therefore, was very strong. Although the level of technology employed was often inferior to that of Europe, the number of endeavors in which machines replaced men in the United States was higher than in the Old World. This process was greatly facilitated by its independence. For it was only with the protection of extremely high tariffs, an option that the nation would have been denied had it remained a colony, that the nascent industries were able to survive.[3]

Yet, in the meantime, a serious obstacle to industrial development via the capitalist mode of production was being created. During the colonial era, slavery had not threatened to become the dominant mode of production, largely because no appropriate staple had been discovered.[4] As an institution, it was so relatively unimportant that it was at the center of a number of compromises that were essential to the foundation of the nation. For example, it was prohibited by ordinance in the Northwest Territories, and it was agreed that the importation of slaves would be banned after 1808.

In the interim, however, the invention of Eli Whitney's cotton gin in 1793 converted cotton into the kind of staple best capable of being exploited by concentrated slave labor. This occurred precisely at the time that the growth of the English textile industry was generating an insatiable demand. The possibilities seemed limitless. Soon large concentrations of slaves were working the virgin lands of the southwestern United States. D. A. Farnie notes that "the U. S. acquired . . . the most successful agricultural staple ever known. . . . Upon the basis of that crop . . . [was] reestablished the old alliance between British industry and American agriculture."[5] What he failed to note, however, was that, if cotton helped to redress the U.S. balance of payments, it also established a collision course between two diametrically opposed modes of production. It would not be until this contradiction was resolved that the future direction of the United States would be determined.

The plight of Spanish-speaking America in the postindependence era was even more traumatic. Most problems were directly related to the inability of a variety of actors to reach compromise either during the revolutionary period or in the immediate aftermath. Within a few years of independence, beset by the problems of regional loyalties, mutual jealousies, and paranoic fears of being dominated by regions that apparently would have liked to replace Madrid as the new metropolis, the former viceroyalties began to disintegrate into their component parts. Thus, whereas the former British colonies soon realized that the safeguards to independent action guaranteed by the Articles of Confederation were less beneficial than the gains to be obtained from unity, Spanish Americans chose the opposite course. Moreover, even within the smaller units there was a complete failure of liberals and conservatives to iron out their differences peacefully. As a result, nearly everywhere civil wars, coups d'état, and anarchy prevailed. Prior to 1850, with the notable exception of Chile, there was a total absence of anything resembling a consensus on what political, social, and economic forms should be implemented.[6]

Under these conditions it proved impossible to sustain the momentum that had developed during the later stages of the colonial era. The situation was exacerbated by the collapse of the mining industry. Damaged by the ravages of war and the rust and flooding that resulted from neglect during the war years, and simply because their ore was giving out after centuries of constant exploitation, the great staple of Spanish-speaking America ceased to give forth its bounty in limitless quantities. Not even foreign capital, which deluded itself by believing that it could resurrect the faltering industry, was able to make the mines productive again. Foreign capital, in the form of state loans, was also an important factor in shaping the future. Firmly believing that an infusion of capital was necessary to foment development, each of the new independent republics negotiated a loan on the London money market. Little of this money, however, found its way into constructive enterprises. Rather, most was either dissipated in civil wars or simply disappeared into the pockets of opportunistic politicians. As a result, soon every republic was in default on its debt. To make matters even worse, capital was in extremely short supply, for Spanish merchants, fearing confiscation, had fled the Americas in droves.[7]

With these initial problems continuing to haunt them, trends in the new nations of Spanish-speaking America were to differ greatly from those of the colonial era. In essence, they proved a disappointment both to Europe and to themselves. Europeans, who for centuries had salivated over the possibility of gaining access to the closed Spanish American territories, were profoundly frustrated that the market they had coveted no longer existed. Bankers were equally displeased because few of the republics had begun to resume payment on their debt prior to 1850.

Spanish Americans, on the other hand, could only rue the lapse of their economies into subsistence. Few contemporaries could have been aware that the social framework being established in this period would outlast the economic downturn. In the absence of a market potential or employment possibilities, large numbers of individuals began to drift into tenancies paid in kind, sharecropping arrangements, or even debt peonage. At the same time, large estates, with limited market orientation, became the order of the day. It was against this backdrop that the forces of industrial capital would subsequently intrude. Its railroads and steamships would create the means of communication, and the need to feed the urbanized working classes of the West would provide the incentive to stimulate food production in Spanish-speaking America. With their monopoly on the land, the magnates of the Americas would be able to reap the benefits of renewed commercial contacts with the world economy. Thus would be consolidated a neoserfdom that independence had helped to inaugurate.

Just as the combination of independence and the new economic environment obliged the former dependencies to make radical adjustments, so, too, were the peripheries faced with new challenges in the era of industrial capitalism. Whereas the difficulties experienced in the former colonies of Spain and Britain once again demonstrate the validity of Dobb's observation that there were no guarantees that the journey on the road to capitalism would be successfully completed, the peripheries were presented with problems of a different nature. The new patterns of production and demand that were becoming dominant in the nineteenth century meant that much of what the peripheries had previously supplied was becoming anachronistic. The crisis that loomed in the periphery was social as well as economic. The social systems were intimately linked with the nature of production for the export market, so they could not continue to be reproduced unless an acceptable alternative commodity could be discovered. The ruling classes of the periphery, therefore, engaged in a desperate search to find viable substitutes for the staples that were no longer in demand. Whether a region continued as part of the periphery depended in large measure on the success or failure of this quest.

Eastern Europe was the first periphery to be confronted with the new challenges. Historically, it was unique insofar as it produced a staple that could have been grown in northwestern Europe. Nevertheless, the complete subjection of the Eastern peasantry reduced the cost of Eastern grain to the extent that it was able to compete favorably in Western markets.

Moreover, the ample supplies of this basic foodstuff enabled Western farmers to specialize in more remunerative endeavors.

By the latter stages of the eighteenth century, however, two factors had intruded to upset the equilibrium. On the one hand, agricultural production, especially in England, improved immeasurably in the West. Thus, despite the higher cost of labor, the price of domestically produced wheat fell to levels considerably below that of grain produced in the East. At the same time, grain yields in the East were diminishing at alarming rates as the primitive techniques that had been employed for centuries took their toll on the landscape. Under these conditions, the East could no longer compete in Western markets and hence was deprived of its staple. Although the Eastern lords may have frantically sought an alternative, they failed to find one. Under these circumstances, as Laszlo Mikkai observed, "East-Central Europe began to crack."[8] Significantly, as the conjuncture of forces that had made the resort to extra-economic coercion a rational choice ceased to be operative, serfdom began to die a quiet death throughout the region. Eastern Europe dropped out of the periphery.

The former French colony of San Domingue was the next to exit from the periphery. The circumstances, however, were completely different from those at work in eastern Europe. In fact, Haiti was unique insofar as it was the only region that ceased to be part of the periphery because the producers revolted successfully against the system of extra-economic coercion. Had Toussaint-Louverture, the leader of the revolution, been allowed to implement his plans, the future of the tiny republic might also have been unique and interesting. For he alone seemed to understand that the country would continue to need export earnings. To this end, he forced the workers back to the fields, and by 1802 a remarkable economic recovery had taken place. Yet, although the labor force was now to be remunerated, his decision was extremely unpopular among the former slaves, whose prevailing attitude was summed up in the expression *moin pas esclaves moin pas travayé* (I am not a slave; I don't have to work). Once Toussaint-Louverture was forced into exile by Napoleon, however, his successors took the politically popular but economically unwise decision to abandon cash-crop production.[9] Small farms replaced plantations, subsistence overtook commodity production, and the journey toward ultimate poverty was begun. For all intents and purposes, Haiti also ceased to play a meaningful role in the world economy.

The British Caribbean demonstrated yet another way in which the status of periphery could be terminated. It was to be the victim of the new forces of industrial capitalism that gained ascendancy in nineteenth-century Britain. Prior to this change, the plantocracy of the West Indies had been able to manipulate the system to its own advantage. For example, the planters were able to use their influence in order to maintain artificially high sugar prices. Moreover, Eric Williams notes that in the peace treaty of 1763 the West Indians secured a significant victory by successfully lobbying in favor of the retention of Canada yet convincing the government to return the potentially competitive French islands to France. Quite perceptibly he adds that "Cinderella decked out temporarily in her fancy clothes was enjoying herself too much at the ball to pay any attention to the hands of the clock."[10]

By the nineteenth century, the hands of the clock had indeed moved to a new setting. For the better part of a half century the issue of abolition of the slave trade had been pushed unsuccessfully by a small but dedicated minority in Parliament. Although abolition gradually ceased to be considered the brainchild of radical extremists, it took the crisis of the Napoleonic Wars to create the conditions for a favorable outcome to the campaign. The critical factor was the situation prevailing in the Caribbean as a result of the war. The plantation production of Haiti had been destroyed, but the potential new competitors did not as yet have the human resources with which to compete with the British-owned islands. The logic of the situation was that without abolition two unfavorable prospects faced the British planter. Either currently uncompetitive foreign islands would be stocked with a labor force, or, even worse, they would be conquered by Britain and thus, by gaining preferential access to the British market, prove to be an even more serious source of competition. Even though not all of the West Indian interests were converted to the abolitionist position, the breach in the ranks was sufficient to enable passage of the bill that outlawed participation in the slave trade by British subjects.[11]

Thereafter the British government applied a great deal of pressure on other nations to do likewise. The crucial blow to the West Indies, however, came in 1833, when the institution of slavery was abolished throughout the British empire. Significant in terms of the new forces operative in this era, the act was passed in the first parliamentary session following the passage of the Reform Bill. Its impact on the Caribbean was devastating. William Green succinctly concluded that the act "shattered the West Indian economy."[12] Moreover, its implications for the new world economy were captured by David Geggus, who noted that by the mid-nineteenth century, "not only Saint Domingue but all the British and French islands had become somnolent backwaters ignored by Europe."[13]

Brazil in the nineteenth century faced a fate similar to that of its former Caribbean rivals. Its problem, however, stemmed neither from a slave insurrection nor from an attack launched by a metropolitan bourgeoisie. Rather, the crisis was brought about by the decadence in its own sugar industry. Although the vacuum in the world sugar market that began when Haiti ceased to be a major producer led to a revival of cultivation in the Brazilian northeast, the respite was to be quite temporary. Soon newer producers, such as Cuba, Mauritius, and even Java had appeared on the scene. Improved transportation facilities and soils virgin to sugar cultivation enabled these latecomers to produce much more efficiently than Brazil.

Ironically, Brazil's stubbornness in the face of this competition was to allow it to remain linked to the world economy in its traditional peripheral role. For, in an effort to coax the maximum possible yields from its tired soil, Brazilians continued to import slaves in large numbers. Although by midcentury, a combination of intense British pressure and growing fears of the racial imbalance that the large-scale importation of Africans had created convinced the Brazilian government to cease participation in the trade, the country still possessed a coerced labor force capable of being used if an alternative staple could be found. Tentatively at first, but becoming more established during the later stages of the first half of the nineteenth century, coffee was this substitute. At one level, Brazil was to be turned upside down. Its center of gravity was to be transferred from the decaying northeast to the south, which for the first time was settled intensively. As large numbers of slaves were sent southward, São Paulo, Rio de Janeiro, and Minas Gerais came to supplant Pernambuco and Bahia as the major sites of the nation's activities. At another level, however, the revolution in production preserved the status quo. Partly because Brazil remained one of the few regions where a slave mode of production continued to prevail, Brazilian coffee gained an ascendancy in the world market that Brazilian sugar had long since abdicated. Thus, Brazil was one of the few peripheral regions able to retain its traditional social relations during the era of transition of the world economy.[14]

The demise of the traditional centers of sugar production, such as Brazil and the Caribbean, posed significant obstacles to Africa's continuation in the periphery. Confronted with the abolition of slavery in many parts of the Americas and the attempts to terminate the transatlantic slave trade at its source, the African ruling classes were to be brought face to face with the new challenges emanating from industrial Europe. By the nineteenth century, for a variety of motives, both the humanitarian lobby and British industrialists had been converted to the view that it would be preferable to keep Africans in Africa as consumers of European produce than to transport them to the Americas as laborers. Although other European nations were not as adamant as the British in their desire to end the slave trade and even resented the pressure the English applied, the loss of their colonial empires meant that neither France, Spain, nor Portugal retained much of a stake in this once almost universal practice. Thus, the British were virtually unopposed by other Europeans in their efforts to stop the export of Africans.

Nevertheless, if most of Europe remained passive observers of the campaign, African rulers were unyielding in their refusal to abandon a practice that brought them so many benefits. They staunchly resisted the diplomacy, bribery, threats, and force that Britain used in an effort to compel them to comply with its wishes. In most slave-trading areas methods were adopted that enabled them to evade detection; almost two million Africans were landed in the New World after the British had declared the trade illegal.[15] In fact, rather than suppression in Africa, events in the Americas signaled the death knell of the trade. For it was only with the closing of the doors of Brazil and Cuba to further importation that the transatlantic slave trade effectively came to an end.

Denied the staple that had linked them with the world economy, Africa's ruling classes were faced with a dilemma. As early as the initial British attempts to suppress the trade, however, some groups had seen the handwriting on the wall and had begun to seek an alternative to the export of human beings. Although the first converts to the "legitimate trade," as the English were fond of calling it, had often been those groups most susceptible to British pressure, by the mid-nineteenth century, a remarkably diverse variety of regions were producing new export commodities. Beeswax, cotton, coffee, ivory, kola nuts, wild rubber, and cocoa were among the products that were traded. The two most important new staples, however, were groundnut oil and palm oil. Ironically, one of their major uses was as a lubricant for industrial machinery. During the first half of the nineteenth century, most regions of West Africa contributed to exports, which grew at an astounding rate.[16]

The implications for African society of the conversion from the export of human beings to the export of other commodities were enormous. Unbeknownst to the humanitarians, who naively believed that cash-crop production would lead to the "regeneration" of Africa, the change in emphasis would have few redemptive consequences. Instead of forming cargoes to be shipped to the New World, captives came to be used as factors of production who made possible Africa's continuing participation in the world economy. As a result, slavery as an institution on the African continent became more prominent and the social status of the slave deteriorated. Thus, although Africa had a new role in a new world economy, the dominant pattern of social relations was intensified.[17]

Whereas the new commodities supplied by western Africa and Brazil were produced within the traditional framework, the nineteenth century would usher in changes of a much more radical nature in India. For centuries, although India played an important part in world trade, traditional social relations hardly seemed to have been affected by this commerce. Rather, production and trade remained the prerogatives of the caste categories to which they were ascribed. Able to satisfy its own needs from the domestic market, India had no need to import from the West. Westerners, therefore, were obliged to settle their debts by paying for Indian commodities in bullion.

Two factors, however, were to conspire to upset the balance. The first was the British conquest. Beginning with the Battle of Plassey in 1757, over the course of the next century, they were able to bring the entire subcontinent under their control. Thus imbued with the power to manipulate Indian tariffs and to abolish local customs barriers, the British were able to create a potentially vast market. In and of itself this would have been of minimal significance had it not coincided with the industrial revolution. Because, however, the standardized, machine-produced textiles of England could bear the cost of transport and still undersell those manufactured by the most able Indian craftsmen, the market soon came to be flooded with English cloth. By the 1840s, imports, which had been nearly nonexistent at the turn of the century, had grown tremendously. Thus was initiated the process that has been referred to as the deindustrialization of India. Craftsmen, who for millennia had dominated much of the world market, were driven back to the land, there to swell an already bloated rural population.[18] India, therefore, became a major casualty of the forces of industrial capital.

The desire of industrial capital to create new markets also made the British covetous of gaining access to China. By the second quarter of the nineteenth century, opium that was manufactured in India and traded to China enabled the East India Company to reverse what had once been an unfavorable balance of trade. Silver began to flow out of China in increasing amounts. Nevertheless, the Ch'ing emperors continued to confine foreign merchants to the port of Canton, and the British believed they were being denied access to what they considered to be potentially one of the world's largest markets. Although diplomatic endeavors to remedy the situation failed, the Chinese attempt in the 1840s to enforce the regulations against the illegal importation of opium provided the English with an opportunity to force China to open its doors to the world. As a consequence of the British victory in the Opium War of 1840-1842, the defeated Chinese were obliged to make several concessions. The most important of these was that thereafter the British would be entitled to do business in a larger number of ports. Lord Palmerston summed up the perceived significance of this concession: "There is no doubt that this event, which will form an epoch in the progress of civilization . . . must be attended with the most important advantages to the commercial interests of England."[19] Moreover, as increasingly was to become the practice during a later era, other European nations demanded and received similar concessions. Thus was begun the process that ultimately would threaten China with dismemberment.

Just as there were changes of major proportions throughout the wider world, the nineteenth century also witnessed a significant restructuring within Europe, as some countries continued to flounder while others prospered. The nations of the Iberian peninsula were among those that proved incapable of meeting the challenges of the epoch. Of the two, Portugal suffered the most. One problem was that the reforms of the Marques de Pombal had not been sufficiently far-reaching to restructure the basic fabric of society; the impetus toward domestic manufacture was lost once its driving force had disappeared from the scene. Moreover, competition from a rapidly industrializing Britain, especially in textiles, had a crippling effect on Portugal's incipient manufacturing sector. The most telling blow, however, was delivered by the loss of Brazil, which during its peak years had accounted for 75 percent of Portuguese commerce. After Brazilian independence, Portugal surrendered its share of Brazil's diminishing trade to European competitors, who were better able to supply the former colony with its needs.[20]

A similar fate befell Spain, which also suffered from the loss of its colonies. Not only had the Americas provided it with its major trading partner, but they had supplied the crucial bullion with which the colonial power had balanced its foreign debt. Partly as a result of the great reduction in trade with the Americas, partly because of stiff competition from other European sources, the great revival in the economy envisaged by the eighteenth-century Bourbons never materialized. Rather, Spain remained a basically agrarian society, dominated by large landholders, who, although they lost some of their seigneurial privileges, were nevertheless able to manipulate the tariff structure in favor of high domestic grain prices and hence to provide a further impediment to industrialization. Thus, the social group that had largely been responsible for Spain's retardation in the seventeenth and eighteenth centuries continued to block the path toward a modern society.[21] So complete would this retardation become that Spain would cease to be of any relevance in subsequent European history.

Other regions of western Europe, however, were able to make the transition to capitalism and industrialization more successfully. Ironically, although the turmoil caused by the French revolutionary wars had contributed to the Continent's lagging behind England in industrial development, it also set in motion forces that would free some countries from the shackles that had impeded progress. In France, Napoleon abolished the internal barriers that had long hindered communications. Elsewhere, especially in Germany, the consolidation of many small entities into larger units, a side-effect of the wars, eventually facilitated consolidation and aided in the movement of goods over a wider area. In addition, in most countries, often as a palliative to counter the populist and universalist appeal of revolutionary France, the last vestiges of feudalism were abolished. These modifications established the basis for significant social change.

Although the transformation was painfully slow and contributed to the massive suffering among the poor that was to lead to the revolutions of 1848, a good part of western Europe was making the transition to capitalist relations of production. As private property rights in land became predominant, a proletariat was created from among the surplus rural poor. Sometimes without secure tenures, squeezed by a rapidly growing population, and undermined by the railroad, the poorer peasants flocked to the towns. The presence of this cheap labor supply in turn convinced many who previously had been reluctant to venture their capital in industrial enterprises, that the gamble was worth the risk. Thus, especially in Belgium, France, and Prussia, by the middle of the nineteenth century the economies were poised to take off into sustained economic growth. Although the Continental nations were still far behind Britain, in future England would no longer be able to style itself the exclusive workshop of the world.

## CONCLUSION

By the mid-nineteenth century, the structure of the world economy differed radically from that of the late eighteenth century. Britain still reigned supreme at its center. Yet the nature of its dominance had changed.

Instead of being focused on the movement of goods produced overseas, its supremacy came to be derived from the ascendancy of industrial capital and the tremendous increase in productive capacity that followed in its wake. This transformation, in turn, was accompanied by other changes. In England itself policies designed to facilitate the movement of goods were enacted. This was especially the case with respect to the import of raw materials needed for British industry. Overseas, the English benefited from the freer access to the world market that was brought on by the colonial revolutions. Thus, the new conjuncture of circumstances contributed to England's ability to extend its already unprecedented lead in the world economy.

New circumstances also required significant adjustments in the wider world. The former colonial territories, for example, had to make the transition to independence. In many cases, however, freedom did not prove to be the panacea that its architects had foreseen. During the colonial era, with opposing points of view suppressed by the imperial powers, there was an enforced stability that provided the framework for growth. Independence, however, often unleashed rival ideologies whose conflicts denied the new republics the unity of purpose and direction that had prevailed during the colonial era, even if policy decisions had greatly favored the metropolis.

The degree to which a given region prospered or stagnated usually depended on the relative success or failure in resolving these problems. Even where stability prevailed, however, the wider world was faced with a new pattern of demand emanating from the core and was subjected to the changing priorities that arose during the nineteenth century. Frequently, formerly profitable staples suddenly were devalued. In these instances it became necessary to identify an alternative that could become a viable substitute.

As was the case concerning relative stability, there was great variation among the different regions with respect to how successfully they made the adjustment. In addition to having to cope with the other changes, the wider world was faced with the dilemma of increasingly being viewed as a potential market for industrially produced commodities. In some cases, in fact, if a given region failed to live up to what was perceived to be its potential as a consumer, an increasingly powerful Europe resorted to force in order to create the conditions it considered necessary to correct the situation. The British-backed Monroe Doctrine, the suppression of the slave trade, the conquest of India, and the opening of China were all part of the same phenomenon. As a result, often with catastrophic consequences for local industries, various regions of the world were unable to resist the intrusion of European goods.

Nevertheless, the new world economy was still in the incipient stages of transition. The immediate future would witness the expansion of the core as parts of continental Europe, the United States, and Japan would all successfully make the transition to capitalism and industrialization. The periphery would also expand, although its form would be different: No longer would its producers necessarily suffer from an institutionalized servile status. Nevertheless, if at all, they were only marginally better off than those of the previous epoch, as they still lacked access to the means of production. For, in most regions, the periphery remained under control of a narrow oligarchy that continued to arrogate to itself the artificial surplus derived from its connections with the world economy. Content with their subservient role, the elite organized the production of primary commodities for export. In return, they imported industrially produced goods and capital in the form of loans and foreign investment, all of which tended to perpetuate an increasingly distorted situation. The surplus capital that the industrial world accumulated was reinvested on extemely favorable terms in an expanded periphery. As Hobsbawm observed, "one part of the world thus swept forward . . . another lagged." He concludes that "the phenomena are not unconnected with each other. Economic stagnation, sluggishness, or even regression was the product of economic advance."[22]

# NOTES

## CHAPTER 1

1. Eric Wolf, *Europe and the Peoples Without History* (Univ. of California Press, 1983).

2. See, for example, L. S. Stavrianos, *Global Rift: The Third World Comes of Age* (New York, Morrow, 1981); William McNeill, *A World History* (Oxford Univ. Press, 1971).

3. Douglass North and Robert Thomas, *The Rise of the Western World* (Cambridge Univ. Press, 1973), 26, 157.

4. Walt Rostow, *How It All Began: Origins of the Modern Economy* (New York, McGraw-Hill, 1975), 28, 160.

5. E. L. Jones, *The European Economic Miracle* (Cambridge Univ. Press, 1981), 84, 160.

6. Nathan Rosenberg and L. E. Birdzell, *How the West Grew Rich* (New York, Basic Books, 1986), 20, 60.

7. Immanuel Wallerstein, *The Modern World System*, vol. 2 (New York, Academic Press, 1980), 38–39.

8. *Ibid.*, 7–9.

9. Wolf, *Peoples Without History*, 79, 81, 85, 86, 109; Max Weber, *The Protestant Ethic and the Spirit of Capitalism* (London, Allen and Unwin, 1976); André Gunder Frank, *World Accumulation, 1492–1789* (New York, Monthly Review Press, 1978).

10. Peter Farb, quoted in Jones, *Miracle*, 153.

11. See Rodney Hilton, ed., *The Transition from Feudalism to Capitalism* (London, Verso, 1978), which contains Sweezy's critique of Dobb, Dobb's replies, and the commentaries of many others.

12. Marxists use Marxist terminology in a bewildering variety of ways. It is of little comfort to a reader that this has come about because Marx used the future Marxist terminology in a bewildering variety of ways. Throughout this essay the term *social formation* refers to a geopolitical entity made up of heterogeneous components that are capable of changing composition and boundaries. See Dominique Legros, Donald Hunderfund, and Judith Shapiro, "Economic Base, Mode of Production, and Social Formation: A Discussion of Marx's Terminology," *Dialectical Anthropology*, 4, 3 (1979), 247. Although there are many definitions of *mode of production*, the one provided by Maurice Dobb is perhaps the most intelligible. He writes that a mode of production is "the way in which the means of production were owned and the social relations between men which resulted from their connection with the process of production." Maurice Dobb, *Studies in the Development of Capitalism* (New York, International Publishers, 1963), 9.

13. Alan K. Smith, "Where Was the Periphery?" *Radical History Review*, 39 (Sept. 1987), 35.

14. This position differs from that put forward by Eugene Genovese and Elizabeth Fox-Genovese, *Fruits of Merchant Capital* (Oxford Univ. Press, 1983), 41, where they argue that

because the interests of slaveholders "clashed with those of the dominant class of the larger capitalist world," the question of viability reduces to one of military and political power. Two commentaries appear relevant. The first is that the political location of slaveholders and dominant classes is important. Although conflict is likely where they occupy the same space, a mutuality of interests is probable when their political spheres are different. Second, whereas the industrial capitalist must find slavery economically anathema, the merchant capitalist will appreciate the plundered "savings" of slave production.

15. Wolf, *Peoples Without History*, 24–73.

16. Edwin Reischauer, "Japanese Feudalism," in Rushton Coulborn, ed., *Feudalism in History* (Princeton Univ. Press, 1956), 26.

17. Samir Amin, *Unequal Development* (New York, Monthly Review Press, 1976), 13–59.

18. For discussion of these migrations, see Peter Farb, *Man's Rise to Civilization as Shown by the Indians of North America, From Primeval Times to the Coming of the Industrial State* (New York, Dutton, 1968); David Philipson, *The Later Prehistory of East and Southern Africa* (New York, Africana, 1977).

19. Jacques Gernet, *A History of Chinese Civilization* (Cambridge Univ. Press, 1982), 5–6, 18; John Cady, *South-East Asia: Its Historical Development* (New York, McGraw-Hill, 1964).

20. Friedrich Katz, *The Ancient American Civilizations* (New York, Praeger, 1972).

21. L. S. Stavrianos, *The World Since 1500* (Englewood Cliffs, N.J., Prentice-Hall, 1966), 3.

# CHAPTER 2

1. Christopher Ehret, "On the Antiquity of Agriculture in Ethiopia," *Journal of African History*, 20, 2 (1979), 177; Hans Wolff, *The Traditional Crafts of Persia* (MIT Press, 1966), 242.

2. Friedrich Katz, *The Ancient American Civilizations* (New York, Praeger, 1972), 20; David Grigg, *The Agricultural Systems of the World* (Cambridge Univ. Press, 1974), 19; Lea Williams, *South-East Asia: A History* (Oxford Univ. Press, 1976), 25.

3. Mark Cohen, *The Food Crisis in Prehistory* (Yale Univ. Press, 1977), 277–83; Bennet Bronson, "The Earliest Farming: Demography as Cause and Consequence," in Charles A. Reed, ed., *Origins of Agriculture* (Paris, Mouton, 1977), 29.

4. William T. Sanders, *New World Pre-History* (Englewood Cliffs, N.J., Prentice-Hall, 1970), 28.

5. Eric Wolf, *Sons of the Shaking Earth* (Univ. of Chicago Press, 1966), 51–54; Jack Harlan et al., eds., *Origins of African Plant Domestication* (The Hague, Mouton, 1976).

6. Sanders, *New World*, 85; Wolf, *Sons*, 63–64.

7. Francesca Bray, "Swords into Plowshares: A Study of Agricultural Technology in Early China," *Technology and Culture*, 19, 1 (1976), 24; Joseph Needham, *Science and Civilisation in China*, vol. 1 (Cambridge Univ. Press, 1954), 84.

8. Jon Livingston et al., eds., *The Japan Reader*, vol. 1 (New York, Pantheon, 1973), 26; Francesca Bray, *The Rice Economies: Technology and Development in Asian Societies* (London, Basil Blackwell, 1986), 15.

9. Katz, *Ancient Civilizations*, 105.

10. Andrew Watson, "The Arab Agricultural Revolution and Its Diffusion, 700–1100," *Journal of Economic History*, 34, 1 (1974), 8–18; Elihu Ashtor, *A Social and Economic History of the Near East in the Middle Ages* (Univ. of California Press, 1976), 43–45.

11. S. K. Maity, *Economic Life in Northern India* (Delhi, Motilal Banarsidass, 1970), 102–107, 117.

12. Mark Elvin, *Patterns of the Chinese Past* (Stanford Univ. Press, 1973), 129; Ping-ti Ho, "Early Ripening Rice in Chinese History," *Economic History Review*, 9, 2 (1956), 213–14.

13. Sanders, *New World*, 65.

14. Watson, "Agricultural Revolution," 13; Earl Scott, "Land Use Change in the Harsh Lands of West Africa," *African Studies Review*, 22, 1 (1979), 2, 5; Edward Lanning, *Peru Before the Incas* (Englewood Cliffs, N.J., Prentice-Hall, 1967), 119–20.

15. Quoted in Needham, *Science and Civilisation*, vol. 1, 82.

16. See P. L. Shinnie, ed., *The African Iron Age* (Oxford Univ. Press, 1971); D. N. Jha, "A Marxist View of Ancient Indian History," in D. N. Jha, *Studies in Early Indian History* (Delhi, Anumpa Publications, 1980), 47; Charles Drekmeier, *Kingship and Community in Early India* (Stanford Univ. Press, 1962), 18; Edwin Reischauer, *Japan, Past and Present* (New York, Knopf, 1964), 11; Dilip Chakrabarti, "The Beginnings of Iron in India," *Antiquity*, 50, 198 (June, 1976), 121.

17. Jha, "A Marxist View," 47; Maity, *Economic Life*, 135; David Phillipson, *The Later Prehistory of East and Southern Africa* (New York, Africana, 1977).

18. H. G. Creel, "The Role of the Horse in Chinese History," *American Historical Review*, 70 (1965), 668–69; Grigg, *Agricultural Systems*, 39–44; Katz, *Ancient Civilizations*, 27.

19. Quoted in E. L. Jones, *The European Economic Miracle* (Cambridge Univ. Press, 1981), 153.

20. H.A.R. Gibb, *Mohammedanism* (Oxford Univ. Press, 1962), 7–11; Katz, *Ancient Civilizations*, 60; Williams, *South-East Asia*, 32; William Fagg, *The Art of Western Africa* (New York, Mentor-Unesco, 1967), 5–24; Gargi Balwant, *Theatre in India* (New York, Theatre Arts Books, 1962); Benjamin Rowland, *Art and Architecture of India* (Baltimore, Penguin, 1956).

21. Joseph Needham, "Science and Society in East and West," *Centaurus*, 10 (1964), 190.

22. Romila Thapar, *A History of India*, vol. 1 (Baltimore, Penguin, 1966), 24; B. G. Trigger, "The Rise of Civilisation in Egypt," *Cambridge History of Africa*, vol. 1 (Cambridge Univ. Press, 1976), 525; Joseph Whitecotton, *The Zapotecs* (Univ. of Oklahoma Press, 1977), 75.

23. Yusakazu Takenaka, "Endogamous Formation and the Development of Capitalism in Japan," *Journal of Economic History*, 29, 1 (1969), 143; Ashtor, *Near East*, 89; Katz, *Ancient Civilizations*, 48; Richard Hull, *African Towns and Cities Before the European Conquest* (New York, Norton, 1976), 40–44; Laurence Ma, *Commercial Development and Urban Change in Sung China* (Ann Arbor, Univ. of Michigan Press, 1971), 91.

24. Subhi Labib, "Egyptian Commercial Policy in the Middle Ages," in M. A. Cook, ed., *Studies in the Economic History of the Middle East* (Oxford Univ. Press, 1970), 71; Roderick and Susan McIntosh, "The Inland Niger Delta Before the Empire of Mali: Evidence from Jenne-Jeno," *Journal of African History*, 21, 1 (1980); J. Eric Thompson, *Maya History and Religion* (Univ. of Oklahoma Press, 1970), 89; Robert July, *Pre-Colonial Africa* (New York, Scribner, 1975), 185–88.

25. Ma, *Commercial Development*, 106; Katz, *Ancient Civilizations*, 185.

26. E. S. Edwards, *The Pyramids of Egypt* (Baltimore, Penguin, 1961), 90–211; Michael Coe, *America's First Civilization* (New York, American Heritage, 1968), 55; R. C. Majumdar et al., *An Advanced History of India* (London, Macmillan, 1960), 224–55.

27. Needham, *Science and Civilisation*, vol. 1, 101, 115; Colin George Simkin, *The Traditional Trade of Asia* (Oxford Univ. Press, 1968), 31.

28. Mataji Miyamoto et al., "Economic Development in Pre-Industrial Japan," *Journal of Economic History*, 25, 4 (1965), 542; Simkin, *Traditional Trade*, 62; S. D. Goitein, "Mediterranean Trade in the Eleventh Century: Some Facts and Problems," in M. A. Cook, ed., *Studies in the Economic History of the Middle East* (Oxford Univ. Press, 1970), 56; Paul Lovejoy, "The Role of the Wangara in the Economic Transformation of the Central Sudan in the Fifteenth and Sixteenth Centuries," *Journal of African History*, 19, 2 (1978), 184; Katz, *Ancient Civilizations*, 272; Wolff, *Traditional Crafts*, 175.

29. Maity, *Economic Life*, 135.

30. Robert Hartwell, "A Revolution in the Chinese Iron and Coal Industries During the Northern Sung, 960–1126," *Journal of Asian Studies*, 21 (1961), 155.

31. Robert Hartwell, "A Cycle of Economic Change in Imperial China: Coal and Iron in North-East China, 750-1350," *Journal of Economic and Social History of the Orient*, 10 (1967), 123; Irfan Habib, "Potentialities of Capitalist Development in Mughal India," *Journal of Economic History*, 29, 1 (1969), 69; Maity, *Economic Life*, 130; Robert Hartwell, "Markets, Technology, and the Structure of Enterprise in the Development of the Eleventh Century Chinese Iron and Steel Industry," *Journal of Economic History*, 26, 1 (1966), 32.

32. Ashtor, *Near East*, 100; Habib, "Potentialities," 71; Subhi Labib, "Capitalism in Medieval Islam," *Journal of Economic History*, 29, 1 (1969), 83; George Spencer, "The Politics of Plunder: The Cholas of Eleventh Century Ceylon," *Journal of Asian Studies*, 35, 3 (1975), 414-15.

33. Yoshinobu Shiba, *Commerce and Society in Sung China* (Ann Arbor, Univ. of Michigan Press, 1970), 209; Habib, "Potentialities," 48; Ashtor, *Near East*, 38.

34. Katz, *Ancient Civilizations*, 128; Gibb, *Mohammedanism*, 7; Lovejoy, "The Wangara," 180-81.

35. Quoted in Simkin, *Traditional Trade*, 138; Irfan Habib, "Non-Agricultural Production and Urban Economy," in Tapan Raychaudhuri and Irfan Habib, eds., *The Cambridge Economic History of India, c. 1200-1750*, vol. 1 (Cambridge Univ. Press, 1982), 82, 93.

36. Needham, *Science and Civilisation*, vol. 1, 59; Simkin, *Traditional Trade*, 11; Timothy Garrard, "Myth and Metrology: The Early Trans-Saharan Gold Trade," *Journal of African History*, 23, 4 (1982).

37. Simkin, *Traditional Trade*, 55, 84, 97.

38. John Cady, *South-East Asia: Its Historical Development* (New York, McGraw-Hill, 1964), 161.

39. Ma, *Commercial Development*, 42, 82; Lovejoy, "The Wangara," 176; Goitein, "Mediterranean Trade," 59, 62; Labib, "Egyptian Commercial Policy," 66.

40. Miyamoto et al., "Economic Development," 545; Ma, *Commercial Development*, 83, 125.

41. See, e.g., Hilary Beattie, *Land and Lineage in China* (Cambridge Univ. Press, 1979), 6-7; Ma, *Commercial Development*, 23; Reischauer, *Japan*, 39-40; Whitecotton, *The Zapotecs*, 150-51.

42. Andrew Watson, *Agricultural Innovation in the Early Islamic World* (Cambridge Univ. Press, 1983), 112.

43. Needham, "Science and Society," 10; Beattie, *Land and Lineage*, 9.

44. Edward Calnek, "Patterns of Empire Formation in the Valley of Mexico, Late Post-Classic Period, 1200-1521," in George Collier et al., eds., *The Inca and Aztec States, 1400-1800* (New York, Academic Press, 1982), 56-59; Edwin Reischauer and John Fairbank, *East Asia, the Great Tradition*, vol. 1 of *A History of East Asian Civilization* (Harvard Univ. Press, 1960), 304; Katz, *Ancient Civilizations*, 273-92.

45. Nehemia Levtzion, "The Early States of the Western Sudan," in J.F.A. Ajayi and Michael Crowder, eds., *A History of West Africa*, vol. 1 (Columbia Univ. Press, 1976), 139; Tapan Raychaudhuri and Irfan Habib, eds., *The Cambridge Economic History of India, c. 1200-1750*, vol. 1 (Cambridge Univ. Press, 1982), 1-2.

46. Needham, *Science and Civilisation*, vol. 1, 67.

47. Craig Morris, "The Infrastructure of Inka Control in the Peruvian Central Highlands," in Collier, *Inca and Aztec States*, 156.

48. Drekmeier, *Kingship*, 171; Catherine Julien, "Inca Decimal Administration in the Lake Titicaca Region," in Collier, *Inca and Aztec States*, 121-26.

49. Ma, *Commercial Development*, 86.

50. Drekmeier, *Kingship*, 171; Watson, "Agricultural Revolution," 28.

51. Hartwell, "A Cycle," 154; Hartwell, "Chinese Iron," 155.

52. Lallanji Gopal, *The Economic Life of Northern India* (Delhi, Motilal Banarsidass, 1965), 82-102.

53. Katz, *American Civilizations*, 116-19.

54. Ashtor, Near East, 55, 246; Andrew Hess, The Forgotton Frontier: A History of the Sixteenth Century Ibero-African Frontier (Univ. of Chicago Press, 1978), 25, 48; S. Pines, "What Was Original in Arabic Science," in A. C. Crombie, ed., Scientific Change (New York, Basic Books, 1963), 203.

55. Elvin, Patterns, 203–34, 285–317.

56. Simkin, Traditional Trade, 16; Drekmeier, Kingship, 167.

57. Spencer, "The Cholas," 406; Nigel Davies, The Aztecs (New York, Putnam, 1974), 96, 100–101.

58. Elvin, Patterns, 55; Ashtor, Near East, 16; Drekmeier, Kingship, 86.

59. Ashtor, Near East, 247; Bernard Lewis, "The Arabs in Decline," in Carlo Cipolla, ed., The Economic Decline of Empires (London, Methuen, 1970), 113.

60. Simkin, Traditional Trade, 142–45.

61. Elvin, Patterns, 217–25.

62. Ashtor, Near East, 182; Lewis, "The Arabs," 112; Watson, Agricultural Innovation, 141–44; Roger Owen, The Middle East in the World Economy (London, Methuen, 1981), 33.

63. Ram Sharan Sharma, Indian Feudalism: c. 300–1200 (Univ. of Calcutta Press, 1965), 124.

64. Drekmeier, Kingship, 182; D. C. Sircar, ed., Land Systems and Feudalism in Ancient India (Univ. of Calcutta Press, 1966).

65. Elvin, Patterns, 72–76.

66. Miyamoto et al., "Economic Development," 542–44.

67. Beattie, Land and Lineage, 18; Ping-ti Ho, "Economic and Institutional Factors in the Decline of the Chinese Empire," in Cipolla, Economic Decline, 275; Reischauer, Japan, 62; Maity, Economic Life, 112.

68. Jones, Miracle, 193; Beattie, Land and Lineage, 59, 117, 128.

69. Gibb, Mohammedanism, 108–26.

70. Gopal, Economic Life, 130.

71. Vikas Mishra, Hinduism and Economic Growth (Oxford Univ. Press, 1962), 19.

72. Carlo Cipolla, Guns, Sails, and Empires (New York, Pantheon, 1965), 117; Needham, "Science and Society," 179.

73. Jaime Vicens Vives, An Economic History of Spain (Princeton Univ. Press, 1969), 306; Woodrow Borah and Sherborne Cook, The Aboriginal Population of Central Mexico on the Eve of the Conquest (Univ. of California Press, 1963), 88.

74. Ho, "Institutional Factors," 276; Jones, Miracle, 5–8; David O'Conner, "Egypt, 1552–664 B.C.," Cambridge History of Africa, vol. 1 (Cambridge Univ. Press, 1976), 837.

75. Gordon R. Willey and Dimitri Shimkin, "The Maya Collapse: A Summary View," in T. Patrick Culbert, ed., The Classic Maya Collapse (Univ. of New Mexico Press, 1973), 491; see also William T. Sanders, "The Cultural Ecology of the Lowland Maya: A Re-evaluation," in ibid., 359; Thompson, Maya, 105.

76. S. P. Sangar, "The Lot of the Agriculturalist in Aurangzeb's Time," Journal of Indian History, 45, 1 (1967), 245, 251; Ashtor, Near East, 280.

77. Walt Rostow, How It All Began: Origins of the Modern Economy (New York, McGraw-Hill, 1975), 28.

## CHAPTER 3

1. Robert Latouche, The Birth of the Western Economy (New York, Barnes and Noble, 1961), 10.

2. A.H.M. Jones, The Decline of the Ancient World (New York, Holt, Rinehart, and Winston, 1966), 121–29, 237.

3. Ibid., 287.

4. Robert Lopez, *The Commercial Revolution of the Middle Ages* (Cambridge Univ. Press, 1976), 4.

5. Perry Anderson, *Passages from Antiquity* (London, Verso, 1978), 81.

6. *Ibid.*, 77; Latouche, *Birth*, 18.

7. Latouche, *Birth*, 7.

8. Jones, *Ancient World*, 367.

9. Chris Wickham, "The Other Transition: From the Ancient World to Feudalism," *Past and Present*, 103 (1984), 12.

10. Jones, *Ancient World*, 291; Wickham, "Other Transition," 17.

11. Lopez, *Commercial Revolution*, 10–11, 17; Norman Pounds, *An Economic History of Medieval Europe* (London, Longman, 1974), 37–43.

12. Joan Hussey, *The Byzantine World* (London, Hutchinson, 1967), 29.

13. *Ibid.*, 26.

14. *Ibid.*, 48–65.

15. Latouche, *Birth*, 107–108.

16. *Ibid.*, 154–62.

17. *Ibid.*, 213–18.

18. Pounds, *Medieval Europe*, 88–89; Georges Duby, *The Early Growth of the European Economy* (Cornell Univ. Press, 1974), 113.

19. Marc Bloch, *Feudal Society* (Univ. of Chicago Press, 1961), 332–33; R. W. Southern, *The Making of the Middle Ages* (Yale Univ. Press, 1961), 92.

20. Bloch, *Feudal Society*, 241–55.

21. B. H. Slicher van Bath, *The Agrarian History of Western Europe* (London, Edward Arnold, 1963), 46.

22. Douglass North and Robert Thomas, *The Rise of the Western World* (Cambridge Univ. Press, 1973), 28.

23. Bloch, *Feudal Society*, 237–38; Duby, *Early Growth*, 174.

24. Rodney Hilton, "A Crisis of Feudalism," *Past and Present*, 80 (1978), 8.

25. Georges Duby, *Rural Economy and Country Life in the Medieval West* (Univ. of South Carolina Press, 1968), 71, 102.

26. Slicher van Bath, *Agrarian History*, 121; Duby, *Early Growth*, 15.

27. Georges Duby, *Medieval Agriculture* (London, Fontana, 1969), 19.

28. J. C. Russell, "Population in Europe, 500–1500," in Carlo Cipolla, ed., *The Fontana Economic History of Europe*, vol. 1 (Sussex, Eng., Harvester Press, 1976), 36.

29. Duby, *Early Growth*, 180.

30. Lopez, *Commercial Revolution*, 63–65; John Day, "The Great Bullion Famine of the Fifteenth Century," *Past and Present*, 79 (May, 1978), 7.

31. Marion Malowist, "The Problem of Inequality of Economic Development in Europe in the Later Middle Ages," *Economic History Review*, 19, 1 (1966), 24–25.

32. Lopez, *Commercial Revolution*, 112–13; Charles Verlinden, "The Rise of Spanish Trade in the Middle Ages," *Economic History Review*, 1st series, 10, 1 (1940), 54–57; Bailie Diffie, *Prelude to Empire: Portugal Overseas Before Henry the Navigator* (Univ. of Nebraska Press, 1960),

33. M. M. Postan, "The Economic Foundations of Medieval Agriculture," in M. M. Postan, ed., *Essays on Medieval Agriculture and General Problems of the Medieval Economy* (Cambridge Univ. Press, 1973), 8; Day, "Bullion Famine," 6.

34. Pounds, *Medieval Europe*, 100–101.

35. David Nicholas, *Town and Countryside: Social, Economic, and Political Tensions in Fourteenth Century Flanders* (Bruges, de Tempel, 1971), 53, 218.

36. Sylvia Thrupp, "The Gilds," in M. M. Postan, E. E. Rich, and Edward Miller, eds., *The Cambridge Economic History of Europe*, vol. 3 (Cambridge Univ. Press, 1965), 232–46; A. B. Hibbert, "The Economic Policies of Towns," in *ibid.*, 198–206.

37. Hilton, "Crisis," 8; Maurice Dobb, *Studies in the Development of Capitalism* (New York, International Publishers, 1963), 41.

38. Paul Sweezy, "A Critique of *Studies in the Development of Capitalism*," in Rodney Hilton, ed., *The Transition from Capitalism to Feudalism* (London, Verso, 1978), 33–57.

39. Maurice Dobb, "A Reply," and "A Further Comment," in Hilton, *Transition*.

40. Robert Brenner, "Agrarian Class Structure and Economic Development in Pre-Industrial Europe," *Past and Present*, 70 (1976), 44.

41. Slicher van Bath, *Agrarian History*, 53.

42. Duby, *Rural Economy*, 125.

43. Postan, "Economic Foundations," 17.

44. Harry Miskimin, *The Economy of Early Renaissance Europe* (Yale Univ. Press, 1977), 26; Guy Bois, *The Crisis of Feudalism; Economy and Society in Eastern Normandy, c. 1300–1550* (Cambridge Univ. Press, 1984), 271.

45. J.M.W. Bean, "Plague, Population and Economic Decline in the Later Middle Ages," *Economic History Review*, 15, 3 (1963), 425.

46. Pounds, *Medieval Europe*, 440–41.

47. Carlo Cipolla, *Before the Industrial Revolution* (New York, Norton, 1976), 157.

48. Bean, "Plague," 426–27.

49. Georges Duby, "Medieval Agriculture," in Carlo Cipolla, ed., *The Fontana Economic History of Europe*, vol. 1 (Sussex, Eng., Harvester Press, 1976), 213–15.

50. Miskimin, *Renaissance Europe*, 64; Pounds, *Medieval Europe*, 480; Robert Brenner, "The Agrarian Roots of European Capitalism," *Past and Present*, 97 (1982), 113.

51. Miskimin, *Renaissance Europe*, 90.

52. Perry Anderson, *Lineages of the Absolutist State* (London, Verso, 1974), 199; Slicher van Bath, *Agrarian History*, 106; Eric Wolf, *Europe and the Peoples Without History* (Univ. of California Press, 1983), 107; J. A. van Houtte, "The Rise and Decline of the Market of Bruges," *Economic History Review*, 19, 1 (1966), 33, 43, 46; Bois, *Crisis*, 269.

53. Gene Brucker, *Renaissance Florence* (New York, Wiley, 1969), 87; Denys Hay, *The Italian Renaissance and Its Historical Background* (Cambridge Univ. Press, 1962), 54, 89; Anderson, *Lineages*, 160; Richard Goldwaite, "The Medici Bank and the World of Florentine Capitalism," *Past and Present*, 114 (1987), 8.

54. Lopez, *Commercial Revolution*, 63–65.

55. Duby, *Rural Economy*, 109–10.

56. Lynn White, ed., *Medieval Religion and Technology* (Univ. of California Press, 1979), 22.

57. Philippe Braunstein, "Innovation in Mining and Metal Production in Europe in the Late Middle Ages," *Journal of European Economic History*, 12 (1983), 580–89; Day, "Bullion," 37.

58. Elanora Carus-Wilson, "The Woolen Industry," in M. M. Postan and E. E. Rich, eds., *The Cambridge Economic History of Europe*, vol. 2 (Cambridge Univ. Press, 1952), 393–94, 412–13; Patrick Chorley, "The Cloth Exports of Flanders and Northern France During the Thirteenth Century: A Luxury Trade?" *Economic History Review*, 40, 3 (1987), 359. Chorley points out, however, that these towns continued to produce other types of cloth as well.

59. Frederick C. Lane, *Venice, a Maritime Republic* (Johns Hopkins Univ. Press, 1973), 120; Lynn White, "The Expansion of Technology," in Cipolla, *Fontana Economic History*, vol. 1, 166–68.

60. Carlo Cipolla, *Guns, Sails, and Empires* (New York, Pantheon, 1965), 93.

61. Cipolla, *Before*, 157.

62. Ragaei El Mallakh and Dorothy El Mallakh, "Trade and Commerce," in John R. Hayes, ed., *The Genius of Arab Civilization: Source of the Renaissance* (MIT Press, 1983), 233.

63. Edwin Reischauer and John Fairbank, *East Asia, the Great Tradition* (Boston, Heath, 1960), 280–85.

64. Lynn White, "Technology and Invention in the Middle Ages," in White, *Medieval Religion,* 22.

65. Joseph Needham, *The Grand Titration, Science and Society in East and West* (Univ. of Toronto Press, 1969), 117.

66. Hilton, "Crisis," 12–14; Bois, *Crisis,* 237.

67. Anderson, *Passages,* 201–202.

68. Pounds, *Medieval Europe,* 445.

69. Rodney Hilton, *Bond Men Made Free* (New York, Viking Press, 1973), 119–20, 155, 184–85.

70. Dobb, *Studies,* 46–47; Brenner, "Agrarian Roots," 66, 83–84.

71. Slicher van Bath, *Agrarian History,* 148.

72. Anderson, *Lineages,* 17–18.

73. Antonio de Oliveira Marques, *History of Portugal,* vol. 1 (Columbia Univ. Press, 1972), 128–32.

74. John Elliott, *Imperial Spain, 1469–1716* (New York, St. Martin's Press, 1964), 23–29; Stanley Payne, *A History of Spain and Portugal,* vol. 1 (Univ. of Wisconsin Press, 1973), 147–55.

75. Charles W. Previté-Orton, *The Shorter Cambridge Medieval History* (Cambridge Univ. Press, 1966), 893–94.

76. *Ibid.,* 998–99.

77. Geoffrey Elton, *England Under the Tudors* (London, Methuen, 1957), 1–42; William McElwee, *A Short History of England* (New York, Praeger, 1969), 105–12.

78. J.H.M. Salmon, *Society in Crisis: France in the Sixteenth Century* (New York, St. Martin's Press, 1975), 21–24.

79. A. R. Bridbury, "Before the Black Death," *Economic History Review,* 30, 3 (1977), 395.

80. Eugene Rice, *The Foundations of Early Modern Europe* (New York, Norton, 1970), 12; Harry Miskimin, *Money, Prices, and Foreign Exchange in Fourteenth Century France* (Yale Univ. Press, 1963), 7.

81. Rice, *Foundations,* 11.

82. Oliveira Marques, *Portugal,* 271–305.

83. Elliott, *Imperial Spain,* 64–75.

84. Previté-Orton, *Cambridge Medieval History,* 894; Anderson, *Lineages,* 87; Salmon, *Crisis,* 21, 96–97.

85. Previté-Orton, *Cambridge Medieval History,* 891–93; Anderson, *Lineages,* 115, 118; McElwee, *Short History of England,* 118; Conrad Russell, *The Crisis of Parliaments* (Oxford Univ. Press, 1971), 40.

86. Frederich Herr, *The Holy Roman Empire* (New York, Praeger, 1968), 2, 23, 53, 56, 59; Anderson, *Lineages,* 145–46.

87. Miskimin, *Renaissance Europe,* 4–5.

88. *Ibid.,* 5–6.

89. Fritz Rorig, *The Medieval Town* (Univ. of California Press, 1967), 63, 66.

90. Anderson, *Lineages,* 143.

91. Rorig, *Medieval Town,* 93; Henri Pirenne, "The Place of the Netherlands in the Economic History of Medieval Europe," *Economic History Review,* 1st series, 2 (1931), 40.

92. Miskimin, *Renaissance Europe,* 98.

93. Karl Marx, *Capital,* vol. 3 (New York, International Publishers, 1967), 295.

94. Dobb, *Studies,* 109.

95. Miskimin, *Renaissance Europe,* 98; Pirenne, "Place," 38.

96. Hermann van der Wee, "Structural Changes and Specialization in the Industry of the Southern Netherlands, 1100-1600," *Economic History Review*, 28, 2 (1975), 215.

97. Marion Gibbs, *Feudal Order* (London, Cobbett Press, 1949), 21.

98. Jack Goody, *The Development of the Family and Marriage in Europe* (Cambridge Univ. Press, 1983), 94.

99. Gibbs, *Feudal Order*, 65-66.

100. Anderson, *Passages*, 66-67.

## CHAPTER 4

1. Eric Hobsbawm, "The Crisis of the Seventeenth Century," in Trevor Aston, ed., *Crisis in Europe, 1560-1660* (New York, Basic Books, 1965), 31-32.

2. Earl J. Hamilton, "American Treasure and the Rise of Capitalism," *Economica*, 5 (Nov., 1929), 338-57.

3. Peter Clark, "Introduction," in Peter Clark, ed., *The European Crisis of the 1590s* (London, Allen and Unwin, 1985), 8-9; Emmanuel Le Roy Ladurie, *The French Peasantry, 1450-1660* (Univ. of California Press, 1987), 135, 410.

4. One of the more extensive treatments of Muslim Iberia is S. M. Imamuddin, *The Economic History of Spain Under the Umayyads* (Dacca, Asiatic Society of Pakistan, 1963).

5. Jaime Vicens Vives, *An Economic History of Spain* (Princeton Univ. Press, 1969), 125, 131.

6. Stanley Payne, *A History of Spain and Portugal*, vol. 1 (Univ. of Wisconsin Press, 1973), 55-74.

7. Bailie Diffie and George Winius, *The Foundations of the Portuguese Empire, 1415-1580* (Univ. of Minnesota Press, 1977), 13-15.

8. Antonio de Oliveira Marques, *History of Portugal*, vol. 1 (Columbia Univ. Press, 1972), 88, 121, 210.

9. Payne, *Spain and Portugal*, 125.

10. Elana Lourie, "A Society Organized for War: Medieval Spain," *Past and Present*, 35 (Dec., 1966), 56-57, 68.

11. Payne, *Spain and Portugal*, vol. 1, 77.

12. Jean Mariejol, *The Spain of Ferdinand and Isabella* (Rutgers Univ. Press, 1961), 15-38.

13. John Elliott, *Imperial Spain, 1469-1716* (New York, St. Martin's Press, 1964), 80.

14. Jaime Vicens Vives, cited in Roger Highfield, ed., *Spain in the Fifteenth Century, 1369-1516* (London, Macmillan, 1972), 47, 255.

15. For an important corrective of the often-quoted figure of 97 percent for land owned by seigneurs, see David Vassberg, *Land and Society in Golden Age Castile* (Cambridge Univ. Press, 1984), 136; Charles Jago, "The Influence of Debt on Relations Between Crown and Aristocracy in Seventeenth Century Castile," *Economic History Review*, 26 (1973), 233.

16. Vassberg, *Land and Society*, 136.

17. Charles Verlinden, "The Rise of Spanish Trade in the Middle Ages," *Economic History Review*, 1st series, 10, 1 (1940), 48-58; Vives, *Economic History*, 241-78.

18. J. S. Parry, *The Age of Reconnaissance* (New York, Praeger, 1963), 53-114.

19. Diffie and Winius, *Foundations*, 113-18.

20. C. R. Boxer, *Four Centuries of Portuguese Expansion* (Johannesburg, Univ. of Witwatersrand Press, 1965), 5-13.

21. Bailie Diffie, *Prelude to Empire: Portugal Overseas Before Henry the Navigator* (Univ. of Nebraska Press, 1960), 89-90.

22. James Duffy, *Portuguese Africa* (Harvard Univ. Press, 1959), 5-24.

23. Diffie and Winius, *Foundations*, 89, 176.

24. *Ibid.*, 240.

25. John Cady, *South-East Asia, Its Historical Development* (New York, McGraw-Hill, 1964), 173–76.

26. K. M. Panikkar, *Asia and Western Dominance* (London, Allen and Unwin, 1959), 13–15.

27. Ivor Wilks, "Wangara, Akan, and the Portuguese in the Fifteenth and Sixteenth Centuries: The Matter of Bita," *Journal of African History*, 23, 3 (1982), 336; John Vogt, *Portuguese Rule on the Gold Coast, 1469–1682* (Univ. of Georgia Press, 1979), 89.

28. Bernard Lewis, "The Arabs in Decline," in Carlo Cipolla, ed., *The Economic Decline of Empires* (London, Methuen, 1970), 114.

29. Carl Sauer, *The Early Spanish Main* (Univ. of California Press, 1966), 12–37.

30. *Ibid.*, 294; Frank Moya Pons, *Historia Colonial de Santo Domingo* (Santiago, Dominican Republic, Universidad Catolica Madre y Maestra, 1977), 75; Ramiro Guerra y Sanchez, *Sugar and Society in the Caribbean* (Yale Univ. Press, 1964), 34; see also Alfred Crosby, *Ecological Imperialism, the Biological Expansion of Europe* (Cambridge Univ. Press, 1986).

31. Nigel Davies, *The Aztecs* (New York, Putnam, 1974), 233–84.

32. For the most detailed account of the conquest, see John Hemming, *The Conquest of the Incas* (London, Macmillan, 1970).

33. Eric Wolf, *Sons of the Shaking Earth* (Univ. of Chicago Press, 1966), 152.

34. Elliott, *Imperial Spain*, 180.

35. Earl J. Hamilton, *American Treasure and the Price Revolution in Spain, 1501–1650* (New York, Octagon Books, 1977), 42.

36. Philip Longworth, *The Rise and Fall of Venice* (London, Constable, 1974), 150.

37. Quoted in John Lynch, *Spain Under the Habsburgs*, vol. 1 (Oxford Univ. Press, 1964), 35.

38. Elliott, *Imperial Spain*, 125–33.

39. Henry Kamen, *Spain, 1469–1714* (London, Longman, 1983), 86–89.

40. R. Trevor Davies, *The Golden Century of Spain, 1501–1621* (London, Macmillan, 1937), 67–70; Payne, *Spain and Portugal*, vol. 1, 277–81.

41. Fernand Braudel, *The Mediterranean and the Mediterranean World in the Age of Philip II*, vol. 1 (London, Collins, 1972), 511.

42. J. S. Parry, *The Spanish Seaborne Empire* (London, Hutchinson, 1966), 245.

43. Elliott, *Imperial Spain*, 285.

44. Lynch, *Habsburgs*, vol. 1, 56.

45. Braudel, *Mediterranean*, vol. 2, 841.

46. Kamen, *Spain*, 162.

47. See, Gordon Griffeths, "The Revolutionary Character of the Revolution of the Netherlands," *Comparative Studies in Society and History*, 2, 4 (1959–1960); I. Schöffer, "The Dutch Revolution Atomized," *Comparative Studies in Society and History*, 3, 4 (1960–1961).

48. P. J. Bakewell, *Silver Mining and Society in Colonial Mexico* (Cambridge Univ. Press, 1971), 67.

49. Hamilton, *American Treasure*, 42.

50. Braudel, *Mediterranean*, vol. 1, 511; A. W. Lovett, "The Castilian Bankruptcy of 1575," *Historical Journal*, 23 (1980), 899–911.

51. Vassberg, *Land and Society*, 219, 224.

52. Kamen, *Spain*, 167.

53. Vassberg, *Land and Society*, 159, 161, 203.

54. Vives, *Economic History*, 293, 346; Lynch, *Habsburgs*, vol. 2, 2.

55. Lynch, *Habsburgs*, vol. 2, 126; Vives, *Economic History*, 412.

56. James Casey, "Moriscos and the Depopulation of Valencia," *Past and Present*, 50 (1971), 19; Elliott, *Imperial Spain*, 301; Kamen, *Spain*, 219–22.

57. François Chevalier, *Land and Society in Colonial Mexico* (Univ. of California Press, 1963), 41; Vives, *Economic History*, 333, 387.

58. Lynch, *Habsburgs*, vol. 2, 152.

59. *Ibid.*, 149-53.

60. Quoted in Braudel, *Mediterranean*, vol. 1, 476; Vives, *Economic History*, 444; Michael Weisser, "Rural Crisis and Rural Credit in Seventeenth Century Castile," *Journal of European Economic History*, 16, 2 (1987), 311.

61. Vives, *Economic History*, 433.

62. Vassberg, *Land and Society*, 200.

63. Jago, "The Influence of Debt," 233; this privilege was also extended to those who held advanced degrees; see Ruth Pike, *Aristocrats and Traders: Sevillian Society in the Sixteenth Century* (Cornell Univ. Press, 1972).

64. Vives, *Economic History*, 416.

65. H. G. Koenigsberger and George Mosse, *Europe in the Sixteenth Century* (London, Longman, 1968), 50.

66. Immanuel Wallerstein, *The Modern World System*, vol. 1 (New York, Academic Press, 1974), 131.

67. Diffie and Winius, *Foundations*, 312.

68. Vogt, *Portuguese Rule*, 98-113, 170-92.

69. Vitorino Malgalhães Godinho, "Le répli vénitien et égyptien et la route du cap," in *Eventail de l'histoire vivante: Hommage à Lucien Febvre*, vol. 2 (Paris, 1953), 298-300; Diffie and Winius, *Foundations*, 320.

70. Michael Pearson, *Merchants and Rulers in Gujerat* (Univ. of California Press, 1976), 48; Diffie and Winius, *Foundations*, 417.

71. Frederick C. Lane, "Pepper Prices Before da Gama," *Journal of Economic History*, 28, 4 (1968), 596.

72. Donald Lach, *Asia in the Making of Europe*, vol. 1 (Univ. of California Press, 1965), 125-26.

73. Anthony Disney, *Twilight of the Pepper Empire* (Harvard Univ. Press, 1978), 61.

74. Davies, *Golden Century*, 185-86; Alan K. Smith, "The Indian Ocean Zone," in David Birmingham and Phyllis Martin, eds., *History of Central Africa*, vol. 1 (London, Longman, 1983), 223.

75. Caio Prado Junior, *Formação do Brasil Contemporâneo* (São Paulo, Brasiliense, 1971), 86-88.

76. Davies, *Golden Age*, 189-93; Elliott, *Imperial Spain*, 267-68.

77. C. R. Boxer, *The Dutch Seaborne Empire* (London, Knopf, 1965), 87-90, 101-103.

78. Pearson, *Merchants*, 56.

79. Carl Hanson, *Economy and Society in Baroque Portugal, 1668-1703* (Univ. of Minnesota Press, 1981), 265-76.

80. Frederick C. Lane, *Venice, a Maritime Republic* (Johns Hopkins University Press, 1973), 146.

81. Brian Pullan, "Introduction," in Brian Pullan, ed., *Crisis and Change in the Venetian Economy in the Sixteenth and Seventeenth Centuries* (London, Methuen, 1968), 8.

82. Longworth, *Rise and Fall*, 75; A. H. Lybyer, "The Ottoman Turks and the Routes of the Oriental Trade," *English Historical Review*, 30 (1915), 581; Ruth Pike, *Enterprise and Adventure: The Genoese in Seville* (Cornell Univ. Press, 1966), 1-2, 48-83.

83. Lybyer, "Oriental Trade," 585.

84. Richard Rapp, "The Unmaking of the Mediterranean Trade Hegemony: International Trade Rivalry and the Commercial Revolution," *Journal of Economic History*, 35, 3 (1975), 502; Longworth, *Rise and Fall*, 190; Lane, *Venice*, 156.

85. Longworth, *Rise and Fall*, 223.

86. Pullan, "Introduction," 10; Rapp, "Unmaking," 22-23.

87. Domenico Sella, "The Rise and Fall of the Venetian Woolen Industry," in Pullan, Crisis and Change, 121.

88. Richard Rapp, Industry and Economic Decline in Seventeenth Century Venice (Cambridge Univ. Press, 1976), 15.

89. Ibid., 136; Carlo Cipolla, "Economic Decline in Italy," in Cipolla, Economic Decline, 208.

90. Ruggiero Romano, "Italy in the Crisis of the Seventeenth Century," in Peter Earle, ed., Essays in European Economic History, 1500-1800 (Oxford Univ. Press, 1974), 193; S. J. Woolf, "Venice and the Terra Ferma: Problems of the Change from Commercial to Landed Activities," in Pullan, Crisis and Change, 186.

## CHAPTER 5

1. Frederick C. Lane, "Meanings of Capitalism," Journal of Economic History, 29, 1 (1969), 5-13.

2. These paragraphs are derived from various sections of Karl Marx, Capital (New York, International Publishers, 1967).

3. Lawrence Stone, The Crisis of the Aristocracy, 1558-1641 (Oxford Univ. Press, 1965), 15.

4. Maurice Dobb, Studies in the Development of Capitalism (New York, International Publishers, 1963), 18.

5. See, for example, Violet Barbour, Capitalism in Amsterdam (Johns Hopkins Univ. Press, 1950); Charles Wilson, The Dutch Republic (New York, McGraw-Hill, 1968); Pieter Geyl, The Netherlands in the Seventeenth Century, vol. 1 (New York, Barnes and Noble, 1961); C. R. Boxer, The Dutch Seaborne Empire (London, Knopf, 1965).

6. Henri Pirenne, "The Place of the Netherlands in the Economic History of Medieval Europe," Economic History Review, 1st series, 2 (1931), 40.

7. J. A. van Houtte, An Economic History of the Low Countries, 800-1800 (New York, St. Martin's Press, 1977), 70.

8. Elanora Carus-Wilson, "The Woolen Industry," in M. M. Postan and E. E. Rich, eds., The Cambridge Economic History of Europe, vol. 2 (Cambridge Univ. Press, 1952), 398-408.

9. Pirenne, "The Place," 31.

10. Hermann van der Wee, "Structural Changes and Specialization in the Industry of the Southern Netherlands, 1100-1600," Economic History Review, 28, 2 (1976), 213.

11. David Nicholas, Town and Countryside: Social, Economic, and Political Tensions in Fourteenth Century Flanders (Bruges, de Tempel, 1971), 302.

12. J. A. van Houtte, "The Rise and Decline of the Market of Bruges," Economic History Review, 19, 1 (1966), 39, 46.

13. Pirenne, "The Place," 37.

14. Ibid., 38.

15. Dobb, Studies, 156.

16. Jan de Vries, The Dutch Rural Economy in the Golden Age, 1500-1700 (Yale Univ. Press, 1974), 26.

17. Audrey Lambert, The Making of the Dutch Landscape (London, Seminar Press, 1971), 171.

18. de Vries, Rural Economy, 27.

19. Ibid., 28.

20. van Houtte, The Low Countries, 68-69.

21. de Vries, Rural Economy, 36.

22. Ibid., 55.

23. Ibid., 48.

24. Jan de Vries, "On the Modernity of the Dutch Republic," *Journal of Economic History*, 33, 1 (1973), 202.

25. van Houtte, *The Low Countries*, 176–82.

26. H. G. Koenigsberger and George Mosse, *Europe in the Sixteenth Century* (London, Longman, 1968), 50.

27. Maria Bogucka, "Amsterdam and the Baltic in the First Half of the Seventeenth Century," *Economic History Review*, 26, 3 (1973), 447.

28. van Houtte, *The Low Countries*, 146–49.

29. de Vries, *Rural Economy*, 149.

30. J. A. Mertens and A. E. Verhulst, "Yield Ratios in Flanders in the Fourteenth Century," *Economic History Review*, 19 (1966), 177; de Vries, *Rural Economy*, 152.

31. Geyl, *The Netherlands*, vol. 1, 165.

32. Gordon Griffeths, "The Revolutionary Character of the Revolution of the Netherlands," *Comparative Studies in Society and History*, 2, 4 (1959-1960), 460.

33. John Lynch, *Spain Under the Habsburgs*, vol. 1 (Oxford Univ. Press, 1964), 289.

34. van der Wee, "Structural Changes," 217–18; van Houtte, *The Low Countries*, 133–35.

35. Immanuel Wallerstein, *The Modern World System*, vol. 2 (New York, Academic Press, 1980), 44.

36. de Vries, *Rural Economy*, 207.

37. Wilson, *Dutch Republic*, 30–32; van Houtte, *The Low Countries*, 159–70.

38. Lambert, *Dutch Landscape*, 203.

39. Ibid., 189.

40. Boxer, *Dutch Seaborne Empire*, 23–24; 44–48.

41. C. R. Boxer, *The Dutch in Brazil, 1624–1654* (Hamden, Conn., Anchor Books, 1973), 2–16.

42. Wilson, *Dutch Republic*, 32.

43. van Houtte, *The Low Countries*, 145.

44. de Vries, *Rural Economy*, 224.

45. Ibid., 231, 235.

46. Geyl, *The Netherlands*, vol. 1, 163.

47. Lambert, *Dutch Landscape*, 173, 187.

48. Ralph Davis, *The Rise of the Atlantic Economies* (Cornell Univ. Press, 1973), 252–53.

49. See, for example, J. G. van Dillen, "Economic Fluctuations and Trade in the Netherlands, 1650-1750," in Peter Earle, ed., *Essays in European Economic History, 1500–1800* (Oxford Univ. Press, 1974); J. C. Riley, "The Dutch Economy After 1650: Decline or Growth?" *Journal of European Economic History*, 13, 3 (1984), discusses the various points of view with respect to the degree of decline.

50. C. R. Boxer, "The Dutch Economic Decline," in Carlo Cipolla, ed., *The Economic Decline of Empires* (London, Methuen, 1970), 236–37.

51. Davis, *Atlantic Economies*, 193.

52. Wilson, *Dutch Republic*, 39.

53. Boxer, "Dutch Decline," 256–57.

54. The phrase was used by Fernand Braudel in the lectures published in *Afterthoughts on Material Civilization and Capitalism* (Johns Hopkins Univ. Press, 1977).

55. Geyl, *The Netherlands*, vol. 1, 163.

56. Dobb, *Studies*, 195.

57. The issue of Dutch hegemony, its impact on Europe, and the reasons for its decline are considered by a number of scholars in Maurice Aymard, ed., *Dutch Capitalism and World Capitalism* (Cambridge Univ. Press, 1982).

58. Conrad Russell, *The Crisis of Parliaments* (Oxford Univ. Press, 1971), 26.

59. Sidney Pollard and David Crossley, *The Wealth of Britain* (London, Batsford, 1968), 75; M. M. Postan, "The Fifteenth Century," *Economic History Review*, 1st series (1938-1939), 164; John McDonald and G. D. Snooks, *Domesday Economy* (Oxford Univ. Press, 1986), 12; Kathleen Biddick, "Medieval English Peasants and Market Involvement," *Journal of Economic History*, 45, 4 (1985), 831.

60. Leslie Clarkson, *The Pre-Industrial Economy in England, 1500-1750* (London, Batsford, 1971), 62.

61. Robert Brenner, "Agrarian Class Structure and Economic Development in Pre-Industrial Europe," *Past and Present*, 70 (1976), 71.

62. William McElwee, *A Short History of England* (New York, Praeger, 1969), 105-109.

63. Stone, *Crisis*, 265.

64. Lawrence Stone, "Social Mobility in England, 1500-1700," *Past and Present*, 33 (Apr., 1966), 18-20.

65. Y. S. Brenner, "The Inflation of Prices in England, 1551-1650," *Economic History Review*, 15, 2 (1963), 80; Clarkson, *Pre-Industrial England*, 47.

66. Lawrence Stone, *The Causes of the English Revolution, 1529-1642* (London, Routledge and Kegan Paul, 1972), 67.

67. Joan Thirsk, *The Rural Economy of England* (London, Hambledon Press, 1984), 65-85.

68. C. H. George, "The Making of the English Bourgeoisie, 1500-1750," *Science and Society*, 35, 4 (1971), 394-95.

69. Charles Wilson, *England's Apprenticeship* (London, Longman, 1965), 43.

70. Barry Supple, *Commercial Crisis and Change in England, 1600-1642* (Cambridge Univ. Press, 1964), 23-24.

71. Christopher Hill, *Economic Problems of the Church* (Oxford Univ. Press, 1956), 14-50.

72. McElwee, *Short History*, 118.

73. Clarkson, *Pre-Industrial England*, 62.

74. Stone, *Crisis*, 269.

75. *Ibid.*, 381-83.

76. Thirsk, *Rural Economy*, 355.

77. Richard H. Tawney, *The Agrarian Problem in the Sixteenth Century* (London, Longman, 1912), 46, notes that in the sixteenth century, villeinage ceased but the Poor Laws began.

78. Richard H. Tawney, "The Rise of the Gentry, 1558-1640," *Economic History Review*, 1st series, 11, 1 (1941), 4-5.

79. Marx, *Capital*, vol. 3, 614.

80. Robert Brenner, "The Social Basis for English Commercial Expansion, 1550-1650," *Journal of Economic History*, 32, 1 (1972); Marion Gibbs, *Feudal Order* (London, Cobbett Press, 1949), 102; Supple, *Commercial Crisis*, 23.

81. Supple, *Commercial Crisis*, 31, 71; Robert Ashton, "The Parliamentary Agitation for Free Trade in the Opening Years of James I," *Past and Present*, 38 (Dec., 1967), 47; Wilson, *England's Apprenticeship*, 54.

82. J. R. Killett, "The Breakdown of Gild and Corporation Control over the Handicraft and Retail Trade in London," *Economic History Review*, 10, 3 (1958), 381-82.

83. Dobb, *Studies*, 144-51.

84. Stone, *Causes*, 70.

85. R. L. Dunnes, "The Stower Partnership: Landed Capital in the Iron Industry," *Economic History Review*, 3, 1 (1950), 94.

86. Dobb, *Studies*, 143.

87. C. H. George, "The Origins of Capitalism: A Marxist Epitome and a Critique of Immanuel Wallerstein's Modern World System," *Marxist Perspectives*, 3, 2 (1980), 79; Stone, *Causes*, 69, 75.

88. Supple, *Commercial Crisis*, 72.

89. Stone, *Causes*, 59–60, 115; Clarkson, *Pre-Industrial England*, 161; McElwee, *Short History*, 84, 94.

90. Stone, *Causes*, 125–26; Clarkson, *Pre-Industrial England*, 106, 187; Stone, *Crisis*, 120, 126; Wilson, *England's Apprenticeship*, 100–102.

91. Christopher Hill, *The Century of Revolution* (Edinburgh, T. Nelson and Sons, 1961), 34.

92. Wilson, *England's Apprenticeship*, 106.

93. Christopher Hill, "Parliament and People in Seventeenth Century England," *Past and Present*, 92 (Aug., 1981), 108.

94. Russell, *Crisis*, 323–29.

95. *Ibid.*, 330.

96. Stone, *Causes*, 51, 56.

97. R. R. Palmer and Joel Colton, *A History of the Modern World*, vol. 1 (New York, Knopf, 1978), 168.

98. Stone, *Causes*, 72.

99. Christopher Hill, *From Reformation to Industrial Revolution* (London, Weidenfeld and Nicolson, 1967), 76.

100. Tawney, *Agrarian Problem*, 394.

101. J. E. Farnell, "The Navigation Act of 1651, the First Dutch War, and the London Merchant Community," *Economic History Review*, 16, 3 (1964), 446.

102. Pollard and Crossley, *Wealth of Britain*, 143.

103. R. Conquest, "The State and Commercial Expansion: England in the Years 1642–1688," *Journal of European Economic History*, 14, 1 (1985), 160; Patrick O'Brien, "The Political Economy of British Taxation, 1660–1815," *Economic History Review*, 41, 1 (1988), 19.

104. Jan de Vries, *The Economy of Europe in an Age of Crisis, 1600–1750* (Cambridge Univ. Press, 1976), 76.

105. D. C. Coleman, "Labour in the English Economy of the Seventeenth Century," *Economic History Review*, 8, 3 (1956), 284.

106. Pollard and Crossley, *Wealth of Britain*, 130–40.

107. K. G. Davis, "Joint-Stock Investment in the Later Seventeenth Century," *Economic History Review*, 4, 3 (1952), 288.

108. George, "English Bourgeoisie," 396.

## CHAPTER 6

1. André Gunder Frank, *World Accumulation, 1492–1789* (New York, Monthly Review Press, 1978), 4; Patrick O'Brien, "European Economic Development: The Contribution of the Periphery," *Economic History Review*, 35, 1 (1982), 4; Peter Kriedte, *Peasants, Landlords, and Merchant Capitalists in Europe and the World Economy, 1500–1800* (Cambridge Univ. Press, 1983), 124–25, 126.

2. Fernand Braudel, *Civilization and Capitalism* (New York, Harper and Row, 1984), 39.

3. Bruce McGowan, *Economic Life in Ottoman Europe: Taxation, Trade and the Struggle for Land* (Cambridge Univ. Press, 1981), 38.

4. Immanuel Wallerstein, *The Modern World System*, vol. 1 (New York, Academic Press, 1974), 199–200; Immanuel Wallerstein, *The Modern World System*, vol. 2 (New York, Academic Press, 1980), 17.

5. Geoffrey Kay, *Development and Underdevelopment: A Marxist Analysis* (London, Macmillan, 1975), 33; Howard Sherman and E. K. Hunt, *Economics: An Introduction to Traditional and Radical Views* (New York, Harper and Row, 1978), 61.

6. See, for example, Artur Attman, *The Struggle for Baltic Markets: Powers in Conflict, 1558–1618* (Gothenburg, Vetenskaps- O.Vitterhets Samhallet, 1979).

7. W. F. Reddaway et al., eds., *The Cambridge History of Poland*, vol. 2 (Cambridge Univ. Press, 1941), xiv-xvi; Roman Dyboski, *Poland in World Civilization* (New York, J. M. Barrett, 1950); John Stoye, *Europe Unfolding, 1648-1688* (New York, Harper and Row, 1969), 43-60.

8. Jerome Blum, "The Rise of Serfdom in Eastern Europe," *American Historical Review*, 62, 4 (1957), 812-16.

9. *Ibid.*, 814-16.

10. *Ibid.*, 818.

11. Karl von Loewe, "Commerce and Agriculture in Lithuania, 1400-1600," *Economic History Review*, 26, 1 (1973), 33.

12. Marion Malowist, "The Problem of Inequality of Economic Development in Europe in the Later Middle Ages," *Economic History Review*, 19, 1 (1966), 22-25.

13. Antonio Maczak, "Export of Grain and the Problem of the Distribution of National Income in the Years 1550-1650," *Acta Poloniae Historica*, 18 (1968), 91; Marion Malowist, "Poland, Russia, and the Western Trade in the Fifteenth and Sixteenth Centuries," *Past and Present*, 13 (Apr., 1958), 29-30; Maria Bogucka, "Amsterdam and the Baltic in the First Half of the Seventeenth Century," *Economic History Review*, 26, 3 (1973), 440-44.

14. Perry Anderson, *Lineages of the Absolutist State* (London, Verso, 1974), 200; O. Halecki, *A History of Poland* (New York, Roy Publishers, 1956), 153-65.

15. Leonid Zytkowicz, "Grain Yields in Poland, Bohemia, Hungary, and Slovakia in the Sixteenth to the Eighteenth Centuries," *Acta Poloniae Historica*, 24 (1971), 64.

16. Blum, "Serfdom," 820.

17. Hermann Kellenbenz, *The Rise of the European Economy* (New York, Holmes and Meier, 1976), 64.

18. William Wright, *Serf, Seigneur and Sovereign: Agrarian Reform in Eighteenth Century Bohemia* (Univ. of Minnesota Press, 1966), 14.

19. Kellenbenz, *Rise*, 63-64.

20. *Ibid.*, 66.

21. *Ibid.*, 70.

22. von Loewe, "Commerce," 26.

23. Marion Malowist, "The Economic and Social Development of the Baltic Countries from the Fifteenth to the Seventeenth Centuries," *Economic History Review*, 12, 2 (1959), 186.

24. Robert Brenner, "Agrarian Class Structure and Economic Development in Pre-Industrial Europe," *Past and Present*, 70 (1976), 56-57.

25. Jerzy Topolski, "The Manorial Serf Economy in Central Europe in the Sixteenth and Seventeenth Centuries," *Agricultural History*, 48, 3 (1974), 351.

26. Laszlo Mikkai, "Neo-Serfdom: Its Origin and Nature in East-Central Europe," *Slavic Review*, 34, 2 (1975), 237.

27. Witold Kula, *An Economic Theory of the Feudal System: Towards a Model of the Polish Economy, 1500-1800* (London, N.L.B., 1976), 137.

28. H.S.K. Kent, "The Anglo-Norwegian Timber Trade in the Eighteenth Century," *Economic History Review*, 8, 1 (1955), 66-67.

29. McGowan, *Economic Life*, 9.

30. Anderson, *Lineages*, 282.

31. Malowist, "Poland," 37.

32. Richard Sheridan, "Temperate and Tropical: Aspects of European Penetration into the Tropical Regions," *Caribbean Studies*, 3, 2 (1963), 18.

33. E. Bradford Burns, *A History of Brazil* (Columbia Univ. Press, 1980), 31-41.

34. Caio Prado Junior, *Formação do Brasil Contemporâneo* (São Paulo, Brasiliense, 1971), 86-88.

35. Bailie Diffie, *Latin American Civilization* (New York, Octagon Books, 1967), 51-74.

36. Richard Morse, ed., *The Bandeirantes: The Historical Role of the Brazilian Pathfinders* (New York, Knopf, 1965), 25–26; Manoel Cardozo, "Dom Rodrigo de Castel-Branco and the Brazilian El Dorado, 1673–1682," *The Americas*, 1 (1944), 131–59.

37. Alexander Marchant, *From Barter to Slavery* (Johns Hopkins Univ. Press, 1942), 28–47; see also John Hemming, *Red Gold, the Conquest of the Brazilian Indians* (Harvard Univ. Press, 1978).

38. Rae Flory, "Bahian Society in the Mid-Colonial Period: 1680–1720," (Ph.D. dissertation, Univ. of Texas, 1978), 158; Catherine Lugar, "The Portuguese Tobacco Trade and Tobacco Growers in Bahia in the Late Colonial Period," in Dauril Alden and Warren Dean, eds., *Essays Concerning the Socio-Economic History of Brazil and Portuguese India* (Univ. of Florida Press, 1977), 46–49.

39. Manoel Cardozo, "The Collection of the Fifths in Brazil," *Hispanic American Historical Review*, 20 (1940), 371; C. R. Boxer, "Brazilian Gold and British Traders in the First Half of the Eighteenth Century," *Hispanic American Historical Review*, 49, 3 (1969), 458, 460.

40. Burns, *Brazil*, 75.

41. For conflicting views on the inception of the depression in sugar prices, see J. H. Galloway, "North-East Brazil, 1700–1750: The Agricultural Crisis Re-examined," *Journal of Historical Geography*, 1, 1 (1975) and Mathew Edel, "The Brazilian Sugar Cycle of the Seventeenth Century and the Rise of the West Indies' Competition," *Caribbean Studies*, 9 (Apr., 1964).

42. Alan K. Manchester, "The Rise of the Brazilian Aristocracy," *Hispanic American Historical Review*, 11 (1931), 152–53; Stuart Schwartz, "Free Labor in a Slave Society: The Lavradores da Cana of Colonial Brazil," in Dauril Alden, ed., *The Colonial Roots of Modern Brazil* (Univ. of California Press, 1973), 159.

43. Schwartz, "Free Labor," 194.

44. Philip Curtin, *The Atlantic Slave Trade* (Univ. of Wisconsin Press, 1969), 268.

45. J. S. Parry and Philip Sherlock, *A Short History of the West Indies* (London, Macmillan, 1956), 16–17; Frank Moya Pons, *Historia Colonial de Santo Domingo* (Santiago, Dominican Republic, Universidad Catolica Madre y Maestra, 1977), 88.

46. Kenneth Andrews, *The Spanish Caribbean: Trade and Plunder, 1530–1630* (Yale Univ. Press, 1978), 70, 247.

47. Parry and Sherlock, *West Indies*, 49–55.

48. Richard Dunn, *Sugar and Slaves* (Univ. of North Carolina Press, 1972), 52, 58, 60.

49. Richard Pares, *Merchants and Planters* (Cambridge Univ. Press, 1960), 19.

50. Dunn, *Sugar and Slaves*, 189.

51. Pares, *Merchants*, 19.

52. Dunn, *Sugar and Slaves*, 189; Richard B. Sheridan, *Sugar and Slavery: An Economic History of the British West Indies, 1623–1775* (Johns Hopkins Univ. Press, 1974), 231.

53. Ward Barrett, "Caribbean Sugar Production Standards in the Seventeenth and Eighteenth Centuries," in J. Parker, ed., *Merchants and Scholars: Essays in the History of Exploration and Trade* (Univ. of Minnesota, 1965), 149.

54. Dunn, *Sugar and Slaves*, 188.

55. Pares, *Merchants*, 22.

56. Sheridan, *Sugar*, 120–21.

57. Richard Sheridan, "The Plantation Revolution and the Industrial Revolution, 1625–1775," *Caribbean Studies*, 9, 3 (1969), 9.

58. R. P. Thomas, "The Sugar Colonies of the Old Empire: Profit or Loss for Great Britain?" *Economic History Review*, 21, 1 (1968), 30; Richard Sheridan, "The Wealth of Jamaica in the Eighteenth Century," *Economic History Review*, 18, 2 (1965), 307; J. R. Ward, "The Profitability of Sugar Planting in the British West Indies, 1650–1834," *Economic History Review*, 31, 2 (1978), 208.

59. Dunn, *Sugar and Slaves*, 83.

60. Parry and Sherlock, *West Indies*, 69.

61. Dunn, *Sugar and Slaves*, 117.

62. Sheridan, *Sugar*, 122–23; 416.

63. Sheridan, "Jamaica," 303–306.

64. C.L.R. James, *The Black Jacobins* (New York, Vintage Books, 1963), 45; Sheridan, *Sugar*, 416; Alex Dupuy, *Haiti in the World Economy* (Boulder, Colo., Westview Press, 1989), 27.

65. James, *Black Jacobins*, 46.

66. Curtin, *Slave Trade*, 269; Sheridan, "Jamaica," 297–98.

67. Robin Blackburn, *The Overthrow of Colonial Slavery, 1776–1848* (London, Verso, 1988), 20–21; Gwendolyn Hall, *Social Control in Slave Plantation Societies* (Johns Hopkins Univ. Press, 1971), 13–20.

68. Hall, *Plantation Societies*, 62–64; Raymond Kent, "Palmares: An African State in Brazil," *Journal of African History*, 6, 2 (1965), 171, 175.

69. Hall, *Plantation Societies*, 75–76.

70. Blackburn, *Colonial Slavery*, 54–57.

71. *Ibid.*, 167.

72. Curtin, *Slave Trade*, 221; J. E. Inikori, "Measuring the Atlantic Slave Trade: An Assessment of Curtin and Anstey," *Journal of African History*, 17, 2 (1976), 223; J. E. Inikori, ed., *Forced Migration: The Impact of the Export Slave Trade on African Societies* (New York, Africana Press, 1982), 20–25.

73. David Birmingham, "Central Africa, from the Camerouns to the Zambezi," in R. Gray, ed., *Cambridge History of Africa*, vol. 4 (1965), 349, 361.

74. James Rawley, *The Trans-Atlantic Slave Trade* (New York, Norton, 1981), 22; Joseph C. Miller, "The Significance of Drought, Disease, and Famine in the Agriculturally Marginal Zones of West-Central Africa," *Journal of African History*, 23, 1 (1982), 24.

75. David Northrup, *Trade Without Rulers* (Oxford Univ. Press, 1978), 68–79; Patrick Manning, *Slavery, Colonialism, and Economic Growth in Dahomey, 1640–1960* (Cambridge Univ. Press, 1982), 9; Joseph C. Miller, "Imbangala Lineage Slavery," in S. Miers and I. Kopytoff, eds., *Slavery in Africa* (Univ. of Wisconsin, 1977), 212–16.

76. Rawley, *Slave Trade*, 29.

77. Robin Law, "Royal Monopoly and Private Enterprise in the Atlantic Slave Trade: The Case of Dahomey," *Journal of African History*, 18, 4 (1977), 566.

78. Joseph C. Miller, "The Dual Slave Trade in Angola" (mimeograph, UCLA, 1971).

79. Kwame Daaku, *Trade and Politics on the Gold Coast, 1600–1720* (Oxford Univ. Press, 1970), 166.

80. G. I. Jones, *The Trading States of the Oil Rivers* (Oxford Univ. Press, 1963), 51–63, 166–76.

81. David Northrup, "The Growth of Trade Among the Igbo Before 1800," *Journal of African History*, 13, 2 (1972), 232; Birmingham, "Central Africa," 374–75.

82. Miller, "Drought," 31.

83. Paul Lovejoy, *Transformations in Slavery* (Cambridge Univ. Press, 1983), 73–78.

84. Basil Davidson, *A History of West Africa* (London, Longman, 1965), 110–11.

85. David Henige and Marion Johnson, "Agaja and the Slave Trade: Another Look at the Evidence," *History in Africa*, 3 (1976), 59, 64; W.G.L. Randles, *L'ancien royaume du Congo des origines à la fin du dix-neuvième siècle* (Paris, Mouton, 1968), 132.

86. Walter Rodney, *A History of the Upper Guinea Coast, 1545–1800* (Oxford Univ. Press, 1971), 257–58.

87. Philip Curtin, *Economic Change in Pre-Colonial Africa* (Univ. of Wisconsin Press, 1975), 156; Frederick Cooper, "The Problem of Slavery in African Studies," *Journal of African*

*History*, 20, 1 (1979), 116; George Metcalf, "A Microcosm of Why Africans Sold Slaves: Akan Consumption Patterns in the 1770s," *Journal of African History*, 28, 3 (1987), 377–94.

88. J. D. Fage, "Slaves and Society in West Africa, c. 1445–1700," *Journal of African History*, 21, 3 (1980), 297–98.

89. J. E. Inikori, "The Import of Firearms into West Africa, 1750–1807: A Quantitative Assessment," *Journal of African History*, 18, 3 (1977), 361; E. Philip Leveen, "The African Slave Supply Response," *African Studies Review* 18, 1 (Apr., 1975), 22.

90. Cooper, "Problem of Slavery," 122.

91. Roger Anstey, *The Atlantic Slave Trade and the British Abolition* (Atlantic Highlands, N.J., Humanities Press, 1975), 404.

92. Anstey, *Atlantic Slave Trade*, 404; Manning, *Slavery*, 11; Joseph C. Miller, "Chokwe Trade and Conquest," in Richard Gray and David Birmingham, eds., *Pre-Colonial Trade* (Oxford Univ. Press, 1970), 177.

93. Joseph C. Miller, "Slaves, Slavers and Social Change in Nineteenth Century Kasanje," in Franz-Wilhelm Heimer, ed., *Social Change in Angola* (Munich, Weltforum Verlag, 1973), 12–17; Ray Kea, *Settlements, Trade, and Politics in the Seventeenth Century Gold Coast* (Johns Hopkins Univ. Press, 1982), 164–65, 288–98.

94. Northrup, *Trade*, 121–40.

95. Emmanuel Terray, "Long Distance Exchange and the Formation of the State: The Case of the Abron of Gyaman," *Economy and Society*, 3 (1974), 315–45.

96. Lovejoy, *Transformations*, 274.

97. Patrick Manning, "Contours of Slavery and Social Change in Africa," *American Historical Review*, 84, 4 (1983), 845.

98. Jan Hogendorn and Henry A. Gemery, "Abolition and Its Impact on Monies Imported into West Africa," in David Eltis and James Walvin, eds., *The Abolition of the Atlantic Slave Trade: Origins and Effects in Europe, Africa, and the Americas* (Univ. of Wisconsin Press, 1981), 102.

99. Inikori, *Forced Migration*, 16–18, 37.

100. John Thornton, "The Slave Trade in Eighteenth Century Angola: Effects on Demographic Structures," *Canadian Journal of African Studies*, 14, 3 (1980), 424; John Thornton, "Demography and History in the Kingdom of the Kongo, 1550–1750," *Journal of African History*, 18, 4 (1977), 527; Miller, "Drought," 31.

101. Jones, *Oil Rivers*, 89.

102. Inikori, *Forced Migration*, 15.

## CHAPTER 7

1. C.L.R. James, *The Black Jacobins* (New York, Vintage Books, 1963), 46.

2. Colm Regan, "Economic Development in Ireland: The Historical Dimension," *Antipode* (1981), 3.

3. Edmund Curtis, *A History of Medieval Ireland* (New York, Macmillan, 1923), 202.

4. Regan, "Historical Dimension," 2.

5. Margaret MacCurtain, *Tudor and Stuart Ireland* (Dublin, Gill and Macmillan, 1972), 102.

6. Patrick O'Farrell, *Ireland's English Question* (London, Batsford, 1971), 30, 38.

7. James Beckett, *The Making of Modern Ireland, 1603–1923* (New York, Knopf, 1966), 146.

8. Francis James, *Ireland in the Empire, 1688–1770* (Harvard Univ. Press, 1973), 17.

9. Beckett, *Making*, 120.

10. Regan, "Historical Dimension," 4.

11. O'Farrell, *English Question*, 38.

12. James, *The Empire*, 22–33, 229, 232.

13. *Ibid.*, 192, 194, 200.

14. Francis James, "Irish Colonial Trade in the Eighteenth Century," *William and Mary Quarterly*, 20, 5 (1963), 583.

15. James Beckett, *The Anglo-Irish Tradition* (Cornell Univ. Press, 1976), 72.

16. Thomas Bartlett, "An End to Moral Economy: The Irish Militia Disturbances of 1793," *Past and Present*, 99 (May, 1983), 62.

17. James, *The Empire*, 17.

18. K. H. Connell, "The Potato in Ireland," *Past and Present*, 23 (Nov., 1962), 59.

19. David Large, "The Wealth of the Great Irish Landowners," *Irish Historical Studies*, 15 (Mar., 1966), 35.

20. James, *The Empire*, 205.

21. James, "Colonial Trade," 584.

22. Regan, "Economic Development," 7.

23. Beckett, *Anglo-Irish*, 45; Beckett, *Making*, 159.

24. Allan Kuethe and G. Douglas Inglis, "Absolutism and Enlightened Reform: Charles III, the Establishment of the Alcabala, and Commercial Reorganization in Cuba," *Past and Present*, 109 (Nov., 1985), 143; John Phelan, "Authority and Flexibility in Spanish Imperial Bureaucracy," *Administrative Science Quarterly*, 5 (1960), 60.

25. Roland Hussey, *The Caracas Company* (Harvard Univ. Press, 1934), 52.

26. D. A. Brading, *Miners and Merchants in Bourbon Mexico, 1763–1810* (Cambridge Univ. Press, 1971), 7; Robert West, *Colonial Placer Mining in Colombia* (Louisiana State Univ. Press, 1952), 4, 78.

27. Woodrow Borah and Sherborne Cook, *Essays in Population History: Mexico and the Caribbean*, vol. 1 (Univ. of California Press, 1971), 82; West, *Placer Mining*, 80; Leslie Bird Simpson, *The Encomienda in New Spain* (Univ. of California Press, 1982), 28; Noble David Cook, *Demographic Collapse, Indian Peru, 1520–1620* (Cambridge Univ. Press, 1981), 247–56.

28. Alfred Crosby, "Conquistador y Pestilencia: The First New World Pandemic and the Fall of the Great Indian Empires," *Hispanic American Historical Review*, 47, 3 (1967), 323–29. For an interesting discussion of the phenomenon of the spread of disease, see Alfred Crosby, *Ecological Imperialism, the Biological Expansion of Europe* (Cambridge Univ. Press, 1986).

29. François Chevalier, *Land and Society in Colonial Mexico* (Univ. of California Press, 1963), 266–71.

30. *Ibid.*, 83.

31. D. A. Brading, *Haciendas and Ranchos in the Mexican Bajio* (Cambridge Univ. Press, 1978), 62–63.

32. Eric Wolf and Sidney Mintz, "Haciendas and Plantations in Middle America and the Antilles," *Social and Economic Studies*, 6, 3 (1957), 386–96.

33. James Lockhart, "Encomienda and Hacienda: The Evolution of the Great Estate in the Spanish Indies," *Hispanic American Historical Review*, 49 (1969), 427–48; Simpson, *Encomienda*, 29–44.

34. William Taylor, *Landlord and Peasant in Colonial Oaxaca* (Stanford Univ. Press, 1972), 144; Charles Gibson, *The Aztecs Under Colonial Rule* (Stanford Univ. Press, 1964), 224–26, 233–36.

35. Gibson, *Aztecs*, 255–56.

36. Rolando Mellafe, *Negro Slavery in Latin America* (Univ. of California Press, 1975), 90.

37. Brading, *Miners*, 110.

38. Gwendolyn Cobb, "Supply and Transportation for the Potosi Mines, 1545–1640," *Hispanic American Historical Review*, 29 (1949), 45; P. J. Bakewell, *Silver Mining and Society in Colonial Mexico: Zacatecas, 1546–1700* (Cambridge Univ. Press, 1971), 60–69.

39. E. J. Hamilton, *American Treasure and the Price Revolution in Spain, 1501–1650* (New York, Octagon Books, 1977), 34.

40. Bakewell, *Silver Mining*, 117–18.

41. Woodrow Borah, *New Spain's Century of Depression* (Univ. of California Press, 1951), 28.

42. Bakewell, *Silver Mining*, 165–67, 225; M. F. Lang, "New Spain's Mining Depression and the Supply of Quicksilver from Peru," *Hispanic American Historical Review*, 48 (1968), 639–40.

43. Arthur Whitaker, *The Huancavelica Mercury Mines* (Harvard Univ. Press, 1952), 16–21.

44. C. H. Haring, *Trade and Navigation Between Spain and the Indies* (Harvard Univ. Press, 1918), still remains the most complete treatment of the subject. John Fisher, "Silver Production in the Viceroyalty of Peru, 1776–1824," *Hispanic American Historical Review*, 51, 1 (1971), 25; Murdo MacLeod, *Spanish Central America: A Socio-Economic History, 1520–1720* (Univ. of California Press, 1973), 199.

45. Haring, *Trade and Navigation*, 129.

46. J. S. Parry, *The Sale of Public Office in the Spanish Indies Under the Habsburgs* (Univ. of California Press, 1953), 58.

47. MacLeod, *Central America*, 223.

48. Brading, *Miners*, 261.

49. Bakewell, *Silver Mining*, 178–79.

50. *Ibid.*, 118.

51. Brading, *Miners*, 215.

52. Jan Bazant, "Evolution of the Textile Industry of Puebla," *Comparative Studies in Society and History*, 7, 1 (1964–1965), 56–57; Fisher, "Silver Production," 41.

53. Nicolas Sanchez-Albornoz, "The Population of Colonial America," in Leslie Bethell, ed., *Cambridge History of Latin America*, vol. 2 (Cambridge Univ. Press, 1984), 34.

54. John Lynch, *Spain Under the Habsburgs*, vol. 2 (Oxford Univ. Press, 1964), 224–27; Bakewell, *Silver Mining*, 225, 229; Brading, *Haciendas*, 80–82; Jay Kinsbruner, *Chile: A Historical Interpretation* (New York, Harper and Row, 1973), 20; Robert Smith, "Indigo Production and Trade in Colonial Guatemala," *Hispanic American Historical Review*, 39, 2 (1959), 181–212; Troy Floyd, "The Guatemalan Merchants, the Government and the Provincianos, 1750–1800," *Hispanic American Historical Review*, 41, 1 (1961), 90–110.

55. Lynch, *Habsburgs*, vol. 2, 195.

56. Richard Boyer, "Mexico in the Seventeenth Century: Transition of a Colonial Society," *Hispanic American Historical Review*, 57, 3 (1977), 476; Eduardo Arcila Farias, *Economia colonial de Venezuela* (Mexico City, Fondo de Cultura Economica, 1946), 143–44; Kenneth Andrews, *The Spanish Caribbean* (Yale Univ. Press, 1978), 196; John Elliot, *Imperial Spain, 1469–1716* (New York, St. Martin's Press, 1964), 190.

57. Lynch, *Habsburgs*, vol. 2, 200.

58. Brading, *Miners*, 152, 294.

59. Lynch, *Habsburgs*, vol. 2, 219.

60. Karen Spalding, "Tratos mercantiles del corregidor de indios y la formación de la hacienda serrana en el Peru," *América Indígena*, 30, 3 (1970), 596.

61. Hugh Hamill, *The Hidalgo Revolt* (Univ. of Florida Press, 1966), 49.

62. Brading, *Miners*, 149; Brading, *Haciendas*, 114.

63. Enrique Tandeter, "Forced and Free Labour in Late Colonial Potosi," *Past and Present*, 93 (Nov., 1981), 117.

64. Brading, *Miners*, 224.

65. Bakewell, *Silver Mining*, 227.

66. Lynch, *Habsburgs*, vol. 2, 217.

67. Brading, *Haciendas*, 119.

68. Michael Costeloe, *Church Wealth in Mexico* (Cambridge Univ. Press, 1967), 105–106.

69. A. D. Innes, *The Maritime and Colonial Expansion of England Under the Stuarts* (London, S. Low, Marston and Co., 1931), 81–86, 105–11.

70. Fred Shannon, *America's Economic Growth* (New York, Macmillan, 1940), 14–22; Edwin Perkins, *The Economic Growth of Colonial America* (New York, Columbia Univ. Press, 1980), 6.

71. James Horn, "Servant Emigration to the Chesapeake in the Seventeenth Century," in Thad Tate and David Ammerman, eds., *The Chesapeake in the Seventeenth Century* (Univ. of North Carolina Press, 1979), 94–95; Abbot Emerson Smith, *Colonists in Bondage* (Univ. of North Carolina Press, 1947), 91, 103.

72. David Galenson, "White Servitude and the Growth of Black Slavery in America," *Journal of Economic History*, 41, 1 (1981), 40; Perkins, *Colonial America*, 7, 72.

73. Perkins, *Colonial America*, 81.

74. Quoted in John McCusker and Russell Menard, *The Economy of British North America, 1607–1789* (Univ. of North Carolina Press, 1985), 326.

75. One of the most extensive treatments is to be found in Howard S. Russell, *A Long, Deep Furrow: Three Centuries of Farming in New England* (Hanover, N.H., Univ. Press of New England, 1976).

76. Similarly, the most detailed account of southern agriculture is Lewis Gray, *History of Agriculture in the Southern United States to 1860*, vol. 1 (Washington, Carnegie Institution of Washington, 1933); see also Merrill Jensen, "The American Revolution and American Agriculture," *Agricultural History*, 43, 1 (1969), 111–12.

77. Allan Kulikoff, "The Economic Growth of the Eighteenth Century Chesapeake Colonies," *Journal of Economic History*, 39, 1 (1979), 276; T. M. Devine, "The Colonial Trade and Industrial Investment in Scotland, c. 1700–1815," *Economic History Review*, 29, 1 (1976), 3.

78. Peter Coclanis, "Rice Prices in the 1720s and the Evolution of the South Carolina Economy," *Journal of Southern History*, 48, 4 (1982), 542–44; Sam B. Hilliard, "Ante-Bellum Tidewater Rice Culture in South Carolina and Georgia," in James Gibson, ed., *European Settlement and Development in North America* (Univ. of Toronto Press, 1978), 115; G. Terry Sharrer, "The Indigo Bonanza in South Carolina, 1740–1790," *Technology and Culture*, 12, 3 (1971), 448–52.

79. Stephen Saunders Webb, *1676: The End of American Independence* (New York, Knopf, 1984), 211–13.

80. Innes, *Maritime Expansion*, 285–86.

81. Oliver Dickerson, *The Navigation Acts and the American Revolution* (Univ. of Pennsylvania Press, 1951), 7–31.

82. Roger Ranson, "British Policy and Colonial Growth: Some Implications of the Burden from the Navigation Acts," *Journal of Economic History*, 28, 3 (1968), 431, 434.

83. Robert Thomas, "A Quantitative Approach to the Study of the Effects of British Imperial Policy upon Colonial Welfare," *Journal of Economic History*, 25, 4 (1965), 638; Sharrer, "Bonanza," 453; Robert Albion, *Forests and Sea Power* (Harvard Univ. Press, 1929), 251.

84. Gary Walton and James Shepherd, *The Economic Rise of Early America* (Cambridge Univ. Press, 1979), 174.

85. Governor William Weeden, quoted in Stuart Bruchey, *The Roots of American Economic Growth, 1607–1861* (New York, Harper and Row, 1968), 69.

86. Perkins, *Colonial America*, 22.

87. James Lydon, "Fish and Flour for Gold: Southern Europe and the Colonial Balance of Payments," *Business History Review*, 39, 2 (1965), 173–79.

88. Jacob Price, "A Note on the Value of Colonial Exports of Shipping," *Journal of Economic History*, 36, 3 (1976), 22; McCusker and Menard, *British North America*, 82.

89. Walton and Shepherd, *Early America*, 4.

90. Jackson Turner Main, *The Social Structure of Revolutionary America* (Princeton Univ. Press, 1965), 9, 183.

91. Perkins, *Colonial America*, 12–13.

92. Walton and Shepherd, *Early America*, 158.

## CHAPTER 8

1. W. E. Minchinton, "Introduction," in W. E. Minchinton, ed., *The Growth of English Overseas Trade in the Seventeenth and Eighteenth Centuries* (London, Methuen, 1969), 11.

2. E. L. Jones, "Agriculture and Economic Growth in England, 1660-1750: Agricultural Change," *Journal of Economic History*, 25, 1 (1965), 3–4.

3. J. D. Chambers and G. E. Mingay, *The Agricultural Revolution, 1750-1880* (New York, Schocken Books, 1966), 42, 78.

4. Arthur John, "Agricultural Productivity and Economic Growth in England, 1700-1760," *Journal of Economic History*, 25, 1 (1965), 24.

5. William Scott, *The Constitution and Finance of English, Scottish and Irish Joint Stock Companies to 1720*, vol. 1 (Gloucester, Mass., Peter Smith, 1968), 460; John Carswell, *The South Sea Bubble* (Stanford Univ. Press, 1960), 56–57.

6. Scott, *Joint Stock*, vol. 3, 314–18; Carswell, *Bubble*, 23, 248.

7. Charles Wilson, *England's Apprenticeship, 1603-1763* (London, Longman, 1965), 270–71.

8. Margaret Priestly, "The Anglo-French Trade and the 'Unfavorable' Balance Controversy, 1660-1685," *Economic History Review*, 4, 1 (1951), 42–43; Kenneth Maxwell, "Pombal and the Nationalization of the Luso-Brazilian Economy," *Hispanic American Historical Review*, 48, 4 (1968), 612.

9. H.S.K. Kent, "The Anglo-Norwegian Timber Trade in the Eighteenth Century," *Economic History Review*, 8, 1 (1955), 62; H.S.K. Kent, *War and Trade in Northern Seas* (Cambridge University Press, 1973), 59, 80, 110–11; Jan Federowicz, "Anglo-Polish Commercial Relations in the First Half of the Seventeenth Century," *Journal of European Economic History*, 5, 2 (1976), 365–67.

10. Arnost Klima, "English Merchant Capital in the Eighteenth Century," *Economic History Review*, 12, 1 (1959), 37.

11. Bruce McGowan, *Economic Life in Ottoman Europe: Taxation, Trade and the Struggle for Land* (Cambridge Univ. Press, 1981), 15.

12. H.E.S. Fisher, *The Portugal Trade: A Study of Anglo-Portuguese Commerce, 1700-1770* (London, Methuen, 1971), 4–6; Ralph Davis, "English Foreign Trade, 1700-1774," in Minchinton, *Overseas Trade*, 100.

13. Fisher, *Portugal Trade*, 19; S. Sideri, *Trade and Power: Informal Colonialism in Anglo-Portuguese Relations* (Rotterdam Univ. Press, 1970), 22.

14. C. R. Boxer, "Brazilian Gold and British Traders in the First Half of the Eighteenth Century," *Hispanic American Historical Review*, 49, 3 (1969), 470; Fisher, *Portugal Trade*, 138.

15. Lucy Sutherland, *The East India Company in Eighteenth Century Politics* (Oxford Univ. Press, 1952), 26.

16. Wilson, *England's Apprenticeship*, 173.

17. Sutherland, *East India Company*, 2.

18. Sukumar Bhattacharrya, *The East India Company and the Economy of Bengal from 1704 to 1740* (London, Luzac, 1954), 36–41.

19. K. N. Chaudhuri, "European Trade with India," in Tapan Raychaudhuri and Irfan Habib, eds., *The Cambridge Economic History of India*, vol. 1 (Cambridge Univ. Press, 1982), 395–404; Albert Craig, John Fairbank, and Edwin Reischauer, *East Asia, the Modern Transformation*, vol. 2 (Harvard Univ. Press, 1965), 75–76.

20. Pamela Nightingale, *Trade and Empire in Western India* (Cambridge Univ. Press, 1970), 239–40.

21. Quoted in Ramkrishna Mukherjee, *The Rise and Fall of the East India Company* (Berlin, Veb Deutscher Verlag der Wissenschaften, 1958), 251–52.

22. C. A. Bayly, *The New Cambridge History of India, Indian Society and the Making of the British Empire* (Cambridge Univ. Press, 1988), 51–53; Dhires Bhattacharrya, *A Concise History of the East India Company* (Calcutta, Progressive Publishers, 1972), 8–15.

23. Nightingale, *Western India*, 233.

24. James Rawley, *The Trans-Atlantic Slave Trade* (New York, Norton, 1981), 165; Richard B. Sheridan, "The Commercial and Financial Organization of the British Slave Trade, 1750–1807," *Economic History Review*, 11, 2 (1958–1959), 252; Gilian Ostrander, "The Making of the Triangular Myth," *William and Mary Quarterly*, 30, 4 (Oct., 1973), 635–44.

25. Walter Dorn, *Competition for Empire* (New York, Harper and Brothers, 1940), 123.

26. Kenneth Davies, *The Royal Africa Company* (London, Longman, 1957), 135–52.

27. Robert Thomas and Richard Bean, "The Fishers of Men: The Profits of the Slave Trade," *Journal of Economic History*, 34, 4 (1974), 887.

28. Richard B. Sheridan, *Sugar and Slavery: An Economic History of the British West Indies, 1623–1775* (Johns Hopkins Univ. Press, 1974), 416.

29. For a very useful survey of the literature on the colonial American economy, see John McCusker and Russell Menard, *The Economy of British North America, 1607–1789* (Univ. of North Carolina Press, 1985).

30. L. M. Cullen, *Anglo-Irish Trade, 1660–1800* (New York, A. M. Kelley, 1968), 46.

31. Leslie Clarkson, *The Pre-Industrial Economy in England, 1500–1750* (London, Batsford, 1971), 214; Ralph Davis, *The Industrial Revolution and British Overseas Trade* (Leicester Univ. Press, 1979), 34–36; Ralph Davis, "English Foreign Trade, 1700–1774," *Economic History Review*, 15, 2 (1962), 289–92.

32. Peter Kriedte, *Peasants, Landlords, and Merchant Capitalists in Europe and the World Economy, 1500–1800* (Cambridge Univ. Press, 1983), 91, 129.

33. Sidney Pollard and David Crossley, *The Wealth of Britain* (London, Batsford, 1968), 168.

34. Immanuel Wallerstein, *The Modern World System* (New York, Academic Press, 1974), vol. 1, 171.

35. Robert Stein, "Measuring the French Slave Trade, 1713–1792-93," *Journal of African History*, 19, 4 (1978), 519.

36. Robert Stein, *The French Slave Trade in the Eighteenth Century: An Old Regime Business* (Univ. of Wisconsin Press, 1979), 196–97.

37. *Ibid.*, 133–37.

38. François Crouzet, "England and France in the Eighteenth Century," in Marc Ferro, ed., *Social Historians in Contemporary France* (New York, Harper and Row, 1972), 63.

39. Shepard Clough and Charles Cole, *Economic History of Europe* (Boston, Heath, 1952), 318–23.

40. *Ibid.*, 332–40.

41. Eugene Asher, *The Resistance to the Maritime Classes: The Survival of Feudalism in the France of Colbert* (Univ. of California Press, 1960), 3.

42. Clough and Cole, *Economic History*, 331; Pierre Goubert, *Louis XIV and Twenty Million Frenchmen* (New York, Pantheon, 1966), 237; J. S. Parry, *Trade and Dominion: The European Overseas Empires in the Eighteenth Century* (London, Weidenfeld and Nicolson, 1971), 43.

43. Dorn, *Competition*, 369; Holden Furber, *Rival Empires in the Orient Trade* (Univ. of Minnesota Press, 1976), 334.

44. Crouzet, "England and France," 60.

45. Asher, *Resistance*, 94.

46. James C. Riley, *The Seven Years War and the Old Regime in France* (Princeton Univ. Press, 1986), 54; Franklin Ford, *Robe and Sword: The Regrouping of the French Aristocracy After Louis XIV* (Harvard Univ. Press, 1953), 27, 106.

47. Asher, *Resistance*, 94.

48. Guy Chaussinand-Nogaret, *The French Nobility in the Eighteenth Century* (Cambridge Univ. Press, 1985), 90–95, 114.

49. Pierre Goubert, *The French Peasantry in the Seventeenth Century* (Cambridge Univ. Press, 1986), 109; Robert Forster, "Obstacles to Agricultural Growth in Eighteenth Century France," *American Historical Review*, 75, 6 (1970), 1611–12; Philip T. Hoffman, "Taxes and Agrarian Life in Early Modern France: Land Sales, 1550–1730," *Journal of Economic History*, 46, 1 (1986), 43.

50. Catharina Lis and Hugo Soly, *Poverty and Capitalism in Pre-Industrial Europe* (Atlantic Highlands, N.J., Humanities Press, 1979), 99.

51. Albert Soboul, "The French Rural Community in the Eighteenth and Nineteenth Centuries," *Past and Present*, 10 (1956), 84.

52. Goubert, *Louis XIV*, 37.

53. Richard Herr, *The Eighteenth Century Revolution in Spain* (Princeton Univ. Press, 1958).

54. Stanley Payne, *A History of Spain and Portugal*, vol. 2 (Univ. of Wisconsin Press, 1973), 356–57.

55. David Ringrose, "Transportation and Economic Stagnation in Eighteenth Century Castile," *Journal of Economic History*, 28, 1 (1968), 54.

56. Payne, *Spain and Portugal*, vol. 2, 378–82; Herr, *Eighteenth Century*, 110, 118.

57. E. J. Hamilton, "Money and Economic Recovery in Spain Under the First Bourbon, 1701–1746," *Journal of Modern History*, 15, 3 (1943), 206.

58. Carl Hanson, *Economy and Society in Baroque Portugal, 1668–1703* (Univ. of Minnesota Press, 1981), 160–85.

59. For opposing views on the significance of the treaty, see Fisher, *Portugal Trade*, 38, and Sideri, *Trade and Power*, 45.

60. Maxwell, "Pombal," 609–10.

61. Sideri, *Trade and Power*, 99.

62. Payne, *Spain and Portugal*, vol. 2, 407.

63. Sideri, *Trade and Power*, 99–104.

64. Kenneth Maxwell, *Conflicts and Conspiracies: Brazil and Portugal, 1750–1808* (Cambridge Univ. Press, 1973), 40.

65. Sideri, *Trade and Power*, 111.

66. J. E. Farnell, "The Navigation Act of 1651, the First Dutch War, and the London Merchant Community," *Economic History Review*, 16, 3 (1964), 446.

67. Charles Wilson, *Profit and Power: A Study of England and the Dutch Wars* (London, Longman, 1957), 77, 93, 97, 135, 151, 156–57; Jan de Vries, *The Economy of Europe in an Age of Crisis, 1600–1750* (Cambridge Univ. Press, 1976), 122.

68. Dorn, *Competition*, 128; Parry, *Trade and Dominion*, 125.

69. Dorn, *Competition*, 164, 174–75.

70. P.G.M. Dickson, *The Financial Revolution in England* (New York, St. Martin's Press, 1967), 9.

71. Riley, *Seven Years War*; Patrick K. O'Brien, "The Political Economy of British Taxation, 1660–1815," *Economic History Review*, 41, 1 (1988), 1; James C. Riley, *International Government Finance and the Amsterdam Capital Market* (Cambridge Univ. Press, 1980), 123.

72. J. S. Parry and Philip Sherlock, *A Short History of the West Indies* (London, Macmillan, 1956), 127.

73. Parry, *Trade and Dominion*, 133.

74. Benjamin Labaree and Ian Christie, *Empire or Independence* (New York, Norton, 1976) 30.

75. Quoted in *ibid.*, 124.

76. Quoted in John Lynch, *The Spanish American Revolutions, 1808-1826* (London, Weidenfeld and Nicolson, 1973), 5.

77. Quoted in Maxwell, *Conflicts*, 78-79.

# CHAPTER 9

1. Quoted in Ward Barrett, "Caribbean Sugar Production Standards in the Seventeenth and Eighteenth Centuries," in J. Parker, ed., *Merchants and Scholars: Essays in the History of Exploration and Trade* (Univ. of Minnesota Press, 1965), 148.

2. Louis Gottschalk and Donald Lach, *Toward the French Revolution* (New York, Scribner, 1973), 77.

3. Gary Walton and James Shepherd, *The Economic Rise of Early America* (Cambridge Univ. Press, 1979), 161.

4. Michael Kammen, *Empire and Interest: The American Colonies and the Politics of Mercantilism* (Cornell Univ. Press, 1970), 16-24, describes the long-term thinking of the English establishment.

5. Benjamin Labaree and Ian Christie, *Empire or Independence* (New York, Norton, 1976), 41-49.

6. Gottschalk and Lach, *Toward the French Revolution*, 155.

7. Reginald Coupland, *The American Revolution and the British Empire* (New York, Russell and Russell, 1965), 74.

8. Edmund Morgan, *The Birth of the American Republic, 1763-1789* (Univ. of Chicago Press, 1956), 27.

9. Arthur Schlesinger, "The American Revolution Reconsidered," *Political Science Quarterly*, 34 (Mar., 1919), 74-75.

10. John Bullion, *A Great and Necessary Measure: George Grenville and the Genesis of the Stamp Act, 1763-1765* (Univ. of Missouri Press, 1982), 204.

11. Cecilia Kenyon, "Republicanism and Radicalism in the American Revolution: An Old Fashioned Interpretation," *William and Mary Quarterly*, 3rd series, 19 (Apr., 1962), 164.

12. Merrill Jensen, *The New Nation* (New York, Knopf, 1950), 32.

13. J. S. Parry and Philip Sherlock, *A Short History of the West Indies* (London, Macmillan, 1956), 135-36; William Stinchcombe, *The American Revolution and the French Alliance* (Syracuse Univ. Press, 1969), 11, 23; Gottschalk and Lach, *Toward the French Revolution*, 176.

14. Jensen, *New Nation*, 18.

15. Georges Lefebvre, *The Coming of the French Revolution* (Princeton Univ. Press, 1947), 21.

16. William Doyle, *Origins of the French Revolution* (Oxford Univ. Press, 1980), 94.

17. Theda Skocpol, *States and Social Revolutions* (Cambridge Univ. Press, 1979), 62.

18. Lynn Hunt, *Politics, Culture, and Class in the French Revolution* (Univ. of California Press, 1984), 213.

19. Colin Lucas, "Nobles, Bourgeois, and the Origins of the French Revolution," *Past and Present*, 60 (1973), 92.

20. Albert Soboul, *Understanding the French Revolution* (New York, International Publishers, 1988), 32.

21. James C. Riley, *The Seven Years War and the Old Regime in France* (Princeton Univ. Press, 1986), 28; Doyle, *Origins*, 194-201; Skocpol, *States*, 123.

22. George V. Taylor, "Non-Capitalist Wealth and the Origins of the French Revolution," *American Historical Review*, 72, 2 (1967) 492.

23. M. J. Sydenham, *The French Revolution* (Westport, Conn., Greenwood Press, 1985), 112–26.

24. *Ibid.*, 162–77; M. J. Sydenham, *The First French Republic, 1792–1804* (Univ. of California Press, 1973), 20.

25. Geoffrey Bruun, *Europe and the French Imperium, 1799–1814* (New York, Harper and Brothers, 1938), 25–29, 109–33; Robert R. Palmer, *The Age of Democratic Revolution*, vol. 2 (Princeton Univ. Press, 1964), 256–60.

26. Eugene Tarlé, *Bonaparte* (New York, Knight Publications, 1937), 132–33.

27. Bruun, *French Imperium*, 97–102; Tarlé, *Bonaparte*, 182.

28. Maurice O'Connell, *Irish Politics and Social Conflict in the Age of the American Revolution* (Univ. of Pennsylvania Press, 1965), 25–37.

29. Francis James, *Ireland in the Empire, 1688–1770* (Harvard Univ. Press, 1973), 258.

30. James Beckett, *The Making of Modern Ireland, 1603–1923* (New York, Knopf, 1969), 225.

31. Coupland, *British Empire*, 130, 147.

32. Beckett, *Making*, 249.

33. Eric Strauss, *Irish Nationalism and British Democracy* (Columbia Univ. Press, 1951), 52–55, 60–65.

34. Alex Dupuy, *Haiti in the World Economy: Class, Race, and Underdevelopment Since 1700* (Boulder, Colo., Westview Press, 1989), 25–26.

35. Robert Stein, *The French Slave Trade in the Eighteenth Century: An Old Regime Business* (Univ. of Wisconsin Press, 1979), 33.

36. Dupuy, *Haiti*, 28–30.

37. David Geggus, *Slavery, War, and Revolution: The British Occupation of Saint Domingue, 1793–1798* (Oxford Univ. Press, 1982), 30.

38. Robin Blackburn, *The Overthrow of Colonial Slavery, 1776–1848* (London, Verso, 1988), 183.

39. Geggus, *Slavery*, 289.

40. Thomas Ott, *The Haitian Revolution* (Univ. of Tennessee Press, 1973), 82–83; T. Lothrop Stoddard, *The French Revolution in San Domingue* (Negro Universities Press, 1970), 248.

41. Blackburn, *Slavery*, 240.

42. Ott, *Haitian Revolution*, 134–35.

43. C.L.R. James, *The Black Jacobins* (New York, Vintage Books, 1963), 369–70.

44. On the revolt of Tupac Amaru, see Lillian Fisher, *The Last Inca Revolt* (Univ. of Oklahoma Press, 1966).

45. On the *comunero* revolt, see John Phelan, *People of the King: The Comunero Revolt in Colombia* (Univ. of Wisconsin Press, 1978); for other rebellions, see Eduardo Arcila Farias, *Economia colonial de Venezuela* (Mexico City, Fondo de Cultura Economica, 1946), 220–24; John Lynch, *The Spanish American Revolutions, 1808–1826* (London, Weidenfeld and Nicolson, 1973), 192.

46. John Lynch, *Spanish American Colonial Administration, 1782–1810* (London, Athlone Press, 1958), 46–56.

47. R. A. Humphreys and John Lynch, eds., *The Origins of the Latin American Revolutions* (New York, Knopf, 1965), 15.

48. Allan Kuethe and G. Douglas Inglis, "Absolutism and Enlightened Reform: Charles III, the Establishment of the Alcabala, and Commercial Reorganization in Cuba," *Past and Present*, 109 (Nov., 1985), 143.

49. John Fisher, *Commerical Relations Between Spain and Spanish America in the Era of Free Trade, 1778–1796* (Univ. of Liverpool, Centre for Latin American Studies, 1985), 45–46.

50. Humphreys and Lynch, *Latin American Revolutions*, 6.

51. Lynch, *Spanish American Revolutions*, 7.

52. John Fisher, *Government and Society in Colonial Peru: The Intendant System, 1784–1814* (Univ. of London, 1970), 155.

53. Hugh Hamill, *The Hidalgo Revolt* (Univ. of Florida Press, 1966), 23–27.

54. Fisher, *Free Trade*, 90.

55. Jan Bazant, *A Concise History of Mexico* (Cambridge Univ. Press, 1971), 6.

56. Raymond Carr, *Spain, 1808–1975* (Oxford Univ. Press, 1982), 81–87.

57. Chileans, for example, began to talk of independence in 1809–1810 and began to act independently by 1812. See Simon Collier, *Ideas and Politics of Chilean Independence, 1808–1833* (Cambridge Univ. Press, 1967), 80, 95.

58. Lynch, *Spanish American Revolutions*, 137; David Bushnell, "The Independence of Spanish South America," in Leslie Bethell, ed., *The Independence of Latin America* (Cambridge Univ. Press, 1987), 114.

59. Stanley Payne, *A History of Spain and Portugal*, vol. 2 (Univ. of Wisconsin Press, 1973), 428.

60. Lynch, *Spanish American Revolutions*, 203–05.

61. Charles Griffin, "Economic and Social Aspects of the Era of Spanish American Independence," *Hispanic American Historical Review*, 29 (1949), 170, 178–79, 185–87.

62. Lynch, *Spanish American Revolutions*, 142–45.

63. Michael Meyer and William Sherman, *The Course of Mexican History* (Oxford Univ. Press, 1987), 285–96.

64. Caio Prado Junior, *The Colonial Background of Modern Brazil* (Univ. of California Press, 1967), 424.

65. E. Bradford Burns, "The Intellectuals as Agents of Change and the Independence of Brazil, 1724–1822," in A.J.R. Russell-Wood, ed., *From Colony to Nation: Essays on the Independence of Brazil* (Johns Hopkins Univ. Press, 1975), 245–46.

66. Emilio Viotti da Costa, "The Political Emancipation of Brazil," in Russell-Wood, *From Colony to Nation*, 79–80.

67. Maria Odila Silva Dias, "The Establishment of the Royal Court in Brazil," in Russell-Wood, *From Colony to Nation*, 99.

68. Prado Junior, *Modern Brazil*, 424–25.

69. da Costa, "Emancipation," 79–80.

70. George Unwin, *Studies in Economic History* (London, Frank Cass, 1958), 15.

71. J. U. Nef, "The Progress of Technology and the Growth of Large-Scale Industry in Great Britain, 1540–1640," in E. H. Carus-Wilson, ed., *Essays in Economic History* (London, E. Arnold, 1954), 100.

72. H. Heaton, "The Industrial Revolution," in R. M. Hartwell, ed., *The Causes of the Industrial Revolution in England* (London, Methuen, 1967), 38.

73. T. S. Ashton, *The Industrial Revolution, 1760–1830* (Oxford Univ. Press, 1969), 40–41.

74. J. U. Nef, "The Industrial Revolution Reconsidered," *Journal of Economic History*, 3 (1943), 24.

75. Sidney Pollard and David Crossley, *The Wealth of Britain* (London, Batsford, 1968), 182.

76. Phyllis Deane, "The Industrial Revolution in Great Britain," in Carlo Cipolla, ed., *The Fontana Economic History of Europe*, vol. 4, part 1 (Sussex, Eng., Harvester Press, 1976), 166.

77. Ibid., 163.

78. David Landes, *The Unbound Prometheus* (Cambridge Univ. Press, 1969), 1.

79. R. M. Hartwell, "The Causes of the Industrial Revolution: An Essay in Methodology," *Economic History Review*, 18, 1 (1965), 169–76.

80. Ralph Davis, *The Industrial Revolution and British Overseas Trade* (Leicester Univ. Press, 1979), 16; Landes, *Unbound Prometheus*, 41–42.

81. B. R. Mitchell, "The Coming of the Railway and United Kingdom Economic Growth," *Journal of Economic History*, 24, 3 (1964), 324; Eric Hobsbawm, *Industry and Empire: An Economic History of Britain Since 1750* (London, Weidenfeld and Nicolson, 1968), 53.

82. Phyllis Deane, *The First Industrial Revolution* (Cambridge Univ. Press, 1979), 129.

83. *Ibid.*, 166.

84. Eric Hobsbawm, *The Age of Revolution* (London, Sphere Books, 1977), 44.

85. Pollard and Crossley, *Wealth*, 189.

86. Patrick K. O'Brien, "European Economic Development: The Contribution of the Periphery," *Economic History Review*, 35, 1 (Feb., 1982), 19.

87. Davis, *Overseas Trade*, 10.

88. Walt Rostow, *How It All Began: Origins of the Modern Economy* (New York, McGraw-Hill, 1975), 131.

89. Robert Hartwell, "Introduction," in Hartwell, *Causes*, 26.

90. Deane, "Industrial Revolution in Britain," 168.

91. Maurice Dobb, *Studies in the Development of Capitalism* (New York, International Publishers, 1963), 294–95.

92. Hobsbawm, *Industry and Empire*, 32.

93. *Ibid.*, 33–34.

94. This issue remains as polarized as ever. The standard for the pessimists was established by J. L. Hammond and B. Hammond, *The Rise of Modern Industry* (New York, Harcourt, Brace, 1926); nevertheless, there are still modern studies such as Elizabeth Gilboy, "Demand as a Factor in the Industrial Revolution," in Hartwell, *Causes*, 133–35, which place emphasis on what they deem to be the positive achievements of the era.

95. J. D. Chambers, "Enclosure and Labour Supply in the Industrial Revolution," *Economic History Review*, 5, 3 (1953), 338–39.

96. Pollard and Crossley, *Wealth*, 192.

97. *Ibid.*, 209.

98. E. P. Thompson, *The Making of the English Working Class* (New York, Pantheon, 1964), 212.

99. Michael Brock, *The Great Reform Act* (London, Hutchinson, 1973), 18–24.

100. *Ibid.*, 39.

101. *Ibid.*, 197–98, 205–207.

102. *Ibid.*, 314–36.

103. Quoted in Thompson, *Making*, 832.

104. *Ibid.*, 807–808.

105. P. J. Cain, *Economic Foundations of British Overseas Expansion, 1815–1914* (London, Macmillan, 1980), 17–20.

106. Davis, *Overseas Trade*, 52.

## CHAPTER 10

1. Merrill Jensen, *The New Nation* (New York, Knopf, 1950), 400.

2. A classic study is A. P. Thornton, *The Imperial Idea and Its Enemies* (London, Macmillan, 1959); see also C. A. Bodelsen, *Studies in Mid-Victorian Imperialism* (London, Gyldendal Nordisk Forlag, 1924).

3. George Rogers Taylor, *The Transportation Revolution, 1815–1860* (New York, Rinehart, 1951), deals with much more than transportation.

4. Carville Earle, "A Staple Interpretation of Slavery and Free Labor," *Geographical Review*, 68 (1978), 64.

5. D. A. Farnie, *The English Cotton Industry and the World Market, 1815–1896* (Oxford Univ. Press, 1979), 14.

6. Tulio Halperin Donghi, *The Aftermath of Revolution in Latin America* (New York, Harper and Row, 1973), 1–44.

7. Benjamin Keen and Mark Wasserman, *A History of Latin America* (Boston, Houghton Mifflin, 1988), 174–78.

8. Laszlo Mikkai, "Neo-Serfdom: Its Origin and Nature in East-Central Europe," *Slavic Review*, 34, 2 (1975), 238.

9. Quoted in Robin Blackburn, *The Overthrow of Colonial Slavery, 1776–1848* (London, Verso, 1988), 241–47.

10. Eric Williams, *Capitalism and Slavery* (Univ. of North Carolina Press, 1944), 84.

11. Blackburn, *Colonial Slavery*, 304–10, 314; other contributions to the debate on the reasons for the abolition of the slave trade are Roger Anstey, *The Atlantic Slave Trade and the British Abolition* (Atlantic Highlands, N.J., Humanities Press, 1975), and Theodore Drescher, *Econocide: British Slavery in the Era of Abolition* (Univ. of Pittsburgh Press, 1977).

12. William Green, *British Slave Emancipation* (Oxford Univ. Press, 1976), 84.

13. David Geggus, *Slavery, War, and Revolution: The British Occupation of Saint Domingue, 1793–1798* (Oxford Univ. Press, 1982), 388.

14. Leslie Bethell, *The Abolition of the Brazilian Slave Trade* (Cambridge Univ. Press, 1970), 72–73; Robert Conrad, *The Destruction of Brazilian Slavery, 1850–1888* (Cambridge Univ. Press, 1972), 22–23.

15. Paul Lovejoy, "The Volume of the Atlantic Slave Trade: A Synthesis," *Journal of African History*, 23, 4 (1982), 496.

16. Anthony Hopkins, *An Economic History of West Africa* (Columbia Univ. Press, 1973), 125–35.

17. Paul Lovejoy, *Transformations in Slavery* (Cambridge Univ. Press, 1983), 176–84.

18. Amiya Kumar Bagchi, "De-Industrialization in India During the Nineteenth Century: Some Theoretical Implications," *Journal of Development Studies*, 12, 2 (1975–1976), 142; K. N. Chaudhuri, "India's Foreign Trade and the Cessation of the East India Company's Trading Activities, 1828–1845," *Economic History Review*, 19, 2 (1966), 361.

19. Quoted in Michael Greenberg, *British Trade and the Opening of China, 1800–1842* (Cambridge Univ. Press, 1951), 214–15.

20. S. Sideri, *Trade and Power: Informal Colonialism in Anglo-Portuguese Relations* (Rotterdam Univ. Press, 1970), 111.

21. Stanley Payne, *A History of Spain and Portugal* (Univ. of Wisconsin Press, 1973), vol. 2, 481–82.

22. Eric Hobsbawm, *The Age of Revolution* (London, Sphere Books, 1977), 220.

# BIBLIOGRAPHY

Albert, William. *The Turnpike Road System in England, 1663–1840*. Cambridge Univ. Press, 1972.

Albion, Robert. *Forests and Sea Power*. Harvard Univ. Press, 1929.

Alden, Dauril, ed. *The Colonial Roots of Modern Brazil*. Univ. of California Press, 1973.

_____. *Royal Government in Colonial Brazil*. Univ. of California Press, 1968.

Alden, Dauril, and Warren Dean, eds. *Essays Concerning the Socio-Economic History of Brazil and Portuguese India*. Univ. of Florida Press, 1977.

Amin, Samir. *Unequal Development*. New York, Monthly Review Press, 1976.

Anderson, Perry. *Lineages of the Absolutist State*. London, Verso, 1974.

_____. *Passages from Antiquity*. London, Verso, 1978.

Andrews, Kenneth. *The Spanish Caribbean: Trade and Plunder, 1530–1630*. Yale Univ. Press, 1978.

Anstey, Roger. *The Atlantic Slave Trade and the British Abolition*. Atlantic Highlands, N.J., Humanities Press, 1975.

Arasaratnam, Sinnapah. *Dutch Power in Ceylon*. Amsterdam, Djambatan, 1958.

Arcila Farias, Eduardo. *Economia colonial de Venezuela*. Mexico City, Fondo de Cultura Economica, 1946.

Asher, Eugene. *The Resistance to the Maritime Classes: The Survival of Feudalism in the France of Colbert*. Univ. of California Press, 1960.

Ashton, Robert. "The Parliamentary Agitation for Free Trade in the Opening Years of James I," *Past and Present*. 38 (Dec., 1967), 40–56.

Ashton, T. S. *The Industrial Revolution, 1760–1830*. Oxford Univ. Press, 1969.

Ashtor, Elihu. *A Social and Economic History of the Near East in the Middle Ages*. Univ. of California Press, 1976.

Attman, Artur. *The Struggle for Baltic Markets: Powers in Conflict, 1558–1618*. Gothenburg, Vetenskaps- O. Vitterhets Samhallet, 1979.

Atwell, William. "International Bullion Flows and the Chinese Economy, 1530–1655," *Past and Present*. 95 (1982), 63–91.

Aymard, Maurice, ed. *Dutch Capitalism and World Capitalism*. Cambridge Univ. Press, 1982.

Bagchi, Amiya Kumar. "De-Industrialization in India During the Nineteenth Century: Some Theoretical Implications," *Journal of Development Studies*. 12, 2 (1975–1976), 135–64.

Bakewell, P. J. *Silver Mining and Society in Colonial Mexico: Zacatecas, 1546–1700*. Cambridge Univ. Press, 1971.

Balwant, Gargi. *Theatre in India*. New York, Theatre Arts Books, 1962.

Barber, Elinor. *The Bourgeoisie in Eighteenth Century France*. Princeton Univ. Press, 1955.

Barbour, Violet. *Capitalism in Amsterdam*. Johns Hopkins Univ. Press, 1950.

Barrett, Ward. "Caribbean Sugar Production Standards in the Seventeenth and Eighteenth Centuries," in J. Parker, ed., *Merchants and Scholars: Essays in the History of Exploration and Trade*. Univ. of Minnesota Press, 1965, 145–70.

Bartlett, Thomas. "An End to Moral Economy: The Irish Militia Disturbances of 1793," *Past and Present*. 99 (May, 1983), 41–64.

Bayly, C. A. *The New Cambridge History of India, Indian Society and the Making of the British Empire*. Cambridge Univ. Press, 1988.

Bazant, Jan. *A Concise History of Mexico*. Cambridge Univ. Press, 1971.

——— . "The Evolution of the Textile Industry of Puebla," *Comparative Studies in Society and History*. 7, 1 (1964–1965), 56–70.

Bean, J.M.W. "Plague, Population and Economic Decline in the Later Middle Ages," *Economic History Review*. 15, 3 (1963), 423–37.

Beattie, Hilary. *Land and Lineage in China*. Cambridge Univ. Press, 1979.

Beckett, James. *The Anglo-Irish Tradition*. Cornell Univ. Press, 1976.

——— . *The Making of Modern Ireland, 1603–1923*. New York, Knopf, 1966.

Benson, Nettie Lee, ed. *Mexico and the Spanish Cortes, 1810–1822*. Univ. of Texas Press, 1966.

Bethell, Leslie. *The Abolition of the Brazilian Slave Trade*. Cambridge Univ. Press, 1970.

——— , ed. *Cambridge History of Latin America*. Cambridge Univ. Press, 1984.

——— . *The Independence of Latin America*. Cambridge Univ. Press, 1987.

Bhattacharrya, Dhires. *A Concise History of the East India Company*. Calcutta, Progressive Publishers, 1972.

Bhattacharrya, Sukumar. *The East India Company and the Economy of Bengal from 1704 to 1740*. London, Luzac, 1954.

Biddick, Kathleen. "Medieval English Peasants and Market Involvement," *Journal of Economic History*. 45, 4 (1985), 823–31.

Birmingham, David. "Central Africa, from Camerouns to the Zambezi," in Richard Gray, ed., *Cambridge History of Africa*, vol. 4. Cambridge Univ. Press, 1965, 325–83.

Blackburn, Robin. *The Overthrow of Colonial Slavery, 1776–1848*. London, Verso, 1988.

Blanchard, Ian. "Population Change, Enclosure and the Tudor Economy," *Economic History Review*. 23, 4 (1970), 427–46.

Bloch, Marc. *Feudal Society*. Univ. of Chicago Press, 1961.

Blum, Jerome. "The Rise of Serfdom in Eastern Europe," *American Historical Review*. 62, 4 (1957), 807–36.

Bodelson, C. A. *Studies in Mid-Victorian Imperialism*. London, Gyldendal Nordisk Forlag, 1924.

Bogucka, Maria. "Amsterdam and the Baltic in the First Half of the Seventeenth Century," *Economic History Review*. 26, 3 (1973), 433–48.

Bois, Guy. *The Crisis of Feudalism: Economy and Society in Eastern Normandy, c. 1300–1550*. Cambridge Univ. Press, 1984.

Borah, Woodrow. *New Spain's Century of Depression*. Univ. of California Press, 1951.

Borah, Woodrow, and Sherborne Cook. *The Aboriginal Population of Central Mexico on the Eve of Conquest*. Univ. of California Press, 1963.

——— , eds. *Essays in Population History: Mexico and the Caribbean*. vol. 1. Univ. of California Press, 1971.

Bowser, Frederick. *The African Slave in Colonial Peru, 1524–1650*. Stanford Univ. Press, 1974.

Boxer, C. R. "Brazilian Gold and British Traders in the First Half of the Eighteenth Century," *Hispanic American Historical Review*. 49, 3 (1969), 454–73.

——— . "The Dutch Economic Decline," in Carlo Cipolla, ed., *The Economic Decline of Empires*. London, Methuen, 1970.

——— . *The Dutch in Brazil, 1624–1654*. Hamden, Conn., Anchor Books, 1973.

——— . *The Dutch Seaborne Empire*. London, Knopf, 1965.

_____ . *Four Centuries of Portuguese Expansion.* Johannesburg, Univ. of Witwatersrand Press, 1965.

Boyd-Bowman, Peter. *Patterns of Spanish Emigration to the New World (1493–1580).* Buffalo, State Univ. of New York, 1973.

Boyer, Richard. "Mexico in the Seventeenth Century: Transition of a Colonial Society," *Hispanic American Historical Review.* 57, 3 (1977), 454–78.

Brading, D. A. *Haciendas and Ranchos in the Mexican Bajio.* Cambridge Univ. Press, 1978.

_____ . *Miners and Merchants in Bourbon Mexico, 1763–1810.* Cambridge Univ. Press, 1971.

Braudel, Fernand. *Afterthoughts on Material Civilization and Capitalism.* Johns Hopkins Univ. Press, 1977.

_____ . *Capitalism and Material Life.* 2 vols. New York, Harper and Row, 1973.

_____ . *Civilization and Capitalism.* New York, Harper and Row, 1984.

_____ . *The Mediterranean and the Mediterranean World in the Age of Philip II.* 2 vols., London, Collins, 1972.

Braunstein, Philippe. "Innovation in Mining and Metal Production in Europe in the Late Middle Ages," *Journal of European Economic History.* 12 (1983), 573–92.

Bray, Francesca. *The Rice Economies: Technology and Development in Asian Societies.* London, Basil Blackwell, 1986.

_____ . "Swords into Plowshares: A Study of Agricultural Technology in Early China," *Technology and Culture.* 19, 1 (1976), 1–32.

Brenner, Robert. "Agrarian Class Structure and Economic Development in Pre-Industrial Europe," *Past and Present.* 70, 1976, 30–75.

_____ . "The Agrarian Roots of European Capitalism," *Past and Present.* 97, 1982, 16–113.

_____ . "The Social Basis for English Commercial Expansion, 1550–1650," *Journal of Economic History.* 32, 1, 1972, 361–85.

Brenner, Y. S. "The Inflation of Prices in England, 1551–1650," *Economic History Review.* 15, 2, 1963, 266–85.

Bridbury, A. R. "Before the Black Death," *Economic History Review.* 30, 3, 1977, 393–411.

Brock, Michael, *The Great Reform Act.* London, Hutchinson, 1973.

Bronson, Bennet. "The Earliest Farming: Demography as Cause and Consequence," in Charles A. Reed, ed., *Origins of Agriculture.* Paris, Mouton, 1977.

Bruchey, Stuart. *The Roots of American Economic Growth, 1607–1861.* New York, Harper and Row, 1968.

Brucker, Gene. *Florentine Politics and Society, 1343–1378.* Princeton Univ. Press, 1962.

_____ . *Renaissance Florence.* New York, Wiley, 1969.

Bruun, Geoffrey. *Europe and the French Imperium, 1799–1814.* New York, Harper and Brothers, 1938.

Bullion, John. *A Great and Necessary Measure: George Grenville and the Genesis of the Stamp Act, 1763–1765.* Univ. of Missouri Press, 1982.

Burns, E. Bradford. *A History of Brazil.* Columbia Univ. Press, 1980.

_____ . "The Intellectuals as Agents of Change and the Independence of Brazil, 1724–1822," in A.J.R. Russell-Wood, ed., *From Colony to Nation: Essays on the Independence of Brazil.* Johns Hopkins Univ. Press, 1975, 211–46.

Bushnell, David. "The Independence of Spanish South America," in Leslie Bethell, ed., *The Independence of Latin America.* Cambridge Univ. Press, 1987.

Cady, John. *South-East Asia: Its Historical Development.* New York, McGraw-Hill, 1964.

Cain, P. J. *Economic Foundations of British Overseas Expansion, 1815–1914.* London, Macmillan, 1980.

Calhoun, Craig. *The Question of the Class Struggle.* Univ. of Chicago Press, 1982.

Callahan, William. *Honor, Commerce and Industry in Eighteenth Century Spain.* Cambridge, Baker Library, Harvard School of Business Administration, 1972.

Calnek, Edward. "Patterns of Empire Formation in the Valley of Mexico: Late Post-Classic Period, 1200-1521," in George A. Collier, Renato Rosaldo, and John Wirth, eds., *The Inca and Aztec States, 1400-1800*. New York, Academic Press, 1982.

Cardozo, Manoel. "The Collection of the Fifths in Brazil," *Hispanic American Historical Review*. 20, 1940, 359-79.

———. "Dom Rodrigo de Castel-Branco and the Brazilian El Dorado, 1673-1682," *The Americas*. 1, 1944, 131-59.

Carr, Raymond. *Spain, 1808-1975*. Oxford Univ. Press, 1982.

Carswell, John. *The South Sea Bubble*. Stanford Univ. Press, 1960.

Carus-Wilson, Elanora. "The Woolen Industry," in M. M. Postan and E. E. Rich, eds., *The Cambridge Economic History of Europe*, vol. 2. Cambridge Univ. Press, 1952, 355-429.

Casey, James. "Moriscos and the Depopulation of Valencia," *Past and Present*. 50 (1971), 19-40.

Chafee, John. *The Thorny Gates of Learning in Sung China: A Social History of Examinations*. Cambridge Univ. Press, 1985.

Chakrabarti, Dilip. "The Beginnings of Iron in India," *Antiquity*. 50, 198 (June, 1976), 114-24.

Chambers, J. D. "Enclosure and Labour Supply in the Industrial Revolution," *Economic History Review*. 5, 3 (1953), 318-42.

Chambers, J. D., and G. E. Mingay, *The Agricultural Revolution, 1750-1880*. New York, Schocken Books, 1966.

Chance, John. *Race and Class in Colonial Mexico*. Stanford Univ. Press, 1978.

Chaudhuri, K. N. "European Trade with India," in Tapan Raychaudhuri and Irfan Habib, eds., *The Cambridge Economic History of India*, vol. 1. Cambridge Univ. Press, 1982, 382-407.

———. "India's Foreign Trade and the Cessation of the East India Company's Trading Activities, 1828-1845," *Economic History Review*. 19, 2 (1966), 345-64.

Chaussinand-Nogaret, Guy. *The French Nobility in the Eighteenth Century*. Cambridge Univ. Press, 1985.

Chevalier, François. *Land and Society in Colonial Mexico*. Univ. of California Press, 1963.

Chorley, Patrick. "The Cloth Exports of Flanders and Northern France During the Thirteenth Century: A Luxury Trade?" *Economic History Review*. 40, 3 (1987), 349-79.

Cipolla, Carlo. *Before the Industrial Revolution: European Society and Economy, 1000-1700*. New York, Norton, 1976.

———. "Currency Depreciation in Medieval Europe," *Economic History Review*. 15 (1963), 413-22.

———. "Economic Decline in Italy," in Carlo Cipolla, ed., *The Economic Decline of Empires*. London, Methuen, 1970, 196-215.

———. *The Economic History of World Population*. Baltimore, Penguin, 1962.

———. *Guns, Sails, and Empires*. New York, Pantheon, 1965.

Clark, Peter, ed. *The European Crisis of the 1590s*. London, Allen and Unwin, 1985.

Clarkson, Leslie. *The Pre-Industrial Economy in England, 1500-1750*. London, Batsford, 1971.

Clough, Sheperd, and Charles Cole. *Economic History of Europe*. Boston, Heath, 1952.

Coatsworth, John. "The Limits of Colonial Absolutism: The State in Eighteenth Century Mexico," in Karen Spalding, ed., *Essays in the Political, Economic, and Social History of Latin Colonial America*. Univ. of Delaware Press, 1982, 25-52.

Cobb, Gwendolyn. "Supply and Transportation for the Potosi Mines, 1545-1640," *Hispanic American Historical Review*. 29 (1949), 25-45.

Coclanis, Peter. "Rice Prices in the 1720s and the Evolution of the South Carolina Economy," *Journal of Southern History*. 48, 4 (1982), 531-44.

Coe, Michael. *America's First Civilization*. New York, American Heritage, 1968.

Cohen, Mark Nathan. *The Food Crisis In Prehistory.* Yale Univ. Press, 1977.

Cohn, Samuel Kline. *The Laboring Classes in Renaissance Florence.* New York, Academic Press, 1980.

Cole, Jeffrey. *The Potosi Mita, 1573-1700.* Stanford Univ. Press, 1985.

Coleman, D. C. "Labour in the English Economy of the Seventeenth Century," *Economic History Review.* 8, 3 (1956), 280-96.

Collier, Simon. *Ideas and Politics of Chilean Independence, 1808-1833.* Cambridge Univ. Press, 1967.

Connell, K. H. "The Potato in Ireland," *Past and Present.* 23 (Nov., 1962), 57-71.

Conquest, R. "The State and Commercial Expansion: England in the Years 1642-1688," *Journal of European Economic History.* 14, 1 (1985), 155-72.

Conrad, Robert. *The Destruction of Brazilian Slavery, 1850-1888.* Cambridge Univ. Press, 1972.

Cook, Noble David. *Demographic Collapse: Indian Peru, 1520-1620.* Cambridge Univ. Press, 1981.

Cooper, Frederick. "The Problem of Slavery in African Studies," *Journal of African History.* 20, 1 (1979), 103-25.

Costeloe, Michael. *Church Wealth in Mexico.* Cambridge Univ. Press, 1967.

Coupland, Reginald. *The American Revolution and the British Empire.* New York, Russell and Russell, 1965.

_____. *The British Anti-Slavery Movement.* London, T. Butterworth, 1933.

Creel, H. G. "The Role of the Horse in Chinese History," *American Historical Review.* 70 (1965), 647-72.

Crosby, Alfred. "Conquistador y Pestilencia: The First New World Pandemic and the Fall of the Great Indian Empires," *Hispanic American Historical Review.* 47, 3 (1967), 324-38.

_____. *Ecological Imperialism, the Biological Expansion of Europe.* Cambridge Univ. Press, 1986.

Crouzet, François. "England and France in the Eighteenth Century," in Marc Ferro, ed., *Social Historians in Contemporary France.* New York, Harper and Row, 1972, 59-87.

Culbert, T. Patrick, ed. *The Classic Maya Collapse.* Univ. of New Mexico Press, 1973.

Cullen, L. M. *Anglo-Irish Trade, 1660-1800.* New York, A. M. Kelley, 1968.

_____. *An Economic History of Ireland Since 1660.* London, Batsford, 1972.

Curtin, Philip. *The Atlantic Slave Trade: A Census.* Univ. of Wisconsin Press, 1969.

_____. *Cross-Cultural Trade in World History.* Cambridge Univ. Press, 1984.

_____. *Economic Change in Pre-Colonial Africa.* Univ. of Wisconsin Press, 1975.

Curtis, Edmund. *A History of Medieval Ireland.* New York, Macmillan, 1923.

Daaku, Kwame. *Trade and Politics on the Gold Coast, 1600-1720.* Oxford Univ. Press, 1970.

Davidson, Basil. *A History of West Africa.* London, Longman, 1965.

Davidson, David. "How the Brazilian West Was Won: Freelance and State on the Mato Grosso Frontier, 1737-1752," in Dauril Alden, ed., *The Colonial Roots of Modern Brazil.* Univ. of California Press, 1973, 61-106.

Davies, Kenneth. *The North Atlantic World in the Seventeenth Century.* Univ. of California Press, 1974.

_____. *The Royal Africa Company.* London, Longman, 1957.

Davies, Nigel. *The Aztecs.* New York, Putnam, 1974.

Davies, R. Trevor. *The Golden Century of Spain, 1501-1621.* London, Macmillan, 1937.

Davis, K. G. "Joint-Stock Investment in the Later Seventeenth Century," *Economic History Review.* 4, 3 (1952), 283-301.

Davis, Ralph. "English Foreign Trade, 1700-1774," in W. E. Minchinton, ed., *The Growth of English Overseas Trade in the Seventeenth and Eighteenth Centuries.* London, Methuen, 1969, 99-120.

_____. *The Industrial Revolution and British Overseas Trade.* Leicester Univ. Press, 1979.

———. *The Rise of the Atlantic Economies*. Cornell Univ. Press, 1973.

Day, John. "The Great Bullion Famine of the Fifteenth Century," *Past and Present*. 79 (May, 1978), 3–55.

Deane, Phyllis. *The First Industrial Revolution*. Cambridge Univ. Press, 1979.

———. "The Industrial Revolution in Great Britain," in Carlo Cipolla, ed., *The Fontana Economic History of Europe*. vol. 4, part 1. Sussex, Eng., Harvester Press, 1976.

Devine, T. M. "The Colonial Trade and Industrial Investment in Scotland, c. 1700–1815," *Economic History Review*. 29, 1 (1976), 1–14.

de Vries, Jan. *The Dutch Rural Economy in the Golden Age, 1500–1700*. Yale Univ. Press, 1974.

———. *The Economy of Europe in an Age of Crisis, 1600–1750*. Cambridge Univ. Press, 1976.

———. *European Urbanization, 1500–1800*. Harvard Univ. Press, 1984.

———. "On the Modernity of the Dutch Republic," *Journal of Economic History*. 33, 1 (1973), 191–203.

Dickerson, Oliver. *The Navigation Acts and the American Revolution*. Univ. of Pennsylvania Press, 1951.

Dickson, P.G.M. *The Financial Revolution in England*. New York, St. Martin's Press, 1967.

Diehl, Charles. "The Economic Decay of Byzantium," in Carlo Cipolla, ed., *The Economic Decline of Empires*. London, Methuen, 1970, 92–101.

Diffie, Bailie, *Latin American Civilization*. New York, Octagon Books, 1967.

———. *Prelude to Empire: Portugal Overseas Before Henry the Navigator*. Univ. of Nebraska Press, 1960.

Diffie, Bailie, and George Winius. *The Foundations of the Portuguese Empire, 1415–1580*. Univ. of Minnesota Press, 1977.

Disney, Anthony. *Twilight of the Pepper Empire*. Harvard Univ. Press, 1978.

Dobb, Maurice. "A Further Comment," in Rodney Hilton, ed., *The Transition from Feudalism to Capitalism*. London, Verso, 1978, 98–102.

———. "A Reply," in Rodney Hilton, ed., *The Transition from Feudalism to Capitalism*. London, Verso, 1978, 57–68.

———. *Studies in the Development of Capitalism*. New York, International Publishers, 1963.

Dorn, Walter. *Competition for Empire*. New York, Harper and Brothers, 1940.

Douglas, David. "The Norman Conquest and English Feudalism," *Economic History Review*. 1st series, 9 (1938–1939), 128–43.

Doyle, William. *Origins of the French Revolution*. Oxford Univ. Press, 1980.

Drekmeier, Charles. *Kingship and Community in Early India*. Stanford Univ. Press, 1962.

Drescher, Theodore. *Econocide: British Slavery in the Era of Aboliton*. Univ. of Pittsburgh Press, 1977.

Duby, Georges. *The Early Growth of the European Economy*. Cornell Univ. Press, 1974.

———. *Medieval Agriculture*. London, Fontana, 1969.

———. *Rural Economy and Country Life in the Medieval West*. Univ. of South Carolina Press, 1968.

Duffy, James. *Portuguese Africa*. Harvard Univ. Press, 1959.

Dunn, Richard. *Sugar and Slaves*. Univ. of North Carolina Press, 1972.

Dunnes, R. L. "The Stower Partnership: Landed Capital in the Iron Industry," *Economic History Review*. 3, 1 (1950), 90–96.

Dupuy, Alex. *Haiti in the World Economy: Class, Race, and Underdevelopment Since 1700*. Boulder, Colo., Westview Press, 1989.

Dyboski, Roman. *Poland in World Civilization*. New York, J. M. Barrett, 1950.

Earle, Carville. "A Staple Interpretation of Slavery and Free Labor," *Geographical Review*. 68 (1978), 51–65.

Earle, Peter, ed. *Essays in Economic History, 1500–1800*. Oxford Univ. Press, 1974.

Edel, Mathew. "The Brazilian Sugar Cycle of the Seventeenth Century and the Rise of West Indies' Competition," *Caribbean Studies*. 9 (Apr., 1964), 24-44.

Edwards, E. S. *The Pyramids of Egypt*. Baltimore, Penguin, 1961.

Egnal, Marc. "The Economic Development of the Thirteen American Colonies, 1720-1775," *William and Mary Quarterly*. 32 (1975), 191-222.

Egnal, Marc, and Joseph Ernst. "An Economic Interpretation of the American Revolution," *William and Mary Quarterly*. 29 (1972), 3-32.

Ehret, Christopher. "On the Antiquity of Agriculture in Ethiopia," *Journal of African History*. 20, 2 (1979), 161-78.

Elliott, John. *Imperial Spain, 1469-1716*. New York, St. Martin's Press, 1964.

El Mallakh, Ragaei, and Dorothy El Mallakh. "Trade and Commerce," in John R. Hayes, ed., *The Genius of Arab Civilization: Source of the Renaissance*. MIT Press, 1983.

Elton, Geoffrey. *England Under the Tudors*. London, Methuen, 1957.

Elvin, Mark. "The Last Thousand Years of Chinese History: Changing Patterns of Land Tenure," *Modern Asian Studies*. 4 (1970), 97-114.

_____ . *Patterns of the Chinese Past*. Stanford Univ. Press, 1973.

Engels, Friedrich. *The Origin of the Family, Private Property and the State*. New York, International Publishers, 1972.

Ernst, Joseph. *Money and Politics in America, 1755-1775*. Univ. of North Carolina Press, 1973.

Fage, J. D. "Slaves and Society in West Africa, c. 1445-1700," *Journal of African History*. 21, 3 (1980), 288-310.

Fagg, William. *The Art of Western Africa*. New York, Mentor-Unesco, 1967.

Fairbank, John, Edwin Reischauer, and Albert Craig. *East Asia: Tradition and Transformation*. London, Allen and Unwin, 1973.

Farb, Peter. *Man's Rise to Civilization as Shown by the Indians of North America, from Primeval Times to the Coming of the Industrial State*. New York, Dutton, 1968.

Farnell, J. E. "The Navigation Act of 1651, the First Dutch War, and the London Merchant Community," *Economic History Review*. 16, 3 (1964), 439-55.

Farnie, D. A. "The Commercial Empire of the Atlantic, 1607-1783," *Economic History Review*. 15 (1962), 205-18.

_____ . *The English Cotton Industry and the World Market, 1815-1896*. Oxford Univ. Press, 1979.

Federowicz, Jan. "Anglo-Polish Commercial Relations in the First Half of the Seventeenth Century," *Journal of European Economic History*. 5, 2 (1976), 359-78.

Fernandez-Armesto, Felipe. *Before Columbus: Exploration and Colonization from the Mediterranean to the Atlantic, 1229-1492*. Univ. of Pennsylvania Press, 1987.

Ferro, Marc, ed. *Social Historians in Contemporary France*. New York, Harper and Row, 1972.

Fisher, H.E.S. "Anglo-Portuguese Trade, 1700-1770," *Economic History Review*. 16, 2 (1963), 219-33.

_____ . *The Portugal Trade: A Study of Anglo-Portuguese Commerce, 1700-1770*. London, Methuen, 1971.

Fisher, John. *Commercial Relations Between Spain and Spanish America in the Era of Free Trade, 1778-1796*. Univ. of Liverpool, Centre for Latin American Studies, 1985.

_____ . *Government and Society in Colonial Peru: The Intendant System, 1784-1814*. Univ. of London, 1970.

_____ . "Silver Production in the Viceroyalty of Peru, 1776-1824," *Hispanic American Historical Review*. 51, 1 (1971), 25-44.

Fisher, Lillian. *The Last Inca Revolt*. Univ. of Oklahoma Press, 1966.

Flory, Rae. "Bahian Society in the Mid-Colonial Period: The Sugar Planters, Tobacco Growers, Merchants, and Artisans of Salvador and the Reconcâvo, 1680-1725." Ph.D. dissertation, Univ. of Texas, 1978.

Floyd, Troy. "The Guatemalan Merchants, the Government and the Provincianos, 1750–1800," *Hispanic American Historical Review.* 41, 1 (1961), 90–110

Ford, Franklin. *Robe and Sword: The Regrouping of the French Aristocracy After Louis XIV.* Harvard Univ. Press, 1953.

Forster, Robert. "Obstacles to Agricultural Growth in Eighteenth Century France," *American Historical Review.* 75, 6 (1970), 1600–15.

Fox, Edward Whiting. *History in Geographic Perspective.* New York, Norton, 1971.

Frank, André Gunder. *World Accumulation, 1492–1789.* New York, Monthly Review Press, 1978.

Frykenberg, Robert. *Land Control and Social Structure in Indian History.* Univ. of Wisconsin Press, 1969.

Furber, Holden. *Rival Empires in the Orient Trade.* Univ. of Minnesota Press, 1976.

Galenson, David. "The Slave Trade to the English West Indies, 1673–1724," *Economic History Review.* 32 (1979), 241–50.

——— . "White Servitude and the Growth of Black Slavery in America," *Journal of Economic History.* 41, 1 (1981), 39–47.

——— . *White Servitude in Colonial America: An Economic Analysis.* Cambridge Univ. Press, 1981.

Galloway, J. H. "North-East Brazil, 1700–1750: The Agricultural Crisis Re-examined," *Journal of Historical Geography.* 1, 1 (1975), 21–38.

Garrard, Timothy. "Myth and Metrology: The Early Trans-Saharan Gold Trade," *Journal of African History.* 23, 4 (1982), 443–62.

Geggus, David. *Slavery, War and Revolution: The British Occupation of Saint Domingue, 1793–1798.* Oxford Univ. Press, 1982.

Genovese, Eugene. *The World the Slaveholders Made.* New York, Pantheon, 1969.

Genovese, Eugene, and Elizabeth Fox-Genovese. *Fruits of Merchant Capital.* Oxford Univ. Press, 1983.

George, C. H. "The Making of the English Bourgeoisie, 1500–1750," *Science and Society.* 35, 4 (1971), 385–414.

——— . "The Origins of Capitalism: A Marxist Epitome and a Critique of Immanuel Wallerstein's Modern World System," *Marxist Perspectives.* 3, 2 (1980), 70–102.

Gernet, Jacques. *A History of Chinese Civilization.* Cambridge Univ. Press, 1982.

Geyl, Pieter. *The Netherlands in the Seventeenth Century.* 2 vols. New York, Barnes and Noble, 1961.

Gibb, H.A.R. *Mohammedanism.* Oxford Univ. Press, 1962.

Gibbs, Marion. *Feudal Order: An Historical Survey.* London, Cobbett Press, 1949.

Gibson, Charles. *The Aztecs Under Colonial Rule.* Stanford Univ. Press, 1964.

Gilboy, Elizabeth. "Demand as a Factor in the Industrial Revolution," in R. M. Hartwell, ed., *The Causes of the Industrial Revolution.* London, Methuen, 1967, 121–39.

Glamann, Kristoff. *Dutch Asiatic Trade, 1620–1740.* Copenhagen, Danish Science Press, 1958.

Goitein, S. D. "Mediterranean Trade in the Eleventh Century: Some Facts and Problems," in M. A. Cook, ed., *Studies in the Economic History of the Middle East.* Oxford Univ. Press, 1970, 51–63.

Goldwaite, Richard. "The Medici Bank and the World of Florentine Capitalism," *Past and Present.* 114 (1987), 3–31.

Goody, Jack. *The Development of the Family and Marriage in Europe.* Cambridge Univ. Press, 1983.

——— . "Feudalism in Africa?" *Journal of African History.* 4 (1963), 1–18.

Gopal, Lallanji. *The Economic Life of Northern India.* Delhi, Motilal Banarsidass, 1965.

Gottschalk, Louis, and Donald Lach. *Toward the French Revolution.* New York, Scribner, 1973.

Goubert, Pierre. *The French Peasantry in the Seventeenth Century.* Cambridge Univ. Press, 1986.

_____ . *Louis XIV and Twenty Million Frenchmen.* New York, Pantheon, 1966.

Gould, J. D. "The Price Revolution Reconsidered," *Economic History Review.* 17, 2 (1964), 249-66.

Gray, Lewis. *History of Agriculture in the Southern United States to 1860,* vol. 1. Washington, D.C., Carnegie Institution of Washington, 1933.

Green, William. *British Slave Emancipation: The Sugar Colonies and the Great Experiment.* Oxford Univ. Press, 1976.

Greenberg, Michael. *British Trade and the Opening of China, 1800-1842.* Cambridge Univ. Press, 1951.

Griffeths, Gordon. "The Revolutionary Character of the Revolution of the Netherlands," *Comparative Studies in Society and History.* 2, 4 (1959-1960), 452-72.

Griffin, Charles. "Economic and Social Aspects of the Era of Spanish American Independence," *Hispanic American Historical Review.* 29 (1949), 170-87.

Grigg, David. *The Agricultural Systems of the World.* Cambridge Univ. Press, 1974.

Guerra y Sanchez, Ramiro. *Sugar and Society in the Caribbean.* Yale Univ. Press, 1964.

Habakkuk, H. J. "English Landownership, 1600-1740," *Economic History Review.* 1st series, 10 (1940), 3-17.

_____ . "Landowners and the Civil War," *Economic History Review.* 18 (1965), 130-52.

Habib, Irfan. "Potentialities of Capitalist Development in Mughal India," *Journal of Economic History.* 29, 1 (1969), 32-78.

Halecki, O. *A History of Poland.* New York, Roy Publishers, 1956.

Hall, Gwendolyn. *Social Control in Slave Plantation Societies.* Johns Hopkins Univ. Press, 1971.

Halperin Donghi, Tulio. *The Aftermath of Revolution in Latin America.* New York, Harper and Row, 1973.

Hamill, Hugh. *The Hidalgo Revolt.* Univ. of Florida Press, 1966.

Hamilton, Earl J. *American Treasure and the Price Revolution in Spain, 1501-1650.* New York, Octagon Books, 1977.

_____ . "American Treasure and the Rise of Capitalism," *Economica.* 5 (Nov., 1929), 338-57.

_____ . "Money and Economic Recovery in Spain Under the First Bourbon, 1701-1746," *Journal of Modern History.* 15, 3 (1943), 192-207.

Hammond, J. L., and B. Hammond. *The Rise of Modern Industry.* New York, Harcourt, Brace, 1926.

Hamnett, Brian. *Politics and Trade in Southern Mexico, 1750-1821.* Cambridge Univ. Press, 1971.

Hanna, Willard. *Indonesian Banda.* Philadephia, Institute for the Study of Human Issues, 1978.

Hanson, Carl. *Economy and Society in Baroque Portugal, 1668-1703.* Univ. of Minnesota Press, 1981.

Haring, C. H. *Trade and Navigation Between Spain and the Indies.* Harvard Univ. Press, 1918.

Harlan, Jack et al., eds., *Origins of African Plant Domestication.* The Hague, Mouton, 1976.

Harris, Robert. "French Finances and the American War, 1777-1783," *Journal of Modern History.* 48 (1976), 233-58.

Hartwell, R. M. "The Causes of the Industrial Revolution: An Essay in Methodology," *Economic History Review.* 18, 1 (1965), 164-82.

_____ , ed. *The Causes of the Industrial Revolution.* London, Methuen, 1967.

Hartwell, Robert. "A Cycle of Economic Change in Imperial China: Coal and Iron in North-East China, 750-1350," *Journal of Economic and Social History of the Orient.* 10 (1967).

———. "Markets, Technology and the Structure of Enterprise in the Development of the Eleventh Century Chinese Iron and Steel Industry," *Journal of Economic History*. 26, 1 (1966), 29–58.

———. "A Revolution in the Chinese Iron and Coal Industries During the Northern Sung, 960–1126," *Journal of Asian Studies*. 21 (1961), 153–62.

Hay, Denys. *The Italian Renaissance and Its Historical Background*. Cambridge Univ. Press, 1962.

Heaton, Herbert. "The Industrial Revolution," in R. M. Hartwell, ed., *The Causes of the Industrial Revolution in England*. London, Methuen, 1967, 31–52.

Hemming, John. *The Conquest of the Incas*. London, Macmillan, 1970.

———. *Red Gold: The Conquest of the Brazilian Indians*. Harvard Univ. Press, 1978.

Henige, David, and Marion Johnson. "Agaja and the Slave Trade: Another Look at the Evidence," *History in Africa*. 3 (1976), 57–69.

Herbert, P. A. *Under the Brilliant Emperor*. Canberra, Australian National Univ. Press, 1978.

Herr, Frederich. *The Holy Roman Empire*. New York, Praeger, 1968.

Herr, Richard. *The Eighteenth Century Revolution in Spain*. Princeton Univ. Press, 1958.

Hess, Andrew. *The Forgotten Frontier: A History of the Sixteenth Century Ibero-African Frontier*. Univ. of Chicago Press, 1978.

Hibbert, A. B. "The Economic Policies of Towns," in M. M. Postan, E. E. Rich, and Edward Miller, eds., *The Cambridge Economic History of Europe*, vol. 3. Cambridge Univ. Press, 1965, 157–229.

Highfield, Roger, ed. *Spain in the Fifteenth Century, 1369–1516*. London, Macmillan, 1972.

Higonnet, Patrice Louis-René. "The Origins of the Seven Years War," *Journal of Modern History*. 40 (1968), 57–90.

Hill, Christopher. *The Century of Revolution*. Edinburgh, T. Nelson and Sons, 1961.

———. *Economic Problems of the Church*. Oxford Univ. Press, 1956.

———. *From Reformation to Industrial Revolution: A Social and Economic History of Britain, 1530–1780*. London, Weidenfeld and Nicolson, 1967.

———. "Parliament and People in Seventeenth Century England," *Past and Present*. 92 (Aug., 1981), 100–25.

Hilliard, Sam. B. "Ante-Bellum Tidewater Rice Culture in South Carolina and Georgia," in James Gibson, ed., *European Settlement and Development in North America*. Univ. of Toronto Press, 1978, 91–115.

Hilton, Rodney. *Bond Men Made Free*. New York, Viking Press, 1973.

———. "Capitalism: What's in a Name?" in Rodney Hilton, ed., *The Transition from Feudalism to Capitalism*. London, Verso, 1978.

———. "A Crisis of Feudalism," *Past and Present*. 80 (1978), 3–20.

———, ed. *The Transition From Feudalism to Capitalism*. London, Verso, 1978.

Ho, Ping-ti. "Early Ripening Rice in Chinese History," *Economic History Review*. 9, 2 (1956), 200–19.

———. "Economic and Institutional Factors in the Decline of the Chinese Empire," in Carlo Cipolla, ed., *The Economic Decline of Empires*. London, Methuen, 1970, 264–77.

Hobsbawm, Eric. *The Age of Revolution*. London, Sphere Books, 1977.

———. "The Crisis of the Seventeenth Century," in Trevor Ashton, ed., *Crisis in Europe, 1560–1660*. New York, Basic Books, 1965, 5–55.

———. *Industry and Empire*. London, Weidenfeld and Nicolson, 1968.

Hoffman, Philip T. "Taxes and Agrarian Life in Early Modern France: Land Sales, 1550–1730," *Journal of Economic History*. 46, 1 (1986), 37–55.

Hogendorn, Jan, and Henry A. Gemery. "Abolition and Its Impact on Monies Imported into West Africa," in David Eltis and James Walvin, eds., *The Abolition of the Atlantic Slave*

*Trade: Origins and Effects in Europe, Africa, and the Americas.* Univ. of Wisconsin Press, 1981, 99–116.

Hopkins, Anthony. *An Economic History of West Africa.* Columbia Univ. Press, 1973.

Hoppit, Julian. "Financial Crisis in Eighteenth Century England," *Economic History Review.* 39 (1986), 39–58.

Horn, James. "Servant Emigration to the Chesapeake in the Sevententh Century," in Thad Tate and David Ammerman, eds., *The Chesapeake in the Seventeenth Century.* Univ. of North Carolina Press, 1979, 51–95.

Hull, Richard. *African Towns and Cities Before the European Conquest.* New York, Norton, 1976.

Humphreys, Robert A., and John Lynch, eds. *The Origins of the Latin American Revolutions.* New York, Knopf, 1965.

Hunt, Lynn. *Politics, Culture, and Class in the French Revolution.* Univ. of California Press, 1984.

Hussey, Joan. *The Byzantine World.* London, Hutchinson, 1967.

Hussey, Roland. *The Caracas Company.* Harvard Univ. Press, 1934.

Hymes, Robert. *Statesmen and Gentlemen.* Cambridge Univ. Press, 1986.

Imamuddin, S. M. *The Economic History of Spain Under the Umayyads.* Dacca, Asiatic Society of Pakistan, 1963.

Inikori, J. E. *Forced Migration: The Impact of the Export Slave Trade on African Societies.* New York, Africana Press, 1982.

———. "The Import of Firearms into West Africa, 1750–1807: A Quantitative Assessment," *Journal of African History.* 18, 3 (1977), 339–69.

———. "Measuring the Atlantic Slave Trade: An Assessment of Curtin and Anstey," *Journal of African History.* 17, 2 (1976), 197–223.

Innes, A. D. *The Maritime and Colonial Expansion of England Under the Stuarts.* London, S. Low, Marston and Co., 1931.

Israel, Jonathan. *Race, Class, and Politics in Colonial Mexico, 1610–1670.* Oxford Univ. Press, 1975.

Jago, Charles. "The Influence of Debt on Relations Between Crown and Aristocracy in Seventeenth Century Castile," *Economic History Review.* 26 (1973), 218–36.

James, C.L.R. *The Black Jacobins.* New York, Vintage Books, 1963.

James, Francis. *Ireland in the Empire, 1688–1770.* Harvard Univ. Press, 1973.

———. "Irish Colonial Trade in the Eighteenth Century," *William and Mary Quarterly.* 20, 5 (1963), 575–84.

Jennings, Francis. *The Invasion of America: Indians, Colonialism, and the Cant of Conquest.* Univ. of North Carolina Press, 1975.

Jensen, Merrill. "The American Revolution and American Agriculture," *Agricultural History.* 43, 1 (1969), 107–24.

———. *The New Nation.* New York, Knopf, 1950.

Jha, D. N. *Studies in Early Indian History.* Delhi, Anupama Publications, 1980.

John, Arthur. "Agricultural Productivity and Economic Growth in England, 1700–1760," *Journal of Economic History.* 25, 1 (1965), 19–35.

Jones, A.H.M. *The Decline of the Ancient World.* New York, Holt, Rinehart, and Winston, 1966.

Jones, Andrew. "The Rise and Fall of the Manorial System: A Critical Comment," *Journal of Economic History.* 32 (1972), 938–45.

Jones, E. L. "Agriculture and Economic Growth in England, 1660–1750: Agricultural Change," *Journal of Economic History.* 25, 1 (1965), 1–18.

———. *The European Economic Miracle.* Cambridge Univ. Press, 1981.

Jones, G. I. *The Trading States of the Oil Rivers.* Oxford Univ. Press, 1963.

Julien, Catherine. "Inca Decimal Administration in the Lake Titicaca Region," in George Collier et al., eds., *The Inca and Aztec States, 1400–1800.* New York, Academic Press, 1982, 121–52.

July, Robert. *Pre-Colonial Africa.* New York, Scribner, 1975.

Kalik, Juban. *Peasant and Lord in the Process of Transition from Feudalism to Capitalism in the Baltic.* Academy of Sciences of the Estonian SSR, 1982.

Kamen, Henry. *Spain, 1469–1714.* London, Longman, 1983.

———. *The War of Succession in Spain, 1700–1715.* Indiana Univ. Press, 1969.

Kammen, Michael. *Empire and Interest: The American Colonies and the Politics of Mercantilism.* Cornell Univ. Press, 1970.

Katz, Friedrich. *The Ancient American Civilizations.* New York, Praeger, 1972.

Kay, Geoffrey. *Development and Underdevelopment: A Marxist Analysis.* London, Macmillan, 1975.

Kea, Ray. *Settlements, Trade, and Politics in the Seventeenth Century Gold Coast.* Johns Hopkins Univ. Press, 1982.

Keen, Benjamin, and Mark Wasserman. *A History of Latin America.* Boston, Houghton Mifflin, 1988.

Keith, Robert. *Conquest and Agrarian Change: The Emergence of the Hacienda System on the Peruvian Coast.* Harvard Univ. Press, 1976.

Kellenbenz, Hermann. *The Rise of the European Economy.* New York, Holmes and Meier, 1976.

Kent, H.S.K. "The Anglo-Norwegian Timber Trade in the Eighteenth Century," *Economic History Review.* 8, 1 (1955), 62–74.

———. *War and Trade in Northern Seas.* Cambridge Univ. Press, 1973.

Kent, Raymond. "Palmares: An African State in Brazil," *Journal of African History.* 6, 2 (1965), 161–75.

Kenyon, Cecilia. "Republicanism and Radicalism in the American Revolution: An Old Fashioned Interpretation," *William and Mary Quarterly.* 3rd series, 19 (Apr., 1962), 153–82.

Killett, J. R. "The Breakdown of Gild and Corporation Control over the Handicraft and Retail Trade in London," *Economic History Review.* 10, 3 (1958), 381–95.

Kinsbruner, Jay. *Chile: A Historical Interpretation.* New York, Harper and Row, 1973.

Klima, Arnost. "English Merchant Capital in the Eighteenth Century," *Economic History Review.* 12, 1 (1959), 34–48.

Koenigsberger, H. G. "Property and the Price Revolution: Hainault, 1474–1573," *Economic History Review.* 9 (1956), 1–15.

Koenigsberger, H. G., and George Mosse. *Europe in the Sixteenth Century.* London, Longman, 1968.

Kriedte, Peter. *Peasants, Landlords, and Merchant Capitalists in Europe and the World Economy, 1500–1800.* Cambridge Univ. Press, 1983.

Kuethe, Allan, and G. Douglas Inglis. "Absolutism and Enlightened Reform: Charles III, the Establishment of the Alcabala, and Commercial Reorganization in Cuba," *Past and Present.* 109 (Nov., 1985), 118–43.

Kula, Witold. *An Economic Theory of the Feudal System: Towards a Model of the Polish Economy, 1500–1800.* London, N.L.B., 1976.

Kulikoff, Allan. "The Economic Growth of the Eighteenth Century Chesapeake Colonies," *Journal of Economic History.* 39, 1 (1979), 275–89.

Labaree, Benjamin, and Ian Christie. *Empire or Independence: A British-American Dialogue on the Coming of the American Revolution.* New York, Norton, 1976.

Labib, Subhi. "Capitalism in Medieval Islam," *Journal of Economic History.* 29, 1 (1969), 79–96.

———. "Egyptian Commercial Policy in the Middle Ages," in M. A. Cook, ed., *Studies in the Economic History of the Middle East.* Oxford Univ. Press, 1970.

Lach, Donald. *Asia in the Making of Europe*, vol. 1. Univ. of California Press, 1965.

Lambert, Audrey. *The Making of the Dutch Landscape*. London, Seminar Press, 1971.

Landes, David. *The Unbound Prometheus*. Cambridge Univ. Press, 1969.

Lane, Frederick C. "Meanings of Capitalism," *Journal of Economic History*. 29, 1 (1969), 5-13.

_____. "Pepper Prices Before da Gama," *Journal of Economic History*. 28, 4 (1968), 590-97.

_____. *Venice, a Maritime Republic*. Johns Hopkins Univ. Press, 1973.

Lang, M. F. "New Spain's Mining Depression and the Supply of Quicksilver from Peru," *Hispanic American Historical Review*. 48 (1968), 632-42.

Lanning, Edward. *Peru Before the Incas*. Englewood Cliffs, N.J., Prentice-Hall, 1967.

Large, David. "The Wealth of the Great Irish Landowners," *Irish Historical Studies*. 15 (Mar., 1966), 21-47.

Latouche, Robert. *The Birth of the Western Economy*. New York, Barnes and Noble, 1961.

Lavrosky, V. M. "Expropriation of the English Peasantry in the Eighteenth Century," *Economic History Review*. 9 (1959), 271-82.

Law, Robin. "Royal Monopoly and Private Enterprise in the Atlantic Slave Trade: The Case of Dahomey," *Journal of African History*. 18, 4 (1977), 555-79.

Lefebvre, Georges. *The Coming of the French Revolution*. Princeton Univ. Press, 1947.

Legros, Dominique, Donald Hunderfund, and Judith Shapiro, "Economic Base, Mode of Production, and Social Formation: A Discussion of Marx's Terminology," *Dialectical Anthropology*, 4, 3 (1979), 243-49.

Le Roy Ladurie, Emmanuel. *The French Peasantry, 1450-1660*. Univ. of California Press, 1987.

Leveen, E. Philip. "The African Slave Supply Response," *African Studies Review*. 18, 1 (Apr., 1975), 9-28.

Levtzion, Nehemia. "The Early States of the Western Sudan," in J.F.A. Ajayi and Michael Crowder, eds., *A History of West Africa*, vol. 1. Columbia Univ. Press, 1976, 120-57.

Lewis, Bernard. "The Arabs in Decline," in Carlo Cipolla, ed., *The Economic Decline of Empires*. London, Methuen, 1970, 112-20.

Lis, Catharina, and Hugo Soly. *Poverty and Capitalism in Pre-Industrial Europe*. Atlantic Highlands, N.J., Humanities Press, 1979.

Liss, Peggy. *The Atlantic Empires*. Johns Hopkins Univ. Press, 1983.

Livermore, H. L. *A New History of Portugal*. Cambridge Univ. Press, 1966.

Livingston, Jon, et al., eds. *The Japan Reader*, vol. 1. New York, Pantheon, 1973.

Lockhart, James. "Encomienda and Hacienda: The Evolution of the Great Estate in the Spanish Indies," *Hispanic American Historical Review*. 49 (1969), 411-29.

_____. *Spanish Peru, 1532-1560: A Colonial Society*. Univ. of Wisconsin Press, 1968.

Longworth, Philip. *The Rise and Fall of Venice*. London, Constable, 1974.

Lopez, Robert. *The Commercial Revolution of the Middle Ages*. Cambridge Univ. Press, 1976.

Lourie, Elana. "A Society Organized for War: Medieval Spain," *Past and Present*. 35 (Dec., 1966), 54-77.

Lovejoy, Paul. "The Role of the Wangara in the Economic Transformation of the Central Sudan in the Fifteenth and Sixteenth Centuries," *Journal of African History*. 19, 2 (1978), 173-93.

_____. *Transformations in Slavery*. Cambridge Univ. Press, 1983.

_____. "The Volume of the Atlantic Slave Trade: A Synthesis," *Journal of African History*. 23, 4 (1982), 473-501.

Lovett, A. W. "The Castilian Bankruptcy of 1575," *Historical Journal*. 23 (1980), 899-911.

Lucas, Colin. "Nobles, Bourgeois, and the Origins of the French Revolution," *Past and Present*. 60 (1973), 84-126.

Lugar, Catherine. "The Portuguese Tobacco Trade and the Tobacco Growers of Bahia in the Late Colonial Period," in D. Alden and Warren Dean, eds., *Essays Concerning the Socio-Economic History of Brazil and Portuguese India*. Univ. of Florida Press, 1977, 20-70.

Lybyer, A. H. "The Ottoman Turks and the Routes of the Oriental Trade," *English Historical Review*. 30 (1915), 576–88.

Lydon, James. "Fish and Flour for Gold: Southern Europe and the Colonial Balance of Payments," *Business History Review*. 39, 2 (1965), 171–84.

Lynch, John. *Spain Under the Habsburgs.* 2 vols., Oxford Univ. Press, 1964.

———. *Spanish American Colonial Administration, 1782–1810.* London, Athlone Press, 1958.

———. *The Spanish American Revolutions, 1808–1826.* London, Weidenfeld and Nicolson, 1973.

Ma, Laurence. *Commercial Development and Urban Change in Sung China.* Ann Arbor, University of Michigan Press, 1971.

MacCurtain, Margaret. *Tudor and Stuart Ireland.* Dublin, Gill and Macmillan, 1972.

MacLeod, Murdo. "The Primitive State, Delegations of Functions, and Results: Some Examples from Early Colonial Central America," in Karen Spalding, ed., *Essays on the Political, Economic, and Social History of Colonial Latin America.* Univ. of Delaware Press, 1982, 53–69.

———. *Spanish Central America: A Socio-Economic History, 1520–1720.* Univ. of California Press, 1973.

Maczak, Antonio. "Export of Grain and the Problem of the Distribution of National Income in the Years 1550–1650," *Acta Poloniae Historica.* 18 (1968), 75–98.

Main, Jackson Turner. *The Social Structure of Revolutionary America.* Princeton Univ. Press, 1965.

Maity, S. K. *Economic Life in Northern India in the Gupta Period.* Delhi, Motilal Banarsidass, 1970.

Majumdar, R. C., et al. *An Advanced History of India.* London, Macmillan, 1960.

Malgalhães Godinho, Vitorino. "Le répli vénitien et égyptien et la route du cap," in *Eventail de l'histoire vivante: Hommage à Lucien Febvre,* vol. 2. Paris, 1953, 283–300.

Malowist, Marion. "The Economic and Social Development of the Baltic Countries from the Fifteenth to the Seventeenth Centuries," *Economic History Review.* 12, 2 (1959), 177–87.

———. "Poland, Russia, and the Western Trade in the Fifteenth and Sixteenth Centuries," *Past and Present.* 13 (Apr., 1958), 26–41.

———. "The Problem of Inequality of Economic Development in Europe in the Later Middle Ages," *Economic History Review.* 19, 1 (1966), 15–29.

Manchester, Alan K. "The Rise of the Brazilian Aristocracy," *Hispanic American Historical Review.* 11 (1931), 145–68.

Manning, Patrick. "Contours of Slavery and Social Change in Africa," *American Historical Review.* 84, 4 (1983), 835–59.

———. *Slavery, Colonialism, and Economic Growth in Dahomey, 1640–1960.* Cambridge Univ. Press, 1982.

Marchant, Alexander. *From Barter to Slavery: The Economic Relations of Portuguese and Indians in the Settlement of Brazil, 1500–1580.* Johns Hopkins Univ. Press, 1942.

Mariejol, Jean. *The Spain of Ferdinand and Isabella.* Rutgers Univ. Press, 1961.

Marx, Karl. *Capital.* 3 vols. New York, International Publishers, 1967.

Maxwell, Kenneth. *Conflicts and Conspiracies: Brazil and Portugal, 1750–1808.* Cambridge Univ. Press, 1973.

———. "Pombal and the Nationalization of the Luso-Brazilian Economy," *Hispanic American Historical Review.* 48, 4 (1968), 608–31.

McCusker, John, and Russell Menard. *The Economy of British North America, 1607–1789.* Univ. of North Carolina Press, 1985.

McDonald, John, and G. D. Snooks. *Domesday Economy.* Oxford Univ. Press, 1986.

McElwee, William. *A Short History of England.* New York, Praeger, 1969.

McGowan, Bruce. *Economic Life in Ottoman Europe: Taxation, Trade and the Struggle for Land.* Cambridge Univ. Press, 1981.

McIntosh, Roderick, and Susan McIntosh. "The Inland Niger Delta Before the Empire of Mali: Evidence from Jenne-Jeno," *Journal of African History.* 21, 1 (1980), 1–22.

McNeill, William. *A World History.* Oxford Univ. Press, 1971.

Mellafe, Rolando. *Negro Slavery in Latin America.* Univ. of California Press, 1975.

Mertens, J. A., and A. E. Verhulst. "Yield Ratios in Flanders in the Fourteenth Century," *Economic History Review.* 19 (1966), 175–82.

Metcalf, George. "A Microcosm of Why Africans Sold Slaves: Akan Consumption Patterns in the 1770s," *Journal of African History.* 28, 3 (1987), 377–94.

Meyer, Michael, and William Sherman. *The Course of Mexican History.* Oxford Univ. Press, 1987.

Mikkai, Laszlo. "Neo-Serfdom: Its Origins and Nature in East-Central Europe," *Slavic Review.* 34, 2 (1975), 225–38.

Millar, Fergus. "The Mediterranean and the Roman Revolution: Politics, War, and the Economy," *Past and Present.* 102 (1984), 3–24.

Miller, Joseph C. "Chokwe Trade and Conquest," in Richard Gray and David Birmingham, eds., *Pre-Colonial African Trade.* Oxford Univ. Press, 1970, 175–201.

———. "The Dual Slave Trade in Angola." Mimeograph, UCLA, 1971.

———. "Imbangala Lineage Slavery," in S. Miers and I. Kopytoff, eds., *Slavery in Africa.* Univ. of Wisconsin Press, 1977, 205–35.

———. "The Paradoxes of Impoverishment in the Atlantic Zone," in David Birmingham and Phyllis Martin, eds., *History of Central Africa,* vol. 1. London, Longman, 1983, 118–60.

———. "The Significance of Drought, Disease, and Famine in the Agriculturally Marginal Zones of West-Central Africa," *Journal of African History.* 23, 1 (1982), 17–63.

———. "Slaves, Slavers and Social Change in Nineteenth Century Kasanje," in Franz-Wilhelm Heimer, ed., *Social Change in Angola.* Munich, Weltforum Verlag, 1973, 9–30.

Minchinton, W. E., ed. *The Growth of English Overseas Trade in the Seventeenth and Eighteenth Centuries.* London, Methuen, 1969.

Mintz, Sidney. *Sweetness and Power.* New York, Viking, 1985.

Mishra, Vikas. *Hinduism and Economic Growth.* Oxford Univ. Press, 1962.

Miskimin, Harry. *The Economy of Early Renaissance Europe.* Yale Univ. Press, 1977.

———. *Money and Power in Fifteenth Century France.* Yale Univ. Press, 1984.

———. *Money, Prices, and Foreign Exchange in Fourteenth Century France.* Yale Univ. Press, 1963.

Mitchell, B. R. "The Coming of the Railway and United Kingdom Economic Growth," *Journal of Economic History.* 24, 3 (1964), 315–37.

Miyamoto, Mataji, et al. "Economic Development in Pre-Industrial Japan," *Journal of Economic History.* 25, 4 (1965), 541–65.

Morgan, Edmund. *The Birth of the American Republic, 1763–1789.* Univ. of Chicago Press, 1956.

Morison, Samuel Eliot. *The European Discovery of America.* Oxford Univ. Press, 1971–1974.

Morison, Samuel Eliot, and Henry Steele Commager. *The Growth of the American Republic.* 2 vols. Oxford Univ. Press, 1962.

Morris, Craig. "The Infrastructure of Inka Control in the Peruvian Central Highlands," in George Collier et al., eds., *The Inca and Aztec States, 1400–1800.* New York, Academic Press, 1982.

Morse, Richard, ed. *The Bandeirantes: The Historical Role of the Brazilian Pathfinders.* New York, Knopf, 1965.

Mukherjee, Ramkrishna. *The Rise and Fall of the East India Company.* Berlin, Veb Deutscher Verlag der Wissenschaften, 1958.

Neal, Larry. "The Integration of the London and Amsterdam Stock Markets in the Eighteenth Century," *Journal of Economic History.* 47 (1987), 97–116.

Neale, Walter. "Land Is to Rule," in Robert Eric Frykenberg, ed., *Land Control and Social Structure in Indian History.* Univ. of Wisconsin Press, 1969, 3–17.

Needham, Joseph. *The Grand Titration, Science and Society in East and West.* Univ. of Toronto Press, 1969.

———. "Poverties and Triumphs of the Chinese Scientific Tradition," in A. C. Crombie, ed., *Scientific Change.* Oxford Univ. Press, 1961.

———. *Science and Civilisation in China.* 5 vols., Cambridge Univ. Press, 1954–1986.

———. "Science and Society in East and West," *Centaurus.* 10 (1964), 174–97.

Nef, J. U. "The Industrial Revolution Reconsidered," *Journal of Economic History.* 3 (1943), 1–32.

———. "The Progress of Technology and the Growth of Large-Scale Industry in Great Britain, 1540–1640," in E. H. Carus-Wilson, ed., *Essays in Economic History.* London, E. Arnold, 1954.

Nettels, Curtis. "England and the Spanish American Trade, 1680–1715," *Journal of Social History.* 7 (1931), 1–32.

Newman, K. "Hamburg in the European Economy, 1660–1750," *Journal of European Economic History.* 14 (1985), 57–95.

Nicholas, David. *Town and Countryside: Social, Economic, and Political Tensions in Fourteenth Century Flanders.* Bruges, de Tempel, 1971.

Nightingale, Pamela. *Trade and Empire in Western India.* Cambridge Univ. Press, 1970.

North, Douglass, and Robert Thomas. *The Rise of the Western World.* Cambridge Univ. Press, 1973.

Northrup, David. "The Growth of Trade Among the Igbo Before 1800," *Journal of African History.* 13, 2 (1972), 217–37.

———. *Trade Without Rulers.* Oxford Univ. Press, 1978.

O'Brien, Patrick K. "European Economic Development: The Contribution of the Periphery," *Economic History Review.* 35, 1 (Feb., 1982), 1–19.

———. "The Political Economy of British Taxation, 1660–1815," *Economic History Review.* 41, 1 (1988), 1–33.

O'Connell, Maurice. *Irish Politics and Social Conflict in the Age of the American Revolution.* Univ. of Pennsylvania Press, 1965.

O'Conner, David. "Egypt, 1552–664 B.C.," *Cambridge History of Africa*, vol. 1. Cambridge Univ. Press, 1976, 830–940.

O'Farrell, Patrick. *Ireland's English Question.* London, Batsford, 1971.

Oliveira Marques, Antonio de. *History of Portugal.* 2 vols., Columbia Univ. Press, 1972.

Ostrander, Gilian. "The Making of the Triangular Myth," *William and Mary Quarterly.* 30, 4 (Oct., 1973), 635–44.

Ott, Thomas. *The Haitian Revolution.* Univ. of Tennessee Press, 1973.

Owen, Roger. *The Middle East in the World Economy.* London, Methuen, 1981.

Paddock, John, ed. *Ancient Oaxaca: Discoveries in Mexican Archeology and History.* Stanford Univ. Press, 1966.

Palmer, Colin. *Slaves of the White God: Blacks in Mexico, 1570–1650.* Harvard Univ. Press, 1976.

Palmer, Robert R. *The Age of Democratic Revolution.* 2 vols., Princeton Univ. Press, 1964.

Palmer, Robert R., and Joel Colton. *A History of the Modern World.* 2 vols., New York, Knopf, 1978.

Panikkar, K. M. *Asia and Western Dominance.* London, Allen and Unwin, 1959.

Pares, Richard. *Merchants and Planters.* Cambridge Univ. Press, 1960.

Parry, John S. *The Age of Reconnaissance.* New York, Praeger, 1963.

———. *The Sale of Public Office in the Spanish Indies Under the Habsburgs*. Univ. of California Press, 1953.

———. *The Spanish Seaborne Empire*. London, Hutchinson, 1966.

———. *Trade and Dominion: The European Overseas Empires in the Eighteenth Century*. London, Weidenfeld and Nicolson, 1971.

Parry, John S., and Philip Sherlock. *A Short History of the West Indies*. London, Macmillan, 1956.

Payne, Stanley. *A History of Spain and Portugal*. 2 vols., Univ. of Wisconsin Press, 1973.

Pearson, Michael. *Merchants and Rulers in Gujerat*. Univ. of California Press, 1976.

Penson, Lillian. "The West Indies and the Spanish American Trade, 1713-1748," in J. Holland Rose, ed., *Cambridge History of the British Empire*, vol. 1. Cambridge Univ. Press, 1960.

Perkins, Edwin. *The Economic Growth of Colonial America*. Columbia Univ. Press, 1980.

Perroy, Edouard. *The Hundred Years War*. New York, Capricorn Books, 1965.

Phelan, John. "Authority and Flexibility in Spanish Imperial Bureaucracy," *Administrative Science Quarterly*. 5 (1960), 47-65.

———. *The Kingdom of Quito in the Seventeenth Century: Bureaucratic Politics in the Spanish Empire*. Univ. of Wisconsin Press, 1967.

———. *People of the King: The Comunero Revolt in Colombia*. Univ. of Wisconsin Press, 1978.

Phillipson, David. *The Later Prehistory of East and Southern Africa*. New York, Africana, 1977.

Pike, Ruth. *Aristocrats and Traders: Sevillian Society in the Sixteenth Century*. Cornell Univ. Press, 1972.

———. *Enterprise and Adventure: The Genoese in Seville*. Cornell Univ. Press, 1966.

Pines, S. "What Was Original in Arabic Science," in A. C. Crombie, ed., *Scientific Change*. New York, Basic Books, 1963.

Pirenne, Henri. "The Place of the Netherlands in the Economic History of Medieval Europe," *Economic History Review*. 1st series, 2 (1931), 20-41.

Pollard, Sidney, and David Crossley. *The Wealth of Britain*. London, Batsford, 1968.

Pons, Frank Moya. *Historia Colonial de Santo Domingo*. Santiago, República Dominicana, UCMM, 1977.

Postan, M. M. "The Economic Foundations of Medieval Agriculture," in M. M. Postan, ed., *Essays on Medieval Agriculture and General Problems of the Medieval Economy*. Cambridge Univ. Press, 1973, 3-28.

———. "The Fifteenth Century," *Economic History Review*. 1st series (1938-1939), 160-69.

Pounds, Norman. *An Economic History of Medieval Europe*. London, Longman, 1974.

Prado Junior, Caio. *The Colonial Background of Modern Brazil*. Univ. of California Press, 1967.

———. *Formação do Brasil Contemporâneo*. São Paulo, Brasiliense, 1971.

Prakash, Om. *The Dutch East India Company and the Economy of Bengal, 1630-1720*. Princeton Univ. Press, 1985.

Previté-Orton, Charles W. *The Shorter Cambridge Medieval History*. Cambridge Univ. Press, 1966.

Price, Jacob. "A Note on the Value of Colonial Exports of Shipping," *Journal of Economic History*. 36, 3 (1976), 704-24.

Priestly, Margaret. "The Anglo-French Trade and the 'Unfavorable' Balance Controversy, 1660-1685," *Economic History Review*. 4, 1 (1951), 37-52.

Pullan, Brian, ed. *Crisis and Change in the Venetian Economy in the Sixteenth and Seventeenth Centuries*. London, Methuen, 1968.

Randles, W.G.L. *L'ancien royaume du Congo des origines à la fin du dix-neuvième siècle*. Paris, Mouton, 1968.

Ranson, Roger. "British Policy and Colonial Growth: Some Implications of the Burden from the Navigation Acts," *Journal of Economic History.* 28, 3 (1968), 427–36.

Rapp, Richard. *Industry and Economic Decline in Seventeenth Century Venice.* Cambridge Univ. Press, 1976.

——— . "The Unmaking of the Mediterranean Trade Hegemony: International Trade Rivalry and the Commercial Revolution," *Journal of Economic History.* 35, 3 (1975), 499–525.

Rawley, James. *The Trans-Atlantic Slave Trade.* New York, Norton, 1981.

Raychaudhuri, Tapan, and Irfan Habib, eds. *The Cambridge Economic History of India, c. 1200–1750,* vol. 1. Cambridge Univ. Press, 1982.

Reddaway, W. F., et al., eds. *The Cambridge History of Poland.* Cambridge Univ. Press, 1941.

Reed, Charles, ed. *Origins of Agriculture.* Paris, Mouton, 1977.

Regan, Colm. "Economic Development in Ireland: The Historical Dimension," *Antipode.* 12, 1 (1980), 1–15.

Reischauer, Edwin. *Japan, Past and Present.* New York, Knopf, 1964.

——— . "Japanese Feudalism," in Rushton Coulborn, ed., *Feudalism in History.* Princeton Univ. Press, 1956, 26–49.

Reischauer, Edwin, and John Fairbank. *East Asia: The Great Tradition.* Vol. 1 of *A History of East Asian Civilization.* Harvard University Press, 1960.

Rice, Eugene. *The Foundations of Early Modern Europe.* New York, Norton, 1970.

Richet, Denis. "Economic Growth and Its Setbacks in France from the Fifteenth to the Eighteenth Centuries," in Marc Ferro, ed., *Social Historians in Contemporary France.* New York, Harper and Row, 1972.

Riley, James C. "The Dutch Economy After 1650: Decline or Growth?" *Journal of European Economic History.* 13, 3 (1984), 521–71.

——— . *International Government Finance and the Amsterdam Capital Market.* Cambridge Univ. Press, 1980.

——— . *The Seven Years War and the Old Regime in France.* Princeton Univ. Press, 1986.

Ringrose, David. "Transportation and Economic Stagnation in Eighteenth Century Castile," *Journal of Economic History.* 28, 1 (1968), 51–79.

Rodney, Walter. "African Slavery and Other Forms of Social Oppression on the Upper Guinea Coast in the Context of the African Slave Trade," *Journal of African History.* 7 (1966), 431–43.

——— . *A History of the Upper Guinea Coast, 1545–1800.* Oxford Univ. Press, 1971.

Rogers, Edward. "The Iron and Steel Industry in Colonial and Imperial Brazil," *The Americas.* 19 (1962–1963), 172–84.

Romano, Ruggiero. "Italy in the Crisis of the Seventeenth Century," in Peter Earle, ed., *Essays in European Economic History, 1500–1800.* Oxford Univ. Press, 1974, 185–98.

Rorig, Fritz. *The Medieval Town.* Univ. of California Press, 1967.

Rosenberg, Nathan, and L. E. Birdzell. *How the West Grew Rich.* New York, Basic Books, 1986.

Rostow, Walt. *How It All Began: Origins of the Modern Economy.* New York, McGraw-Hill, 1975.

Rout, Leslie B. *The African Experience in Spanish America.* Cambridge Univ. Press, 1976.

Rowland, Benjamin. *Art and Architecture in India.* Baltimore, Penguin, 1956.

Russell, Conrad. *The Crisis of Parliaments.* Oxford Univ. Press, 1971.

Russell, Howard S. *A Long, Deep Furrow: Three Centuries of Farming in New England.* Hanover, N.H., Univ. Press of New England, 1976.

Russell, J. C. "Population in Europe, 500–1500," in Carlo Cipolla, ed., *The Fontana Economic History of Europe,* vol. 1. Sussex, Eng., Harvester Press, 1976, 25–70.

Russell-Wood, A.J.R. *The Black Man in Slavery and Freedom in Colonial Brazil.* New York, Norton, 1982.

———. "Technology and Society: The Impact of Gold Mining on the Institution of Slavery in Portuguese America," *Journal of Economic History.* 37 (1977), 59–84.

———, ed. *From Colony to Nation: Essays on the Independence of Brazil.* Johns Hopkins Univ. Press, 1975.

Salmon, J.H.M. *Society in Crisis: France in the Sixteenth Century.* New York, St. Martin's Press, 1975.

Sanders, William T. "The Cultural Ecology of the Lowland Maya: A Re-evaluation," in T. Patrick Culbert, ed., *The Classic Maya Collapse.* Univ. of New Mexico Press, 1973, 325–67.

———. *New World Pre-History.* Englewood Cliffs, N.J., Prentice-Hall, 1970.

Sangar, S. P. "The Lot of the Agriculturalist in Aurangzeb's Time," *Journal of Indian History.* 45, 1 (1967), 245–51.

Sauer, Carl. *The Early Spanish Main.* Univ. of California Press, 1966.

Schlesinger, Arthur. "The American Revolution Reconsidered," *Political Science Quarterly.* 34 (Mar., 1919), 61–78.

Schöffer, I. "The Dutch Revolution Atomized," *Comparative Studies in Society and History.* 3, 4 (1960–1961), 470–77.

Schwartz, Stuart. "Free Labor in a Slave Society: The Lavradores da Cana of Colonial Brazil," in Dauril Alden, ed., *The Colonial Roots of Modern Brazil.* Univ. of California Press, 1973, 147–98.

———. *Sovereignty and Society in Colonial Brazil.* University of California Press, 1973.

Scott, Earl. "Land Use Change in the Harsh Lands of West Africa," *African Studies Review.* 22, 1 (1979), 1–24.

Scott, William Robert. *The Constitution and Finance of English, Scottish and Irish Joint Stock Companies to 1720.* 3 vols., Gloucester, Mass., Peter Smith, 1968.

Sella, Domenico. "The Rise and Fall of the Venetian Woolen Industry," in Brian Pullan, ed., *Crisis and Change in the Venetian Economy in the Sixteenth and Seventeenth Centuries.* London, Methuen, 1968, 106–26.

Shannon, Fred. *America's Economic Growth.* New York, Macmillan, 1940.

Sharma, Ram Sharan. *Indian Feudalism: c. 300–1200.* Univ. of Calcutta Press, 1965.

Sharrer, G. Terry. "The Indigo Bonanza in South Carolina, 1740–1790," *Technology and Culture.* 12, 3 (1971), 447–55.

Sheridan, Richard B. "The Commercial and Financial Organization of the British Slave Trade, 1750–1807," *Economic History Review.* 11, 2 (1958–1959), 249–64.

———. "The Molasses Act and the Market Strategy of the British Sugar Planters," *Journal of Economic History.* 18 (1958), 62–83.

———. "The Plantation Revolution and the Industrial Revolution, 1625–1775," *Caribbean Studies.* 9, 3 (1969), 5–25.

———. *Sugar and Slavery: An Economic History of the British West Indies, 1623–1775.* Johns Hopkins Univ. Press, 1974.

———. "Temperate and Tropical: Aspects of European Penetration into Tropical Regions," *Caribbean Studies.* 3, 2 (1963), 5–22.

———. "The Wealth of Jamaica in the Eighteenth Century," *Economic History Review.* 18, 2 (1965), 292–311.

Sherman, Howard, and E. K. Hunt. *Economics: An Introduction to Traditional and Radical Views.* New York, Harper and Row, 1978.

Shiba, Yoshinobu. *Commerce and Society in Sung China.* Univ. of Michigan Press, 1970.

Shinnie, P. L., ed. *The African Iron Age.* Oxford Univ. Press, 1971.

Sideri, S. *Trade and Power: Informal Colonialism in Anglo-Portuguese Relations.* Rotterdam Univ. Press, 1970.

Silva Dias, Maria Odila. "The Establishment of the Royal Court in Brazil," in A.J.R. Russell-Wood, ed., *From Colony to Nation: Essays on the Indpendence of Brazil*. Johns Hopkins Univ. Press, 1975.

Simkin, Colin George. *The Traditional Trade of Asia*. Oxford Univ. Press, 1968.

Simpson, Leslie Bird. *The Encomienda in New Spain*. Univ. of California Press, 1982.

Sinha, Narendra. *The Economic History of Bengal, 1757-1905*. Univ. of Calcutta Press, 1967.

Sircar, D. C., ed. *Land Systems and Feudalism in Ancient India*. Univ. of Calcutta Press, 1966.

Skocpol, Theda. *States and Social Revolutions*. Cambridge Univ. Press, 1979.

Slicher van Bath, B. H. *The Agrarian History of Western Europe*. London, Edward Arnold, 1963.

Smith, Abbot Emerson. *Colonists in Bondage*. Univ. of North Carolina Press, 1947.

Smith, Alan K. "The Indian Ocean Zone," in David Birmingham and Phyllis Martin, eds., *History of Central Africa*, vol. 1. London, Longman, 1983, 205-45.

———. "Where Was the Periphery? The Wider World and the Core of the World Economy," *Radical History Review*. 39 (Sept., 1987), 28-50.

Smith, Robert. "Indigo Production and Trade in Colonial Guatemala," *Hispanic American Historical Review*. 39, 2 (1959), 181-211.

Soboul, Albert. "The French Rural Community in the Eighteenth and Nineteenth Centuries," *Past and Present*. 10 (1956), 78-95.

———. *A Short History of the French Revolution, 1789-1799*. Univ. of California Press, 1977.

———. *Understanding the French Revolution*. New York, International Publishers, 1988.

Southern, R. W. *The Making of the Middle Ages*. Yale Univ. Press, 1961.

Spalding, Karen, ed. *Essays on the Political, Economic, and Social History of Colonial Latin America*. Univ. of Delaware Press, 1982.

———. "Tratos mercantiles del corregidor de indios y la formación de la hacienda serrana en el Peru," *América Indígena*. 30, 3 (1970), 595-608.

Spencer, George. "The Politics of Plunder: The Cholas of Eleventh Century Ceylon," *Journal of Asian Studies*. 35, 3 (1975), 405-19.

Stavrianos, L. S. *Global Rift: The Third World Comes of Age*. New York, Morrow, 1981.

———. *The World Since 1500*. Englewood Cliffs, N.J., Prentice-Hall, 1966.

Stein, Robert. *The French Slave Trade in the Eighteenth Century: An Old Regime Business*. Univ. of Wisconsin Press, 1979.

———. "Measuring the French Slave Trade, 1713-1792-93," *Journal of African History*. 19, 4 (1978), 515-21.

Stinchcombe, William. *The American Revolution and the French Alliance*. Syracuse Univ. Press, 1969.

Stoddard, T. Lothrop. *The French Revolution in San Domingue*. Negro Universities Press, 1970.

Stone, Lawrence. "The Bourgeois Revolution of Seventeenth Century England Revisited," *Past and Present*. 109 (1985), 44-55.

———. *The Causes of the English Revolution, 1529-1642*. London, Routledge and Kegan Paul, 1972.

———. *The Crisis of the Aristocracy, 1558-1641*. Oxford Univ. Press, 1965.

———. "Social Mobility in England, 1500-1700," *Past and Present*. 33 (Apr., 1966), 16-55.

Stoye, John. *Europe Unfolding, 1648-1688*. New York, Harper and Row, 1969.

Strauss, Eric. *Irish Nationalism and British Democracy*. Columbia Univ. Press, 1951.

Supple, Barry. *Commercial Crisis and Change in England, 1606-1642*. Cambridge Univ. Press, 1964.

Sutherland, Lucy. *The East India Company in Eighteenth Century Politics*. Oxford Univ. Press, 1952.

Sweezy, Paul. "A Critique of *Studies in the Development of Capitalism*," in Rodney Hilton, ed., *The Transition from Feudalism to Capitalism*. London, Verso, 1978, 33-57.

Sydenham, M. J. *The First French Republic, 1792–1804*. Univ. of California Press, 1973.
_____. *The French Revolution*. Westport, Conn., Greenwood Press, 1985.
Takenaka, Yusakazu. "Endogamous Formation and the Development of Capitalism in Japan," *Journal of Economic History*. 29, 1 (1969), 141–62.
Tandeter, Enrique. "Forced and Free Labour in Late Colonial Potosi," *Past and Present*. 93 (Nov., 1981), 98–137.
Tarlé, E. V. *Bonaparte*. New York, Knight Publications, 1937.
Tawney, Richard H. *The Agrarian Problem in the Sixteenth Century*. London, Longman, 1912.
_____. "The Rise of the Gentry, 1558–1640," *Economic History Review*. 1st series, 11, 1 (1941), 1–39.
Taylor, George Rogers. *The Transportation Revolution, 1815–1860*. New York, Rinehart, 1951.
Taylor, George V. "Non-Capitalist Wealth and the Origins of the French Revolution," *American Historical Review*. 72, 2 (1967), 469–97.
Taylor, William. *Landlord and Peasant in Colonial Oaxaca*. Stanford Univ. Press, 1972.
Terray, Emmanuel. "Long Distance Exchange and the Formation of the State: The Case of the Abron of Gyamon," *Economy and Society*. 3 (1974), 315–45.
Thapar, Romila. *A History of India*, vol. 1. Baltimore, Penguin, 1966.
Thirsk, Joan, ed. *The Agrarian History of England and Wales, 1500–1640*. Cambridge Univ. Press, 1967.
_____. *The Rural Economy of England*. London, Hambledon Press, 1984.
Thomas, R. P. "A Quantitative Approach to the Study of the Effects of British Imperial Policy upon Colonial Welfare," *Journal of Economic History*. 25, 4 (1965), 615–38.
_____. "The Sugar Colonies of the Old Empire: Profit or Loss for Great Britain?" *Economic History Review*. 21, 1 (1968), 30–46.
Thomas, R. P., and Richard Bean. "The Fishers of Men: The Profits of the Slave Trade," *Journal of Economic History*. 34, 4 (1974), 885–915.
Thompson, E. P. *The Making of the English Working Class*. New York, Pantheon, 1964.
Thompson, F.M.L. *English Landed Society in the Nineteenth Century*. London, Routledge and Kegan Paul, 1963.
_____. "The Social Distribution of Landed Property Since the Sixteenth Century," *Economic History Review*. 19 (1966), 505–18.
Thompson, J. Eric. *Maya History and Religion*. Univ. of Oklahoma Press, 1970.
_____. *The Rise and Fall of the Maya Civilization*. Univ. of Oklahoma Press, 1966.
Thornton, A. P. *The Imperial Idea and Its Enemies*. London, Macmillan, 1959.
Thornton, John. "Demography and History in the Kingdom of the Kongo, 1550–1750," *Journal of African History*. 18, 4 (1977), 507–30.
_____. "The Slave Trade in Eighteenth Century Angola: Effects on Demographic Structures," *Canadian Journal of African Studies*. 14, 3 (1980), 417–29.
Thrupp, Sylvia. "The Gilds," in M. M. Postan, E. E. Rich, and Edward Miller, eds., *The Cambridge Economic History of Europe*, vol. 3. Cambridge Univ. Press, 1965, 230–81.
Toch, M. "Lords and Peasants: A Reappraisal of Medieval Economic Relationships," *Journal of European Economic History*. 15 (1986), 163–82.
Topolski, Jerzy. "The Manorial Serf Economy in Central Europe in the Sixteenth and Seventeenth Centuries," *Agricultural History*. 48, 3 (1974), 341–52.
Trigger, B. G. "The Rise of Civilisation in Egypt," *Cambridge History of Africa*, vol. 1. Cambridge Univ. Press, 1976, 478–547.
Tullock, Gordon. "Paper Money—A Cycle in Cathay," *Economic History Review*. 9 (1956), 393–408.
Turner, Michael. "English Open Fields and Enclosure: Retardation on Productivity Improvements," *Journal of Economic History*. 46 (1986), 669–92.
Unwin, George. *Studies In Economic History*. London, Frank Cass, 1958.

van der Wee, Hermann. "Structural Changes and Specialization in the Industry of the Southern Netherlands, 1100–1600," *Economic History Review.* 28, 2 (1976), 203–21.

van Dillen, J. G. "Economic Fluctuations and Trade in the Netherlands, 1650–1750," in Peter Earle, ed., *Essays in European Economic History, 1500–1800.* Oxford Univ. Press, 1974, 109–212.

van Houtte, J. A. *An Economic History of the Low Countries, 800–1800.* New York, St. Martin's Press, 1977.

———. "The Rise and Decline of the Market of Bruges," *Economic History Review.* 19, 1 (1966), 29–47.

Vassberg, David. *Land and Society in Golden Age Castile.* Cambridge Univ. Press, 1984.

Verlinden, Charles. *The Beginnings of Modern Colonization.* Cornell Univ. Press, 1984.

———. "The Rise of Spanish Trade in the Middle Ages," *Economic History Review.* 1st series, 10, 1 (1940), 44–59.

Vilar, Pierre. "Problems of the Formation of Capitalism," *Past and Present.* 10 (1956), 15–38.

Viotti da Costa, Emilio. "The Political Emancipation of Brazil," in A.J.R. Russell-Wood, ed., *From Colony to Nation: Essays on the Independence of Brazil.* Johns Hopkins Univ. Press, 1975, 43–88.

Vives, Jaime Vicens. *An Economic History of Spain.* Princeton Univ. Press, 1969.

Vlekke, Bernard. *Nusantara: A History of Indonesia.* Chicago, Quadrangle Books, 1959.

Vogt, John. *Portuguese Rule on the Gold Coast, 1469–1682.* Univ. of Georgia Press, 1979.

von Loewe, Karl. "Commerce and Agriculture in Lithuania, 1400–1600," *Economic History Review.* 26, 1 (1973), 23–35.

Wallerstein, Immanuel. *The Modern World System.* 2 vols., New York, Academic Press, 1974 and 1980.

Walton, Gary, and James Shepherd. *The Economic Rise of Early America.* Cambridge Univ. Press, 1979.

Ward, J. R. "The Profitability of Sugar Planting in the British West Indies, 1650–1834," *Economic History Review.* 31, 2 (1978), 197–214.

Watson, Andrew. *Agricultural Innovation in the Early Islamic World.* Cambridge Univ. Press, 1983.

———. "The Arab Agricultural Revolution and Its Diffusion, 700–1100," *Journal of Economic History.* 34, 1 (1974), 8–36.

Webb, Stephen Saunders. *1676: The End of American Independence.* New York, Knopf, 1984.

Weber, Max. *The Protestant Ethic and the Spirit of Capitalism.* London, Allen and Unwin, 1976.

Weisser, Michael. "Rural Crisis and Rural Credit in Seventeenth Century Castile," *Journal of European Economic History.* 16, 2 (1987), 297–313.

West, Robert. *Colonial Placer Mining in Colombia.* Louisiana State Univ. Press, 1952.

Whitaker, Arthur. *The Huancavelica Mercury Mines.* Harvard Univ. Press, 1952.

White, Lynn. "The Expansion of Technology," in Carlo Cipolla, ed., *The Fontana Economic History of Europe,* vol. 1. Sussex, Eng., Harvester Press, 1976, 143–74.

———. "What Accelerated Technological Progress in the Western Middle Ages," in A. C. Crombie, ed., *Scientific Change.* New York, Basic Books, 1963, 272–92.

———, ed. *Medieval Religion and Technology.* Univ. of California Press, 1979.

Whitecotton, Joseph. *The Zapotecs.* Univ. of Oklahoma Press, 1977.

Wickham, Chris. "The Other Transition: From the Ancient World to Feudalism," *Past and Present.* 103 (1984), 3–36.

Wilks, Ivor. "Wangara, Akan, and the Portuguese in the Fifteenth and Sixteenth Centuries: The Matter of Bita," *Journal of African History.* 23, 3 (1982), 333–50.

Willey, Gordon, and Dimitri Shimkin. "The Maya Collapse: A Summary View," in T. Patrick Culbert, ed., *The Classic Maya Collapse.* Univ. of New Mexico Press, 1973, 457–503.

Williams, Eric. *Capitalism and Slavery*. Univ. of North Carolina Press, 1944.

Williams, Lea. *South-East Asia: A History*. Oxford Univ. Press, 1976.

Wilson, Charles. *The Dutch Republic*. New York, McGraw-Hill, 1968.

_____ . *England's Apprenticeship*. London, Longman, 1965.

_____ . *Profit and Power: A Study of England and the Dutch Wars*. London, Longman, 1957.

Wolf, Eric. *Europe and the Peoples Without History*. Univ. of California Press, 1983.

_____ . *Sons of the Shaking Earth*. Univ. of Chicago Press, 1966.

Wolf, Eric, and Sidney Mintz. "Haciendas and Plantations in Middle America and the Antilles," *Social and Economic Studies*. 6, 3 (1957), 380–412.

Wolff, Hans. *The Traditional Crafts of Persia*. MIT Press, 1966.

Wolpert, Stanley. *A New History of India*. Oxford Univ. Press, 1982.

Woodruff, William. *The Impact of Western Man: A Study of Europe's Role in the World Economy, 1750–1960*. London, Macmillan, 1966.

Woolf, S. J. "Venice and the Terra Firma: Problems of the Change from Commercial to Landed Activities," in Brian Pullan, ed., *Crisis and Change in the Venetian Economy in the Sixteenth and Seventeenth Centuries*. London, Methuen, 1968, 175–203.

Wright, William. *Serf, Seigneur, and Sovereign: Agrarian Reform in Eighteenth Century Bohemia*. Univ. of Minnesota Press, 1966.

Zytkowicz, Leonid. "Grain Yields in Poland, Bohemia, Hungary, and Slovakia in the Sixteenth to Eighteenth Centuries," *Acta Poloniae Historica*. 24 (1971), 51–73.

# ABOUT THE BOOK
# AND AUTHOR

This is an exploration in world history that examines complex and intriguing questions concerning the origins of the first truly global economy, centered in Europe, which served in turn as a solid basis for the later emergence of the modern world system.

Professor Smith first examines the remarkable progress achieved by many cultures around the world, achievements that for some time far exceeded anything then found in Europe. The study then probes beyond "traditionalism" as a sufficient explanation of the inability of these societies to maintain the economic momentum that had begun so auspiciously and carefully examines the experience of European societies by way of comparison, finding that remarkably similar processes tended to unfold at first: regions of Europe that made the earliest gains in material progress were, like other parts of the world, unable to sustain these advances.

Still, in some parts of Europe—particularly the Netherlands and England—a new alignment of social forces was yielding the social system that would eventually evolve into capitalism. This breakthrough allowed for continued dynamic material progress, particularly for the English. Able to establish an unprecedented commercial dominance in vast reaches of the world, the British found themselves at the hub of a new world economy much more complex than any earlier intercultural commercial system.

The book delineates the systemic roles assumed by the various regions of the world and by European merchant capital and explains the tensions within this system that ensured its continued dynamism and eventual transformation into the current world economic system. *Creating a World Economy* combines an epic sweep with a mastery of historical detail and is sure to stimulate discussion among sociologists and historians interested in questions of a global nature.

Alan K. Smith is associate professor of history at Syracuse University.

# INDEX